Hands-On Data Science
Marketing

Improve your marketing strategies with machine learning
using Python and R

Yoon Hyup Hwang

BIRMINGHAM - MUMBAI

Hands-On Data Science for Marketing

Commissioning Editor: Sunith Shetty
Acquisition Editor: Joshua Nadar
Content Development Editor: Chris D'cruz
Technical Editor: Sushmeeta Jena
Copy Editor: Safis Editing
Project Coordinator: Hardik Bhinde
Proofreader: Safis Editing
Indexer: Pratik Shirodkar
Graphics: Tom Scaria
Production Coordinator: Jisha Chirayil

First published: March 2019

Production reference: 1280319

Published by Packt Publishing Ltd.
Livery Place
35 Livery Street
Birmingham
B3 2PB, UK.

ISBN 978-1-78934-634-3

www.packtpub.com

`mapt.io`

Mapt is an online digital library that gives you full access to over 5,000 books and videos, as well as industry leading tools to help you plan your personal development and advance your career. For more information, please visit our website.

Why subscribe?

- Spend less time learning and more time coding with practical eBooks and Videos from over 4,000 industry professionals

- Improve your learning with Skill Plans built especially for you

- Get a free eBook or video every month

- Mapt is fully searchable

- Copy and paste, print, and bookmark content

Packt.com

Did you know that Packt offers eBook versions of every book published, with PDF and ePub files available? You can upgrade to the eBook version at `www.packt.com` and as a print book customer, you are entitled to a discount on the eBook copy. Get in touch with us at `customercare@packtpub.com` for more details.

At `www.packt.com`, you can also read a collection of free technical articles, sign up for a range of free newsletters, and receive exclusive discounts and offers on Packt books and eBooks.

Contributors

About the author

Yoon Hyup Hwang is a seasoned data scientist in the marketing and financial sectors with expertise in predictive modeling, machine learning, statistical analysis, and data engineering. He has 8+ years' experience of building numerous machine learning models and data products using Python and R. He holds an MSE in computer and information technology from the University of Pennsylvania and a BA in economics from the University of Chicago.

In his spare time, he enjoys practicing various martial arts, snowboarding, and roasting coffee. Born and raised in Busan, South Korea, he currently works in New York and lives in New Jersey with his artist wife, Sunyoung, and a playful dog, Dali (named after Salvador Dali).

I'd like to thank my wife, Sunyoung, for keeping me sane throughout the process of writing this book. I cannot thank her enough for all the sacrifices she made over the past year. I'd also like to thank my family, who were there when I needed mental support. Without them, I wouldn't even have had the opportunity to work on this amazing book. Lastly, I'd like to thank all of my editors and reviewers for pushing me hard to write quality content.

About the reviewer

Rohan Dhupar is in the final semester of his degree computer science and engineering from the Rustamji Institute of Technology. Since November 2017, he has done a number of internships, mainly in relation to natural language processing for both US and Indian companies, focusing on machine and deep learning. He has undertaken numerous projects and achieved much in his academic life. He ranks in the top 1% of Kaggle experts, has been a Microsoft Student Partner since 2017, and has received numerous invitations from established companies to join their data science software engineering teams. He is currently working as a data scientist, focusing mainly on image processing projects, for Innovations Labs, a US firm based in India.

> *I would like to thank Ali Mehndi Hasan Abidi and Hardik Bhinde, who provided me with the support required to write well-formatted and properly documented reviews.*

Packt is searching for authors like you

If you're interested in becoming an author for Packt, please visit `authors.packtpub.com` and apply today. We have worked with thousands of developers and tech professionals, just like you, to help them share their insight with the global tech community. You can make a general application, apply for a specific hot topic that we are recruiting an author for, or submit your own idea.

Table of Contents

Preface

The adoption of data science and machine learning for marketing has been on the rise, from small to large organizations. With data science, you can better understand the drivers behind the successes and failures of previous marketing strategies and you can better understand customer behavior and interaction with your products. With data science, you can also predict customer behavior and create better targeted and personalized marketing strategies for better cost per acquisition, higher conversion rates, and higher net sales. With this book, you will be able to apply various data science techniques to create data-driven marketing strategies.

This book serves as a practical guide to performing simple-to-advanced tasks in marketing. You will use data science to understand what drives sales and customer engagement. You will use machine learning to forecast which customer is likely to engage with products more and has the highest expected lifetime value. You will also use machine learning to understand what data tells you about different customer segments and recommend the right products for individual customers that they are most likely to purchase. By the end of this book, you will be well-versed with various data science and machine learning techniques and how they can be utilized for different marketing goals.

Personally, I would have benefited from books such as this. When I was embarking on my career in data science and marketing, there were abundant resources on theories and details of different data science and machine learning techniques, but not so much on how to use these technologies and techniques for marketing specifically. Learning about the theories was vastly different from actually utilizing and applying them to real-world business use cases in marketing. In this book, I hope to share my experience and the knowledge acquired through significant instances of trial and error in applying data science and machine learning to different marketing goals. By the end of this book, you will have a good understanding of what types of technologies and techniques are used for different marketing use cases, where to find additional resources, and what to study next after this book.

In this book, Python and R will be used for data science and machine learning exercises. As you may already be aware, Python and R are two of the most frequently used programming languages for data scientists, data analysts, and machine learning engineers on account of their ease of use, the abundant resources that are available in relation to data science and machine learning, and the broad community of users. In each chapter, we will guide you through the different packages and libraries used and how to install them, so you do not need to worry about what to install on your computer before you start this book.

Who this book is for

This book is for marketing professionals, data scientists and analysts, machine learning engineers, and software engineers who have some working knowledge of Python and R and some basic understanding of machine learning and data science. Even if you do not have any in-depth knowledge of the theory behind data science and machine learning algorithms, don't worry! This book is for practitioners with a focus on the practicality of machine learning, so that you can quickly pick things up and start utilizing them in relation to your next marketing strategies. If you have studied data science and machine learning previously, then this book will be great for you. It will guide you through how to apply your knowledge and experience of data science and machine learning in marketing to real-life examples. If you are a marketing professional with a passion and interest in data science, then great! This book will be perfect for you. You will learn how data science can help you improve your marketing strategies and how predictive machine learning models can be used to fine-tune targeted marketing. This book will guide you through each step of utilizing data science and machine learning to achieve your marketing goals.

This book is really designed for anyone with a passion for using data science and machine learning for marketing. If you are interested in building data-driven marketing strategies, making sense of customer behavior from data, forecasting how customers will react, and predicting what customers will respond do, then you have come to the right place!

What this book covers

Chapter 1, *Data Science and Marketing*, covers the basics of how data science is used for marketing. It will briefly introduce frequently used data science and machine learning techniques and how those techniques are applied when it comes to creating better marketing strategies. It also covers how to set up your Python and R environments for upcoming projects.

Chapter 2, *Key Performance Indicators and Visualizations*, goes over some of the **key performance indicators (KPIs)** to track in marketing. This chapter discusses how Python and R can be used to compute such KPIs and how to build visualizations of those KPIs.

Chapter 3, *Drivers behind Marketing Engagement*, demonstrates how to use regression analysis to understand what drives engagement from customers. This chapter covers how to fit linear regression models in Python and R and how to extract the intercept and coefficients from a model. With the insights gathered from regression analysis, we will examine how we can potentially improve a marketing strategy for a higher engagement rate.

Chapter 4, *From Engagement to Conversion*, discusses how to use different machine learning models to understand what drives conversion. This chapter introduces you to how to build decision tree models in Python and R, as well as how to interpret the results and extract the drivers behind the conversions.

Chapter 5, *Product Analytics*, guides you through exploratory product analysis. This chapter walks you through various data aggregation and analysis methods in Python and R to obtain further insights into the trends and patterns in products.

Chapter 6, *Recommending the Right Products*, covers how to improve product visibility and recommend the right products that individual customers are most likely to purchase. It discusses how to use the collaborative filtering algorithm in Python and R in order to build a recommendation model. Then, it covers how these recommendations can be used for marketing campaigns.

Chapter 7, *Exploratory Analysis for Customer Behavior*, dives deeper into data. This chapter discusses various metrics that can be used to analyze how customers behave and interact with the product. Using Python and R, this chapter broadens your knowledge to encompass data visualization and different charting techniques.

Chapter 8, *Predicting the Likelihood of Marketing Engagement*, discusses how to build a machine learning model to predict the likelihood of customer engagement. This chapter covers how to train machine learning algorithms using Python and R. It then discusses how to evaluate the performance of the model and how these models can be used to achieve better target marketing.

Chapter 9, *Customer Lifetime Value*, covers how to get the lifetime value of individual customers. This chapter discusses how to build regression models using Python and R and how to evaluate them. It also covers how the computed customer lifetime value can be used for building better marketing strategies.

Chapter 10, *Data-Driven Customer Segmentation*, dives into segmenting the customer base using a data-driven approach. This chapter introduces clustering algorithms to build different customer segments from data using Python and R.

Chapter 11, *Retaining Customers*, discusses how to predict the likelihood of customer churn and focuses on building classification models using Python and R and how to evaluate their performances. This chapter will cover how to build an **artificial neural network (ANN)** model, which is the backbone of deep learning, in Python and R using the keras library.

Chapter 12, *A/B Testing for Better Marketing Strategy*, introduces a data-driven approach to making better decisions on marketing strategies. This chapter discusses the concept of A/B testing and how to implement and evaluate it using Python and R. It then discusses the real-life applications and benefits of A/B testing in relation to better marketing strategies.

Chapter 13, *What's Next?*, summarizes what has been discussed in this book, as well as real-life challenges in using data science for marketing. This chapter also introduces other data science and machine learning packages and libraries, as well as other machine learning algorithms that can be used for your future data science projects.

To get the most out of this book

To get the most out of this book, I highly recommend that you work through the programming exercises in each chapter thoroughly. Each exercise is meant to lay a solid foundation for more advanced exercises, so it is critical that you follow each and every step in the programming exercises. I also recommend you be adventurous. Different technologies and techniques discussed in each chapter can be mixed with those from other chapters. A technique used in one chapter is not meant to be exclusively applicable to that specific chapter. You can apply the technology and techniques learned from one chapter to other chapters, so it will be beneficial for you to go through the examples from the beginning again and try to mix up different techniques learned from other chapters when you finish this book.

Download the example code files

You can download the example code files for this book from your account at www.packt.com. If you purchased this book elsewhere, you can visit www.packt.com/support and register to have the files emailed directly to you.

You can download the code files by following these steps:

1. Log in or register at www.packt.com.
2. Select the **SUPPORT** tab.
3. Click on **Code Downloads & Errata**.
4. Enter the name of the book in the **Search** box and follow the onscreen instructions.

Once the file is downloaded, please make sure that you unzip or extract the folder using the latest version of:

- WinRAR/7-Zip for Windows
- Zipeg/iZip/UnRarX for Mac
- 7-Zip/PeaZip for Linux

The code bundle for the book is also hosted on GitHub at https://github.com/ PacktPublishing/Hands-On-Data-Science-for-Marketing. In case there's an update to the code, it will be updated on the existing GitHub repository.

We also have other code bundles from our rich catalog of books and videos available at https://github.com/PacktPublishing/. Check them out!

Download the color images

We also provide a PDF file that has color images of the screenshots/diagrams used in this book. You can download it here: https://www.packtpub.com/sites/default/files/downloads/9781789346343_Color Images.pdf.

Conventions used

There are a number of text conventions used throughout this book.

CodeInText: Indicates code words in text, database table names, folder names, filenames, file extensions, pathnames, dummy URLs, user input, and Twitter handles. Here is an example: "Mount the downloaded WebStorm-10*.dmg disk image file as another disk in your system."

A block of code is set as follows:

```
# total number of conversions
df.conversion.sum()
# total number of clients in the data (= number of rows in the data)
df.shape[0]
```

When we wish to draw your attention to a particular part of a code block, the relevant lines or items are set in bold:

```
# total number of conversions
df.conversion.sum()
# total number of clients in the data (= number of rows in the data)
df.shape[0]
```

Any command-line input or output is written as follows:

```
$ mkdir css
$ cd css
```

Bold: Indicates a new term, an important word, or words that you see on screen. For example, words in menus or dialog boxes appear in the text like this. Here is an example: "Select **System info** from the **Administration** panel."

Warnings or important notes appear like this.

Tips and tricks appear like this.

Get in touch

Feedback from our readers is always welcome.

General feedback: If you have questions about any aspect of this book, mention the book title in the subject of your message and email us at customercare@packtpub.com.

Errata: Although we have taken every care to ensure the accuracy of our content, mistakes do happen. If you have found a mistake in this book, we would be grateful if you would report this to us. Please visit www.packt.com/submit-errata, selecting your book, clicking on the Errata Submission Form link, and entering the details.

Piracy: If you come across any illegal copies of our works in any form on the internet, we would be grateful if you would provide us with the location address or website name. Please contact us at copyright@packt.com with a link to the material.

If you are interested in becoming an author: If there is a topic that you have expertise in, and you are interested in either writing or contributing to a book, please visit authors.packtpub.com.

Reviews

Please leave a review. Once you have read and used this book, why not leave a review on the site that you purchased it from? Potential readers can then see and use your unbiased opinion to make purchase decisions, we at Packt can understand what you think about our products, and our authors can see your feedback on their book. Thank you!

For more information about Packt, please visit packt.com.

Section 1: Introduction and Environment Setup

This section will introduce you to data science for marketing and setting up Python and R environments for the upcoming projects.

This section consists of the following chapter:

- Chapter 1, *Data Science and Marketing*

Data Science and Marketing

1

Welcome to the first chapter of *Hands-On Data Science for Marketing*! As you may be familiar already, the importance and application of data science in the marketing industry have been rising significantly over the past few years. Yet, marketing data science is a relatively new field and the amount of resources available for education and references lags behind the momentum. However, the amount of data gathered and available to the process has been growing exponentially each year, which opens up even more opportunities to learn and bring insight from the data.

With the growing amount of data and applications of data science in marketing, we can easily find examples of the usage of data science to marketing efforts. Companies are starting to use data science to better understand customer behaviors and identify different customer segments based on their activity patterns. Many organizations also use machine learning to predict future customer behaviors, such as what items are they likely to purchase, which websites are they likely to visit, and who are likely to churn. With endless use cases of data science for marketing, companies of all sizes can benefit from using data science and machine learning for their marketing efforts. After this brief introductory chapter, we will learn about how to apply data science and machine learning for individual marketing tasks.

In this chapter, we will cover the following topics:

- Trends in marketing
- Applications of data science in marketing
- Setting up the Python environment
- Setting up the R environment

Technical requirements

You will require Python and R installed to run most of the code throughout this book, and you can find the installation code at the following link: `https://github.com/ PacktPublishing/Hands-On-Data-Science-for-Marketing/tree/master/Chapter01`.

Trends in marketing

As the amount of data available and gathered increases exponentially every year and access to such valuable datasets becomes easier, data science and machine learning have become an integral part of marketing. The applications of data science in marketing range from building insightful reports and dashboards to utilizing complicated machine learning algorithms to predict customer behaviors or engage customers with the products and contents. The trends in marketing in recent years have been toward more data-driven target marketing. We will discuss some of the trends we see in the marketing industry:

- **Rising importance of digital marketing**: As people spend more time online than ever before, the importance and effectiveness of digital marketing have been rising with time. Lots of marketing activities are now happening on digital channels, such as search engines, social network, email, and websites. For example, Google Ads helps your brand to get more exposure to potential customers through its search engine, Gmail, or YouTube. You can easily customize your target audience, to whom you want your advertisements to be shown. Facebook and Instagram are two of the well-known social networks, where you can post your advertisements to reach your target customers. In the era of the internet, these marketing channels have become more cost-effective than traditional marketing channels, such as television advertising. The following is an example of different digital marketing channels that Google provides (`https://ads.google.com/start/how-it-works/?subid=us-en-ha-g-aw-c-dr_df_1-b_ex_pl!o2~-1072012490-284305340539-kwd-94527731`):

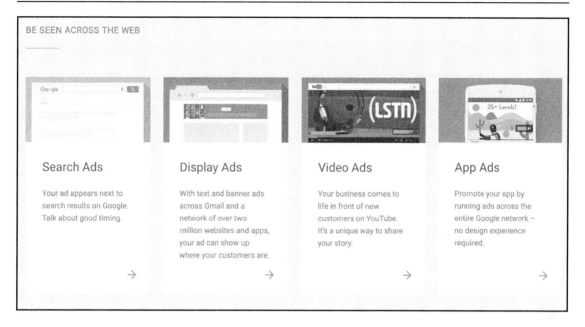

- **Marketing analytics**: Marketing analytics is a way of monitoring and analyzing the performances of marketing efforts. Not only does it help you to understand how much sales or exposure you gain from marketing, but it can also help you gain deeper insights into more individual level patterns and trends. In e-commerce businesses, you can analyze and visualize the different types and segments of customers and which type of customers drives the revenue for your business the most with marketing analytics. In media businesses, with marketing analytics, you can analyze which content attracts the users the most and what the trends in keyword searches are. Marketing analytics also helps you to understand the cost-effectiveness of your marketing campaigns. By looking into the **return on investment (ROI)**, you can further optimize your future marketing campaigns. As the adoption and usage of marketing analytics rise, it is not difficult to find various software products for marketing analytics.

- **Personalized and target marketing**: With the rising applications of data science and machine learning in marketing, another trend in marketing is individual-level target marketing. Various organizations of different sizes utilize machine learning algorithms to learn from the user history data and apply different and specialized marketing strategies to smaller and more specific subgroups of their user base, which results in lower cost per acquisition and higher return on investment. In retail businesses, many companies implement artificial intelligence and machine learning to predict which customers are more likely to purchase and which items they are going to buy from their stores. Using these predictions, they customize the marketing messages to each of their customers. Many of media businesses also utilize artificial intelligence and machine learning to drive higher engagement from individual users to grow their user base. As these customized and target marketing result in higher ROI, there are many SaaS companies, such as Sailthru and Oracle, that provide platforms for personalized marketing. Sailthru recently published a *Retail Personalization Index* report, which analyzes how various retail companies use personalized marketing in different marketing channels. In this report, we can find that retail companies, such as Sephora, JustFab, and Walmart, use personalized marketing heavily in their websites, emails, and other marketing channels. This report can be found at this link: https://www.sailthru.com/personalization-index/sailthru100/.

The overall trends in marketing have been toward more data-driven and quantitative approaches. Companies of all sizes have been investing in marketing analytics and technologies more and more. According to the February 2018 CMO survey, the reliance on marketing analytics has gone up from 30% to 42% in the past 5 years. The reliance on marketing analytics is even higher for B2C companies with a 55% increase. Also, the number of firms using quantitative tools to demonstrate the impact of marketing has increased by 28% in the past 5 years. Lastly, the CMO survey suggests that the percentage of companies utilizing artificial intelligence and machine learning is expected to increase to 39% over the next 3 years. You can find more details on this February 2018 CMO survey report at the following link: https://www.forbes.com/sites/christinemoorman/2018/02/27/marketing-analytics-and-marketing-technology-trends-to-watch/#4ec8a8431b8a.

Applications of data science in marketing

We have discussed the trends in marketing and how the trend has been toward more data-driven and quantitative marketing, often using data science and machine learning. There are various ways to apply data science and machine learning in the marketing industry and it will be beneficial for us to discuss the typical tasks and usage of data science and machine learning.

In this section, we will cover the basics of machine learning, the different types of learning algorithms, and, typical data science workflow and process.

Descriptive versus explanatory versus predictive analyses

As we work through the exercises and projects in the upcoming chapters, there are mainly three different types of analyses that we are going to conduct throughout this book: descriptive, explanatory, and predictive analyses:

- **Descriptive analysis:** This is conducted to understand and describe the given dataset better. The purpose of this analysis is to quantitatively and statistically summarize the information that the data contains. For example, if you are conducting a descriptive analysis on user purchase history data, you will be answering such questions as *What is the best selling item? What were the monthly sales like in the past year? What is the average price of the items that are sold?* Throughout this book, we will be conducting descriptive analysis, whenever we introduce a new dataset. Especially, in Chapter 2, *Key Performance Indicators and Visualizations*, we will be discussing in more detail how to use descriptive analysis to analyze and compute key summary statistics, as well as visualizing the analysis results.
- **Explanatory analysis**: When the purpose of descriptive analysis is to answer the *what* and *how* from the data, explanatory analysis is to answer *why* using the data. This type of analysis is typically conducted when you have a specific question that you want to answer. As an example for e-commerce businesses, if you want to analyze what drives your users to make purchases, you would conduct explanatory analysis, not descriptive analysis. We will be discussing more detail about this type of analysis with examples in Chapter 3, *Drivers behind Marketing Engagement*; and Chapter 4, *From Engagement to Conversion*, where we are going to use explanatory analyses to answer such questions as *What drives users to engage with our marketing campaigns more?* and *What makes users purchase items from our retail shop?*

- **Predictive analysis**: This analysis is conducted when there is a specific future event that you would like to predict. The purpose of this analysis is to build machine learning models that learn from the historical data and make predictions about events that will happen in the future. Similar to the previous examples of e-commerce and purchase history data, one of the questions you can answer from this type of analysis may be, *Which user is the most likely to make a purchase within the next seven days?* Typically, in order to conduct predictive analysis, you will have to first run descriptive and explanatory analyses to have a better understanding of the data and generate ideas on what types of learning algorithms and approaches to use for the given project. We will be discussing in more detail predictive analysis and its applications in marketing in Chapter 6, *Recommending the Right Products*, Chapter 8, *Predicting the Likelihood of Marketing Engagement*, and Chapter 11, *Retaining Customers*.

Types of learning algorithms

Let's now discuss more about machine learning and machine learning algorithms. Broadly speaking, there are three types of machine learning algorithms: supervised learning, unsupervised learning, and reinforcement learning. Let's first learn how these three different types of machine learning algorithms differ from each other:

- **Supervised learning algorithms:** These algorithms are used when the prediction target or outcome is known. For example, if we want to use machine learning to predict who will make purchases in the next few days, then we will use supervised learning algorithms. Here, the prediction target or outcome is whether this person made a purchase within the given time window or not. Based on the historical purchase data, we will need to build features, which describe each data point, such as a user's age, address, last purchase date, and then supervised learning algorithms will learn from this data how to map these features to the prediction target or outcome. We will be exploring how to use such algorithms in marketing in Chapter 3, *Drivers behind Marketing Engagement;* Chapter 4, *From Engagement to Conversion;* Chapter 8, *Predicting the Likelihood of Marketing Engagement*, and, lastly, Chapter 11, *Retaining Customers*.

- **Unsupervised learning algorithms:** Unlike supervised learning algorithms, unsupervised learning algorithms are used when we do not have a specific prediction target or outcome. This type of machine learning algorithm is frequently used in clustering and recommendation systems. As an example, you can use unsupervised learning algorithms to cluster your customer base into different subgroups or segments, based on their behaviors. In this case, we do not have a specific target or outcome that we want to predict. We are just grouping similar customers together into different segments. We will be exploring how to use unsupervised learning algorithms in marketing in Chapter 6, *Recommending the Right Products*, and Chapter 10, *Data-Driven Customer Segmentation*.

- **Reinforcement learning algorithms:** These algorithms are used when we want the model to continuously learn and train itself without prior knowledge or experience. In the case of reinforcement learning, the model learns how to make predictions after lots of trials and errors. One example of the application of reinforcement learning in marketing is when there are multiple marketing strategies you'd like to test and choose the one that works the best. In this case, you can run a reinforcement learning algorithm, where it randomly picks one strategy at a time and gets rewarded when a positive outcome occurs. After multiple iterations of trials and errors, the reinforcement learning model will have learned to choose the best marketing strategy, based on the total rewards each marketing strategies have earned.

Data science workflow

Now that we have covered the basics and different types of machine learning algorithms, let's discuss the workflow in data science. A typical workflow looks like the following:

1. **Problem definition**: Typically, any data science and machine learning project starts with problem definition. In this first step, you need to define the problems that you are trying to solve with data science, the scope of the project, and the approaches to solving this problem. When you are thinking about some of the approaches to solving your problem, you will need to brainstorm on what types of analyses (descriptive versus explanatory versus predictive) and types of learning algorithms (supervised versus unsupervised versus reinforcement learning) that we discussed previously will be suitable for solving the given problem.

2. **Data collection**: Once you have a clear definition of the project, you will then move on to the data collection step. This is where you gather all the data you need to proceed with your data science project. It is not uncommon that you will need to purchase data from third-party vendors, scrape and extract data from the web, or use publicly available data. In some cases, you will also need to collect data from your internal systems for your project. Depending on the cases, the data collection step can be trivial or it can also be tedious.

3. **Data preparation**: When you have gathered all of the data you need from the data collection step, then the next step is data preparation. The goal of this step is to transform your data and prepare it for future steps. If the formats of the data sources are different, then you will have to transform and unify the data. If the data doesn't have a certain structure, then you will have to structure the data, typically in tabular format, so that you can easily conduct different analyses and build machine learning models.

4. **Data analysis**: When you are done with the data preparation step, then you will have to start looking into the data. In the data analysis step, typically, descriptive analyses are conducted to compute some descriptive summary statistics and build visual plots to better understand the data. Quite often, you can find some recognizable patterns and draw some insight from data during this step. You may also be able to find any anomalies in the data, such as missing values, corrupted data, or duplicate records, from this step.

5. **Feature engineering**: Feature engineering is the most important part of data science and machine learning, as it directly affects the performance of predictive models. Feature engineering requires expertise and good domain knowledge of the data, as it requires you to transform the raw data into more informative data for your algorithms to learn from. One good example of feature engineering is transforming text data into numerical data. As the machine learning algorithms can only learn from numerical data, you will need to come up with an idea and strategy to translate textual data into numerical data. As we work through this book and as we build machine learning models, we will discuss and experiment with various feature engineering techniques.

6. **Model building**: Once you are done with the feature engineering step, then you can start training and testing your machine learning models. In this step, you can experiment with various learning algorithms to figure out which one works the best for your use case. One thing to keep in mind in this step is the validation metrics. It is important to have a good measure of your model performance, as machine learning algorithms will try to optimize on the given performance measure. As we start building machine learning models in the following chapters, we will discuss more in detail regarding what metrics to use depending on the type of problems that we are working on.

The following diagram shows the overall workflow for typical data science projects:

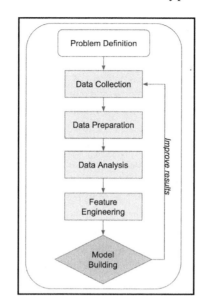

As you can see from this diagram, quite often, the data science work does not end in one iteration. You may have to repeat the data collection step when you notice that the model is not performing well and when you notice you can improve on the quality of the input data. You may have to revisit the feature engineering step when you come up with better ideas and strategies on building features from the raw dataset. You also may have to repeat the model building step more than once, if you think you can improve the model results by tuning the hyperparameters of the learning algorithms. As we work through the following chapters and as we work on actual projects and exercises in this book, we are going to discuss in more detail certain steps and different techniques we can use.

Setting up the Python environment

Now that we have discussed some of the basics of data science and its applications to marketing, let's start getting our development environments ready for the upcoming chapters and projects. For those of you who will be using the R language for the exercises, you can skip this section and move to the *Setting up the R environment* section. For those of you who are planning to use the Python language for the exercises, it will be beneficial for you to follow these steps to install all the required Python packages and get your Python environment ready, even if you are already familiar with Python.

Installing the Anaconda distribution

For data science and machine learning tasks in this book, we will be using lots of different Python packages. To name a few, we will be using the `pandas` package for data munging and data analysis. You can find more information about this package at the following link: `https://pandas.pydata.org/`. We will also be using the `scikit-learn` package for building machine learning models. For more information about this package, you can visit the following page: `http://scikit-learn.org/stable/`. Another Python package that we will be using frequently is `numpy`. This package will come in handy when we need to run mathematical and scientific operations on multi-dimensional data. You can find more information about this package at this page: `http://www.numpy.org/`. Aside from these three packages we just mentioned, we will be using some other Python libraries as well and will discuss them individually in more detail when we use them.

Since we need various Python libraries for data science and machine learning tasks, it can sometimes be cumbersome to install them separately. Thanks to the Anaconda distribution, we can install all of the required packages at once. In order to download the Anaconda distribution, visit `https://www.anaconda.com/download/` to install it. When you follow this link, the webpage should look as follows:

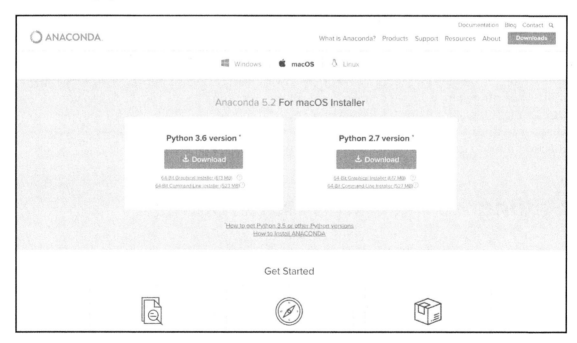

In this book, we will be using Anaconda 5.2 in Python 3. Once you have downloaded the Anaconda distribution, you can install all of the packages using the installer. On macOS, the installer looks as follows:

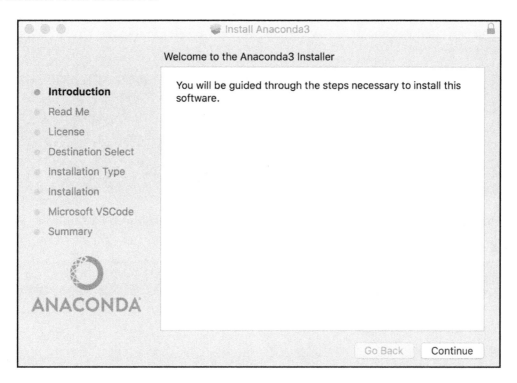

Once you follow the steps in the installer and finish this Anaconda distribution installation, we are now ready to start running data science and machine learning tasks. In the following section, we will build a simple logistic regression model to get familiar with how we can use the key Python libraries that we just installed for future exercises.

A simple logistic regression model in Python

Now that we have all of the packages installed, let's test to see if we can use them. We will be using Jupyter Notebook for all future data analysis, data visualization, and machine learning tasks. Jupyter Notebook is an open source web application, where you can easily write code, display charts, and share notebooks with others. You can find more information about Jupyter Notebook at this link: `http://jupyter.org/`.

As the Jupyter Notebook is part of the Anaconda distribution that we just installed in the previous section, you should have it installed in your computer already.

To start the Jupyter Notebook, you can open a Terminal window and type in the following command:

```
jupyter notebook
```

When you type in this command, you should see some output that looks similar to the following screenshot:

In the end, it should open a web application on your browser. The web UI should look like the following:

As you can see from this screenshot, you can create a new Jupyter Notebook by clicking the **New** button on the top-right corner and then clicking on **Python 3**. This will create a new empty notebook using Python 3 as the choice of programming language. The new notebook should look like the following:

In order to change the name of this notebook, you can simply click on the top bar, where it says Untitled, and name it differently.

Now that we have created a notebook, let's start using some of the Python libraries to build a simple logistic regression model. In the first cell, we are going to import the numpy and scikit-learn packages. The code looks like the following:

```
import numpy as np
from sklearn.linear_model import LogisticRegression
```

As you can see from this code snippet, we have imported the numpy package and given it an alias of np. This is a standard alias for the numpy library. Also, we are only importing the LogisticRegression module in the scikit-learn package's linear_model module (sklearn.linear_model).

In order to build a model, we need data. For demo and test purposes in this chapter, we will create two-dimensional input data and a binary output. The following code shows how we created the input and output data:

```
input_data = np.array([
    [0, 0],
    [0.25, 0.25],
    [0.5, 0.5],
    [1, 1],
])

output_data = [
    0,
    0,
    1,
    1
]
```

As you can see from this code snippet, we created 4 x 2 input data with the `numpy` array datatype. The output is binary, where it can only take 0 or 1.

With this data, we can train a logistic regression model, as shown in the following code:

```
logit_model = LogisticRegression()
logit_model.fit(input_data, output_data)
```

As you can see from this code, we instantiated a model object with `LogisticRegression`. Then, we used the `fit` function, where it takes the input and output data, to train a logistic regression model. You can retrieve the coefficients and intercept of this logistic regression model, as shown in the following code:

```
logit_model.coef_      # output: array([[0.43001235, 0.43001235]])
logit_model.intercept_     # output: array([-0.18498028])
```

Our Jupyter Notebook up to this point looks as follows:

```
In [1]:  import numpy as np
         from sklearn.linear_model import LogisticRegression

In [2]:  input_data = np.array([
             [0, 0],
             [0.25, 0.25],
             [0.5, 0.5],
             [1, 1],
         ])

In [3]:  output_data = [
             0,
             0,
             1,
             1
         ]

In [4]:  logit_model = LogisticRegression()

In [5]:  logit_model.fit(input_data, output_data)
Out[5]:  LogisticRegression(C=1.0, class_weight=None, dual=False, fit_intercept=True,
                     intercept_scaling=1, max_iter=100, multi_class='ovr', n_jobs=1,
                     penalty='l2', random_state=None, solver='liblinear', tol=0.0001,
                     verbose=0, warm_start=False)

In [6]:  logit_model.coef_
Out[6]:  array([[0.43001235, 0.43001235]])

In [7]:  logit_model.intercept_
Out[7]:  array([-0.18498028])
```

In order to make predictions on the new data, you can use the `predict` function of the logistic regression model object, `logit_model`. This function will return the predicted output class for each input. The code looks like the following:

```
predicted_output = logit_model.predict(input_data)
```

So far, we have experimented with how to use the `numpy` and `scikit-learn` packages for building a machine learning model. Let's familiarize ourselves with one more package for data visualization. Throughout this book's chapters, we will be heavily utilizing the `matplotlib` library to visualize any data analysis results. For more information, you can visit this page: `https://matplotlib.org/`.

Let's first look at the following code:

```
import matplotlib.pyplot as plt

plt.scatter(
    x=input_data[:,0],
    y=input_data[:,1],
    color=[('red' if x == 1 else 'blue') for x in output_data]
)
plt.xlabel('X')
plt.ylabel('Y')
plt.title('Actual')
plt.grid()
plt.show()
```

As you can see from this code snippet, you can easily import the `matplotlib` package as in the first line of this code. In order to build a scatterplot, we are using the `scatter` function, which takes x and y values, as well as the `color` of each point. You can use the `xlabel` function to change the label of the *x*-axis and the `ylabel` function to change the label of the *y*-axis. Using the `title` function, you can change the title of the chart. The `grid` function will show grids within the plot and you will need to call the `show` function to actually display the plot.

The Jupyter Notebook should look like the following:

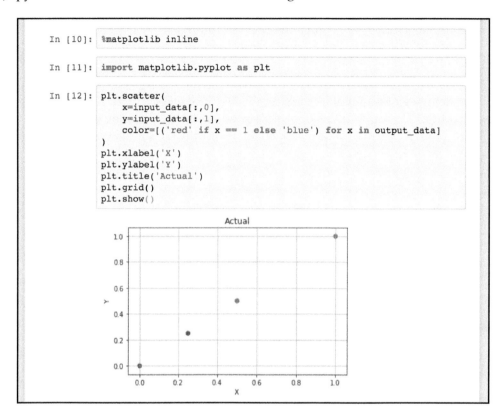

One thing to note here is the following code:

```
%matplotlib inline
```

This is required to display the plots within the web applications. Without this line of code, the plots will not be shown in the web UI. In order to compare the actual output against the model's predictions, we built another scatterplot with the predicted values.

The code and plot look like the following:

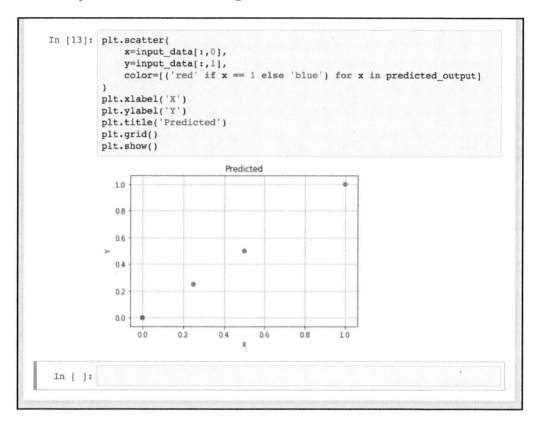

```
In [13]: plt.scatter(
             x=input_data[:,0],
             y=input_data[:,1],
             color=[('red' if x == 1 else 'blue') for x in predicted_output]
         )
         plt.xlabel('X')
         plt.ylabel('Y')
         plt.title('Predicted')
         plt.grid()
         plt.show()
```

If you compare this chart with the previous one, you can see that the model predicted the output correctly three out of four times and incorrectly predicted one point.

 You can download the full Jupyter Notebook that we used in this section from the following link: https://github.com/yoonhwang/hands-on-data-science-for-marketing/blob/master/ch.1/python/Setting%20Up%20Python%20Environment.ipynb.

We will be using these three Python libraries, which we just experimented with, frequently throughout this book. As we progress through the chapters, we will be covering more advanced features and functions of these Python libraries and how to fully utilize them for our data science and machine learning tasks.

Setting up the R environment

For those of you who are planning to use the R language for the upcoming exercises and projects, we will discuss how to get your R environment ready for data science and machine learning tasks in this book. We will start by installing R and RStudio and then build a simple logistic regression model using R to familiarize ourselves with R for data science.

Installing R and RStudio

Along with Python, R is one of the most frequently used languages for data science and machine learning. The fact that it is very easy to use, and that there is a large number of R libraries for machine learning, attracts many data scientists. In order to use this language, you will need to download it from the following link: `https://www.r-project.org/`. If you go to this web page, it will look something like the following screenshot:

The R Project for Statistical Computing

[Home]

Download

CRAN

R Project

About R
Logo
Contributors
What's New?
Reporting Bugs
Conferences
Search
Get Involved: Mailing Lists
Developer Pages
R Blog

R Foundation

Foundation
Board
Members
Donors
Donate

Help With R

Getting Help

Getting Started

R is a free software environment for statistical computing and graphics. It compiles and runs on a wide variety of UNIX platforms, Windows and MacOS. To **download R**, please choose your preferred CRAN mirror.

If you have questions about R like how to download and install the software, or what the license terms are, please read our answers to frequently asked questions before you send an email.

News

- **R version 3.5.3 (Great Truth) prerelease versions** will appear starting Friday 2019-03-01. Final release is scheduled for Monday 2019-03-11.
- **R version 3.5.2 (Eggshell Igloo)** has been released on 2018-12-20.
- The R Foundation Conference Committee has released a call for proposals to host useR! 2020 in North America.
- You can now support the R Foundation with a renewable subscription as a supporting member
- The R Foundation has been awarded the Personality/Organization of the year 2018 award by the professional association of German market and social researchers.

News via Twitter

 The R Foundation
@_R_Foundation

One week to go now.

You can find more information about R on this web page. In order for you to download, follow the **download R** link in this page. It will ask you to choose a CRAN mirror. You can choose the location that is closest to you and download R. Once you download it, you can follow the steps in the installer and install R in your computer. The installer on macOS is shown in the following screenshot:

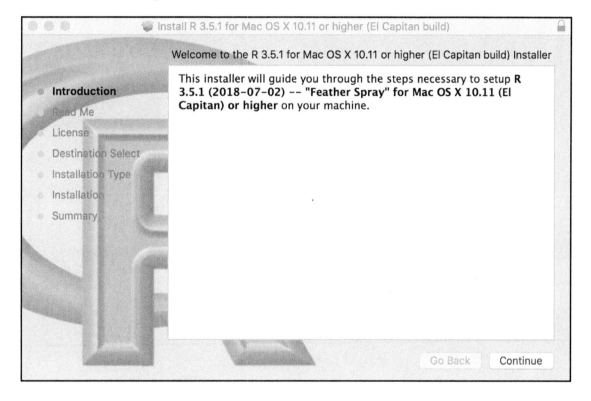

Once you have finished installing R, we are going to install one more thing for our R development environment. In this book, we will be using RStudio, which is a popular IDE for the R programming language. You can download RStudio at the following link: `https://www.rstudio.com/products/rstudio/download/`. When you go to this RStudio download page, it should look like the following screenshot:

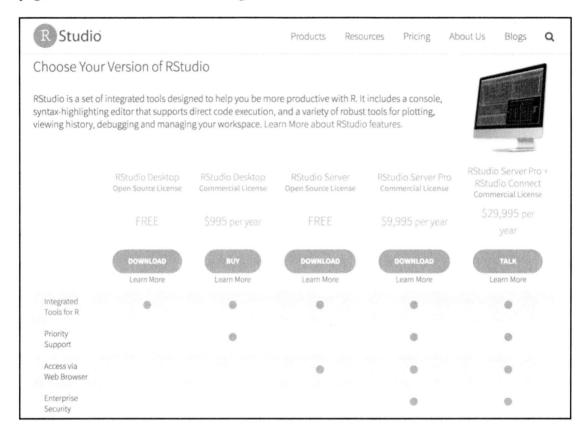

We will be using the **RStudio Desktop Open Source License** version in this book, but feel free to use other versions if you already have a license for others. Once you download and install RStudio, you will see something like the following screenshot when you open RStudio:

Now that we have our R environment ready, let's build a simple logistic regression model to familiarize ourselves with R a little more.

A simple logistic regression model in R

Let's test our environment setup by building a simple logistic regression model in R. Open RStudio and create a new **R Script** file. You can create a data frame in R, using the following code:

```
# Input Data
data <- data.frame(
    "X"=c(0, 0.25, 0.5, 1),
    "Y"=c(0, 0.5, 0.5, 1),
    "output"=c(0, 0, 1, 1)
)
```

As you can see from this code snippet, we built a dataframe with columns X, Y, and output. The X column takes values of 0, 0.25, 0.5, and 1. The Y column has values of 0, 0.5, 0.5, and 1. output is a binary class, where it can be either 0 or 1. data looks as follows:

```
> data
     X    Y output
1 0.00 0.0      0
2 0.25 0.5      0
3 0.50 0.5      1
4 1.00 1.0      1
```

Now that we have the data to train a logistic regression model with, let's take a look at the following code:

```
# Train logistic regression
logit.fit <- glm(
    output ~ X + Y,
    data = data,
    family = binomial
)
```

As shown in this code snippet, we are using the glm function in R to fit a logistic regression model. Since the glm function is used to fit any linear models, we need to define the variable family of the model we want to train. In order to train a logistic regression, we use binomial for the family argument in the glm function. The first argument, output ~ X + Y, defines the formula for this model and the data argument is used to define the dataframe to use to train the model with.

In R, you can use the summary function to get the details of the fitted logistic regression model, as shown in the following code:

```
# Show Fitted Results
summary(logit.fit)
```

This will output something like the following screenshot:

```
> # Show Fitted Results
> summary(logit.fit)

Call:
glm(formula = output ~ X + Y, family = binomial, data = data)

Deviance Residuals:
           1            2            3            4
-1.140e-05   -6.547e-06    1.516e-05    2.110e-08

Coefficients:
              Estimate Std. Error z value Pr(>|z|)
(Intercept)     -23.46   75250.33       0        1
X               189.81  570847.71       0        1
Y               -97.12  556850.90       0        1

(Dispersion parameter for binomial family taken to be 1)

    Null deviance: 5.5452e+00  on 3  degrees of freedom
Residual deviance: 4.0252e-10  on 1  degrees of freedom
AIC: 6

Number of Fisher Scoring iterations: 23
```

As you can see from this output, we can easily find the coefficients and the intercept of the model. We will use this summary function frequently throughout this book to better understand the trained models.

With a trained model, we can predict on new data with the following code:

```
# Predict Class Probabilities
logit.probs <- predict(
  logit.fit,
  newdata=data,
  type="response"
)

# Predict Classes
logit.pred <- ifelse(logit.probs > 0.5, 1, 0)
logit.pred    # output: 0 0 1 1
```

As you can see from this code snippet, we are using the `predict` function to make a prediction with the trained model, `logit.fit`, and with new data defined in the argument, `newdata`. This `predict` function will output the probabilities or likelihoods for each example in the new data; in order to transform this output into a binary class, we can use the `ifelse` function to encode any output that is above a threshold (in this case, `0.5`) as `1` and the rest as `0`.

Lastly, let's quickly look at how we can build plots in R. We will be using an R package, `ggplot2`, for plotting throughout this book. So, it will be beneficial for you to get familiar with how to import this plotting library and use it for data visualizations. If it is your first time using this package, then you will most likely see the following error message when you try to import the `ggplot2` package:

```
> # Plotting Library
> require(ggplot2)
Loading required package: ggplot2
Warning message:
In library(package, lib.loc = lib.loc, character.only = TRUE, logical.return = TRUE,  :
  there is no package called 'ggplot2'
```

As the message says, the package, `ggplot2`, is not yet installed on your machine. In order to install any R package, you can simply run the following command:

```
install.packages('ggplot2')
```

If you run this command, you will see output like the following:

```
> install.packages("ggplot2")
also installing the dependencies 'colorspace', 'RColorBrewer', 'dichromat', 'munsell', 'labeli
ng', 'digest', 'gtable', 'lazyeval', 'plyr', 'reshape2', 'scales', 'viridisLite', 'withr'

trying URL 'https://cran.rstudio.com/bin/macosx/el-capitan/contrib/3.4/colorspace_1.3-2.tgz'
Content type 'application/x-gzip' length 443683 bytes (433 KB)
==================================================
downloaded 433 KB
```

Once the installation of this library is complete, then you can import and use this library. We are going to build a simple scatterplot using the `ggplot2` library, as shown in the following code snippet:

```
# Plotting Library
library(ggplot2)

# Simple Scatterplot
```

```
ggplot(data, aes(x=X, y=Y, color=output)) +
  geom_point(size=3, shape=19) +
  ggtitle('Actual') +
  theme(plot.title = element_text(hjust = 0.5))
```

As you can see from this code snippet, you can build a scatterplot with data, using the ggplot function of ggplot2 package. In order to change the shape and size of the points on the scatterplot, you can use the geom_point function. You can also use the ggtitle function to change the title of the plot. When you run this code, you will see the following chart:

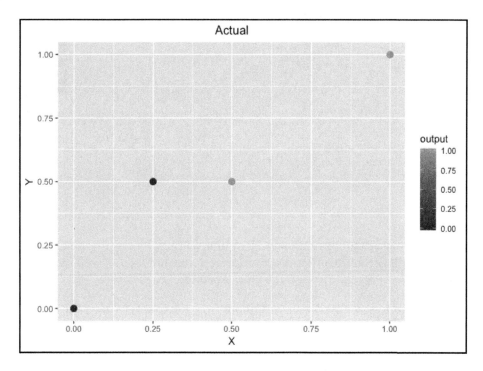

We will run the same task for the prediction results. The code looks as follows:

```
ggplot(data, aes(x=X, y=Y, color=logit.pred)) +
  geom_point(size=3, shape=19) +
  ggtitle('Predicted') +
  theme(plot.title = element_text(hjust = 0.5))
```

The output appears as follows:

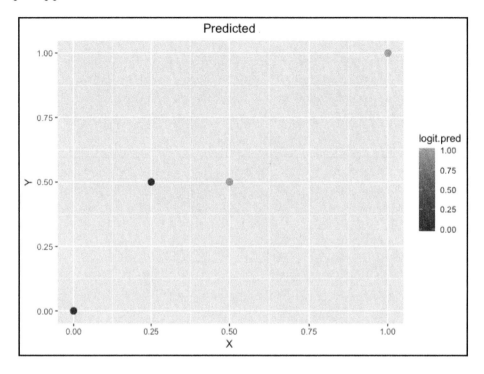

We will be heavily utilizing these functions and the plotting library, ggplot2, throughout this book, so you will get more and more comfortable coding in R, as well as using these other libraries, as we progress through the chapters and exercises.

 You can view and download the full R code that was used for this section from the following link: https://github.com/yoonhwang/hands-on-data-science-for-marketing/blob/master/ch.1/R/SettingUpREnvironment.R.

Summary

In this chapter, we discussed the overall trends in marketing and learned the rising importance of data science and machine learning in the marketing industry. As the amount of data increases and as we observe the benefits of utilizing data science and machine learning for marketing, companies of all sizes are investing in building more data-driven and quantitative marketing strategies.

We also learned different types of analysis methods, especially the three types of analysis that we will be using frequently in this book—descriptive, explanatory, and predictive —and different use cases of these analyses. In this chapter, we covered different types of machine learning algorithms, as well as the typical workflow in data science. Lastly, we spent some time setting up our development environments in Python and R and testing our environment setup by building a simple logistic regression model.

In the next chapter, we are going to go over some of the **key performance indicators (KPIs)** and how to visualize these key metrics. We will learn how to compute and build visual plots of these KPIs in Python, using different packages, such as `pandas`, `numpy`, and `matplotlib`. For those of you who are following the exercises in this book using the R language, we will also discuss how to use R to compute and plot these KPIs in R, using various statistical and mathematical functions in R and the `ggplot2` package for visualizations.

Section 2: Descriptive Versus Explanatory Analysis

2

In this section, you will learn the Key Performance Indicators (KPIs) that are commonly used in the marketing industry, how to use charting libraries in Python and R to visualize metrics, and how to use machine learning algorithms to understand what drives the successes and failures of marketing campaigns.

This section consists of the following chapters:

- Chapter 2, *Key Performance Indicators and Visualizations*
- Chapter 3, *Drivers behind Marketing Engagement*
- Chapter 4, *From Engagement to Conversion*

2
Key Performance Indicators and Visualizations

When you run marketing campaigns or any other marketing efforts, you would most likely want to know how well each of them performs and understand the weaknesses and strengths of each of your marketing efforts. In this chapter, we are going to discuss commonly used **key performance indicators** (**KPIs**) that help you track the performances of your marketing efforts. More specifically, we will cover such KPIs as sales revenue, **cost per acquisition** (**CPA**), digital marketing KPIs, and site traffic. We will learn how these KPIs can help you stay on track toward your marketing goals.

After discussing some of the commonly used KPIs, we will then learn how we can use Python and/or R to compute such KPIs and build visualizations of those KPIs. In this chapter, we will use a bank marketing dataset that showcases a real-world case of marketing campaigns for finance organizations. For the Python project, we will learn how we can use the `pandas` and `matplotlib` libraries to analyze data and build visualizations. For the R project, we will introduce the `dplyr` and `ggplot2` libraries to analyze and manipulate data and build visualizations.

In particular, we will cover the following topics in this chapter:

- KPIs to measure performances of different marketing efforts
- Computing and visualizing KPIs using Python
- Computing and visualizing KPIs using R

KPIs to measure performances of different marketing efforts

Every marketing effort costs money to the company. When you run marketing campaigns through emails, sending each email costs some money. When you are running marketing efforts on social network services or broadcast media, it also requires some capital. As every marketing effort is associated with some costs, it is critical to look at the performances of marketing campaigns and track the **return on investments (ROI)** of your marketing campaigns. We will mainly discuss how to track sales revenue, CPA, and digital marketing KPIs in this section.

Sales revenue

It is clear that the goal of every marketing effort is to generate and grow more revenue for the company. No company wants to spend more money on marketing than it generates. In order to correctly report the sales revenue, you will need to clearly define how you want to attribute sales to each of your marketing efforts. Some sales might come from email marketing campaigns, while some others might come from advertisements placed on TV or public transportation. Some sales could even come naturally, without any attributions to any of your marketing campaigns.

In order to correctly report how much sales revenue each of your marketing efforts drives, you will have to clearly define the rules to attribute your sales to each of your marketing efforts. For example, if you are an ecommerce company and promoting special offers through email and TV marketing campaigns, you might want to put a different URL in the emails than the URL in your TV commercials. This way, you can identify and differentiate those sales from email marketing campaigns from those sales from marketing efforts through TV.

Depending on your needs, you might also want to report time-series sales revenue data. You can report it in a spreadsheet format, such as the following:

	Date	TotalSales
1	2010–12–01	748957.020
2	2011–01–01	560000:260
3	2011–02–01	498062.650
4	2011–03–01	683267.080
5	2011–04–01	493207.121
6	2011–05–01	723333.510
7	2011–06–01	691123.120
8	2011–07–01	681300.111
9	2011–08–01	682680.510
10	2011–09–01	1019687.622
11	2011–10–01	1070704.670
12	2011–11–01	1461756.250
13	2011–12–01	433668.010

You can also report time-series sales revenue data in a line chart, such as the following:

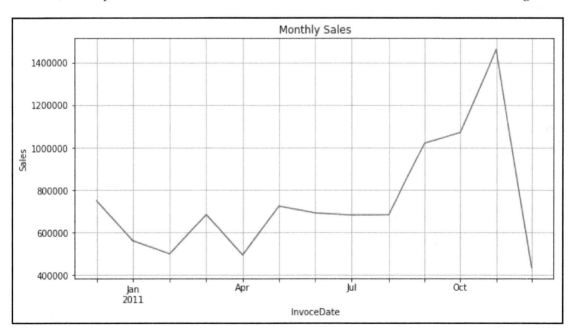

We will discuss more about the different types of plots and data visualizations you can use for reporting KPIs when we work through the Python and R exercises toward the end of this chapter.

Cost per acquisition (CPA)

Another way to look at the effectiveness of your marketing efforts is CPA. This KPI metric tells you how much it costs you to acquire a customer through your marketing efforts. A high CPA means it costs more to acquire a new customer, while a low CPA clearly means it costs less to acquire a new customer. Depending on the type of business, you can still have a very profitable marketing campaign with high CPA. For example, if you are selling a very luxurious and high-end product, where the pool of targeted customers is small and it costs more to acquire such customers, your CPA might be high, but the value of each customer you acquired might be even higher and result in a profitable marketing campaign.

We will take a look at the following hypothetical case:

Campaign	Cost	Customers Acquired	CPA	Sales	Sales per Customer	Value of Campaign
Happy Hour Event	$25,000	40	$625	$50,000	$1,250	$25,000
Webinar	$2,000	10	$200	$5,000	$500	$3,000
Radio Commercial	$7,000	50	$140	$6,000	$120	($1,000)

If you look at this spreadsheet, **Happy Hour Event** was the most expensive marketing event, in terms of both the total cost and CPA. However, it generated the most **Sales** and **Sales per Customer**; thus, it was the most valuable campaign. On the other hand, **Radio Commercial** was the lowest CPA marketing campaign, even though the total cost is the second highest, because it helped the business to acquire the most number of customers. However, the total sales from these customers did not exceed the total cost of this campaign and introduced a net loss to the company.

Even though this is a hypothetical situation, a similar case can happen in real life. Marketing efforts, such as **Happy Hour Event** and **Webinar** have better-targeted customers than **Radio Commercial**. The quality of customers acquired through highly-targeted marketing campaigns is many times better compared to non-targeted marketing campaigns.

Now that we have seen how we can break down the marketing campaign results to analyze the cost-effectiveness in more depth, we will look at some of the commonly used KPIs for digital marketing.

Digital marketing KPIs

As the choices of marketing channels grow into online space, such as on social network services, blogs, and search engines, reporting the performances of digital marketing efforts has become more and more important. Previously discussed KPIs, sales revenue, and cost per acquisition, apply in the digital marketing space as well.

As an example, based on individual attribution logic, you can analyze how much sales are generated through different social network services, such as Facebook, LinkedIn, and Instagram. You can also analyze how many customers are acquired through such marketing channels and see what individual digital marketing campaigns' CPAs and generated values are. Let's discuss some more digital marketing KPIs:

- **Click-through rate (CTR)** is another KPI that is commonly looked at for digital marketing efforts. CTR is the percentage of people who viewed your advertisement and then went on to click the advertisement. The formula looks as follows:

$$CTR = \frac{Number\ of\ Clicks}{Number\ of\ Views}$$

  CTR is an important measure in digital marketing channels, as it measures how effective your online marketing is in bringing traffic to your website.

- Then, you can use **lead ratio** to measure how much of the website traffic can be converted into leads. Typically, only a subset of website traffic is a good fit to become your customers. These **marketing qualified leads (MQL)** are the leads that are ready to be marketed to and meet business-specific criteria to become customers who are likely to make purchases, based on their characteristics. As you start marketing to these qualified leads, you should also look at conversion rates.

- The **conversion rate** is the percentage of leads that are converted into active customers. You can define what should be considered as conversions, based on your marketing goals. If your goal is to see what percentage of leads became paying customers, then you can compute the conversion rate somewhat similar to the following formula:

$$Conversion\ Rate = \frac{Number\ of\ Paying\ customer}{Number\ of\ Leads}$$

If your goal is to see what percentage of leads signed up on your website, then you can compute the conversion rate as in the following formula:

$$Conversion\ Rate = \frac{Number\ of\ Sign - Ups}{Number\ of\ Leads}$$

We have looked at various KPIs so far and discussed how these KPIs can help you track the progress and performances of your marketing efforts. We will now look at how to use Python and/or R to compute such KPIs and build visualizations. If you plan on using one of the two programming languages, Python and R, used in this book, you can skip to the section that you'd like to work on.

Computing and visualizing KPIs using Python

In this section, we are going to discuss how we can use Python to compute and visualize the KPIs we have discussed in the previous sections. We will primarily focus on analyzing conversion rates using bank marketing data. For those readers who would like to use R for this exercise, you can skip to the next section. We will be using the `pandas` and `matplotlib` libraries in Python to manipulate and analyze data and build various charts to accurately report the progress and performances of marketing efforts.

For the exercise in this section, we are going to use the *UCI's Bank Marketing Data Set*, which can be found at this link: `https://archive.ics.uci.edu/ml/datasets/bank+marketing`. You can follow this link and download the data by clicking the `Data Folder` link in the top-left corner. For this exercise, we downloaded the `bank-additional.zip` data and we will use the `bank-additional-full.csv` file in that zipped file.

When you open this `bank-additional-full.csv` file, you will notice that a semi-colon (`;`) is used as a separator, instead of a comma (`,`). In order to load this data, you can use the following code to read in this data into a `pandas DataFrame`:

```
import pandas as pd

df = pd.read_csv('../data/bank-additional-full.csv', sep=';')
```

As you can see from this code, we are importing the `pandas` library with the alias, `pd`, and we are using the `read_csv` function to load the data. For separators other than commas, you can define a custom separator with the `sep` argument within the `read_csv` function.

If you look at the field description in the data download page (https://archive.ics.uci.edu/ml/datasets/bank+marketing), the output variable, `y`, which has information on whether a client has subscribed to a term deposit, is encoded as `'yes'` or `'no'`. In order to simplify our conversion rate computations, we will encode this variable as 1 for `'yes'` and 0 for `'no'`. You can use the following code for this encoding:

```
df['conversion'] = df['y'].apply(lambda x: 1 if x == 'yes' else 0)
```

As you can see from this code snippet, we are using the `apply` function to encode `'yes'` as 1 and `'no'` as 0 for the variable, `y`, and then adding this encoded data as a new column, `conversion`. The code and the loaded data in our Jupyter Notebook will look like the following:

```
import pandas as pd

df = pd.read_csv('../data/bank-additional-full.csv', sep=';')

df['conversion'] = df['y'].apply(lambda x: 1 if x == 'yes' else 0)

df.head()
```

	age	job	marital	education	default	housing	loan	contact	month	day_of_week	...	pdays	previous	poutcome	emp.var.rate	cons.price.idx
0	56	housemaid	married	basic.4y	no	no	no	telephone	may	mon	...	999	0	nonexistent	1.1	93.994
1	57	services	married	high.school	unknown	no	no	telephone	may	mon	...	999	0	nonexistent	1.1	93.994
2	37	services	married	high.school	no	yes	no	telephone	may	mon	...	999	0	nonexistent	1.1	93.994
3	40	admin.	married	basic.6y	no	no	no	telephone	may	mon	...	999	0	nonexistent	1.1	93.994
4	56	services	married	high.school	no	no	yes	telephone	may	mon	...	999	0	nonexistent	1.1	93.994

5 rows × 22 columns

Now that we have successfully read the data into a `pandas` `DataFrame`, we will start looking at how to analyze and visualize conversion rates, using various methods and plots.

Aggregate conversion rate

First, we are going to look at the aggregate conversion rate. We can calculate this metric by dividing the total number of clients subscribed to a term deposit by the total number of clients in the data. Since we have already encoded the output variable as 1 for those who have converted and 0 for those who have not, in a column named `conversion`, we can simply sum over this column to get the total number of conversions.

The following code snippet shows how we can sum over the `conversion` column and get the total number of clients in the data:

```
# total number of conversions
df.conversion.sum()
# total number of clients in the data (= number of rows in the data)
df.shape[0]
```

The following is what our code for conversion rate calculations in the Jupyter Notebook look like:

```
print('total conversions: %i out of %i' % (df.conversion.sum(), df.shape[0]))

total conversions: 4640 out of 41188

print('conversion rate: %0.2f%%' % (df.conversion.sum() / df.shape[0] * 100.0))

conversion rate: 11.27%
```

As you can see from this code output in the Jupyter Notebook, we have 4640 converted clients out of a total of 41188 bank clients, which suggests the aggregate conversion rate is 11.27%. In the following section, we are going to analyze how these conversion rates vary by different age groups.

Conversion rates by age

Aggregate conversion rate tells us the overall performance of our marketing campaign. However, it does not give us that much insight. When we are reporting and tracking the progress of marketing efforts, we typically would want to dive deeper into the data and break down the customer base into multiple segments and compute KPIs for individual segments. We will first break our data into smaller segments by `age` and see how the conversion rates differ by different age groups.

We will look at the following code first:

```
conversions_by_age = df.groupby(
    by='age'
)['conversion'].sum() / df.groupby(
    by='age'
)['conversion'].count() * 100.0
```

As you can see from this code, we are using the `groupby` function to calculate conversion rates by each age.

We first group by a variable name, `age`, and sum over the `conversion` column, using the `sum` function, to get the total number of conversions by each age. Then, we group by `age` again and count the number of records in each `age` group by using the `count` function.

Using these two computations, we can calculate the conversion rates for each `age`, as shown in the code. A part of the calculated conversion rates for each `age` looks as follows:

age	conversion
17	40.000000
18	42.857143
19	47.619048
20	35.384615
21	28.431373
22	26.277372
23	21.238938
24	18.574514
25	15.551839

Another way to look at conversion rates across client ages is by plotting a line chart, as shown in the following screenshot:

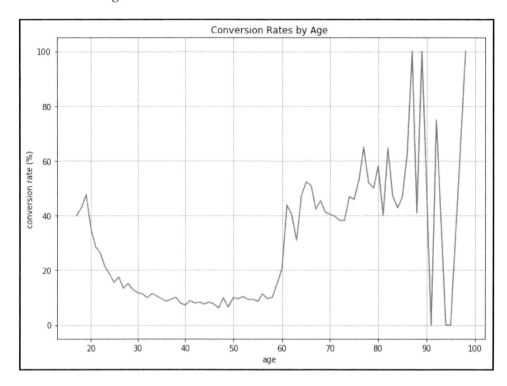

The code to visualize conversion rates across different ages looks as follows:

```
ax = conversions_by_age.plot(
    grid=True,
    figsize=(10, 7),
    title='Conversion Rates by Age'
)

ax.set_xlabel('age')
ax.set_ylabel('conversion rate (%)')

plt.show()
```

As this code shows, we are using the `conversions_by_age` variable that we built previously and the `plot` function for a line chart. As you can see from this code, you can change the size of a figure by an argument, named `figsize`, and the title of the chart with an argument, named `title`. In order to change the labels of the *x*-axis and *y*-axis, you can use the `set_xlabel` and `set_ylabel` functions.

One thing that is noticeable in the previous line chart is the fact that there seems to be lots of noise in old age groups. Conversion rates for those who are 70 or older vary a lot and if you look at the data, this is mostly because the number of clients in this age group is relatively small, compared to other age groups.

In order to reduce this unwanted noise, we can group multiple ages together. In this exercise, we group bank clients into six different groups, based on their age—between 18 and 30, between 30 and 40, between 40 and 50, between 50 and 60, between 60 and 70, and 70 and older. The following code can be used to group the clients into their corresponding groups:

```
df['age_group'] = df['age'].apply(
    lambda x: '[18, 30)' if x < 30 else '[30, 40)' if x < 40 \
        else '[40, 50)' if x < 50 else '[50, 60)' if x < 60 \
        else '[60, 70)' if x < 70 else '70+'
)
```

If you look at this code, we are using the `apply` function on the column, `age`, to group clients into six different age groups and add this data to a new column, named `age_group`. In order to calculate the conversion rates for these newly created age groups, we can use the following code:

```
conversions_by_age_group = df.groupby(
    by='age_group'
)['conversion'].sum() / df.groupby(
    by='age_group'
)['conversion'].count() * 100.0
```

Similar to the previous case, we are using the `groupby`, `sum`, and `count` functions to calculate conversion rates for these six different age groups. The resulting data looks like the following screenshot:

age_group	conversion
70+	47.121535
[18, 30)	16.263891
[30, 40)	10.125162
[40, 50)	7.923238
[50, 60)	10.157389
[60, 70)	34.668508

As you can see from this, the variations by each age group are much smaller than before, especially in old age groups. We can visualize this data using a bar plot, as shown in the following screenshot:

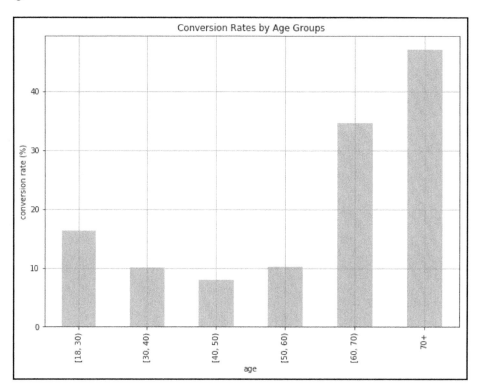

The code to build this bar plot looks like the following:

```
ax = conversions_by_age_group.loc[
    ['[18, 30)', '[30, 40)', '[40, 50)', '[50, 60)', '[60, 70)', '70+']
].plot(
    kind='bar',
    color='skyblue',
    grid=True,
    figsize=(10, 7),
    title='Conversion Rates by Age Groups'
)

ax.set_xlabel('age')
ax.set_ylabel('conversion rate (%)')

plt.show()
```

As you can see from this code, we are using the same `plot` function that we used before to build a line plot. The only difference is the `kind` argument, with which we can define different types of plots we would like to build. Here, we are giving a value of `bar` to this `kind` argument to build a bar plot.

 You can find the full code in the following repository: `https://github.com/yoonhwang/hands-on-data-science-for-marketing/blob/master/ch.2/python/ConversionRate.ipynb`.

Conversions versus non-conversions

One other thing we can look at is the demographic differences between the converted clients and non-converted clients. This type of analysis can help us identify what differentiates converted groups from non-converted groups in our marketing campaigns and help us understand our target clients better and what types of customers respond better to our marketing efforts. In this exercise, we will compare the distributions of the marital status among the conversions and non-conversions groups.

We will first count the number of conversions and non-conversions for each marital status. The following code shows how we can compute this using `pandas` functions:

```
pd.pivot_table(df, values='y', index='marital', columns='conversion',
aggfunc=len)
```

As you can see from this code, we are using the `pivot_table` function in the `pandas` library. We are grouping by the columns, `marital` and `conversion`, where `marital` will become the index and `conversion` will become the column of the new `DataFrame`. With the `aggfunc` argument, we can supply the type of aggregation we want to perform. Here, we are using the `len` function to simply count the number of clients for each group. The resulting data looks like the following screenshot:

marital	non_conversions	conversions
divorced	4136	476
married	22396	2532
single	9948	1620
unknown	68	12

Another way to represent this data is by using pie charts, as follows:

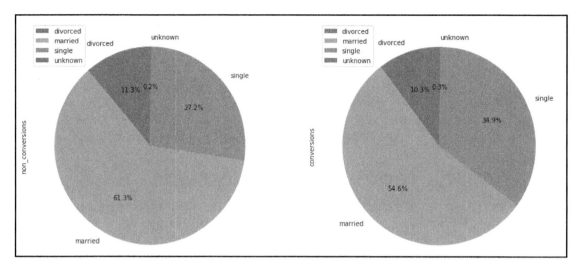

The following code shows how we can build these pie charts:

```
conversions_by_marital_status_df.plot(
    kind='pie',
    figsize=(15, 7),
    startangle=90,
    subplots=True,
    autopct=lambda x: '%0.1f%%' % x
)

plt.show()
```

As you can see from this code, we are using the same `plot` function as before, but using `pie` as the kind of plot that we would like to build. You can use the `autopct` argument to format the label for each group in the pie charts.

Compared to the tabular format of the data output, pie charts make it much easier to understand the overall distributions of the data. With pie charts, we can easily see that the `married` group takes up the largest proportions in both conversions and non-conversions groups, while the `single` group comes as the second. Using pie charts, we can easily visualize the similarities and differences between two groups.

Conversions by age and marital status

So far, we have aggregated our data by one criterion. However, there are cases where you want to group the data by more than one column. In this section, we will discuss how we can analyze and report conversion rates by more than one criterion. As an exercise, we will use age groups that we have built in the previous section and the marital status as the two columns to group by.

Let's first look at the code:

```
age_marital_df = df.groupby(['age_group',
'marital'])['conversion'].sum().unstack('marital').fillna(0)

age_marital_df = age_marital_df.divide(
    df.groupby(
        by='age_group'
    )['conversion'].count(),
    axis=0
)
```

As you can see from this code, we are grouping our data by the two columns, `age_group` and `marital`, and summing the number of conversions. Then, we divide this by the total number of clients in each group. The resulting data looks like the following screenshot:

marital	divorced	married	single	unknown
age_group				
70+	0.136461	0.321962	0.012793	0.000000
[18, 30)	0.002117	0.027871	0.132475	0.000176
[30, 40)	0.007557	0.052958	0.040383	0.000354
[40, 50)	0.011970	0.054627	0.012350	0.000285
[50, 60)	0.017342	0.077674	0.006412	0.000146
[60, 70)	0.037293	0.301105	0.006906	0.001381

As you can see from this data, we can now see the distribution of conversion rates based on two criteria, age group and martial status. For example, the conversion rate of clients who are single and between **18** and **30** years old is 13.25%, while the conversion rate of clients who are married and between **60** and **70** years old is 30.11%. Another way to visualize this data is to use a bar plot that looks like the following:

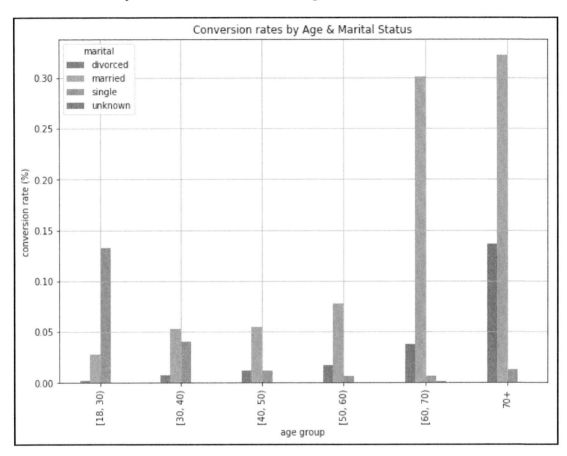

In this bar chart, we can easily see the distributions of conversion rates for each of the age and marital status groups. The code we used to build this bar plot looks is shown here:

```
ax = age_marital_df.loc[
    ['[18, 30)', '[30, 40)', '[40, 50)', '[50, 60)', '[60, 70)', '70+']
].plot(
    kind='bar',
    grid=True,
    figsize=(10,7)
)

ax.set_title('Conversion rates by Age & Marital Status')
ax.set_xlabel('age group')
ax.set_ylabel('conversion rate (%)')

plt.show()
```

Similar to previous cases, we are using the `plot` function of the `pandas` library and passing `bar` to the `kind` argument of the function. Since the `DataFrame`, age_marital_df, has four columns for each of the marital statuses and is indexed by age groups, the `plot` function builds a bar plot with four bars for each of the marital statuses for each of the age groups.

If you would like to stack those four bars for each age group, then you can use the following code for a stacked bar plot:

```
ax = age_marital_df.loc[
    ['[18, 30)', '[30, 40)', '[40, 50)', '[50, 60)', '[60, 70)', '70+']
].plot(
    kind='bar',
    stacked=True,
    grid=True,
    figsize=(10,7)
)

ax.set_title('Conversion rates by Age & Marital Status')
ax.set_xlabel('age group')
ax.set_ylabel('conversion rate (%)')

plt.show()
```

As you can see from this code, the only difference is the argument, `stacked`, that we used in this code. When this argument is set to `True`, it will build a stacked bar plot, which looks like the following:

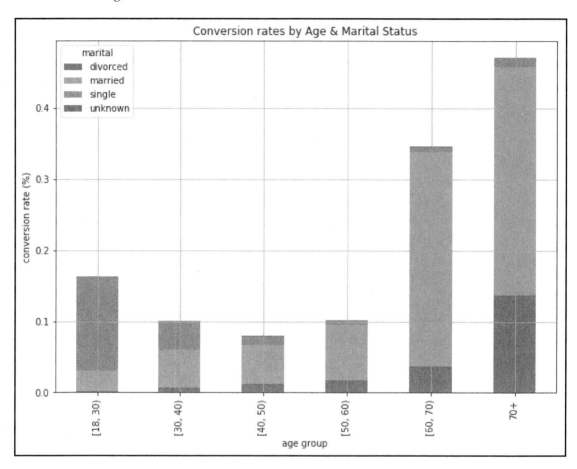

As you can see from this stacked bar plot, different marital statuses are stacked on top of each other for each of the age groups. This way, we can not only easily see the overall trends in conversion rates across different age groups, but also the proportions of converted clients with different marital statuses for each age group.

The full code and Jupyter Notebook that we used for this Python exercise can be found in the following repository: `https://github.com/yoonhwang/hands-on-data-science-for-marketing/blob/master/ch.2/python/ConversionRate.ipynb`.

Computing and visualizing KPIs using R

In this section, we are going to discuss how we can use R to compute and visualize the KPIs we have discussed in the previous sections. We will primarily focus on analyzing conversion rates using bank marketing data. For those readers, who would like to use Python for this exercise, you can find the Python exercise in the previous section. We will be using the `dplyr` and `ggplot2` libraries in R to manipulate and analyze data and build various charts to accurately report the progress and performances of marketing efforts. The `dplyr` library provides various functionalities for data manipulation for data science and machine learning tasks.

For the exercise in this section, we are going to use the **UCI**'s **Bank Marketing Data Set**, which can be found at this link: `https://archive.ics.uci.edu/ml/datasets/bank+marketing`. You can follow this link and download the data by clicking the `Data Folder` link in the top-left corner. For this exercise, we downloaded the `bank-additional.zip` data and we will use the `bank-additional-full.csv` file in that zipped file.

When you open this `bank-additional-full.csv` file, you will notice that a semi-colon (`;`) is used as a separator, instead of a comma (`,`). In order to load this data, you can use the following code to read in this data into a `DataFrame`:

```
conversionsDF <- read.csv(
   file="~/Documents/data-science-for-marketing/ch.2/data/bank-additional-
full.csv",
   header=TRUE,
   sep=";"
)
```

As you can see from this code, we are using the `read.csv` function to load the data. For separators other than commas, you can define a custom separator with the `sep` argument within the `read.csv` function. If your data file contains a row for the header, you can set the argument, `header`, to `TRUE`. On the other hand, if your data file does not contain a row for the header and the data starts from the first row, you can set it to `FALSE`.

If you look at the field description in the data download page (`https://archive.ics.uci.edu/ml/datasets/bank+marketing`), the output variable, `y`, which has information on whether a client has subscribed to a term deposit, is encoded as `'yes'` or `'no'`. In order to simplify our conversion rate computations, we will encode this variable as `1` for `'yes'` and `0` for `'no'`. You can use the following code for this encoding:

```
# Encode conversions as 0s and 1s
conversionsDF$conversion <- as.integer(conversionsDF$y) - 1
```

As you can see from this code snippet, we are using the `as.integer` function to encode `'yes'` as 1 and `'no'` as 0 for the variable, y, and then adding this encoded data as a new column, `conversion`. Since the `as.integer` function will use 1 and 2 for `'no'` and `'yes'` encodings by default, we are subtracting the values by 1. The data now looks like the following in our RStudio:

	age	job	marital	education	default	housing	loan	contact	month	day_of_week	duration	campaign	pdays	previous	poutcome
1	56	housemaid	married	basic.4y	no	no	no	telephone	may	mon	261	1	999	0	nonexistent
2	57	services	married	high.school	unknown	no	no	telephone	may	mon	149	1	999	0	nonexistent
3	37	services	married	high.school	no	yes	no	telephone	may	mon	226	1	999	0	nonexistent
4	40	admin.	married	basic.6y	no	no	no	telephone	may	mon	151	1	999	0	nonexistent
5	56	services	married	high.school	no	no	yes	telephone	may	mon	307	1	999	0	nonexistent
6	45	services	married	basic.9y	unknown	no	no	telephone	may	mon	198	1	999	0	nonexistent
7	59	admin.	married	professional.course	no	no	no	telephone	may	mon	139	1	999	0	nonexistent
8	41	blue-collar	married	unknown	unknown	no	no	telephone	may	mon	217	1	999	0	nonexistent
9	24	technician	single	professional.course	no	yes	no	telephone	may	mon	380	1	999	0	nonexistent

Now that we have successfully read the data into an R `DataFrame`, we will start looking at how to analyze and visualize conversion rates, using various methods and plots.

Aggregate conversion rate

First, we are going to look at is the aggregate conversion rate. We can calculate this metric by dividing the total number of clients subscribed to a term deposit by the total number of clients in the data. Since we have already encoded the output variable as 1 for those who have converted and 0 for those who have not in a column, named `conversion`, we can simply sum over this column to get the total number of conversions. The following code snippet shows how we can sum over the `conversion` column and get the total number of clients in the data:

```
# total number of conversions
sum(conversionsDF$conversion)

# total number of clients in the data (= number of records in the data)
nrow(conversionsDF)
```

As you can see from this code snippet, we are using the `sum` function in R to calculate the total number of conversions and the `nrow` function to count the number of rows in our dataset. On a side note, as with `nrow`, you can use the `ncol` function to count the number of columns of a `DataFrame`.

The following screenshot shows what the code looks like on our RStudio:

```
> #### 1. Aggregate Conversion Rate ####
> sprintf("total conversions: %i out of %i", sum(conversionsDF$conversion), nrow(conversionsDF))
[1] "total conversions: 4640 out of 41188"
> sprintf("conversion rate: %0.2f%%", sum(conversionsDF$conversion)/nrow(conversionsDF)*100.0)
[1] "conversion rate: 11.27%"
```

As you can see from this code output in the RStudio, we have `4640` converted clients out of a total of `41188` bank clients, which suggests the aggregate conversion rate is `11.27%`. In the following section, we are going to analyze how these conversion rates vary by different age groups. We are using the `sprintf` function to format a string with integers and floating point numbers.

Conversion rates by age

Aggregate conversion rate tells us the overall performance of our marketing campaign. However, it does not give us that much insight. When we are reporting and tracking the progress of marketing efforts, we typically would want to dive deeper into the data and break down the customer base into multiple segments and compute KPIs for individual segments. We will first break our data into smaller segments by age and see how the conversion rates differ by different age groups.

We will look at the following code first:

```
conversionsByAge <- conversionsDF %>%
  group_by(Age=age) %>%
  summarise(TotalCount=n(), NumConversions=sum(conversion)) %>%
  mutate(ConversionRate=NumConversions/TotalCount*100.0)
```

The pipe operator, `%>%`, in this code, is the way you can apply different functions sequentially. In this code snippet, we are passing `conversionDF` to a `group_by` function, then passing the results of this `group_by` function to the `summarise` function, and lastly to the `mutate` function.

In the `group_by` function, we are grouping the `DataFrame` by the column `age`. Then, for each age group, we are counting the number of records in each group, by using a function, `n()`, and naming it `TotalCount`. Also, we are summing over the column, `conversion`, for each age group, by using the `sum` function, and naming it `NumConversions`.

Lastly, we are using the `mutate` function, which adds new variables, while preserving the original `DataFrame`, to compute conversion rates for each age group. As you can see, we are simply dividing `NumConversion` by `TotalCount` and multiplying it by `100.0` to get the conversion rates.

The resulting data is shown in the following screenshot:

	Age	TotalCount	NumConversions	ConversionRate
1	17	5	2	40.000000
2	18	28	12	42.857143
3	19	42	20	47.619048
4	20	65	23	35.384615
5	21	102	29	28.431373
6	22	137	36	26.277372
7	23	226	48	21.238938
8	24	463	86	18.574514
9	25	598	93	15.551839
10	26	698	122	17.478510
11	27	851	114	13.396005
12	28	1001	151	15.084915
13	29	1453	186	12.801101
14	30	1714	202	11.785298
15	31	1947	220	11.299435
16	32	1846	184	9.967497
17	33	1833	210	11.456628
18	34	1745	184	10.544413

Another way to look at conversion rates across client ages is by plotting a line chart, as shown in the following screenshot:

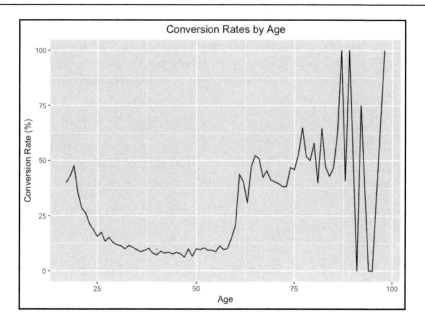

The code to visualize conversion rates across different ages is shown here:

```
# line chart
ggplot(data=conversionsByAge, aes(x=Age, y=ConversionRate)) +
  geom_line() +
  ggtitle('Conversion Rates by Age') +
  xlab("Age") +
  ylab("Conversion Rate (%)") +
  theme(plot.title = element_text(hjust = 0.5))
```

As you can see from this code, we are using the `ggplot` function to initialize a `ggplot` object with `conversionsByAge` as the data and the column, `Age`, as the *x*-axis and the column, `ConversionRate`, as the *y*-axis.

Then, we use `geom_line` function to connect the observations and create a line chart. You can change the title of a plot, by using `ggtitle` function. Also, you can use `xlab` and `ylab` functions to rename the x-axis label and y-axis label respectively.

One thing that is noticeable in the previous line chart is the fact that there seems to be lots of noise in older age groups. Conversion rates for those who are 70 or older vary a lot and if you look at the data, this is mostly because the number of clients in this age group is relatively small, compared to other age groups.

In order to reduce this unwanted noise, we can group multiple ages together. In this exercise, we group bank clients into six different groups, based on their age—between 18 and 30, between 30 and 40, between 40 and 50, between 50 and 60, between 60 and 70, and 70 and older. The following code can be used to group the clients into their corresponding groups:

```
# b. by age groups
conversionsByAgeGroup <- conversionsDF %>%
    group_by(AgeGroup=cut(age, breaks=seq(20, 70, by = 10)) ) %>%
    summarise(TotalCount=n(), NumConversions=sum(conversion)) %>%
    mutate(ConversionRate=NumConversions/TotalCount*100.0)

conversionsByAgeGroup$AgeGroup <-
as.character(conversionsByAgeGroup$AgeGroup)
conversionsByAgeGroup$AgeGroup[6] <- "70+"
```

As with the previous case, we are using the `group_by` function to group the `conversionsDF` data by the `age` column. The difference here is how we used the `cut` function to create the age range for each age group.

The `breaks` argument defines the points at which the `cut` function is going to divide the `DataFrame`. The argument, `seq(20, 70, by = 10)`, means we are going to create a sequence from 20 to 70 in increments of 10. Once the data is grouped by these age groups, the rest are the same as before. We are using the `summarise` and `mutate` functions to compute for the `TotalCount`, `NumConversions`, and `ConversionRate` columns.

The resulting `DataFrame` is shown in the following screenshot:

	AgeGroup	TotalCount	NumConversions	ConversionRate
1	(20,30]	7243	1067	14.731465
2	(30,40]	16385	1597	9.746720
3	(40,50]	10240	837	8.173828
4	(50,60]	6270	668	10.653907
5	(60,70]	488	212	43.442623
6	70+	562	259	46.085409

As you can see from this, the variations by each age group are much smaller than before, especially in old age groups. We can visualize this data using a bar plot, as shown here:

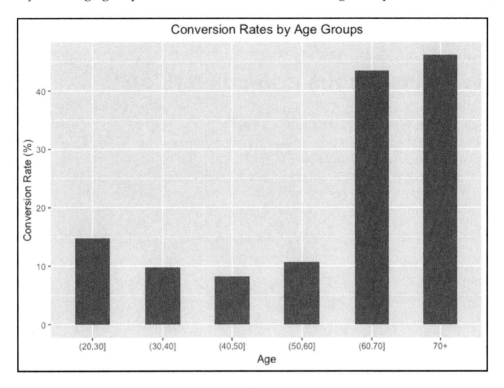

The code to build this bar plot is shown here:

```
# bar chart
ggplot(conversionsByAgeGroup, aes(x=AgeGroup, y=ConversionRate)) +
    geom_bar(width=0.5, stat="identity") +
    ggtitle('Conversion Rates by Age Groups') +
    xlab("Age") +
    ylab("Conversion Rate (%)") +
    theme(plot.title = element_text(hjust = 0.5))
```

As you can see from this code, we are passing the conversionsByAgeGroup data to the ggplot object with the AgeGroup column as the *x*-axis and the ConversionRate column as the *y*-axis. We are using the geom_bar function to build a bar plot.

The width argument defines the width of each bar in the bar plot. Similar to the previous line chart, you can use ggtitle to rename the title of the plot and the xlab and ylab functions to rename the labels of the *x*-axis and *y*-axis.

You can find the full code in the following repository: `https://github.com/yoonhwang/hands-on-data-science-for-marketing/blob/master/ch.2/R/ConversionRate.R`.

Conversions versus non-conversions

One other thing we can look at is the demographic differences between the converted clients and non-converted clients. This type of analysis can help us identify what differentiates converted groups from non-converted groups in our marketing campaigns and helps us understand our target clients better and what types of customers respond better to our marketing efforts. In this exercise, we will compare the distributions of the marital status among the conversions and non-conversions groups.

We will first count the number of conversions and non-conversions for each marital status. The following code shows how we can compute this using R functions:

```
conversionsByMaritalStatus <- conversionsDF %>%
  group_by(Marital=marital, Conversion=conversion) %>%
  summarise(Count=n())
```

As you can see from this code, we are using the pipe operator, `%>%`, in the `dplyr` package to pass the DataFrame, `conversionsDF` to the `group_by` function and then to the `summarise` function. In the `group_by` function, we are grouping by two columns, `marital` and `conversion`. In the `summarise` function, we are simply counting the number of records in each group, by using the `n` function.

The resulting data is shown in the following screenshot:

	Marital	Conversion	Count
1	divorced	0	4136
2	divorced	1	476
3	married	0	22396
4	married	1	2532
5	single	0	9948
6	single	1	1620
7	unknown	0	68
8	unknown	1	12

Another way to represent this data is by using pie charts:

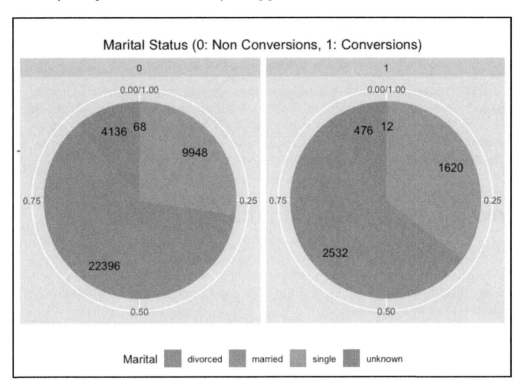

The following code shows how we can build these pie charts in R:

```
# pie chart
ggplot(conversionsByMaritalStatus, aes(x="", y=Count, fill=Marital)) +
  geom_bar(width=1, stat = "identity", position=position_fill()) +
  geom_text(aes(x=1.25, label=Count), position=position_fill(vjust = 0.5))
+
  coord_polar("y") +
  facet_wrap(~Conversion) +
  ggtitle('Marital Status (0: Non Conversions, 1: Conversions)') +
  theme(
    axis.title.x=element_blank(),
    axis.title.y=element_blank(),
    plot.title=element_text(hjust=0.5),
    legend.position='bottom'
  )
```

For building a pie chart in R, we are using the same `geom_bar` function, just as if we are building a bar chart. The difference here is `coord_polar("y")`, which transforms a bar chart into a pie chart. Then, we are using the `facet_wrap` function to create two columns of pie charts by the column, `Conversion`. This builds two pie charts, one for the conversions group and another for the non-conversions group.

Compared to the tabular format of the data output, pie charts make it much easier to understand the overall distributions of the data. With pie charts, we can easily see that the `married` group takes up the largest proportions in both conversions and non-conversions groups, while the `single` group comes second. Using pie charts, we can easily visualize the similarities and differences between two groups.

Conversions by age and marital status

So far, we have aggregated our data by one criterion. However, there are cases where you want to group the data by more than one column. In this section, we will discuss how we can analyze and report conversion rates by more than one criterion. As an exercise, we will use the age groups that we have built in the previous section and the marital status as the two columns to group by.

Let's first look at the code:

```
#### 5. Conversions by Age Groups & Marital Status ####
conversionsByAgeMarital <- conversionsDF %>%
  group_by(AgeGroup=cut(age, breaks= seq(20, 70, by = 10)),
Marital=marital) %>%
  summarise(Count=n(), NumConversions=sum(conversion)) %>%
  mutate(TotalCount=sum(Count)) %>%
  mutate(ConversionRate=NumConversions/TotalCount)

conversionsByAgeMarital$AgeGroup <-
as.character(conversionsByAgeMarital$AgeGroup)
conversionsByAgeMarital$AgeGroup[is.na(conversionsByAgeMarital$AgeGroup)]
<- "70+"
```

Similar to when we built custom age groups, we are using the `cut` function in `group_by` to create age groups from 20 to 70 in increments of 10. However, we are grouping by the column, `marital`, as well this time.

Then, we are using the `summarise` function to compute the number of records in each group `Count`, and the number of conversions in each group, `NumConversions`. Then, using the `mutate` function, we calculate the total counts in each age group, named `TotalCount`, and the conversion rates in each group, named `ConversionRate`.

The resulting data is shown in the following screenshot:

	AgeGroup	Marital	Count	NumConversions	TotalCount	ConversionRate
1	(20,30]	divorced	229	18	7243	0.0024851581
2	(20,30]	married	2389	242	7243	0.0334115698
3	(20,30]	single	4612	804	7243	0.1110037277
4	(20,30]	unknown	13	3	7243	0.0004141930
5	(30,40]	divorced	1505	135	16385	0.0082392432
6	(30,40]	married	9705	867	16385	0.0529142508
7	(30,40]	single	5139	591	16385	0.0360695758
8	(30,40]	unknown	36	4	16385	0.0002441257
9	(40,50]	divorced	1548	126	10240	0.0123046875
10	(40,50]	married	7383	588	10240	0.0574218750
11	(40,50]	single	1295	120	10240	0.0117187500
12	(40,50]	unknown	14	3	10240	0.0002929687

As you can see from this data, we can now see the distribution of conversion rates based on two criteria, age group and martial status. For example, the conversion rate of clients who are single and between **20** and **30** years old is 11.10%, while the conversion rate of clients who are married and between **40** and **50** years old is 5.74%.

Another way to visualize this data is to use a bar plot:

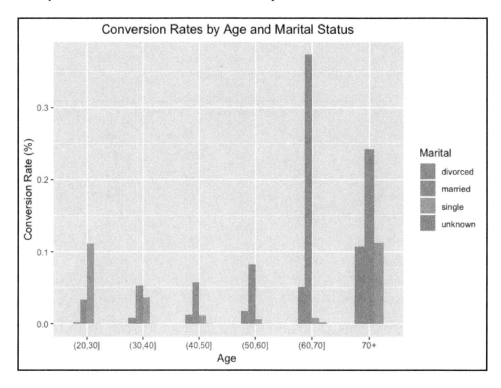

In this bar chart, we can easily see the distributions of conversion rates for each of the age and marital status groups. The code we used to build this bar plot is shown here:

```
# bar chart
ggplot(conversionsByAgeMarital, aes(x=AgeGroup, y=ConversionRate,
fill=Marital)) +
    geom_bar(width=0.5, stat="identity", position="dodge") +
    ylab("Conversion Rate (%)") +
    xlab("Age") +
    ggtitle("Conversion Rates by Age and Marital Status") +
    theme(plot.title=element_text(hjust=0.5))
```

Here, we are creating a ggplot object with the conversionsByAgeMarital data. We are using AgeGroup for the *x*-axis and ConversionRate for the *y*-axis, while we are using Marital column to use different colors for different types of marital status. Then, we are building a bar plot by using the geom_bar function. With this configuration, ggplot builds a bar plot of conversion rates against age groups with breakdowns by marital status, which we saw in the previous bar chart.

If you would like to stack those four bars for each age group, then you can use the following code for a stacked bar plot:

```
# stacked bar chart
ggplot(conversionsByAgeMarital, aes(x=AgeGroup, y=ConversionRate,
fill=Marital)) +
  geom_bar(width=0.5, stat="identity", position="stack") +
  ylab("Conversion Rate (%)") +
  xlab("Age") +
  ggtitle("Conversion Rates by Age and Marital Status") +
  theme(plot.title=element_text(hjust=0.5))
```

As you can see from this code, the only difference is the code, `position="stack"`, in the `geom_bar` function. If you pass the value, `"dodge"`, to this `position` argument of the `geom_bar` function, it will create an unstacked bar plot. Whereas, if you pass the value, `"stack"`, to this `position` argument of the `geom_bar` function, it will build a stacked bar plot, which looks like the following:

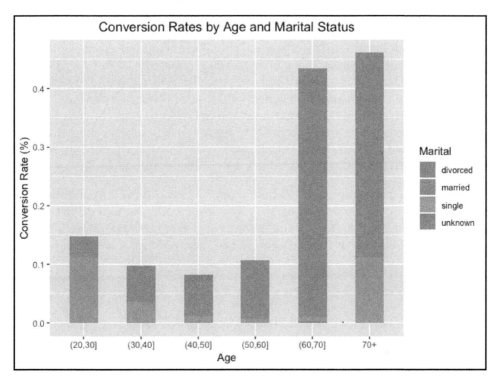

As you can see from this stacked bar plot, different marital statuses are stacked on top of each other for each of the age groups. This way, we can not only easily see the overall trends in conversion rates across different age groups, but also the proportions of converted clients with different marital statuses for each age group.

 The full code that we used for this R exercise can be found in the following repository: `https://github.com/yoonhwang/hands-on-data-science-for-marketing/blob/master/ch.2/R/ConversionRate.R`.

Summary

In this chapter, we have discussed how to use descriptive analysis for reporting and analytics on the progress and performances of marketing efforts. We have discussed various KPIs that are often used in marketing to track the progress of marketing campaigns. We have learned how important it is to look at how much sales revenue each marketing strategy generates. When analyzing the sales revenue metrics, we have seen that it is important to approach it from different angles. You might want to look at not only the aggregate sales revenue, but also time-series (monthly, quarterly, or yearly) sales revenue. You might also want to look at sales attributed to each individual marketing campaigns and how much revenue each campaign generated for your company. We have also discussed CPA metrics, with which you can tell the cost-effectiveness of your marketing strategies. We have learned various metrics to analyze for digital marketing channels as well, such as CTR, lead ratio, and conversion rates. As we have seen and experimented in the Python and R exercises, we can go multiple levels deeper into these KPI metrics.

In the next chapter, we are going to learn how we can apply data science and machine learning techniques for explanatory analysis. More specifically, we will discuss how we can use regression analysis and models to understand the drivers behind marketing engagement. We will also cover how we can interpret the regression analysis results in the following chapter.

3
Drivers behind Marketing Engagement

When you run marketing campaigns, one of the important measures that you will want to look at and analyze is customer engagement with your marketing efforts. For example, in email marketing, customer engagement can be measured by how many of your marketing emails were opened or ignored by your customers. Customer engagement can also be measured by the amount of website visits from individual customers. Successful marketing campaigns will draw a lot of engagement from your customers, while ineffective marketing campaigns will not only drive a lower amount of engagement from your customers, but will also negatively impact your business. Customers might mark emails from your business as spam or unsubscribe from your mailing list.

In order to understand what affects customer engagement, in this chapter, we will discuss how we can use explanatory analysis (more specifically, regression analysis). We will briefly cover the definition of explanatory analysis, what regression analysis is, and how to use a logistic regression model for explanatory analysis. Then, we will cover how to build and interpret regression analysis results in Python, using the `statsmodels` package. For R programmers, we will discuss how we can build and interpret regression analysis results with `glm`.

In this chapter, we will cover the following topics:

- Using regression analysis for explanatory analysis
- Regression analysis with Python
- Regression analysis with R

Using regression analysis for explanatory analysis

In Chapter 2, *Key Performance Indicators and Visualizations*, we discussed what **descriptive analysis** is and how it is used to better understand a dataset. We experimented using various visualization techniques and building different types of plots in Python and R.

In this chapter, we are going to expand our knowledge and start to discuss why, when, and how to use **explanatory analysis** for marketing.

Explanatory analysis and regression analysis

As we briefly discussed in Chapter 1, *Data Science and Marketing*, the purpose of explanatory analysis is to answer why we are using the data, whereas the purpose of descriptive analysis is to answer what we are using the data for, and how we are using it. When you run different marketing campaigns, often times, you will notice that some marketing campaigns perform much better than others; you might wonder why it is that some of your marketing campaigns work so well, while others do not. For example, you might want to understand what types and groups of customers typically open your marketing emails more often than others. As another example, you might want to analyze what attributes of the customer base are highly correlated with higher conversion rates and item purchases.

With explanatory analysis, you can analyze and understand the key factors that are highly and significantly correlated with the outcomes that you want. **Regression analysis** and regression models are frequently used to model the relationships between the attributes and the outcomes. Simply put, regression analysis estimates the values of output variables by finding a function of the attributes or features that best approximates the output values. One of the frequently used forms of regression analysis is **linear regression**. As the name suggests, in linear regression, we try to estimate the output variables via linear combinations of the features. If we use Y for the output variable and X_i for each of the features, where i is the ith feature, then the linear regression formula will look as follows:

$$Y = a + b_1 \times X_1 + b_2 \times X_2 + b_3 \times X_3 + \cdots$$

As you can see from the preceding formula, the output variable Y is expressed as a linear combination of the features, X_i. The purpose of the linear regression models is to find the intercept, a, and the coefficients, b_i, that best estimate the output variable, using the given features. A fitted linear regression line will look something like the following (image from `https://towardsdatascience.com/linear-regression-using-python-b136c91bf0a2`):

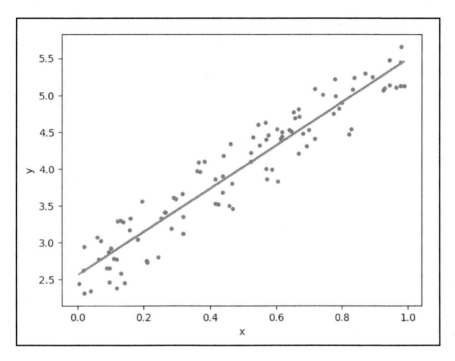

The blue dots in this diagram are the data points, and the red line is the fitted, or trained, linear regression line. As you can see in the graph, linear regression tries to estimate the target variable through a linear combination of the features.

In this chapter, we will discuss how we can use regression analysis, and, more specifically, **logistic regression** models, to understand what drives higher customer engagement.

Logistic regression

Logistic regression is a type of regression analysis that is used when the output variable is binary (one for a positive outcome versus zero for a negative outcome). Like any other linear regression models, logistic regression models estimate the output from linear combinations of the feature variables. The only difference is what the model estimates. Unlike other linear regression models, logistic regression models estimate the log odds of an event, or, in other words, the log ratios between the probabilities of positive and negative events. The equation looks as follows:

$$\log(\frac{P(y=1)}{1 - P(y=1)}) = a + b_1 \times X_1 + b_2 \times X_2 + b_3 \times X_3 + \cdots$$

The ratio on the left is the odds of success, which represents the ratio between the probability of success and the probability of failure. The curve of the log odds, also called the **logit curve**, looks as follows:

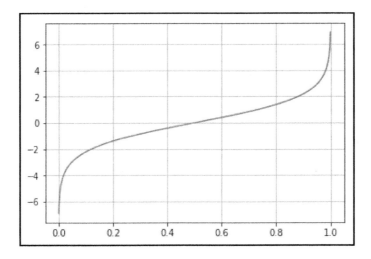

The logistic regression model output is simply the inverse of logit, which ranges from zero to one. In this chapter, we are going to use regression analysis to understand what drives customer engagement, and the output variable will be whether a customer responded to marketing calls. Hence, logistic regression fits perfectly in this case, as the output is a binary variable that can take two values: responded versus did not respond. In the following sections, we will discuss how we can use and build logistic regression models in Python and R, and then we will cover how we can interpret regression analysis results in order to understand what attributes of customers are highly correlated with higher marketing engagement.

Regression analysis with Python

In this section, you will learn how to use the `statsmodels` package in Python to conduct regression analysis. For those readers that would like to use R instead of Python, for this exercise, you can skip to the next section. We will start this section by looking at the data more closely, using the `pandas` and `matplotlib` packages, and then we will discuss how to build regression models and interpret the results by using the `statsmodels` library.

For this exercise, we will be using one of the publicly available datasets from IBM Watson, which can be found at https://www.ibm.com/communities/analytics/watson-analytics-blog/marketing-customer-value-analysis/. You can follow the link and download the data file in a CSV format. In order to load this data into your Jupyter Notebook, you can run the following code:

```
import matplotlib.pyplot as plt
import pandas as pd

df = pd.read_csv('../data/WA_Fn-UseC_-Marketing-Customer-Value-
Analysis.csv')
```

Similar to what we did in Chapter 2, *Key Performance Indicators and Visualizations*, we are importing the `matplotlib` and `pandas` packages first; using the `read_csv` function in `pandas`, we can read the data into a `pandas` DataFrame. We will use `matplotlib` later, for data analysis and visualizations.

The loaded DataFrame, `df`, looks as follows:

```
df.shape
```
```
(9134, 24)
```
```
df.head()
```

	Customer	State	Customer Lifetime Value	Response	Coverage	Education	Effective To Date	EmploymentStatus	Gender	Income	...	Months Since Policy Inception	Number of Open Complaints	Number of Policies	
0	BU79786	Washington	2763.519279	No	Basic	Bachelor	2/24/11	Employed	F	56274	...	5	0	1	C
1	QZ44356	Arizona	6979.535903	No	Extended	Bachelor	1/31/11	Unemployed	F	0	...	42	0	8	
2	AI49188	Nevada	12887.431650	No	Premium	Bachelor	2/19/11	Employed	F	48767	...	38	0	2	
3	WW63253	California	7645.861827	No	Basic	Bachelor	1/20/11	Unemployed	M	0	...	65	0	7	C
4	HB64268	Washington	2813.692575	No	Basic	Bachelor	2/3/11	Employed	M	43836	...	44	0	1	

5 rows × 24 columns

As we discussed in Chapter 2, *Key Performance Indicators and Visualizations*, a DataFrame shape attribute tells us the number of rows and columns in the DataFrame, and the head function will display the first five records of the dataset. Once you have successfully read the data into a pandas DataFrame, your data should look like it does in the screenshot.

Data analysis and visualizations

Before we dive into regression analysis, we will first take a more detailed look at the data, in order to have a better understanding of what data points we have and what patterns we can see in the data. If you look at the data, you will notice a column named Response. It contains information on whether a customer responded to marketing calls. We will use this field as a measure of customer engagement. For future computations, it will be better to encode this field with numerical values. Let's take a look at the following code:

```
df['Engaged'] = df['Response'].apply(lambda x: 0 if x == 'No' else 1)
```

As you can see in this code, using the apply function of a pandas DataFrame, we are encoding those who did not respond to marketing calls (No) with a value of 0 and those who did respond (Yes) with a value of 1. We are creating a new field named Engaged with these encoded values.

Engagement rate

The first thing that we are going to look at is the aggregate engagement rate. This engagement rate is simply the percentage of customers that responded to the marketing calls. Take a look at the following code:

```
engagement_rate_df = pd.DataFrame(
    df.groupby('Engaged').count()['Response'] / df.shape[0] * 100.0
)
```

As you can see from this code, we are grouping by the newly created field, Engaged, using the groupby function of a pandas DataFrame. Then, we are counting the number of records (or customers) in each Engaged group with the count function. By dividing by the total number of customers in the DataFrame and multiplying by 100.0, we get the engagement rate. The results are as follows:

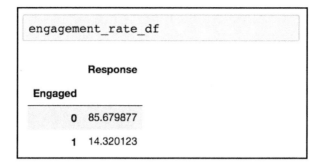

To make this easier to read, we can transpose the DataFrame, meaning that we can flip the rows and columns in the DataFrame. You can transpose a `pandas` DataFrame by using the `T` attribute of a DataFrame. It looks as follows:

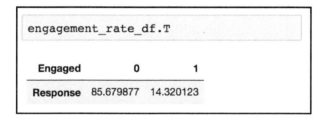

As you can see, about 14% of the customers have responded to marketing calls, and the remaining 86% of the customers have not responded.

Sales channels

Now, let's see whether we can find any noticeable patterns in the sales channel and engagement. We are going to analyze how the engaged and non-engaged customers are distributed among different sales channels. Let's first look at the following code:

```
engagement_by_sales_channel_df = pd.pivot_table(
    df, values='Response', index='Sales Channel', columns='Engaged',
aggfunc=len
).fillna(0.0)

engagement_by_sales_channel_df.columns = ['Not Engaged', 'Engaged']
```

As you can see in this code snippet, we are using the `pivot_table` function in the `pandas` library to group by the `Sales Channel` and `Response` variables. Once you run this code, `engagement_by_sales_channel_df` will have the following data:

Sales Channel	Not Engaged	Engaged
Agent	2811	666
Branch	2273	294
Call Center	1573	192
Web	1169	156

As you will have noticed in the previous section, there are significantly more customers that are not engaged with the marketing efforts, so it is quite difficult to look at the differences in the sales channel distributions between the engaged and non-engaged customers from raw numbers. To make the differences more visually identifiable, we can build pie charts using the following code:

```
engagement_by_sales_channel_df.plot(
    kind='pie',
    figsize=(15, 7),
    startangle=90,
    subplots=True,
    autopct=lambda x: '%0.1f%%' % x
)

plt.show()
```

Once you run this code, you will see the following pie charts, which show the distributions of engaged and non-engaged customers across different sales channels:

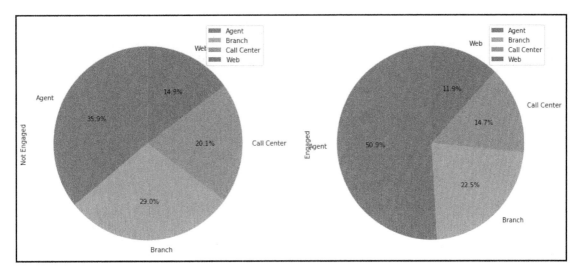

Compared to the previous table that shows raw counts of engaged and non-engaged customers in each sales channel, these pie charts help us to visually spot the differences in the distributions more easily. As you can see from these charts, more than half of the engaged customers were from agents, whereas non-engaged customers are more evenly distributed across all four different channels. As you can see from these charts, analyzing and visualizing data can help us to notice interesting patterns in the data, which will further help when we run regression analysis in the later parts of this chapter.

Total claim amounts

The last thing that we are going to look at before we dive into the regression analysis are the differences in the distributions of `Total Claim Amount` between the engaged and non-engaged groups. We are going to visualize this by using box plots. Let's first look at how we can build box plots in Python, as follows:

```
ax = df[['Engaged', 'Total Claim Amount']].boxplot(
    by='Engaged',
    showfliers=False,
    figsize=(7,5)
)

ax.set_xlabel('Engaged')
ax.set_ylabel('Total Claim Amount')
```

```
ax.set_title('Total Claim Amount Distributions by Engagements')

plt.suptitle("")
plt.show()
```

As you can see in this code, it is quite straightforward to build box plots from a `pandas` DataFrame. You can simply call the `boxplot` function. Box plots are a great way to visualize the distributions of continuous variables. They show the min, max, first quartile, median, and third quartile, all in one view. The following box plots show the distributions of the `Total Claim Amount` between the engaged and non-engaged groups:

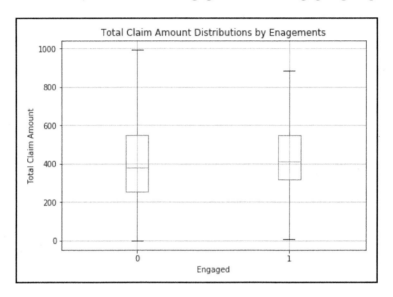

The central rectangle spans from the first quartile to the third quartile, and the green line shows the median. The lower and upper ends show the minimum and maximum of the distribution, respectively. One thing to note from the previous code is the `showfliers=False` argument. Let's see what happens when we set that argument to `True`, using the following code:

```
ax = df[['Engaged', 'Total Claim Amount']].boxplot(
    by='Engaged',
    showfliers=True,
    figsize=(7,5)
)

ax.set_xlabel('Engaged')
ax.set_ylabel('Total Claim Amount')
ax.set_title('Total Claim Amount Distributions by Engagements')
```

```
plt.suptitle("")
plt.show()
```

Using this code and the `showfliers=True` flag, the resulting box plots now look as follows:

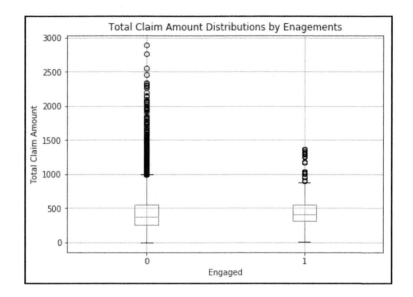

As you notice in these box plots, they plot many dots above the upper boundary lines, which suggested maximum values in the previous box plots. The dots above the upper boundary line show the suspected outliers that are decided based on the **Interquartile range (IQR)**. The IQR is simply the range between the first and third quartiles, and the points that fall `1.5*IQR` above the third quartile or `1.5*IQR` below the first quartile are suspected outliers and are shown with the dots.

Regression analysis

So far, we have analyzed the types of fields that we have in the data and how the patterns differ between the engaged group and the non-engaged group. Now, we are going to discuss how to conduct and interpret regression analysis in Python by using the `statsmodels` package. We will first build a logistic regression model with continuous variables, and you'll learn how to interpret the results. Then, we are going to discuss different ways to handle categorical variables when fitting regression models, and what impact those categorical variables have on the fitted logistic regression model.

Continuous variables

In linear regression, including logistic regression, it is straightforward to fit a regression model when the feature variables are continuous, as it just needs to find a linear combination of feature variables with numerical values for estimating the output variables. In order to fit a regression model with continuous variables, let's first take a look at how to get the data types of the columns in a `pandas` DataFrame. Take a look at the following:

```
df['Income'].dtype

dtype('int64')

df['Customer Lifetime Value'].dtype

dtype('float64')
```

As you can see from this Jupyter Notebook screenshot, the `dtype` attribute of a `pandas` `Series` object tells you what type of data it contains. As you can see from this snapshot, the `Income` variable has integers and the `Customer Lifetime Value` feature has floating point numbers. In order to take a quick look at the distributions of variables with numerical values, you can also do the following:

```
df.describe()
```

	Customer Lifetime Value	Income	Monthly Premium Auto	Months Since Last Claim	Months Since Policy Inception	Number of Open Complaints	Number of Policies	Total Claim Amount	Engaged
count	9134.000000	9134.000000	9134.000000	9134.000000	9134.000000	9134.000000	9134.000000	9134.000000	9134.000000
mean	8004.940475	37657.380009	93.219291	15.097000	48.064594	0.384388	2.966170	434.088794	0.143201
std	6870.967608	30379.904734	34.407967	10.073257	27.905991	0.910384	2.390182	290.500092	0.350297
min	1898.007675	0.000000	61.000000	0.000000	0.000000	0.000000	1.000000	0.099007	0.000000
25%	3994.251794	0.000000	68.000000	6.000000	24.000000	0.000000	1.000000	272.258244	0.000000
50%	5780.182197	33889.500000	83.000000	14.000000	48.000000	0.000000	2.000000	383.945434	0.000000
75%	8962.167041	62320.000000	109.000000	23.000000	71.000000	0.000000	4.000000	547.514839	0.000000
max	83325.381190	99981.000000	298.000000	35.000000	99.000000	5.000000	9.000000	2893.239678	1.000000

As you can see in this Jupyter Notebook snapshot, the `describe` function of a `pandas` DataFrame shows the distributions of all of the columns with numerical values. For example, you can see that there are a total of 9134 records in the `Customer Lifetime Value` column, with a mean of 8004.94 and ranges from 1898.01 to 83325.38.

We are going to store this list of the names of continuous variables in a separate variable, named `continuous_vars`. Take a look at the following code:

```
continuous_vars = [
    'Customer Lifetime Value', 'Income', 'Monthly Premium Auto',
    'Months Since Last Claim', 'Months Since Policy Inception',
    'Number of Open Complaints', 'Number of Policies',
    'Total Claim Amount'
]
```

Now that we know which columns are continuous variables, let's start to fit a logistic regression model. In order to do that, we need to first import the `statsmodels` package, as shown in the following code:

```
import statsmodels.formula.api as sm
```

With the `statsmodels` package imported, the code to initiate a logistic regression model is quite simple, and looks as follows:

```
logit = sm.Logit(
    df['Engaged'],
    df[continuous_vars]
)
```

As you can see from this code, we are using the `Logit` function within the `statsmodels` package. We are supplying the `Engaged` column as the output variable, which the model will learn to estimate, and the `continuous_vars` that contain all of the continuous variables as the input variables. Once a logistic regression object is created with the output and input variables defined, we can train or fit this model by using the following code:

```
logit_fit = logit.fit()
```

As you can see in this code, we are using the `fit` function of the logistic regression object, `logit`, to train a logistic regression model. Once this code is run, the trained model, `logit_fit`, will have learned the optimal solution that best estimates the output variable, `Engaged`, by using the input variables. In order to get a detailed description of the trained model, you can use the following code:

```
logit_fit.summary()
```

When you run this code, the `summary` function will display the following output in the Jupyter Notebook:

Logit Regression Results			
Dep. Variable:	Engaged	**No. Observations:**	9134
Model:	Logit	**Df Residuals:**	9126
Method:	MLE	**Df Model:**	7
Date:	Tue, 04 Sep 2018	**Pseudo R-squ.:**	-0.02546
Time:	17:00:30	**Log-Likelihood:**	-3847.1
converged:	True	**LL-Null:**	-3751.6
		LLR p-value:	1.000

	coef	std err	z	P>|z|	[0.025	0.975]
Customer Lifetime Value	-6.741e-06	5.04e-06	-1.337	0.181	-1.66e-05	3.14e-06
Income	-2.857e-06	1.03e-06	-2.766	0.006	-4.88e-06	-8.33e-07
Monthly Premium Auto	-0.0084	0.001	-6.889	0.000	-0.011	-0.006
Months Since Last Claim	-0.0202	0.003	-7.238	0.000	-0.026	-0.015
Months Since Policy Inception	-0.0060	0.001	-6.148	0.000	-0.008	-0.004
Number of Open Complaints	-0.0829	0.034	-2.424	0.015	-0.150	-0.016
Number of Policies	-0.0810	0.013	-6.356	0.000	-0.106	-0.056
Total Claim Amount	0.0001	0.000	0.711	0.477	-0.000	0.000

Let's take a closer look at this model output. `coef` represents the coefficients for each of the input variables, and `z` represents the z-score, which is the number of standard deviations from the mean. The `P>|z|` column represents the *p*-value, which means how likely it is to observe the relationship between the feature and the output variable by chance. So, the lower the value of `P>|z|` is, the more likely it is that the relationship between the given feature and the output variable is strong and is not by chance. Typically, `0.05` is a good cut-off point for the *p*-value, and any value less than `0.05` signifies a strong relationship between the given feature and the output variable.

Looking at this model output, we can see that `Income`, `Monthly Premium Auto`, `Months Since Last Claim`, `Months Since Policy Inception`, and `Number of Policies` variables have significant relationships with the output variable, `Engaged`. For example, `Number of Policies` variable is significant and is negatively correlated with `Engaged`. This suggests that the more policies that the customers have, the less likely they are to respond to marketing calls. As another example, the `Months Since Last Claim` variable is significant and is negatively correlated with the output variable, `Engaged`. This means that the longer it has been since the last claim, the less likely that the customer is going to respond to marketing calls.

As you can see from these examples, you can interpret the regression analysis results quite easily by looking at the *p*-values and coefficients of the features from the model output. This is a good way to understand which attributes of customers are significantly and highly correlated with your outcomes of interest.

Categorical variables

As you saw in the case of continuous variables in the previous section, it is quite straightforward to understand the relationships between the input and output variables from the coefficients and *p*-values. However, it becomes not so straightforward when we introduce **categorical variables**. Categorical variables often do not have any natural order, or they are encoded with non-numerical values, but in linear regression, we need the input variables to have numerical values that signify the order or magnitudes of the variables. For example, we cannot easily encode the `State` variable in our dataset with certain orderings or values. That is why we need to handle categorical variables differently from continuous variables when conducting regression analysis. In Python, there are multiple ways to handle categorical variables when using the `pandas` package. Let's first look at factorizing categorical variables, as shown in the following code:

```
gender_values, gender_labels = df['Gender'].factorize()
```

The `pandas` function, `factorize`, encodes categorical variables with numerical values by enumerating through the values. Let's take a look at the following output first:

```
gender_values
array([0, 0, 0, ..., 1, 1, 1])

gender_labels
Index(['F', 'M'], dtype='object')
```

As you can see from this output, the values of this `Gender` variable are encoded with zeros and ones, where `0` symbolizes female (`F`) and `1` symbolizes male (`M`). This is a quick way to encode categorical variables with numerical values. However, this function does not work when we want to embed natural orderings into the encoded values. For example, the `Education` variable in our dataset has five different categories: `High School or Below`, `Bachelor`, `College`, `Master`, and `Doctor`. We might want to embed the orderings when encoding different categories within this `Education` variable.

The following code shows another way to encode categorical variables with orderings when using `pandas`:

```
categories = pd.Categorical(
    df['Education'],
    categories=['High School or Below', 'Bachelor', 'College', 'Master',
'Doctor']
)
```

As you can see in this code, we are using the `pd.Categorical` function to encode the values of `df['Education']`. We can define the orderings that we want with the argument, `categories`. In our example, we are giving values of 0, 1, 2, 3, and 4 for the `High School or Below`, `Bachelor`, `College`, `Master`, and `Doctor`, categories respectively. The output looks as follows:

We will now add these encoded variables to the pandas DataFrame, `df`, as shown in the following code:

```
df['GenderFactorized'] = gender_values
df['EducationFactorized'] = categories.codes
```

With these encodings for the two categorical variables, `Gender` and `Education`, we can now fit a logistic regression model using the following code:

```
logit = sm.Logit(
    df['Engaged'],
    df[[
        'GenderFactorized',
        'EducationFactorized'
    ]]
)

logit_fit = logit.fit()
```

Similar to how we fit a logistic regression model with continuous variables previously, we can fit a logistic regression model with the encoded categorical variables, `GenderFactorized` and `EducationFactorized`, by using the `Logit` function in the `statsmodels` package. Using the `summary` function of the fitted logistic regression model object, we will get the following output:

```
logit_fit.summary()
```

Logit Regression Results

Dep. Variable:	Engaged	No. Observations:	9134
Model:	Logit	Df Residuals:	9132
Method:	MLE	Df Model:	1
Date:	Tue, 04 Sep 2018	Pseudo R-squ.:	-0.2005
Time:	17:31:15	Log-Likelihood:	-4503.7
converged:	True	LL-Null:	-3751.6
		LLR p-value:	1.000

	coef	std err	z	P>|z|	[0.025	0.975]
GenderFactorized	-1.1266	0.047	-24.116	0.000	-1.218	-1.035
EducationFactorized	-0.6256	0.021	-29.900	0.000	-0.667	-0.585

As you can see in this output and by looking at the *p*-values in the P>|z| column, both the `GenderFactorized` and `EducationFactorized` variables seem to have significant relationships with the output variable `Engaged`. If we look at the coefficients of these two variables, we can see that both are negatively correlated with the output. This suggests that male customers, encoded with 1 in the `GenderFactorized` variable, are less likely to be engaged with marketing calls, as compared to female customers, encoded with 0 in the `GenderFactorized` variable. Similarly, the higher the customers' education levels are, the less likely that they will be engaged with marketing calls.

We have discussed two ways of handling categorical variables in `pandas`, using the `factorize` and `Categorical` functions. With these techniques, we can understand how different categories of categorical variables are correlated with the output variable.

Combining continuous and categorical variables

The last Python exercise that we are going to do in this chapter involves combining continuous and categorical variables for our regression analysis. We can fit a logistic regression model by using both categorical and continuous variables, as shown in the following code:

```
logit = sm.Logit(
    df['Engaged'],
    df[['Customer Lifetime Value',
        'Income',
        'Monthly Premium Auto',
        'Months Since Last Claim',
        'Months Since Policy Inception',
        'Number of Open Complaints',
        'Number of Policies',
        'Total Claim Amount',
        'GenderFactorized',
        'EducationFactorized'
    ]]
)

logit_fit = logit.fit()
```

The only difference from the previous codes is the features that we selected to fit a logistic regression model. As you can see in this code, we are now fitting a logistic regression model with the continuous variables, as well as the two encoded categorical variables, `GenderFactorized` and `EducationFactorized`, that we created in the previous section. The results look as follows:

```
logit_fit.summary()
```

Logit Regression Results

Dep. Variable:	Engaged	No. Observations:	9134
Model:	Logit	Df Residuals:	9124
Method:	MLE	Df Model:	9
Date:	Tue, 04 Sep 2018	Pseudo R-squ.:	-0.02454
Time:	17:30:53	Log-Likelihood:	-3843.7
converged:	True	LL-Null:	-3751.6
		LLR p-value:	1.000

	coef	std err	z	P>|z|	[0.025	0.975]
Customer Lifetime Value	-6.909e-06	5.03e-06	-1.373	0.170	-1.68e-05	2.96e-06
Income	-2.59e-06	1.04e-06	-2.494	0.013	-4.63e-06	-5.55e-07
Monthly Premium Auto	-0.0081	0.001	-6.526	0.000	-0.011	-0.006
Months Since Last Claim	-0.0194	0.003	-6.858	0.000	-0.025	-0.014
Months Since Policy Inception	-0.0057	0.001	-5.827	0.000	-0.008	-0.004
Number of Open Complaints	-0.0813	0.034	-2.376	0.017	-0.148	-0.014
Number of Policies	-0.0781	0.013	-6.114	0.000	-0.103	-0.053
Total Claim Amount	0.0001	0.000	0.943	0.346	-0.000	0.000
GenderFactorized	-0.1500	0.058	-2.592	0.010	-0.263	-0.037
EducationFactorized	-0.0070	0.027	-0.264	0.792	-0.059	0.045

Let's take a closer look at this output. The `Income`, `Monthly Premium Auto`, `Months Since Last Claim`, `Months Since Policy Inception`, `Number of Open Complaints`, `Number of Policies`, and `GenderFactorized` variable are significant at a `0.05` significance level, and all of them have negative relationships with the output variable, `Engaged`. Hence, the higher the income is, the less likely that the customer will be engaged with marketing calls. Similarly, the more policies that the customer has, the less likely that he or she will be engaged with marketing calls.

Lastly, male customers are less likely to engage with marketing calls than female customers, which we can see from looking at the coefficient of GenderFactorized. From looking at this regression analysis output, we can easily see the relationships between the input and output variables, and we can understand which attributes of customers are positively or negatively related to customer engagement with marketing calls.

 The full code for the Python exercise in this chapter can be found at https://github.com/yoonhwang/hands-on-data-science-for-marketing/blob/master/ch.3/python/RegressionAnalysis.ipynb.

Regression analysis with R

In this section, you are going to learn how to use the glm function in R to conduct regression analysis. For those readers that would like to use Python instead of R for this exercise, the step-by-step instructions for Python are in the previous section. We will start this section by analyzing the data more closely, using the dplyr package, and then we will discuss how to build regression models and interpret the results using the glm function.

For this exercise, we will be using one of the publicly available datasets from IBM Watson, which can be found at https://www.ibm.com/communities/analytics/watson-analytics-blog/marketing-customer-value-analysis/. You can follow this link and download the data file in a CSV format. In order to load this data into your RStudio, you can run the following code:

```
library(dplyr)
library(ggplot2)

# Load data
df <- read.csv(
  file="~/Documents/data-science-for-marketing/ch.3/data/WA_Fn-UseC_-
Marketing-Customer-Value-Analysis.csv",
  header=TRUE,
  sep=","
)
```

Similar to what we did in Chapter 2, *Key Performance Indicators and Visualizations*, we will first import the dplyr and ggplot2 packages for data analysis and plotting in the following sections. Using the read.csv function in R, we can read the data into a DataFrame. Since this CSV file contains the header in the first row and the fields are separated by commas, we are using the header=TRUE and sep="," flags for the correct parsing.

The following screenshot shows how the raw data looks in the DataFrame:

	Customer	State	Customer.Lifetime.Value	Response	Coverage	Education	Effective.To.Date	EmploymentStatus	Gender	Income	Location.Code
1	BU79786	Washington	2763.519	No	Basic	Bachelor	2/24/11	Employed	F	56274	Suburban
2	QZ44356	Arizona	6979.536	No	Extended	Bachelor	1/31/11	Unemployed	F	0	Suburban
3	AI49188	Nevada	12887.432	No	Premium	Bachelor	2/19/11	Employed	F	48767	Suburban
4	WW63253	California	7645.862	No	Basic	Bachelor	1/20/11	Unemployed	M	0	Suburban
5	HB64268	Washington	2813.693	No	Basic	Bachelor	2/3/11	Employed	M	43836	Rural
6	OC83172	Oregon	8256.298	Yes	Basic	Bachelor	1/25/11	Employed	F	62902	Rural
7	XZ87318	Oregon	5380.899	Yes	Basic	College	2/24/11	Employed	F	55350	Suburban
8	CF85061	Arizona	7216.100	No	Premium	Master	1/18/11	Unemployed	M	0	Urban
9	DY87989	Oregon	24127.504	Yes	Basic	Bachelor	1/26/11	Medical Leave	M	14072	Suburban
10	BQ94931	Oregon	7388.178	No	Extended	College	2/17/11	Employed	F	28812	Urban
11	SX51350	California	4738.992	No	Basic	College	2/21/11	Unemployed	M	0	Suburban
12	VQ65197	California	8197.197	No	Basic	College	1/6/11	Unemployed	F	0	Suburban
13	DP39365	California	8798.797	No	Premium	Master	2/6/11	Employed	M	77026	Urban
14	SJ95423	Arizona	8819.019	Yes	Basic	High School or Below	1/10/11	Employed	M	99845	Suburban
15	IL66569	California	5384.432	No	Basic	College	1/18/11	Employed	M	83689	Urban

Now that we have loaded the data into a DataFrame, let's start to look at and analyze the data more closely, so that we can better understand the structure of the data.

Data analysis and visualization

Before we dive into regression analysis, let's first take a more detailed look at the data, in order to have a better understanding of what data points we have and what patterns we can see in the data. If you look at the data, you will notice a column named Response. It contains information on whether a customer responded to their marketing calls. We will use this field as a measure of customer engagement. For future computations, it will be better to encode this field with numerical values. Let's take a look at the following code:

```
# Encode Response as 0s and 1s
df$Engaged <- as.integer(df$Response) - 1
```

As you can see in this code, using the as.integer function, we are encoding those who did not respond to marketing calls (No) with a value of 0 and those who did respond (Yes) with a value of 1. Because as.integer function encodes values to 1 and 2 by default, we are subtracting the values by 1 to encode the response values with zeros and ones. Then, we are creating a new field named Engaged with these encoded values.

Engagement rate

The first thing that we are going to look at is the aggregate engagement rate. This engagement rate is simply the percentage of customers who responded to the marketing calls. Take a look at the following code:

```
engagementRate <- df %>%
   group_by(Engaged) %>%
   summarise(Count=n()) %>%
   mutate(Percentage=Count/nrow(df)*100.0)
```

As you can see in this code, we are grouping by the newly created field, Engaged, using the group_by function. Then, we are counting the number of records or customers in each Engaged group with the n() function. By dividing by the total number of customers in the DataFrame, df, and multiplying by 100.0, we get the engagement rate. The results look as follows:

	Engaged	Count	Percentage
1	0	7826	85.67988
2	1	1308	14.32012

To make it easier to read, we can transpose the DataFrame, meaning that we can flip the rows and columns in the DataFrame. You can transpose a DataFrame by using the t function in R. The code looks as follows:

```
# Transpose
transposed <- t(engagementRate)

colnames(transposed) <- engagementRate$Engaged
transposed <- transposed[-1,]
```

The transposed DataFrame appears as follows:

	0	1
Count	7826.00000	1308.00000
Percentage	85.67988	14.32012

As you can see, it is easier to see the total number and percentage of engaged and non-engaged customers by transposing the DataFrame. From this data, we can see that about 14% of the customers have responded to marketing calls, and the remaining 86% of the customers have not responded.

Sales channels

Now, let's see if we can find any noticeable patterns in sales channels and engagement. We are going to analyze how the engaged and non-engaged customers are distributed among different sales channels. Let's first look at the following code:

```
salesChannel <- df %>%
  group_by(Engaged, Channel=Sales.Channel) %>%
  summarise(Count=n())
```

As you can see in this code snippet, we are using the `group_by` function in R to group by the `Sales Channel` and `Engaged` variables. Then, using the `n()` function, we will count the number of customers in each group. Once you have run this code, the `salesChannel` DataFrame will look as follows:

	Engaged	Channel	Count
1	0	Agent	2811
2	0	Branch	2273
3	0	Call Center	1573
4	0	Web	1169
5	1	Agent	666
6	1	Branch	294
7	1	Call Center	192
8	1	Web	156

As you will have noticed from the previous section, there are significantly more customers that are not engaged with the marketing efforts, so it is quite difficult to compare and see the differences in the sales channel distributions between the engaged and non-engaged customers with the raw numbers. To make it easier to differentiate visually, we can build pie charts using the following code:

```
# pie chart
ggplot(salesChannel, aes(x="", y=Count, fill=Channel)) +
  geom_bar(width=1, stat = "identity", position=position_fill()) +
  geom_text(aes(x=1.25, label=Count), position=position_fill(vjust = 0.5))
+
  coord_polar("y") +
  facet_wrap(~Engaged) +
  ggtitle('Sales Channel (0: Not Engaged, 1: Engaged)') +
  theme(
    axis.title.x=element_blank(),
    axis.title.y=element_blank(),
    plot.title=element_text(hjust=0.5),
```

```
        legend.position='bottom'
    )
```

Similar to what we did in `Chapter 2`, *Key Performance Indicators and Visualizations*, we are using `ggplot` to build a chart in R. If you remember that chapter, we can build pie charts by using `geom_bar` with `coord_polar("y")`. By using `face_wrap(~Engaged)`, we can split the pie charts in two: one for non-engaged customers and another for engaged customers. Once you have run this code, you will see the following pie charts, which show the distributions of engaged and non-engaged customers across different sales channels:

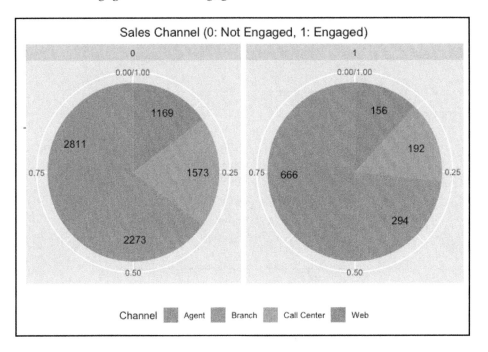

Compared to the previous data table that shows raw counts of engaged and non-engaged customers in each sales channel, these pie charts can help us to visually see the differences in the distributions more easily. As you can see from these charts, more than half of the engaged customers were from agents, whereas non-engaged customers are more evenly distributed across all four different channels. As you can see from these charts, analyzing and visualizing data can help us to notice interesting patterns in the data, which will further help us when we run regression analysis in the later parts of this chapter.

Total claim amounts

The last thing that we are going to look at before we dive into the regression analysis is are the differences in the distributions of `Total Claim Amount` between the engaged and non-engaged groups. We are going to visualize this by using box plots. Let's first look at how we can build box plots in R:

```
ggplot(df, aes(x="", y=Total.Claim.Amount)) +
    geom_boxplot() +
    facet_wrap(~Engaged) +
    ylab("Total Claim Amount") +
    xlab("0: Not Engaged, 1: Engaged") +
    ggtitle("Engaged vs. Not Engaged: Total Claim Amount") +
    theme(plot.title=element_text(hjust=0.5))
```

As you can see in this code, it is quite straightforward to build box plots in R. You can simply call the `ggplot` function with `geom_boxplot`. A box plot is a great way to visualize the distributions of continuous variables. It shows the min, max, first quartile, median, and third quartile, all in one view. The following box plot shows the distributions of `Total Claim Amount` between the engaged and non-engaged groups:

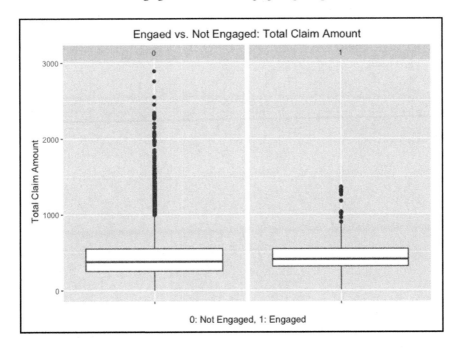

The central rectangle spans from the first quartile to the third quartile, and the line within the rectangle shows the median. The lower and upper ends of the lines from the rectangle show the minimum and maximum of the distribution, respectively. Another thing that you will notice from these box plots are the dots above the upper end of the line.

The dots beyond the end of the upper line show the suspected outliers, which are decided based on the IQR. The IQR is simply the range between the first and third quartiles, which is the same as the height of the rectangle in the box plot that spans from the first quartile to the third quartile. The data points that fall `1.5*IQR` above the third quartile or `1.5*IQR` below the first quartile are suspected outliers, and are shown with the dots.

Depending on your analysis goals, you might not care about (or you might not want to show) the outliers in box plots. Let's take a look at the following code to see how we can remove those outliers from the box plots:

```
# without outliers
ggplot(df, aes(x="", y=Total.Claim.Amount)) +
  geom_boxplot(outlier.shape = NA) +
  scale_y_continuous(limits = quantile(df$Total.Claim.Amount, c(0.1, 0.9))) +
  facet_wrap(~Engaged) +
  ylab("Total Claim Amount") +
  xlab("0: Not Engaged, 1: Engaged") +
  ggtitle("Engaged vs. Not Engaged: Total Claim Amount") +
  theme(plot.title=element_text(hjust=0.5))
```

As you will notice in this code snippet, the only difference between this code and the previous one is `outlier.shape=NA` in the `geom_boxplot` function. Let's take a look at how the box plots look now:

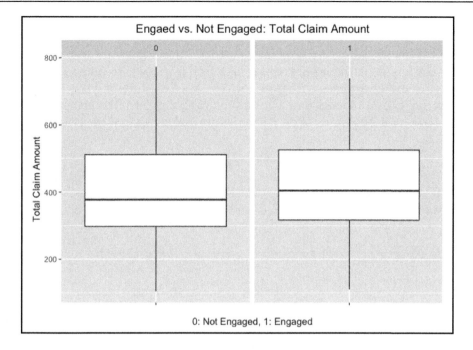

In these plots, we can no longer see the dots beyond the end of the upper line. Depending on what you would like to show and analyze, having outliers in box plots may or may not help.

Regression analysis

So far, we have analyzed the types of fields that we have in the data and how the patterns differ between the engaged group and the non-engaged group. Now, we are going to discuss how to conduct and interpret regression analysis in R, using the `glm` function. We will first build a logistic regression model with continuous variables, and you will learn how to interpret the results. Then, we are going to discuss how to handle categorical variables when fitting regression models in R, and what impact those categorical variables have on the fitted logistic regression model.

Continuous variables

In linear regression, including logistic regression, it is straightforward to fit a regression model when the feature variables are continuous, as it just needs to find a linear combination of feature variables with numerical values for estimating the output variable. In order to fit a regression model with continuous variables, let's first take a look at how to get the data types of the columns in an R DataFrame. Take a look at the following code:

```
# get data types of each column
sapply(df, class)
```

Using the `sapply` function in R, we can apply the `class` function across the columns in a DataFrame, and the `class` function tells us the types of data in each column. The results of this code are as follows:

```
> sapply(df, class)
                Customer                    State      Customer.Lifetime.Value                 Response
                "factor"                 "factor"                     "numeric"                 "factor"
                Coverage                Education           Effective.To.Date         EmploymentStatus
                "factor"                 "factor"                      "factor"                 "factor"
                  Gender                   Income               Location.Code           Marital.Status
                "factor"                "integer"                      "factor"                 "factor"
    Monthly.Premium.Auto Months.Since.Last.Claim Months.Since.Policy.Inception Number.of.Open.Complaints
               "integer"                "integer"                     "integer"                "integer"
       Number.of.Policies              Policy.Type                        Policy          Renew.Offer.Type
               "integer"                 "factor"                      "factor"                 "factor"
           Sales.Channel        Total.Claim.Amount                 Vehicle.Class             Vehicle.Size
                "factor"                "numeric"                      "factor"                 "factor"
                 Engaged
               "numeric"
```

Shown in the preceding screenshot, we can easily see which columns have numerical values and which do not. For example, the type of the `State` column is `"factor"`, which means that the variable is a categorical variable. On the other hand, the type of the `Customer.Lifetime.Value` column is `"numeric"`, and this means that this variable is a continuous variable with numeric values. Aside from this, we can also use an R function, `summary`, to get the summary statistics for each column of a DataFrame, so that we can see not only the types of each column, but can also take a look at a summary of what the distributions for each column look like. The code is as follows:

```
# summary statistics per column
summary(df)
```

When you run this code, you will get output that looks as follows:

```
   Customer          State     Customer.Lifetime.Value Response       Coverage                Education       Effective.To.Date
AA10041:   1   Arizona    :1703   Min.   : 1898        No :7826   Basic   :5568   Bachelor             :2748  1/10/11: 195
AA11235:   1   California:3150    1st Qu.: 3994        Yes:1308   Extended:2742   College              :2681  1/27/11: 194
AA16582:   1   Nevada     : 882   Median : 5780                   Premium : 824   Doctor               : 342  2/14/11: 186
AA30683:   1   Oregon     :2601   Mean   : 8005                                   High School or Below:2622  1/26/11: 181
AA34092:   1   Washington: 798    3rd Qu.: 8962                                   Master               : 741  1/17/11: 180
AA35519:   1                      Max.   :83325                                                               1/19/11: 179
(Other):9128                                                                                                  (Other):8019
```

In this output, we can easily see a snapshot of the distributions of each column in an R DataFrame. For example, for the `State` variable, we can easily see that there are `1703` records or customers from `Arizona` and `3150` customers from `California`. On the other hand, we can easily see that the minimum value for the `Customer.Lifetime.Value` variable is `1898`, whereas, the mean is `8005` and the maximum value is `83325`.

Given this information from the previous code, we can easily select only the columns with numerical values, by using the following code:

```
# get numeric columns
continuousDF <- select_if(df, is.numeric)
colnames(continuousDF)
```

As you can see in this code snippet, we are using the `select_if` function, and the arguments for this function are the DataFrame, `df`, and a conditional statement, `is.numeric`, to define the type of column that we want to sub-select from the DataFrame. Using this function, only the numerical columns in the DataFrame, `df`, are selected and stored as a separate variable, named `continuousDF`. With the `colnames` function, we can see what columns are in the newly created DataFrame, `continuousDF`. You should see an output that looks like the following:

```
> # get numeric columns
> continuousDF <- select_if(df, is.numeric)
> colnames(continuousDF)
[1] "Customer.Lifetime.Value"        "Income"                    "Monthly.Premium.Auto"   "Months.Since.Last.Claim"
[5] "Months.Since.Policy.Inception" "Number.of.Open.Complaints"  "Number.of.Policies"     "Total.Claim.Amount"
[9] "Engaged"
```

We are now ready to fit a logistic regression model with continuous variables. Let's take a look at the following code first:

```
# Fit regression model with continuous variables
logit.fit <- glm(Engaged ~ ., data = continuousDF, family = binomial)
```

In R, you can fit regression models by using the `glm` function, which stands for **generalized linear models**. The R function `glm` can be used for various linear models. By default, the value of the family argument is `gaussian`, which tells the algorithm to fit a simple linear regression model. On the other hand, like in our case, if you use `binomial` for `family`, then it is going to fit a logistic regression model. For more detailed descriptions of the different values that you can use for the `family` argument, you can refer to `https://stat.ethz.ch/R-manual/R-devel/library/stats/html/family.html`.

The other two arguments that we passed on to the `glm` function are `formula` and `data`. The first argument, `formula`, is where you define how you want the model to be fit. The variable on the left side of ~ is the output variable, and the one on the right side of ~ is the input variable. In our case, we are telling the model to learn how to estimate the output variable, `Engaged`, by using all of the other variables as the input variables. If you want to use only a subset of the variables as the input variables, then you can use something like the following for the formula:

```
Engaged ~ Income + Customer.Lifetime.Value
```

In this formula, we are telling the model to learn how to estimate the output variable, `Engaged`, by only using `Income` and `Customer.Lifetime.Value` as the features. Lastly, the second argument in our `glm` function, `data`, defines which data to use to train a regression model.

Now that we have a trained logistic regression model, let's take a look at the following code, which shows how we can get the detailed regression analysis results from this model object:

```
summary(logit.fit)
```

The `summary` function in R provides a detailed description of the regression analysis results, which look as follows:

```
> summary(logit.fit)

Call:
glm(formula = Engaged ~ ., family = binomial, data = continuousDF)

Deviance Residuals:
    Min       1Q   Median       3Q      Max
-0.7629  -0.5704  -0.5477  -0.5216   2.1018

Coefficients:
                               Estimate Std. Error z value Pr(>|z|)
(Intercept)                  -1.787e+00  1.234e-01 -14.476   <2e-16 ***
Customer.Lifetime.Value      -6.327e-06  4.863e-06  -1.301   0.1933
Income                        2.042e-06  1.092e-06   1.869   0.0616 .
Monthly.Premium.Auto         -1.194e-04  1.226e-03  -0.097   0.9224
Months.Since.Last.Claim      -4.489e-03  2.987e-03  -1.503   0.1329
Months.Since.Policy.Inception 2.125e-04  1.073e-03   0.198   0.8429
Number.of.Open.Complaints    -3.257e-02  3.379e-02  -0.964   0.3351
Number.of.Policies           -2.443e-02  1.283e-02  -1.904   0.0569 .
Total.Claim.Amount            2.772e-04  1.463e-04   1.895   0.0581 .
---
Signif. codes:  0 '***' 0.001 '**' 0.01 '*' 0.05 '.' 0.1 ' ' 1

(Dispersion parameter for binomial family taken to be 1)

    Null deviance: 7503.3  on 9133  degrees of freedom
Residual deviance: 7488.1  on 9125  degrees of freedom
AIC: 7506.1

Number of Fisher Scoring iterations: 4
```

Let's take a more detailed look at this output. The `Estimate` column in the `Coefficients` section gives us the computed value for each of the feature coefficients. For example, the coefficient for the `Income` variable is `0.000002042`, and the coefficient for `Number.of.Policies` is `-0.02443`. We can also see that the estimated `Intercept` value is `-1.787`. The column `z value` gives us the z-score, which is the number of standard deviations from the mean of the population, and the column `Pr(>|z|)` is the *p*-value, which means how likely it is to observe the relationship between the feature and the output variable by chance. So, the lower the value of `Pr(>|z|)` is, the more likely it is that the relationship between the given feature and the output variable is strong and is not by chance. Typically, `0.05` is a good cut-off point for the *p*-value, and any value less than `0.05` signifies a strong relationship between the given feature and the output variable.

As you can see from the `Signif. codes` section under the `Coefficients` section in the output, the `***` symbol, next to the *p*-value in the `Coefficients` section, indicates the strongest relationship with the *p*-value at 0; `**` means that the *p*-value is less than 0.001; `*` means that the *p*-value is less than 0.05, and so forth. If you look at the regression analysis output again, only three variables, `Income`, `Number.of.Policies`, and `Total.Claim.Amount`, have significant relationships with the output variable, `Engaged`, at a 0.1 significance level. Also, we can see that `Income` and `Total.Claim.Amount` are positively correlated with `Engaged`, meaning that the higher the income is or the higher the total claim amount is, the more likely that a customer will be engaged with marketing calls. On the other hand, the variable `Number.of.Policies` is negatively correlated with `Engaged`, which suggests that the higher the number of policies that a customer has, the less likely that the given customer will be engaged with marketing calls.

As you can see in these examples, you can interpret the regression analysis results quite easily, by looking at the *p*-values and coefficients of the features from the model output. This is a good way to understand which attributes of customers are significantly and highly correlated with your outcomes of interest.

Categorical variables

As you saw in the case with continuous variables in the previous section, it is quite straightforward to understand the relationships between the input and output variables from the coefficients and *p*-values. However, it becomes not so straightforward when we introduce categorical variables. Categorical variables often do not have any natural order but, in linear regression, we need the `input` variables to have numerical values that signify the orderings or magnitudes of the variables. For example, we cannot easily encode the `State` variable in our dataset with certain orders or values. That is why we need to handle categorical variables differently from continuous variables when conducting regression analysis. In R, the `factor` function helps you to handle these categorical variables easily when running regression analysis. Take a look at the following code:

```
# a. Education
# Fit regression model with Education factor variables
logit.fit <- glm(Engaged ~ factor(Education), data = df, family = binomial)
summary(logit.fit)
```

As you can see in this code, we are fitting a logistic regression model with `Engaged` as the output variable and the factorized `Education` as the input variable. Before we dive deeper into what this means, let's first look at the following regression analysis results:

```
> summary(logit.fit)

Call:
glm(formula = Engaged ~ factor(Education), family = binomial,
    data = df)

Deviance Residuals:
    Min      1Q   Median      3Q      Max
-0.6211  -0.5746  -0.5440  -0.5287   2.0184

Coefficients:
                                      Estimate Std. Error z value Pr(>|z|)
(Intercept)                           -1.83575    0.05538 -33.146   <2e-16 ***
factor(Education)College               0.11816    0.07719   1.531   0.1258
factor(Education)Doctor                0.28819    0.15258   1.889   0.0589 .
factor(Education)High School or Below -0.06137    0.08019  -0.765   0.4441
factor(Education)Master                0.19191    0.11407   1.682   0.0925 .
---
Signif. codes:  0 '***' 0.001 '**' 0.01 '*' 0.05 '.' 0.1 ' ' 1

(Dispersion parameter for binomial family taken to be 1)

    Null deviance: 7503.3  on 9133  degrees of freedom
Residual deviance: 7492.4  on 9129  degrees of freedom
AIC: 7502.4

Number of Fisher Scoring iterations: 4
```

As you can see in this output, the `factor` function created four additional variables: `factor(Education)College`, `factor(Education)Doctor`, `factor(Education)High School or Below`, and `factor(Education)Master`. These variables are encoded with 0 if the given customer does not belong to the given category, or 1 if the given customer belongs to the given category. This way, we can understand the positive or negative relationship between each of the `Education` category and the `output` variable, `Engaged`. For example, the factor variable, `factor(Education)Doctor`, has a positive coefficient, which suggests that if a customer has a doctoral degree, then it is more likely that the given customer will be engaged with marketing calls.

If you look closely, you will notice that this output does not have a separate factor variable for the `Bachelor` category in the `Education` variable. This is because `(Intercept)` contains the information for the `Bachelor` category. If a customer has a bachelor's degree, then all of the other factor variables would have been encoded with 0s. Hence, all of the coefficient values are cancelled out, and only the `(Intercept)` value stays. Since the estimated `(Intercept)` value is negative, if a customer has a `Bachelor` degree, then it is less likely that the given customer will be engaged with marketing calls.

Let's take a look at another example:

```
# b. Education + Gender
# Fit regression model with Education & Gender variables
logit.fit <- glm(Engaged ~ factor(Education) + factor(Gender), data = df,
family = binomial)

summary(logit.fit)
```

As you can see in this code, we are now fitting a regression model with the `Education` and `Gender` variables, and the output looks as follows:

```
> summary(logit.fit)

Call:
glm(formula = Engaged ~ factor(Education) + factor(Gender), family = binomial,
    data = df)

Deviance Residuals:
    Min      1Q   Median      3Q      Max
-0.6247  -0.5713  -0.5409  -0.5256   2.0238

Coefficients:
                                     Estimate Std. Error z value Pr(>|z|)
(Intercept)                          -1.84803    0.06257 -29.537  <2e-16 ***
factor(Education)College              0.11782    0.07720   1.526  0.1269
factor(Education)Doctor               0.28759    0.15259   1.885  0.0595 .
factor(Education)High School or Below -0.06173   0.08019  -0.770  0.4415
factor(Education)Master               0.19223    0.11407   1.685  0.0919 .
factor(Gender)M                       0.02534    0.05979   0.424  0.6717
---
Signif. codes:  0 '***' 0.001 '**' 0.01 '*' 0.05 '.' 0.1 ' ' 1

(Dispersion parameter for binomial family taken to be 1)

    Null deviance: 7503.3  on 9133  degrees of freedom
Residual deviance: 7492.3  on 9128  degrees of freedom
AIC: 7504.3

Number of Fisher Scoring iterations: 4
```

If you look closely at this output, you can only see one additional factor variable, `factor(Gender)M`, for male customers, where the data clearly has female customers. This is because the `Bachelor` category of the `Education` variable and the `F` (female) category of the `Gender` variable are lumped together as `(Intercept)` of this regression model. Thus, the base case, wherein the values of all of the factor variables are `0`, is for `female` customers with a `Bachelor` degree.

For male customers with a `Bachelor` degree, the factor variable `factor(Gender)M` will now have a value of 1, and hence, the estimated value for the output variable, `Engaged`, will be the value of `(Intercept)` plus the coefficient value of `factor(Gender)M`.

As we have discussed so far, we can handle categorical variables by using the `factor` function in R. It is essentially the same as creating one separate input variable per category for each of the categorical variables. Using this technique, we can understand how different categories of categorical variables are correlated with the output variable.

Combining continuous and categorical variables

The last exercise that we are going to do in this chapter involves combining continuous and categorical variables for our regression analysis. Let's first factorize the two categorical variables, `Gender` and `Education`, that we discussed in the previous section, and store them in a DataFrame by using the following code:

```
continuousDF$Gender <- factor(df$Gender)
continuousDF$Education <- factor(df$Education)
```

The DataFrame, `continuousDF`, now contains the following columns:

```
> colnames(continuousDF)
 [1] "Customer.Lifetime.Value"    "Income"                       "Monthly.Premium.Auto"
 [4] "Months.Since.Last.Claim"    "Months.Since.Policy.Inception" "Number.of.Open.Complaints"
 [7] "Number.of.Policies"         "Total.Claim.Amount"           "Engaged"
[10] "Gender"                     "Education"
```

Now, we are going to fit a logistic regression model with both the categorical and continuous variables, using the following code:

```
# Fit regression model with Education & Gender variables
logit.fit <- glm(Engaged ~ ., data = continuousDF, family = binomial)
summary(logit.fit)
```

You should get an output that looks as follows:

```
> summary(logit.fit)

Call:
glm(formula = Engaged ~ ., family = binomial, data = continuousDF)

Deviance Residuals:
    Min      1Q   Median      3Q     Max
-0.7905  -0.5739  -0.5427  -0.5095   2.1431

Coefficients:
                               Estimate Std. Error z value Pr(>|z|)
(Intercept)                   -1.837e+00  1.342e-01 -13.693   <2e-16 ***
Customer.Lifetime.Value       -6.065e-06  4.872e-06  -1.245   0.2132
Income                         2.044e-06  1.094e-06   1.867   0.0618 .
Monthly.Premium.Auto          -4.619e-04  1.237e-03  -0.374   0.7087
Months.Since.Last.Claim       -4.717e-03  2.993e-03  -1.576   0.1150
Months.Since.Policy.Inception  1.856e-04  1.074e-03   0.173   0.8627
Number.of.Open.Complaints     -3.448e-02  3.378e-02  -1.021   0.3075
Number.of.Policies            -2.392e-02  1.285e-02  -1.862   0.0626 .
Total.Claim.Amount             3.471e-04  1.487e-04   2.335   0.0196 *
GenderM                        1.537e-02  6.017e-02   0.255   0.7984
EducationCollege               1.216e-01  7.731e-02   1.573   0.1158
EducationDoctor                3.107e-01  1.532e-01   2.028   0.0425 *
EducationHigh School or Below -7.456e-02  8.056e-02  -0.925   0.3547
EducationMaster                2.065e-01  1.149e-01   1.798   0.0722 .
---
Signif. codes:  0 '***' 0.001 '**' 0.01 '*' 0.05 '.' 0.1 ' ' 1

(Dispersion parameter for binomial family taken to be 1)

    Null deviance: 7503.3  on 9133  degrees of freedom
Residual deviance: 7475.5  on 9120  degrees of freedom
AIC: 7503.5

Number of Fisher Scoring iterations: 4
```

Let's take a closer look at this output. The `Total.Claim.Amount` variables and `EducationDoctor` variables are significant at a `0.05` significance level, and both of them have positive relationships with the output variable, `Engaged`. Hence, the higher the total claim amount is, the more likely that the customer is going to engage with the marketing calls. Also, customers with doctoral degrees are more likely to engage with marketing calls than those with other educational backgrounds. At a `0.1` significance level, we can see that `Income`, `Number.of.Policies`, and `EducationMaster` now have significant relationships with the output variable, `Engaged`. From looking at this regression analysis output, we can easily see the relationships between the input and output variables, and we can understand which attributes of customers are positively or negatively related to customer engagement with marketing calls.

The full code for the R exercise can be found in the repository at `https://github.com/yoonhwang/hands-on-data-science-for-marketing/blob/master/ch.3/R/RegressionAnalysis.R`.

Summary

In this chapter, we discussed how to use explanatory analysis to draw insight on customer behavior. We discussed how regression analysis can be used to dive deeper into understanding customer behavior. More specifically, you learned how to use logistic regression to understand what attributes of customers drive higher engagement rates. In Python and R exercises, we employed the descriptive analysis that we covered in Chapter 2, *Key Performance Indicators and Visualizations*, as well as regression analysis for explanatory analysis. We started the exercises by analyzing the data in order to better understand and identify noticeable patterns in the data. While analyzing the data, you learned one additional way to visualize the data, through box plots, using the `matplotlib` and `pandas` packages in Python and the `ggplot2` library in R.

While fitting regression models, we discussed the two different types of variables: continuous and categorical. You learned about the challenges in handling categorical variables when fitting logistic regression models, and how to handle such variables. For Python, we covered two ways of handling categorical variables: the `factorize` and `Categorical` functions from the `pandas` package. For R, we discussed how we can use the `factor` function to handle categorical variables when fitting a logistic regression model. With the regression analysis results, we showed how you can interpret the results and relationships between the input and output variables by looking at the coefficients and *p*-values. By looking at the regression analysis output, we can understand what attributes of customers show significant relationships with customer marketing engagement.

In the next chapter, we are going to expand your knowledge of explanatory analysis. We will analyze what drives conversions after customer engagements. You will also learn about another machine learning algorithm, decision trees, and how to use them for explanatory analysis.

4
From Engagement to Conversion

In this chapter, we will expand your knowledge of explanatory analysis and show you how to use **decision trees** to understand the drivers behind consumer behavior. We will start by comparing and explaining the differences between logistic regression and decision tree models, and then we will discuss how decision trees are built and trained. Next, we will discuss how a trained decision tree model can be used to extract information about the relationships between the attributes (or features) of individual consumers and the target output variables.

For programming exercises, we will use the bank marketing dataset from the UCI Machine Learning Repository to understand the drivers behind conversions. We will start with some data analysis, so that you can better understand the dataset; then, we will build decision tree models by using the `scikit-learn` package in Python and the `rpart` package in R. Lastly, you will learn how to interpret these trained decision tree models by visualizing them using the `graphviz` package in Python and the `rattle` package in R. By the end of this chapter, you will be familiar with decision trees and will have a better understanding of when and how to use them with Python or R.

In this chapter, we will cover the following topics:

- Decision trees
- Decision trees and interpretations with Python
- Decision trees and interpretations with R

Decision trees

In the previous chapter, we discussed explanatory analysis and regression analysis. We are going to continue with that theme and introduce another machine learning algorithm that we can use to draw insights on customer behavior from data. In this chapter, we will be discussing a machine learning algorithm called **decision trees**: how they learn from the data and how we can interpret their results.

Logistic regression versus decision trees

If you recall from the previous chapter, a **logistic regression** model learns from the data by finding the linear combination of the feature variables that best estimates the log odds of an event occurring. Decision trees, as the name suggests, learn from the data by growing a tree. We are going to discuss how decision tree models grow and to build trees in more detail in the following section, but the main difference between the logistic regression and decision tree models is the fact that logistic regression algorithms search for a single best linear boundary in the feature set, whereas the decision tree algorithm partitions the data to find the subgroups of data that have high likelihoods of an event occurring. It will be easier to explain this with an example. Let's take a look at the following diagram:

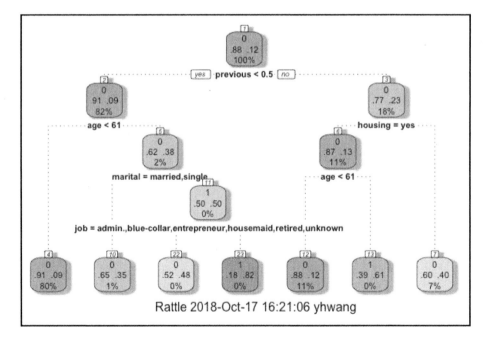

Rattle 2018-Oct-17 16:21:06 yhwang

This is an example of a decision tree model. As you can see in this diagram, it partitions the data with certain criteria. In this example, the root node is split into child nodes by a criterion of `previous < 0.5`. If this condition is met and true, then it traverses to the left child node. If not, then it traverses to the right child node. The left child node is then split into its child nodes by a criterion of `age < 61`. The tree grows until it finds pure nodes (meaning that all of the data points in each node belong to one class) or until it meets certain criteria to stop, such as the maximum depth of the tree.

As you can see in this example, the data are split into seven partitions. The leftmost node or partition at the bottom is for those data points with values less than `0.5` for the `previous` variable and with values less than `61` for the `age` variable. On the other hand, the rightmost node at the bottom is for those data points with values greater than `0.5` for the `previous` variable and with values other than `yes` for the `housing` variable.

One thing that is noticeable here is that there are a lot of interactions between different variables. No single leaf node in this example tree is partitioned with one condition. Every partition in this tree is formed with more than one criterion and interactions between different `feature` variables. This is the main difference from logistic regression models. When there is no linear structure in the data, logistic regression models will not be able to perform well, as they try to find linear combinations among the feature variables. On the other hand, decision tree models will perform better for non-linear datasets, as they only try to partition the data at the purest levels they can.

Growing decision trees

When we are growing decision trees, the trees need to come up with a logic to split a node into child nodes. There are two main methods that are commonly used for splitting the data: **Gini impurity** and **entropy information gain**. Simply put, *Gini* impurity measures how impure a partition is, and entropy information gain measures how much information it gains from splitting the data with the criteria being tested.

Let's take a quick look at the equation to compute the *Gini* impurity measure:

$$Gini = 1 - \sum_{i=1}^{c} p_i^2$$

Here, *c* stands for the class labels, and P_i stands for the probability of a record with the class label *i* being chosen. By subtracting the sum of squared probabilities from one, the *Gini* impurity measure reaches zero, that is, when all records in each partition or node of a tree are pure with a single target class.

The equation to compute the *entropy* looks as follows:

$$Entropy = -\sum_{i=1}^{c} p_i log(p_i)$$

Like before, c stands for the class labels, and P_i stands for the probability of a record with the class label i being chosen. When growing the tree, the entropy of each possible split needs to be calculated and compared against the entropy before the split. Then, the split that gives the biggest change in entropy measures or the highest information gain will be chosen to grow the tree. This process will be repeated until all of the nodes are pure, or until it meets the stopping criteria.

Decision trees and interpretations with Python

In this section, you are going to learn how to use the `scikit-learn` package in Python to build decision tree models and interpret the results via visualizations using Python's `graphviz` package. For those readers that would like to use R instead of Python for this exercise, you can skip to the next section. We will start this section by analyzing the bank marketing dataset in depth, using the `pandas` and `matplotlib` packages, and then we will discuss how to build and interpret decision tree models.

For this exercise, we will be using one of the publicly available datasets from the UCI Machine Learning Repository, which can be found at `https://archive.ics.uci.edu/ml/datasets/bank+marketing`. You can follow the link and download the data in ZIP format. We will use the `bank.zip` file for this exercise. When you unzip this file, you will see two CSV files: `bank.csv` and `bank-full.csv`. We are going to use the `bank-full.csv` file for this Python exercise.

In order to load this data into your Jupyter Notebook, you can run the following code:

```
%matplotlib inline

import matplotlib.pyplot as plt
import pandas as pd

df = pd.read_csv('../data/bank-full.csv', sep=";")
```

As you can see from this code snippet, we use the `%matplotlib inline` command to show plots on the Jupyter Notebook. Then, we import the `matplotlib` and `pandas` packages that we are going to use for the data analysis step. Lastly, we can easily read the data file by using the `read_csv` function in the `pandas` package. One thing to note here is the `sep` argument in the `read_csv` function. If you look at the data closely, you will notice that the fields in the `bank-full.csv` file are separated by semicolons (`;`), not commas (`,`). In order to correctly load the data into a `pandas` DataFrame, we will need to tell the `read_csv` function to use semicolons as the separators, instead of commas.

Once you have loaded the data, it should look like the following screenshot:

```
df.shape
```

```
(45211, 17)
```

```
df.head()
```

	age	job	marital	education	default	balance	housing	loan	contact	day	month	duration	campaign	pdays	previous	poutcome	y
0	58	management	married	tertiary	no	2143	yes	no	unknown	5	may	261	1	-1	0	unknown	no
1	44	technician	single	secondary	no	29	yes	no	unknown	5	may	151	1	-1	0	unknown	no
2	33	entrepreneur	married	secondary	no	2	yes	yes	unknown	5	may	76	1	-1	0	unknown	no
3	47	blue-collar	married	unknown	no	1506	yes	no	unknown	5	may	92	1	-1	0	unknown	no
4	33	unknown	single	unknown	no	1	no	no	unknown	5	may	198	1	-1	0	unknown	no

Data analysis and visualization

Before we start to analyze the data, we will first encode the output variable, `y`, which has information about whether a customer has converted or subscribed to a term deposit, with numerical values. You can use the following code to encode the output variable, `y`, with zeros and ones:

```
df['conversion'] = df['y'].apply(lambda x: 0 if x == 'no' else 1)
```

As you can see from this code snippet, you can use the `apply` function to encode the output variable. We stored these encoded values in a new column, named `conversion`.

Conversion rate

Let's first take a look at the aggregate conversion rate. The **conversion rate** is simply the percentage of customers that subscribed to a term deposit. Take a look at the following code:

```
conversion_rate_df = pd.DataFrame(
    df.groupby('conversion').count()['y'] / df.shape[0] * 100.0
)
```

As you can see from this code snippet, we are grouping by a column, conversion, which is encoded with 1 for those that have subscribed to a term deposit, and with 0 for those that have not. Then, we are counting the number of customers in each group and dividing it by the total number of customers in the dataset. The result looks as follows:

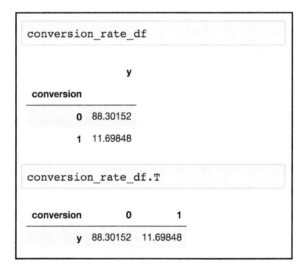

To make it easier to view, you can transpose the DataFrame by using the T attribute of the pandas DataFrame. As you can see, only about 11.7% were converted or subscribed to a term deposit. From these results, we can see that there is a large imbalance between the conversion group and the non-conversion group, which is common and is frequently observed among various marketing datasets.

Conversion rates by job

It might be true that certain job categories tend to convert more frequently than others. Let's take a look at the conversion rates across different job categories. You can achieve this by using the following code:

```
conversion_rate_by_job = df.groupby(
    by='job'
)['conversion'].sum() / df.groupby(
    by='job'
)['conversion'].count() * 100.0
```

Let's take a deeper look at this code. We first group by the column, `job`, which contains information about the job category that each customer belongs to. Then, we sum over the `conversion` column for each job category, from which we get the total number of conversions for each job category. Lastly, we divide these conversion numbers by the total number of customers in each job category, in order to get the conversion rates for each job category.

The results look as follows:

```
conversion_rate_by_job

job
admin.           12.202669
blue-collar       7.274969
entrepreneur      8.271688
housemaid         8.790323
management       13.755551
retired          22.791519
self-employed    11.842939
services          8.883004
student          28.678038
technician       11.056996
unemployed       15.502686
unknown          11.805556
Name: conversion, dtype: float64
```

As you can see from these results, the `student` group tends to convert much more frequently than the others, and the `retired` group comes next. However, it is a bit difficult to compare these from the raw output, and we could present this data better by using a chart. We can build a horizontal bar chart by using the following code:

```
ax = conversion_rate_by_job.plot(
    kind='barh',
    color='skyblue',
    grid=True,
```

```
        figsize=(10, 7),
        title='Conversion Rates by Job'
    )

    ax.set_xlabel('conversion rate (%)')
    ax.set_ylabel('Job')

    plt.show()
```

If you look at this code, we are using the `plot` function of the `pandas` DataFrame, and we defined the type of this plot to be a horizontal bar chart by providing `barh` as the input to the `kind` argument. You can simply adjust the color, size, and title of the chart with the `color`, `figsize`, and `title` arguments, respectively. You can also easily change the *x*-axis and *y*-axis labels, using the `set_xlabel` and `set_ylabel` functions.

The resulting chart looks as follows:

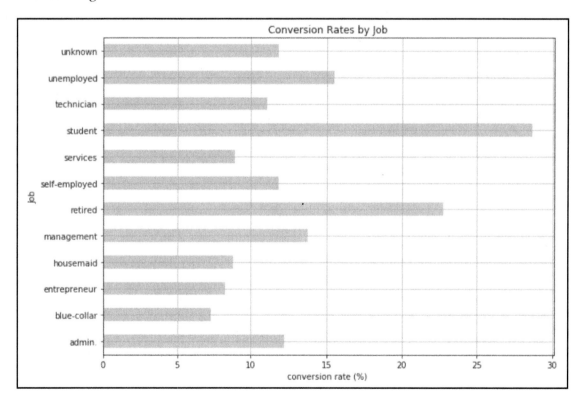

As you can see, it is much easier to spot the differences in the conversion rates by each job category with a horizontal bar chart. We can easily see that the `student` and `retired` groups are the two groups with the highest conversion rates, whereas the `blue-collar` and `entrepreneur` groups are the two groups with the lowest conversion rates.

Default rates by conversions

Another attribute of a customer that would be interesting to see is the default rate, and how it differs between those who subscribed to a term deposit and those who did not. We are going to use the `pivot_table` function in the `pandas` library to analyze the default rates by conversions. Let's take a look at the following code:

```
default_by_conversion_df = pd.pivot_table(
    df,
    values='y',
    index='default',
    columns='conversion',
    aggfunc=len
)
```

As you can see from this code, we are pivoting the DataFrame, `df`, by the `y` and `default` columns. By using `len` as the aggregation function, we can count how many customers fall under each cell of the pivot table. The results look as follows:

default_by_conversion_df		
conversion	**0**	**1**
default		
no	39159	5237
yes	763	52

It is a bit difficult to compare how the default rates differ between the conversion and non-conversion groups by looking at these raw numbers. One way to visualize this data is through a pie chart. You can use the following code to build a pie chart:

```
default_by_conversion_df.plot(
    kind='pie',
    figsize=(15, 7),
    startangle=90,
    subplots=True,
```

```
        autopct=lambda x: '%0.1f%%' % x
    )

plt.show()
```

As you can see from this code, we are simply passing `'pie'` as input to the `kind` argument of the `plot` function. The resulting pie chart appears as follows:

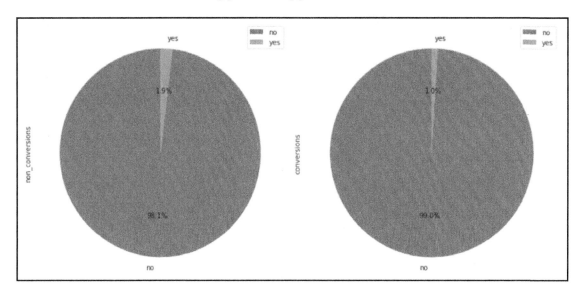

As you can see from these pie charts, it is much easier to compare the default rates between the conversion and non-conversion groups. Although the overall percentage of the previous default is low in both groups, the default rate in the non-conversion group is about twice as high as the conversion group.

Bank balances by conversions

Next, we will try to see if there are any differences in the distributions of bank balances between the conversion and non-conversion groups. A box plot is typically a good way to visualize the distribution of a variable. Let's take a look at the following code:

```
ax = df[['conversion', 'balance']].boxplot(
    by='conversion',
    showfliers=True,
    figsize=(10, 7)
)

ax.set_xlabel('Conversion')
```

```
ax.set_ylabel('Average Bank Balance')
ax.set_title('Average Bank Balance Distributions by Conversion')

plt.suptitle("")
plt.show()
```

You should be familiar with this code by now, as we have discussed how to build box plots using the `pandas` package. Using the `boxplot` function, we can easily build box plots such as the following:

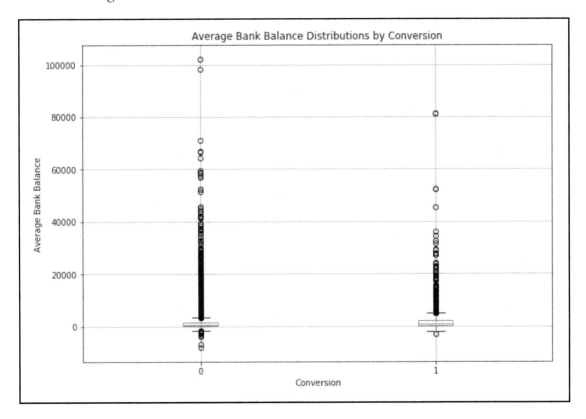

Because there are so many outliers, it is quite difficult to identify any differences between the two distributions. Let's build another box plot without outliers. The only thing that you need to change from the previous code is the `showfliers=True` argument in the `boxplot` function, as you can see in the following code:

```
ax = df[['conversion', 'balance']].boxplot(
    by='conversion',
    showfliers=False,
    figsize=(10, 7)
```

```
)
ax.set_xlabel('Conversion')
ax.set_ylabel('Average Bank Balance')
ax.set_title('Average Bank Balance Distributions by Conversion')

plt.suptitle("")
plt.show()
```

Using this code, you will see the following box plots for the distributions of bank balances between the two groups:

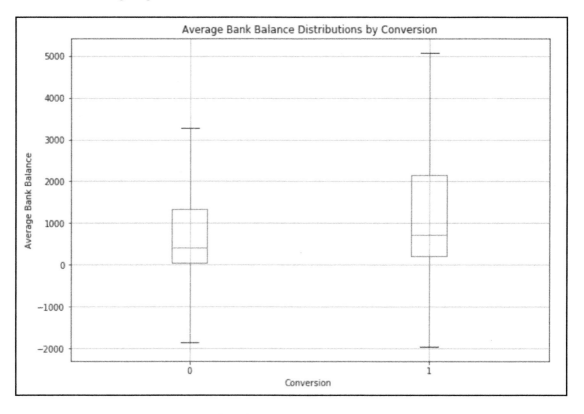

From these box plots, we can see that the median of the bank balance is slightly higher for the conversion group, as compared to the non-conversion group. Also, the bank balances of converted customers seem to vary more than those of non-converted customers.

Conversion rates by number of contacts

Lastly, we will look at how the conversion rates vary by the number of contacts. Typically, in marketing, a higher number of marketing touches can result in marketing fatigue, where the conversion rates drop as you reach out to your customers more frequently. Let's see whether there is any marketing fatigue in our data. Take a look at the following code:

```
conversions_by_num_contacts = df.groupby(
    by='campaign'
)['conversion'].sum() / df.groupby(
    by='campaign'
)['conversion'].count() * 100.0
```

In this code snippet, you can see that we are grouping by the `campaign` column (which has information about the number of contacts performed during the marketing campaign for this customer) and computing the conversion rates for each number of contacts. The resulting data appears as follows:

	conversion
campaign	
1	14.597583
2	11.203519
3	11.193624
4	9.000568
5	7.879819
6	7.126259
7	6.394558
8	5.925926
9	6.422018
10	5.263158

pd.DataFrame(conversions_by_num_contacts)

Like before, it would be easier to look at a chart, rather than raw numbers. We can plot this data by using bar charts, with the following code:

```
ax = conversions_by_num_contacts.plot(
    kind='bar',
    figsize=(10, 7),
    title='Conversion Rates by Number of Contacts',
    grid=True,
```

```
        color='skyblue'
    )

    ax.set_xlabel('Number of Contacts')
    ax.set_ylabel('Conversion Rate (%)')

    plt.show()
```

The plot looks as follows:

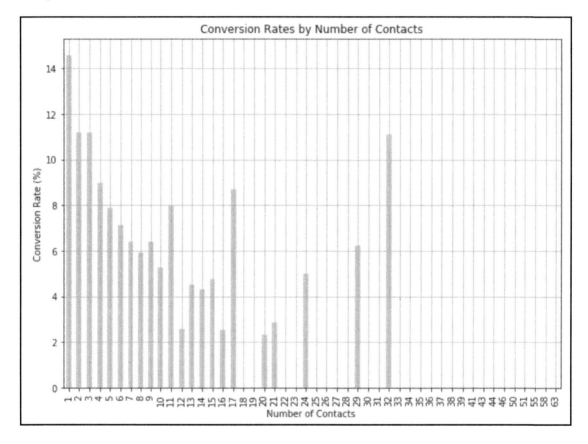

There's some noise in a higher numbers of contacts, as the sample size is smaller for them, but you can easily see the overall downward trend in this bar chart. As the number of contacts increases, the conversion rates slowly decrease. This suggests that the expected conversion rate decreases as you contact a client more frequently for a given campaign.

Encoding categorical variables

There are eight categorical variables in this dataset: job, marital, education, default, housing, loan, contact, and month. Before we start to build decision trees, we need to encode these categorical variables with numerical values. We'll take a look at how we can encode some of these categorical variables in this section.

Encoding months

We all know that there can only be 12 unique values for the month variable. Let's take a quick look at what we have in our dataset. Take a look at the following code:

```
df['month'].unique()
```

The pandas function, unique, helps you to quickly get the unique values in the given column. When you run this code, you will get the following output:

```
df['month'].unique()

array(['may', 'jun', 'jul', 'aug', 'oct', 'nov', 'dec', 'jan', 'feb',
       'mar', 'apr', 'sep'], dtype=object)
```

As expected, we have 12 unique values for the month column, from January to December. Since there is a natural ordering in the values of month, we can encode each of the values with a corresponding number. One way to encode the string values of month with numbers is shown as follows:

```
months = ['jan', 'feb', 'mar', 'apr', 'may', 'jun', 'jul', 'aug', 'sep',
'oct', 'nov', 'dec']

df['month'] = df['month'].apply(
    lambda x: months.index(x)+1
)
```

Using this code, the unique values for the column `month` look as follows:

```
df['month'].unique()
array([ 5,  6,  7,  8, 10, 11, 12,  1,  2,  3,  4,  9])
```

To see how many records we have for each month, we can use the following code:

```
df.groupby('month').count()['conversion']
```

The results are as follows:

```
df.groupby('month').count()['conversion']

month
1      1403
2      2649
3       477
4      2932
5     13766
6      5341
7      6895
8      6247
9       579
10      738
11     3970
12      214
Name: conversion, dtype: int64
```

Encoding jobs

Next, let's look at how we can encode the different categories of the `job` column. We will first look at the unique values in this column, using the following code:

```
df['job'].unique()
```

The unique values in the `job` column look as follows:

```
df['job'].unique()
array(['management', 'technician', 'entrepreneur', 'blue-collar',
       'unknown', 'retired', 'admin.', 'services', 'self-employed',
       'unemployed', 'housemaid', 'student'], dtype=object)
```

As you can see in this output, there is no natural ordering for this variable. One `job` category does not precede the other, so we cannot encode this variable like we did for `month`. We are going to create dummy variables for each of the `job` categories. If you recall from the previous chapter, a **dummy variable** is a variable that is encoded with 1 if a given record belongs to the category, and 0 if not. We can do this easily by using the following code:

```
jobs_encoded_df = pd.get_dummies(df['job'])
jobs_encoded_df.columns = ['job_%s' % x for x in jobs_encoded_df.columns]
```

As you can see from this code snippet, the `get_dummies` function in the `pandas` package creates one dummy variable for each category in the `job` variable, and encodes each record with 1 if the given record belongs to the corresponding category, and 0 if not. Then, we rename the columns by prefixing each column with `job_`. The result looks as follows:

	job_admin.	job_blue-collar	job_entrepreneur	job_housemaid	job_management	job_retired	job_self-employed	job_services	job_student	job_technician	job_unemployed	job_unknown
0	0	0	0	0	1	0	0	0	0	0	0	0
1	0	0	0	0	0	0	0	0	0	1	0	0
2	0	0	1	0	0	0	0	0	0	0	0	0
3	0	1	0	0	0	0	0	0	0	0	0	0
4	0	0	0	0	0	0	0	0	0	0	0	1

As you can see from this screenshot, the first record (or customer) belongs to the `management` job category, while the second record belongs to the `technician` job category. Now that we have created dummy variables for each job category, we need to append this data to the existing DataFrame. Take a look at the following code:

```
df = pd.concat([df, jobs_encoded_df], axis=1)
df.head()
```

Using the `concat` function in the `pandas` package, you can easily add the newly created DataFrame with dummy variables, `jobs_encoded_df`, to the original DataFrame, `df`. The `axis=1` argument tells the `concat` function to concatenate the second DataFrame to the first DataFrame as columns, not as rows. The resulting DataFrame looks as follows:

	age	job	marital	education	default	balance	housing	loan	contact	day	...	job_entrepreneur	job_housemaid	job_management	job_retired
0	58	management	married	tertiary	no	2143	yes	no	unknown	5	...	0	0	1	0
1	44	technician	single	secondary	no	29	yes	no	unknown	5	...	0	0	0	0
2	33	entrepreneur	married	secondary	no	2	yes	yes	unknown	5	...	1	0	0	0
3	47	blue-collar	married	unknown	no	1506	yes	no	unknown	5	...	0	0	0	0
4	33	unknown	single	unknown	no	1	no	no	unknown	5	...	0	0	0	0

As you can see, the newly created dummy variables are added to the original DataFrame as new columns for each record.

Encoding marital

Similar to how we encoded the categorical variable, `job`, we are going to create dummy variables for each category of the `marital` variable. Like before, we are using the following code to encode the `marital` column:

```
marital_encoded_df = pd.get_dummies(df['marital'])
marital_encoded_df.columns = ['marital_%s' % x for x in
marital_encoded_df.columns]
```

The encoding results are as follows:

`marital_encoded_df.head()`			
	marital_divorced	marital_married	marital_single
0	0	1	0
1	0	0	1
2	0	1	0
3	0	1	0
4	0	0	1

As you can see, three new variables are created for the original variable, `marital`: `marital_divorced`, `marital_married`, and `marital_single`, representing whether a given customer is divorced, married, or single, respectively. In order to add these newly created dummy variables to the original DataFrame, we can use the following code:

```
df = pd.concat([df, marital_encoded_df], axis=1)
```

Once you have come this far, your original DataFrame, `df`, should contain all of the original columns, plus newly created dummy variables for the `job` and `marital` columns.

Encoding the housing and loan variables

The last two categorical variables that we are going to encode in this section are `housing` and `loan`. The `housing` variable has two unique values, `'yes'` and `'no'`, and contains information on whether a customer has a housing loan. The other variable, `loan`, also has two unique values, `'yes'` and `'no'`, and tells us whether a customer has a personal loan. We can easily encode these two variables by using the following code:

```
df['housing'] = df['housing'].apply(lambda x: 1 if x == 'yes' else 0)

df['loan'] = df['loan'].apply(lambda x: 1 if x == 'yes' else 0)
```

As you can see, we are using the `apply` function to encode `yes` as `1` and `no` as `0` for both the housing and loan variables. For those categorical variables that we have not discussed in this section, you can use the same techniques that we have discussed to encode them if you wish to explore beyond this exercise.

Building decision trees

Now that we have encoded all of the categorical variables, we can finally start to build decision tree models. We are going to use the following variables as features in our decision tree models:

```
features
['age',
 'balance',
 'campaign',
 'previous',
 'housing',
 'job_admin.',
 'job_blue-collar',
 'job_entrepreneur',
 'job_housemaid',
 'job_management',
 'job_retired',
 'job_self-employed',
 'job_services',
 'job_student',
 'job_technician',
 'job_unemployed',
 'job_unknown',
 'marital_divorced',
 'marital_married',
 'marital_single']
```

In order to build and train a decision tree model with Python, we are going to use the `tree` module in the `scikit-learn` (`sklearn`) package. You can import the required module by using the following line of code:

```
from sklearn import tree
```

Under the `tree` module in the `sklearn` package, there is a class named `DecisionTreeClassifier`, which we can use to train a decision tree model. Take a look at the following code:

```
dt_model = tree.DecisionTreeClassifier(
    max_depth=4
)
```

There are many arguments to the `DecisionTreeClassifier` class, aside from the one that we are using here, `max_depth`. The `max_depth` argument controls how much a tree can grow, and here, we limit it to 4, meaning that the maximum length from the root to a leaf can be 4. You can also use the `criterion` argument to choose between the Gini impurity and the entropy information gain measures for the quality of a split. There are many other ways to tune your decision tree model, and we recommend that, for more information, you take a closer look at the documentation at http://scikit-learn.org/stable/modules/generated/sklearn.tree.DecisionTreeClassifier.html.

In order to train this decision tree model, you can use the following code:

```
dt_model.fit(df[features], df[response_var])
```

As you can see from this code, the `fit` function takes two arguments: the `predictor` or `feature` variables and the `response` or `target` variables. In our case, `response_var` is the `conversion` column of the DataFrame, `df`. Once you have run this code, the decision tree model will learn how to make classifications. In the following section, we will discuss how we can interpret the results of this trained decision tree model.

Interpreting decision trees

Now that we have trained a decision tree model, we need to extract the insights from the model. In this section, we are going to use a package called `graphviz`. You can install this package by using the following command in your Terminal:

```
conda install python-graphviz
```

Once you have installed this package correctly, you should be able to import the package as follows:

```
import graphviz
```

Now that we have set up our environment with the new package, graphviz, let's take a look at the following code to see how we can visualize the trained decision tree:

```
dot_data = tree.export_graphviz(
    dt_model,
    feature_names=features,
    class_names=['0', '1'],
    filled=True,
    rounded=True,
    special_characters=True
)

graph = graphviz.Source(dot_data)
```

As you can see, we first export the trained decision tree model, dt_model, using the export_graphviz function in the tree module of the sklearn package. We can define the feature variables that we used to train this model by using the feature_names argument. Then, we can define the classes (conversion versus non-conversion) that this model is trained to classify. The export_graphviz function exports the trained decision tree model in a DOT format, which is a graphic description language. You can then pass dot_data on to the graphviz Source class. The graph variable now contains a renderable graph. The root node and its direct children look as follows:

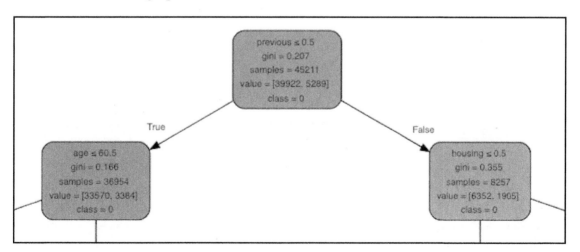

The tree on the left half (or the children of the root node's left child) looks as follows:

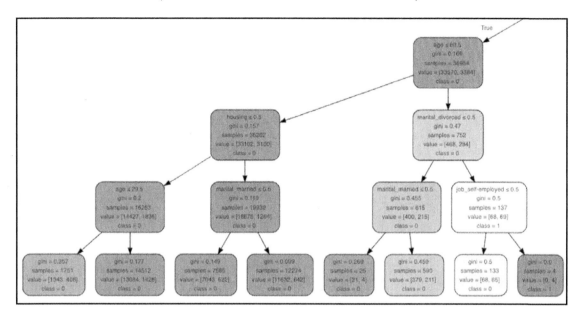

The tree on the right half (or the children of the root node's right child) looks as follows:

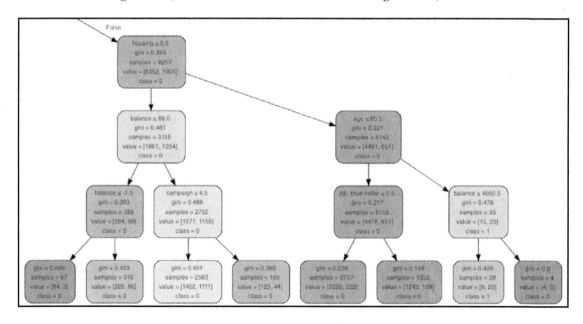

Let's take a closer look at this diagram. Each node contains five lines that describe the information that the given node has. The top line tells us the criteria of the split. The root node, for example, is split into its child nodes based on the value of the previous variable. If the value of this previous variable is less than or equal to 0.5, then it goes to the left child. On the other hand, if the value of this previous variable is larger than 0.5, then it goes to the right child.

The second line tells us the value of the quality measure for the split. Here, we selected the gini impurity measure for the criteria, so we can see the changes in the impurity measures in each node from the second line. The third line tells us the total number of records that belong to the given node. For example, there are 45,211 samples in the root node, and there are 8,257 samples in the right child of the root node.

The fourth line in each node tells us the composition of the records in two different classes. The first element stands for the number of records in the non-conversion group, and the second element stands for the number of records in the conversion group. For example, in the root node, there are 39,922 records in the non-conversion group and 5,289 records in the conversion group. Lastly, the fifth line in each node tells us what the prediction or classification will be for the given node. For example, if a sample belongs to the leftmost leaf, the classification by this decision tree model will be 0, meaning non-conversion. On the other hand, if a sample belongs to the eighth leaf from the left, the classification by this decision tree model will be 1, meaning conversion.

Now that we know what each of the lines in each nodes means, let's discuss how we can draw insights from this tree graph. In order to understand the customers that belong to each leaf node, we need to follow through the tree. For example, those customers that belong to the eighth leaf node from the left are those with a 0 value for the previous variable, age greater than 60.5, a marital_divorced variable with a value of 1, and a job_self-employed variable with a value of 1. In other words, those who were not contacted before this campaign and who are older than 60.5, divorced, and self-employed belong to this node, and have a high chance of converting.

Let's take a look at another example. Those customers that belong to the second leaf node from the right are those with a value of 1 for the previous variable, a value of 1 for the housing variable, age greater than 60.5, and balance less than or equal to 4,660.5. In other words, those customers that were contacted before this campaign and that have a housing loan, are older than 60.5, and have a bank balance less than 4,660.5 belong to this node and 20 out of 29 that belong to this node have converted and subscribed to a term deposit.

As you will have noticed from these two examples, you can draw useful insights about who is more or less likely to convert from trained decision tree models, by visualizing the trained tree. You simply need to follow through the nodes and understand what kinds of attributes are highly correlated with your target class. For this exercise, we restricted the tree to only growing up to a depth of 4, but you can choose to grow a tree larger or smaller than the one we used in this exercise.

 The full code for this chapter's Python exercise can be found in the repository at https://github.com/yoonhwang/hands-on-data-science-for-marketing/blob/master/ch.4/python/From%20Engagement%20to%20Conversions.ipynb.

Decision trees and interpretations with R

In this section, you are going to learn how to use the rpart package in R to build decision tree models and interpret the results via visualizations with the R rattle package. For those readers that would like to use Python instead of R for this exercise, you can work through the Python examples in the previous section. We will start this section by analyzing the bank marketing dataset in depth, using the dplyr and ggplot2 libraries, and then we will discuss how to build and interpret decision tree models.

For this exercise, we will be using one of the publicly available datasets from the UCI Machine Learning Repository, which can be found at https://archive.ics.uci.edu/ml/datasets/bank+marketing. You can follow the link and download the data in ZIP format. We will use the bank.zip file for this exercise. When you unzip this file, you will see two CSV files: bank.csv and bank-full.csv. We are going to use the bank-full.csv file for this exercise.

In order to load this data into your RStudio, you can run the following code:

```
df <- read.csv(
  file="../data/bank-full.csv",
  header=TRUE,
  sep=";"
)
```

As you can see from this code snippet, we can easily read the data file by using the `read.csv` function in R. One thing to note here is the `sep` argument in the `read.csv` function. If you look at the data closely, you will notice that the fields in the `bank-full.csv` file are separated by semicolons (;), not commas (,). In order to correctly load the data into a DataFrame, we will need to tell the `read.csv` function to use semicolons as the separators, instead of commas.

Once you have loaded this data, it should look like the following screenshot:

	age	job	marital	education	default	balance	housing	loan	contact	day	month	duration	campaign	pdays	previous	poutcome	y
1	58	management	married	tertiary	no	2143	yes	no	unknown	5	may	261	1	-1	0	unknown	no
2	44	technician	single	secondary	no	29	yes	no	unknown	5	may	151	1	-1	0	unknown	no
3	33	entrepreneur	married	secondary	no	2	yes	yes	unknown	5	may	76	1	-1	0	unknown	no
4	47	blue-collar	married	unknown	no	1506	yes	no	unknown	5	may	92	1	-1	0	unknown	no
5	33	unknown	single	unknown	no	1	no	no	unknown	5	may	198	1	-1	0	unknown	no
6	35	management	married	tertiary	no	231	yes	no	unknown	5	may	139	1	-1	0	unknown	no
7	28	management	single	tertiary	no	447	yes	yes	unknown	5	may	217	1	-1	0	unknown	no
8	42	entrepreneur	divorced	tertiary	yes	2	yes	no	unknown	5	may	380	1	-1	0	unknown	no
9	58	retired	married	primary	no	121	yes	no	unknown	5	may	50	1	-1	0	unknown	no
10	43	technician	single	secondary	no	593	yes	no	unknown	5	may	55	1	-1	0	unknown	no

Data analysis and visualizations

Before we start to analyze the data, we will first encode the output variable, y, which has information about whether a customer has converted or subscribed to a term deposit, with numerical values. You can use the following code to encode the output variable, y, with zeros and ones:

```
# Encode conversions as 0s and 1s
df$conversion <- as.integer(df$y) - 1
```

As you can see from this code snippet, you can use the `as.integer` function to encode the output variable. Since this function will encode `no` values in the y variable as `1` and `yes` values in the y variable as `2`, we subtract the values by `1` to encode them as `0` and `1`, respectively. We stored these encoded values into a new column, named `conversion`.

Conversion rate

The first thing that we are going to take a look at is the aggregate conversion rate. The conversion rate is simply the percentage of customers that subscribed to a term deposit, or those encoded with 1 in the column `conversion`. Take a look at the following code:

```
sprintf("conversion rate: %0.2f%%", sum(df$conversion)/nrow(df)*100.0)
```

As you can see from this code snippet, we simply sum all of the values in the `conversion` column and divide by the number of records or customers in the DataFrame, `df`. Using the `sprintf` function, we format this conversion rate number with two decimal point numbers. The result looks as follows:

```
> sprintf("conversion rate: %0.2f%%", sum(df$conversion)/nrow(df)*100.0)
[1] "conversion rate: 11.70%"
```

As you can see from this output, only about 11.7% were converted or subscribed to a term deposit. From these results, we can see that there is a large imbalance between the conversion group and the non-conversion group, which is quite common and is frequently observed among various marketing datasets.

Conversion rates by job

It might be true that certain job categories tend to convert more frequently than others. Let's take a look at the conversion rates across different job categories. You can achieve this by running the following code:

```
conversionsByJob <- df %>%
    group_by(Job=job) %>%
    summarise(Count=n(), NumConversions=sum(conversion)) %>%
    mutate(ConversionRate=NumConversions/Count*100.0)
```

Let's take a more detailed look at this code. We first group by the column, `job`, which contains information about the job category that each customer belongs to. Then, we count the total number of customers in a given job category by using the `n()` function, and sum over the `conversion` column for each job category by using the `sum` function. Lastly, we divide the total number of conversions, `NumConversion`, by the total number of customers in each job category, `Count`, and multiply these numbers by `100.0` to get the conversion rates for each job category.

The results look as follows:

	Job	Count	NumConversions	ConversionRate
1	admin.	5171	631	12.202669
2	blue-collar	9732	708	7.274969
3	entrepreneur	1487	123	8.271688
4	housemaid	1240	109	8.790323
5	management	9458	1301	13.755551
6	retired	2264	516	22.791519
7	self-employed	1579	187	11.842939
8	services	4154	369	8.883004
9	student	938	269	28.678038
10	technician	7597	840	11.056996
11	unemployed	1303	202	15.502686
12	unknown	288	34	11.805556

As you can see from these results, the student group tends to convert much more frequently than the others, and the retired group comes next. However, it is a bit difficult to compare these with raw output, and we will be able to better present this data by using a chart. We can build a horizontal bar chart by using the following code:

```
ggplot(conversionsByJob, aes(x=Job, y=ConversionRate)) +
  geom_bar(width=0.5, stat="identity") +
  coord_flip() +
  ggtitle('Conversion Rates by Job') +
  xlab("Job") +
  ylab("Conversion Rate (%)") +
  theme(plot.title = element_text(hjust = 0.5))
```

If you look at this code, we are using the ggplot and geom_bar functions to build a bar chart with the conversionsByJob data (which we built in the previous code), and with the Job variable in the *x*-axis and the ConversionRate variable in the *y*-axis. Then, we use the coord_flip function to flip the vertical bar chart to a horizontal bar chart. You can use the ggtitle, xlab, and ylab functions to change the title, *x*-axis label, and *y*-axis label as you wish.

The resulting chart looks as follows:

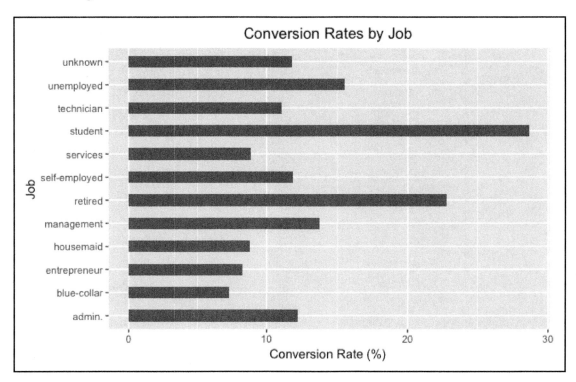

As you can see, it is much easier to see the differences in the conversion rates by each job category with a horizontal bar chart. We can easily see that
the student and retired groups are the two groups with the highest conversion rates, whereas, the blue-collar and entrepreneur groups are the two groups with the lowest conversion rates.

Default rates by conversions

Another attribute of a customer that would be interesting to see is the default rate, and how it differs between those who subscribed to a term deposit and those who did not. Let's take a look at the following R code:

```
defaultByConversion <- df %>%
  group_by(Default=default, Conversion=conversion) %>%
  summarise(Count=n())
```

As you can see from this code, we are grouping the DataFrame, `df`, by the two columns, `default` and `conversion`, using the `group_by` function. By using `n()` as the aggregation function, we can count how many customers fall under each cell of the four cases. Let's look at the following results:

	Default	Conversion	Count
1	no	0	39159
2	no	1	5237
3	yes	0	763
4	yes	1	52

It is a bit difficult to compare how the default rates differ between the conversion and non-conversion groups from looking at these raw numbers. One way to visualize this data is through a pie chart. You can use the following code to build a pie chart:

```
ggplot(defaultByConversion, aes(x="", y=Count, fill=Default)) +
    geom_bar(width=1, stat = "identity", position=position_fill()) +
    geom_text(aes(x=1.25, label=Count), position=position_fill(vjust = 0.5))
+
    coord_polar("y") +
    facet_wrap(~Conversion) +
    ggtitle('Default (0: Non Conversions, 1: Conversions)') +
    theme(
        axis.title.x=element_blank(),
        axis.title.y=element_blank(),
        plot.title=element_text(hjust=0.5),
        legend.position='bottom'
    )
```

As you can see, we are utilizing three functions here: `ggplot`, `geom_bar`, and `coord_polar("y")`. With the `coord_polar("y")` function, we can get the pie chart from a bar chart. Then, we can use the `facet_wrap` function to split it into two pie charts: one for the conversion group and another for the non-conversion group.

Take a look at the following pie chart:

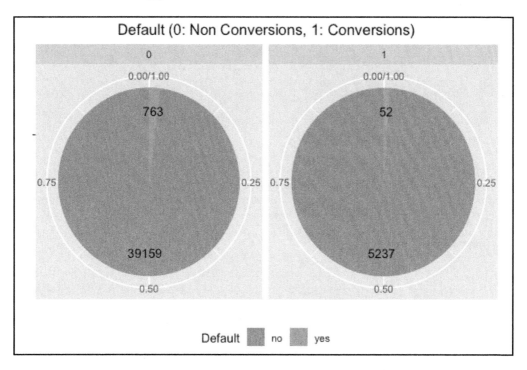

As you can see from these pie charts, it is much easier to compare the default rates between the conversion and non-conversion groups. Although the overall percentage of previous default is low in both groups, the default rate in the non-conversion group is about twice as high as the conversion group.

Bank balance by conversions

Next, we will try to see whether there are any differences in the distributions of the bank balances between the conversion and non-conversion groups. A box plot is typically a good way to visualize the distribution of a variable. Let's take a look at the following code:

```
ggplot(df, aes(x="", y=balance)) +
  geom_boxplot() +
  facet_wrap(~conversion) +
  ylab("balance") +
  xlab("0: Non-Conversion, 1: Conversion") +
  ggtitle("Conversion vs. Non-Conversions: Balance") +
  theme(plot.title=element_text(hjust=0.5))
```

You should be familiar with this code by now, as we discussed how to build box plots in the previous chapter, using the `ggplot` and `geom_boxplot` functions. When you run this code, you will see the following box plot:

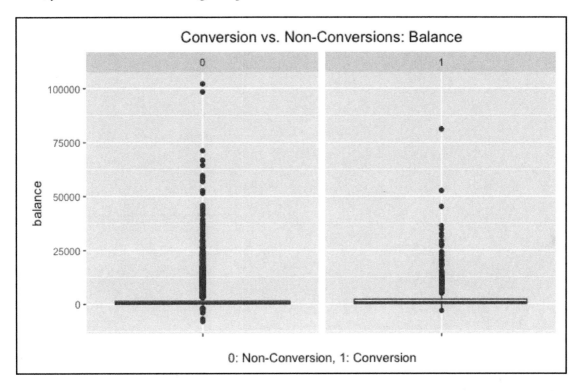

Because there are so many outliers, it is quite difficult to identify any differences between the two distributions. Let's build another box plot without outliers. The only thing that you need to change from the previous code is the `outlier.shape = NA` argument in the `geom_boxplot` function, as you can see in the following code:

```
ggplot(df, aes(x="", y=balance)) +
  geom_boxplot(outlier.shape = NA) +
  scale_y_continuous(limits = c(-2000, 5000)) +
  facet_wrap(~conversion) +
  ylab("balance") +
  xlab("0: Non-Conversion, 1: Conversion") +
  ggtitle("Conversion vs. Non-Conversions: Balance") +
  theme(plot.title=element_text(hjust=0.5))
```

Using this code, you will see the following box plots for the distribution of bank balances between the two groups:

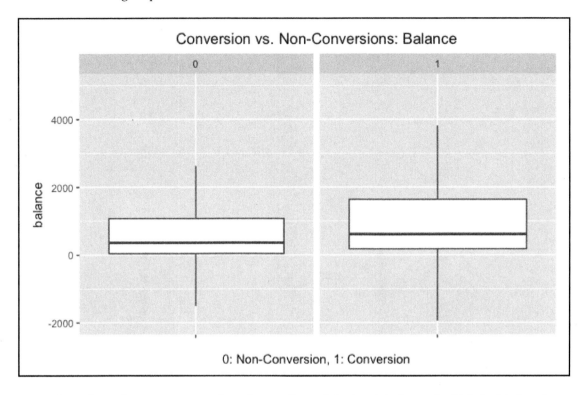

From these box plots, we can see that the median of the bank balance is slightly higher for the conversion group, as compared to the non-conversion group. Also, the bank balances of converted customers seem to vary more than those of non-converted customers.

Conversion rates by number of contacts

Lastly, we will look at how the conversion rates vary by the number of contacts. Typically, in marketing, a higher number of marketing contacts can result in marketing fatigue, wherein the conversion rates drop as you reach out to your customers more frequently. Let's see whether there is any marketing fatigue in our data. Take a look at the following code:

```
conversionsByNumContacts <- df %>%
  group_by(Campaign=campaign) %>%
  summarise(Count=n(), NumConversions=sum(conversion)) %>%
  mutate(ConversionRate=NumConversions/Count*100.0)
```

From this code snippet, you can see that we are grouping by the `campaign` column (which has information about the number of contacts performed during the marketing campaign for this customer) and computing the conversion rate for each number of contacts. The resulting data looks as follows:

	Campaign	Count	NumConversions	ConversionRate
1	1	17544	2561	14.597583
2	2	12505	1401	11.203519
3	3	5521	618	11.193624
4	4	3522	317	9.000568
5	5	1764	139	7.879819
6	6	1291	92	7.126259
7	7	735	47	6.394558
8	8	540	32	5.925926
9	9	327	21	6.422018
10	10	266	14	5.263158
11	11	201	16	7.960199
12	12	155	4	2.580645
13	13	133	6	4.511278
14	14	93	4	4.301075

Like before, it would be easier to look at a chart rather than raw numbers. We can plot this data with bar charts by using the following code:

```
ggplot(conversionsByNumContacts, aes(x=Campaign, y=ConversionRate)) +
    geom_bar(width=0.5, stat="identity") +
    ggtitle('Conversion Rates by Number of Contacts') +
    xlab("Number of Contacts") +
    ylab("Conversion Rate (%)") +
    theme(plot.title = element_text(hjust = 0.5))
```

The plot looks as follows:

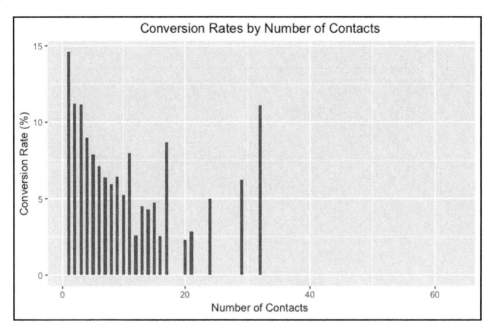

There is some noise in higher numbers of contacts, as the sample size is smaller for them, but you can easily see the overall downward trend in this bar chart. As the number of contacts increases, the conversion rates slowly decrease. This suggests that the expected conversion rate decreases as you contact a client more frequently for a given campaign.

Encoding categorical variables

There are eight categorical variables in this dataset: job, marital, education, default, housing, loan, contact, and month. Before we start to build decision trees, we need to encode some of these categorical variables with numerical values. We'll take a look at how we can encode some of these categorical variables in this section.

Encoding the month

We all know that there can only be 12 unique values for the month variable. Let's take a quick look at what we have in our dataset. Take a look at the following code:

```
unique(df$month)
```

The `unique` function helps you to quickly get the unique values in the given column. When you run this code, you will get the following output:

```
> unique(df$month)
 [1] may jun jul aug oct nov dec jan feb mar apr sep
Levels: apr aug dec feb jan jul jun mar may nov oct sep
```

As we expected, we have 12 unique values for the `month` column, from January to December. Since there is a natural order in the values of `month`, we can encode each of the values with the corresponding number. One way to encode the string values of `month` with numbers is as follows:

```
months = lapply(month.abb, function(x) tolower(x))
df$month <- match(df$month, months)
```

Let's take a closer look at this code. `month.abb` is a built-in R constant that contains the three-letter abbreviated names for the month names, as follows:

```
> month.abb
 [1] "Jan" "Feb" "Mar" "Apr" "May" "Jun" "Jul" "Aug" "Sep" "Oct" "Nov" "Dec"
```

As you can see, the first letters of each abbreviated `month` name are capitalized. However, the month names in the `month` column of our data are all in lowercase. That is why we use the `tolower` function to make all of the values in the `month.abb` constant lowercase. Using the `lapply` function, we can apply this `tolower` function across the `month.abb` list. Then, we use the `match` function, which returns the position of the matching string in an array, to convert the string values in the `month` column of the DataFrame to corresponding numerical values.

Using this code, the unique values for the `month` column look as follows:

```
> match(unique(df$month), months)
 [1]  5  6  7  8 10 11 12  1  2  3  4  9
```

To see how many records we have for each month, we can use the following code:

```
df %>%
  group_by(month) %>%
  summarise(Count=n())
```

The results are as follows:

```
> df %>%
+    group_by(month) %>%
+    summarise(Count=n())
# A tibble: 12 x 2
     month Count
    <fctr> <int>
1      apr  2932
2      aug  6247
3      dec   214
4      feb  2649
5      jan  1403
6      jul  6895
7      jun  5341
8      mar   477
9      may 13766
10     nov  3970
11     oct   738
12     sep   579
```

Encoding the job, housing, and marital variables

Next, we are going to encode the three variables: job, housing, and marital. Since these variables do not have natural orders, we do not need to worry about which category gets encoded with which value. The simplest way to encode categorical variables with no orders in R is to use the factor function. Let's take a look at the following code:

```
df$job <- factor(df$job)
df$housing <- factor(df$housing)
df$marital <- factor(df$marital)
```

As you can see from this code, we are simply applying the factor function for these three variables, job, housing, and marital, and storing the encoded values back to the DataFrame, df. For the categorical variables that we have not discussed in this section, you can use the same techniques that we discussed in this section to encode them if you wish to explore beyond this exercise.

Building decision trees

Now that we have encoded all of the categorical variables, we can finally start to build decision tree models. We are going to use these variables as features for our decision tree models: `age`, `balance`, `campaign`, `previous`, `housing`, `job`, and `marital`. In order to build and train a decision tree model with R, we are going to use the `rpart` package. You can import the required library by using the following line of code:

```
library(rpart)
```

If you do not have the `rpart` package installed, you can install it by using the following command:

```
install.packages("rpart")
```

Once you have imported the required library, you can use the following code to build a decision tree model:

```
fit <- rpart(
    conversion ~ age + balance + campaign + previous + housing + job +
marital,
    method="class",
    data=df,
    control=rpart.control(maxdepth=4, cp=0.0001)
)
```

As you can see, the first argument of the `rpart` model is `formula`, which defines the features and the target variable. Here, we are using the aforementioned variables as the features and `conversion` as the target variable. Then, we define this decision tree model to be a classification model with the `method="class"` input. Lastly, you can fine-tune the decision tree model with the `control` input. There are many parameters that you can tune with the `control` input. In this example, we are only restricting the maximum depth of the tree to be 4 with the `maxdepth` argument, and setting the value for `cp`, which is the complexity parameter, to be small enough for the tree to be able to be split. There are many other ways to tune your decision tree model, and we recommend that you take a closer look at the R documentation for more information, by running the `help(rpart)` or `help(rpart.control)` commands.

Interpreting decision trees

Now that we have trained a decision tree model, we need to extract the insights from the model. In this section, we are going to use a library called `rattle`:

1. You can install this package by using the following command in your RStudio:

    ```
    install.packages("rattle")
    ```

2. Once you have installed this library correctly, you should be able to import the library as follows:

    ```
    library(rattle)
    ```

3. Once you have set up your R environment with this new library, `rattle`, it requires just one line of code to visualize the trained decision tree. Take a look at the following code:

    ```
    fancyRpartPlot(fit)
    ```

4. As you can see, the `fancyRpartPlot` function takes in an `rpart` model object. Here, the model object, `fit`, is the decision tree model that we built in the previous step. Once you run this command, it will show the following diagram:

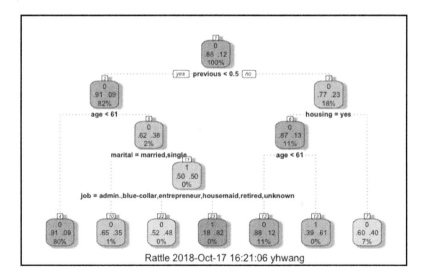

Rattle 2018-Oct-17 16:21:06 yhwang

Let's take a closer look at this tree diagram. Each node contains three lines that describe the information that the given node has. The number on top of the node is the label and the order of the node that was built. We will use this label to refer to each of the nodes in this tree graph. Then, the top line in each node tells us what the prediction or classification will be for the given node. For example, if a sample belongs to the node that is labeled 4, the classification by this decision tree model will be zero, meaning non-conversion. On the other hand, if a sample belongs to the node labeled 23, the classification by this decision tree model will be one, meaning conversion.

The second line in each node tells us the percentage of records in each class for the given node. For example, 52% of the records in node 22 are in the class 0, or the non-conversion group, and the remaining 48% are in the class 1, or the conversion group. On the other hand, 39% of the customers in node 13 are in the class 0, and the remaining 61% of the customers in node 13 are in the class 1. Lastly, the bottom line in each node tells us the percentage of the total number of records that belong to each node. For example, about 80% of the customers fall under the category of node 4, while close to 0% of the customers fall under the category of node 13.

Now that we know what each of the lines in each nodes means, let's discuss how we can draw insights from this tree diagram. In order to understand the customers that belong to each leaf node, we need to follow through the tree. For example, those customers that belong to node 13 are those with values greater than 0.5 for the `previous` variable, with a housing loan and `age` greater than or equal to 61. In other words, those who were contacted before this campaign and who are older than 61, with housing loans, belong to node 13 and have a high chance of converting.

Let's take a look at another example. In order to get to node 22 from the root node, we need to have a 0 value for the `previous` variable, an `age` greater than or equal to 61, a `marital` status other than `married` or `single`, and a `job` in one of these categories: `admin`, `blue-collar`, `entrepreneur`, `housemaid`, `retired`, or `unknown`. In other words, those customers that have not been contacted before this campaign and who are older than 61, divorced, and have a job in one of the previously mentioned categories, belong to the node 22 and have a roughly 50% chance of converting.

As you will have noticed from these two examples, you can draw useful insights on who is more or less likely to convert from trained decision tree models, by visualizing the trained tree. You simply need to follow through the nodes and understand what kinds of attributes are highly correlated with your target class. For this exercise, we restricted the tree to only growing up to a depth of 4, but you can choose to grow a tree larger or smaller than the one that we used in this exercise.

The full code for this chapter's R exercise can be found in the repository at `https://github.com/yoonhwang/hands-on-data-science-for-marketing/blob/master/ch.4/R/FromEngagementToConversions.R`.

Summary

In this chapter, we introduced a new machine learning algorithm, decision trees, which we can use for marketing analytics in order to better understand the data and draw insights on customer behaviors. We discussed how decision tree models are different from logistic regression models, which you learned about in the previous chapter. You saw that decision tree models learn the data by partitioning the data points based on certain criteria. We also discussed the two measures that are frequently used when growing decision trees: the Gini impurity and entropy information gain. Using either of these measures, decision trees can grow until all of the nodes are pure, or until the stopping criteria are met.

During our programming exercises in Python and R, we used the bank marketing dataset from the UCI Machine Learning Repository. We started our programming exercised by analyzing the data in depth, using the `pandas` and `matplotlib` packages in Python and the `dplyr` and `ggplot2` libraries in R. Then, you learned how we can train and grow decision trees, using the `sklearn` package in Python and the `rpart` library in R. With these trained decision tree models, you also learned how to visualize and interpret the results. For visualizations, we used the `graphviz` package in Python and the `rattle` library in R. Moreover, you saw how we can interpret the decision tree results and understand the customer groups that are more likely to convert or subscribe to a term deposit by traversing through the trained decision trees, which is useful when we want to conduct an explanatory analysis of customer behaviors.

In the following chapters, we are going to switch gears and focus on product analytics. In the next chapter, we will discuss the kinds of exploratory analysis that we can run to understand and identify patterns and trends in product data. With the product analytics results from the next chapter, we will show how we can build a product recommendation model.

Section 3: Product Visibility and Marketing

In this section, you will learn how to draw insights from the product purchase history data and how to use machine learning to recommend products that are most likely to be purchased by customers.

This section consists of the following chapters:

5
Product Analytics

From this chapter on, we are going to switch gears from conducting analyses on customer behaviors and start discussing how we can use data science for more granular, product-level analytics. There has been increasing interest and demand from various companies, especially among e-commerce businesses, for utilizing data to understand how customers engage and interact with different products. It has also been proven that rigorous product analytics can help businesses to improve user engagements and conversions that ultimately leads to higher profits. In this chapter, we are going to discuss what product analytics is and how it can be employed for different use cases.

Once we familiarize ourselves with the concept of product analytics, we are going to use the *Online Retail Data Set* from the UCI Machine Learning Repository for our programming exercises. We are going to start by analyzing the overall time series trends we can observe from the dataset. Then, we will look into how the customer engagements and interactions with individual products change over time with the goal of being able to build a simple product recommendation logic or algorithm in the end. For Python exercises, we will mainly utilize the `pandas` and `matplotlib` libraries for data analyses and visualizations. For R exercises, we will mainly use the `dplyr` and `ggplot2` libraries and introduce two other R libraries, `readxl` and `lubridate`.

In this chapter, we will cover the following topics:

- The importance of product analytics
- Product analytics using Python
- Product analytics using R

The importance of product analytics

Product analytics is a way to draw insights from data on how customers engage and interact with products offered, how different products perform, and what some of the observable weaknesses and strengths in a business are. However, product analytics does not just stop at analyzing the data. The ultimate goal of product analytics is really to build actionable insights and reports that can further help optimize and improve product performance and generate new marketing or product ideas based on the findings of product analytics.

Product analytics starts by tracking events. These events can be customer website visits, page views, browser histories, purchases, or any other actions that customers can take with the products that you offer. Then, you can start analyzing and visualizing any observable patterns in these events with the goal of creating actionable insights or reports. Some of the common goals with product analytics are as follows:

- **Improve customer and product retention**: By analyzing what customers viewed and purchased, you can identify what items customers repeatedly purchase and who those repeat customers are. On the other hand, you can also identify what items customers do not buy and the customers who are at risk of churning. Analyzing and understanding the common attributes of the repeatedly purchased items and repeat customers can help you improve your retention strategy.
- **Identify popular and trending products**: As a marketer for retail businesses, it is important to have a good understanding of popular and trending products. These best-selling products are key revenue drivers for the business and provide new selling opportunities, such as cross-sells or bundle sales. With product analytics, you should be able to identify and track these popular and trending products easily and generate new strategies to explore different opportunities using these best-selling products.
- **Segment customers and products based on their key attributes**: With the customer profile and product data, you can segment your customer base and products based on their attributes using product analytics. Some of the ways to segment your product data are based on their profitability, volumes of sales, volumes of reorders, and numbers of refunds. With these segmentations, you can draw actionable insights on which product or customer segments to target next.

- **Develop marketing strategies with higher ROI**: Product analytics can also be used to analyze the **return on investment (ROI)** of your marketing strategies. By analyzing the marketing dollars spent on promoting certain items and the revenue generated from those products, you can understand what works and what does not. Using product analytics for marketing ROI analyses can help you create more efficient marketing strategies.

With what we have discussed here about product analytics, we are going to discuss how to achieve some of these product analytics goals using retail business data in the following programming exercises. We are going to discuss how we can use the data to analyze the patterns of repeat customers and their contributions to overall revenue. Also, we will be covering how we can use product analytics to analyze the behaviors of best-selling products. More specifically, we are going to discuss how to track the trends of popular items over time and then briefly discuss how we can utilize this trending item data for product recommendations in your marketing strategies.

Product analytics using Python

In this section, we are going to discuss how to conduct product analytics using the `pandas` and `matplotlib` packages in Python. For those readers who would like to use R, instead of Python, for this exercise, you can skip to the next section. We will start this section by analyzing the overall time series trends in the revenue and numbers of purchases, and the purchase patterns of repeat purchase customers, and then we will move on to analyze the trends in products being sold.

For this exercise, we will be using one of the publicly available datasets from the UCI Machine Learning Repository, which can be found using this link: http://archive.ics. uci.edu/ml/datasets/online+retail#. From this link, you can download the data in Microsoft Excel format, named `Online Retail.xlsx`. Once you have downloaded this data, you can load it into your Jupyter Notebook by running the following command:

```
%matplotlib inline

import matplotlib.pyplot as plt
import pandas as pd

df = pd.read_excel(io='../data/Online Retail.xlsx', sheet_name='Online
Retail')
```

Similar to the other Python exercises in previous chapters, we use the `%matplotlib`
`inline` command to display plots on the Jupyter Notebook. Then, we can import
the `matplotlib` and `pandas` packages that we will be using for further product analytics.
One thing to note in this code snippet is the new function in the `pandas` package that we
are using here, `read_excel`. This function lets you load any Excel file into your `pandas`
`DataFrame`. As you can see from this code, we are passing two arguments to the
`read_excel` function—`io`, for the path to the data file, and `sheet_name`, for the name of
the Excel sheet that we want to load the data from.

Once you have loaded this data into a `pandas DataFrame`, it should look as shown in the
following screenshot:

```
df.shape

(541909, 8)

df.head()
```

	InvoiceNo	StockCode	Description	Quantity	InvoiceDate	UnitPrice	CustomerID	Country
0	536365	85123A	WHITE HANGING HEART T-LIGHT HOLDER	6	2010-12-01 08:26:00	2.55	17850.0	United Kingdom
1	536365	71053	WHITE METAL LANTERN	6	2010-12-01 08:26:00	3.39	17850.0	United Kingdom
2	536365	84406B	CREAM CUPID HEARTS COAT HANGER	8	2010-12-01 08:26:00	2.75	17850.0	United Kingdom
3	536365	84029G	KNITTED UNION FLAG HOT WATER BOTTLE	6	2010-12-01 08:26:00	3.39	17850.0	United Kingdom
4	536365	84029E	RED WOOLLY HOTTIE WHITE HEART.	6	2010-12-01 08:26:00	3.39	17850.0	United Kingdom

Before we move on to the next step, there is one data-cleaning step we need to take. Let's
look quickly at the distribution of the `Quantity` column. We will visualize the distributions
of `Quantity` by using the following code:

```
ax = df['Quantity'].plot.box(
    showfliers=False,
    grid=True,
    figsize=(10, 7)
)

ax.set_ylabel('Order Quantity')
ax.set_title('Quantity Distribution')

plt.suptitle("")
plt.show()
```

As you can see from this code, we are visualizing the distribution of the `Quantity` column, in a box plot, by using `pandas DataFrame`'s `plot.box` function. The resulting box plot looks as follows:

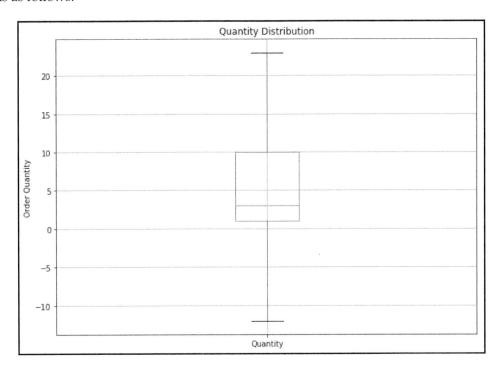

As you can see from this plot, some orders have negative quantities. This is because the cancelled or refunded orders are recorded with negative values in the `Quantity` column of our dataset. For illustration purposes in this exercise, we are going to disregard the cancelled orders. We can filter out all the cancelled orders in our `DataFrame` by using the following code:

```
df = df.loc[df['Quantity'] > 0]
```

Now, we are ready to conduct further analyses and dive into our data.

Time series trends

Before we look at product-level data, as a marketer for an e-commerce business, it will be beneficial to have a better understanding of the overall time series trends in the revenue and the numbers of orders or purchases. This will help us understand whether the business is growing or shrinking in terms of both the overall revenue and the numbers of orders we receive over time.

First, we are going to look into the numbers of orders received over time. Take a look at the following code:

```
monthly_orders_df =
df.set_index('InvoiceDate')['InvoiceNo'].resample('M').nunique()
```

As you can see from this code, we are using the `resample` and `nunique` functions that we have not used in the previous chapters. The `resample` function resamples and converts time series data into the frequency we desire. In our example, we are resampling our time series data into monthly time series data, by using `'M'` as our target frequency and counting the number of distinct or unique invoice numbers. This way, we can get the number of unique purchases or orders month-on-month. The resulting DataFrame looks like the following screenshot:

```
InvoiceDate
2010-12-31    1629
2011-01-31    1120
2011-02-28    1126
2011-03-31    1531
2011-04-30    1318
2011-05-31    1731
2011-06-30    1576
2011-07-31    1540
2011-08-31    1409
2011-09-30    1896
2011-10-31    2129
2011-11-30    2884
2011-12-31     839
Freq: M, Name: InvoiceNo, dtype: int64
```

Often, time series data is better visualized using line charts. Let's take a look at the following code to see how we can visualize this monthly data in a line chart:

```
ax = pd.DataFrame(monthly_orders_df.values).plot(
    grid=True,
    figsize=(10,7),
    legend=False
)
```

```
ax.set_xlabel('date')
ax.set_ylabel('number of orders/invoices')
ax.set_title('Total Number of Orders Over Time')

plt.xticks(
    range(len(monthly_orders_df.index)),
    [x.strftime('%m.%Y') for x in monthly_orders_df.index],
    rotation=45
)

plt.show()
```

As you can see from this code, we are using the `plot` function of a `pandas DataFrame`. Using the `xticks` function of the `matplotlib` package, we can customize the labels of the *x*-ticks. Let's take a look at the following plot first:

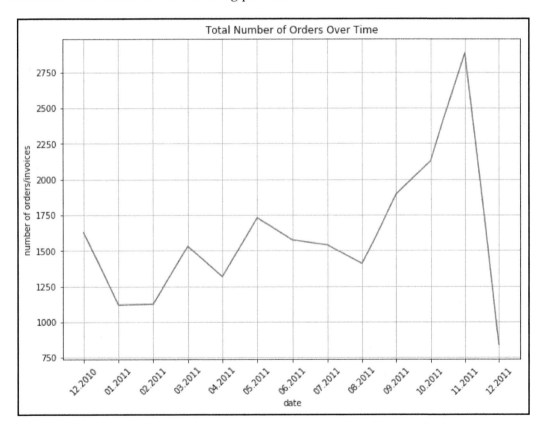

As you may notice from this plot, the tick labels in the *x* axis are formatted by month and year. If you look back at the previous code, we formatted them using `x.strftime('%m.%Y')`, where x is the `Python date` object, `%m` is the placeholder for the month value, and `%Y` is the placeholder for the year value. The `strftime` function of the `Python date` object formats the date into the given format.

One thing that is noticeable from this chart is that there is a sudden radical drop in the number of orders in December 2011. If you look closely at the data, this is simply because we do not have the data for the full month of December 2011. We can verify this by using the following code:

```
invoice_dates = df.loc[
    df['InvoiceDate'] >= '2011-12-01',
    'InvoiceDate'
]

print('Min date: %s\nMax date: %s' % (invoice_dates.min(),
invoice_dates.max()))
```

In this code, we get a series of all invoice dates from December 1, 2011. Then, we print out the minimum and maximum dates. When you run this code, you will get the following output:

```
print('Min date: %s\nMax date: %s' % (invoice_dates.min(), invoice_dates.max()))

Min date: 2011-12-01 08:33:00
Max date: 2011-12-09 12:50:00
```

As you can see from this output, we only have the data from December 1, to December 9, 2011. It would be a misrepresentation if we use this data for analyzing December sales and revenue. For further analyses, we will disregard any data from December 1, 2011. You can use the following code to remove those data points:

```
df = df.loc[df['InvoiceDate'] < '2011-12-01']
```

Now that we have filtered out incomplete data for December 2011, we can redraw the line chart using the previous codes. After removing those data points from December 2011, the line chart looks like the following:

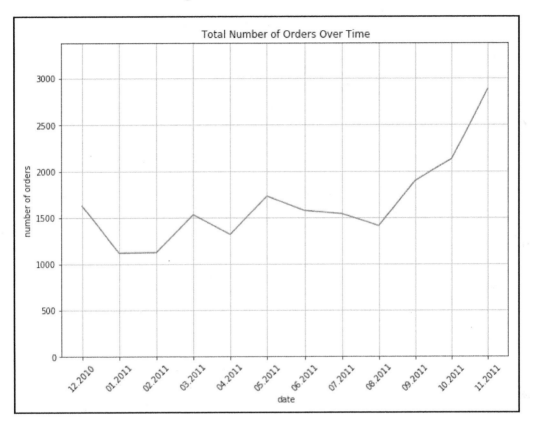

Let's take a closer look at this chart. The monthly number of orders seems to float around 1,500 from December 2010 to August 2011, and then increases significantly from September 2011, and almost doubles by November 2011. One explanation for this could be that the business is actually growing significantly from September 2011. Another explanation could be seasonal effects. In e-commerce businesses, it is not rare to see spikes in sales as it approaches the end of the year. Typically, sales rise significantly from October to January for many e-commerce businesses, and without the data from the previous year, it is difficult to conclude whether this spike in sales is due to a growth in business or due to seasonal effects. When you are analyzing your data, we advise you to compare the current year's data against the previous year's data.

Let's take a quick look at the monthly revenue data by looking at the following code:

```
df['Sales'] = df['Quantity'] * df['UnitPrice']

monthly_revenue_df =
df.set_index('InvoiceDate')['Sales'].resample('M').sum()
```

As you can see from this code, the first thing we do here is to calculate the aggregate sales amount from each order, which is simply the UnitPrice multiplied by the Quantity. Once we have computed and created this Sales column, we can use the resample function with an 'M' flag to resample and convert our time series data into monthly data. Then, using sum as the aggregate function, we can get the monthly sales revenue data. The resulting data looks like the following:

```
monthly_revenue_df

InvoiceDate
2010-12-31      823746.140
2011-01-31      691364.560
2011-02-28      523631.890
2011-03-31      717639.360
2011-04-30      537808.621
2011-05-31      770536.020
2011-06-30      761739.900
2011-07-31      719221.191
2011-08-31      737014.260
2011-09-30     1058590.172
2011-10-31     1154979.300
2011-11-30     1509496.330
Freq: M, Name: Sales, dtype: float64
```

We can visualize this data into a line plot, using the following code:

```
ax = pd.DataFrame(monthly_revenue_df.values).plot(
    grid=True,
    figsize=(10,7),
    legend=False
)

ax.set_xlabel('date')
ax.set_ylabel('sales')
ax.set_title('Total Revenue Over Time')

ax.set_ylim([0, max(monthly_revenue_df.values)+100000])

plt.xticks(
```

```
        range(len(monthly_revenue_df.index)),
        [x.strftime('%m.%Y') for x in monthly_revenue_df.index],
        rotation=45
    )

plt.show()
```

As previously discussed, we can use the `pandas DataFrame` plot function to build a line chart and the `xticks` function of the `matplotlib` package to rename the labels of the ticks on the *x* axis. The line plot looks like the following:

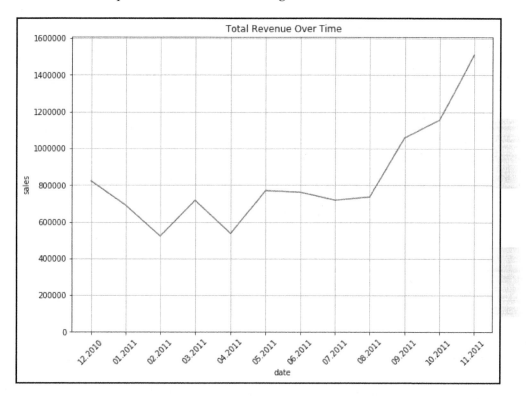

We see a similar pattern to the previous monthly **Total Number of Orders Over Time** chart in this monthly revenue chart. The monthly revenue floats around 700,000 from December 2010 to August 2011 and then it increases significantly from September 2011. As discussed before, to verify whether this significant increase in sales and revenue is due to a growth in business or due to seasonal effects, we need to look further back in the sales history and compare the current year's sales against the previous year's sales.

These types of general and broad time series analyses can help marketers gain a better understanding of the overall performance of the business and identify any potential problems that might be occurring within the business. It is generally a good idea to start with broader analyses, and then drill down into more granular and specific parts of the business for further product analytics.

Repeat customers

Another important factor of a successful business is how well it is retaining customers and how many repeat purchases and customers it has. In this section, we are going to analyze the number of monthly repeat purchases and how much of the monthly revenue is attributable to these repeat purchases and customers. A typical strong and stable business has a steady stream of sales from existing customers. Let's see how much of the sales are from repeat and existing customers of the online retail business that we are currently analyzing in this chapter.

We are going to look at the number of monthly repeat purchases. This means a customer placed more than one order within a given month. Let's take a quick look at the data we have:

```
df.head()
```

	InvoiceNo	StockCode	Description	Quantity	InvoiceDate	UnitPrice	CustomerID	Country	Sales
0	536365	85123A	WHITE HANGING HEART T-LIGHT HOLDER	6	2010-12-01 08:26:00	2.55	17850.0	United Kingdom	15.30
1	536365	71053	WHITE METAL LANTERN	6	2010-12-01 08:26:00	3.39	17850.0	United Kingdom	20.34
2	536365	84406B	CREAM CUPID HEARTS COAT HANGER	8	2010-12-01 08:26:00	2.75	17850.0	United Kingdom	22.00
3	536365	84029G	KNITTED UNION FLAG HOT WATER BOTTLE	6	2010-12-01 08:26:00	3.39	17850.0	United Kingdom	20.34
4	536365	84029E	RED WOOLLY HOTTIE WHITE HEART.	6	2010-12-01 08:26:00	3.39	17850.0	United Kingdom	20.34

As you might have noticed from this snapshot of the data, there are multiple records for one purchase order (`InvoiceNo`). However, what we need is the aggregate data for each order, so that one record in the `DataFrame` represents one purchase order. We can aggregate this raw data for each `InvoiceNo` by using the following code:

```
invoice_customer_df = df.groupby(
    by=['InvoiceNo', 'InvoiceDate']
).agg({
    'Sales': sum,
    'CustomerID': max,
    'Country': max,
}).reset_index()
```

As you can see from this code, we are grouping the `DataFrame`, `df`, by `InvoiceNo` and `InvoiceDate` and summing up all the `Sales`. This way, our new `DataFrame`, `invoice_customer_df`, has one record for each purchase order. The resulting `DataFrame` looks like the following:

	InvoiceNo	InvoiceDate	Sales	CustomerID	Country
		`invoice_customer_df.head()`			
0	536365	2010-12-01 08:26:00	139.12	17850.0	United Kingdom
1	536366	2010-12-01 08:28:00	22.20	17850.0	United Kingdom
2	536367	2010-12-01 08:34:00	278.73	13047.0	United Kingdom
3	536368	2010-12-01 08:34:00	70.05	13047.0	United Kingdom
4	536369	2010-12-01 08:35:00	17.85	13047.0	United Kingdom

As you can see here, each record in the `DataFrame` now has all the information we need for each order. Now, we need to aggregate this data per month and compute the number of customers who made more than one purchase in a given month. Take a look at the following code:

```
monthly_repeat_customers_df =
invoice_customer_df.set_index('InvoiceDate').groupby([
    pd.Grouper(freq='M'), 'CustomerID'
]).filter(lambda x: len(x) > 1).resample('M').nunique()['CustomerID']
```

Let's take a closer look at the `groupby` function in this code. Here, we group by two conditions—`pd.Grouper(freq='M')` and `CustomerID`. The first `groupby` condition, `pd.Grouper(freq='M')`, groups the data by the index, `InvoiceDate`, into each month. Then, we group this data by each `CustomerID`. Using the `filter` function, we can subselect the data by a custom rule. Here, the filtering rule, `lambda x: len(x) > 1`, means we want to retrieve those with more than one record in the group. In other words, we want to retrieve only those customers with more than one order in a given month. Lastly, we resample and aggregate by each month and count the number of unique customers in each month by using `resample('M')` and `nunique`.

The resulting data looks like the following:

```
monthly_repeat_customers_df

InvoiceDate
2010-12-31    263
2011-01-31    153
2011-02-28    153
2011-03-31    203
2011-04-30    170
2011-05-31    281
2011-06-30    220
2011-07-31    227
2011-08-31    198
2011-09-30    272
2011-10-31    324
2011-11-30    541
Freq: M, Name: CustomerID, dtype: int64
```

Let's now compare these numbers against the total number of monthly customers. You can use the following code to compute the total number of monthly customers:

```
monthly_unique_customers_df =
df.set_index('InvoiceDate')['CustomerID'].resample('M').nunique()
```

And the resulting data looks like the following:

```
monthly_unique_customers_df

InvoiceDate
2010-12-31     885
2011-01-31     741
2011-02-28     758
2011-03-31     974
2011-04-30     856
2011-05-31    1056
2011-06-30     991
2011-07-31     949
2011-08-31     935
2011-09-30    1266
2011-10-31    1364
2011-11-30    1665
Freq: M, Name: CustomerID, dtype: int64
```

If you compare these two sets of numbers, roughly about 20 to 30% of the customers are repeat customers. You can use the following code to calculate the percentages of repeat customers for each month:

```
monthly_repeat_percentage =
monthly_repeat_customers_df/monthly_unique_customers_df*100.0
```

Let's visualize all of this data in one chart:

```
ax = pd.DataFrame(monthly_repeat_customers_df.values).plot(
    figsize=(10,7)
)

pd.DataFrame(monthly_unique_customers_df.values).plot(
    ax=ax,
    grid=True
)

ax2 = pd.DataFrame(monthly_repeat_percentage.values).plot.bar(
    ax=ax,
    grid=True,
    secondary_y=True,
    color='green',
    alpha=0.2
)

ax.set_xlabel('date')
ax.set_ylabel('number of customers')
ax.set_title('Number of All vs. Repeat Customers Over Time')

ax2.set_ylabel('percentage (%)')

ax.legend(['Repeat Customers', 'All Customers'])
ax2.legend(['Percentage of Repeat'], loc='upper right')

ax.set_ylim([0, monthly_unique_customers_df.values.max()+100])
ax2.set_ylim([0, 100])

plt.xticks(
    range(len(monthly_repeat_customers_df.index)),
    [x.strftime('%m.%Y') for x in monthly_repeat_customers_df.index],
    rotation=45
)

plt.show()
```

In this code, you will notice a new flag, `secondary_y=True`, to the `plot` function. As the name suggests, if you set this `secondary_y` flag to `True`, then it will create a new *y* axis on the right side of the chart. This is especially useful when you want to visualize two sets of data with different scales. In our case, the scale for one set of our data is the number of users, and the scale for another set of our data is the percentage. Using this `secondary_y` flag, we can easily visualize data with different scales in one plot.

Once you run this code, you will see the following chart:

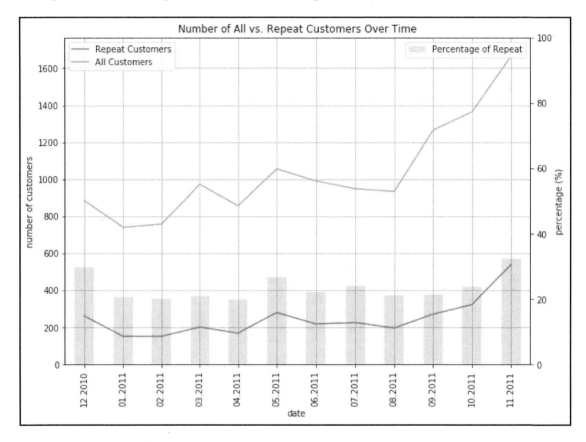

As you can see from this chart, the numbers of both repeat and all customers start to rise significantly from September 2011. The percentage of **Repeat Customers** seems to stay pretty consistent at about 20 to 30%. This online retail business will benefit from this steady stream of **Repeat Customers**, as they will help the business to generate a stable stream of sales. Let's now analyze how much of the monthly revenue comes from these **Repeat Customers**.

The following code shows how to compute the monthly revenue from **Repeat Customers**:

```
monthly_rev_repeat_customers_df =
invoice_customer_df.set_index('InvoiceDate').groupby([
    pd.Grouper(freq='M'), 'CustomerID'
]).filter(lambda x: len(x) > 1).resample('M').sum()['Sales']

monthly_rev_perc_repeat_customers_df =
monthly_rev_repeat_customers_df/monthly_revenue_df * 100.0
```

The only difference between this code and the previous code is the aggregate function, `sum`, that follows `resample('M')`. In the previous case, when we were computing the number of monthly repeat customers, we used the `nunique` function. However, this time we are using the `sum` function to add all the sales from repeat customers for a given month. For visualization, you can use the following code:

```
ax = pd.DataFrame(monthly_revenue_df.values).plot(figsize=(12,9))

pd.DataFrame(monthly_rev_repeat_customers_df.values).plot(
    ax=ax,
    grid=True,
)

ax.set_xlabel('date')
ax.set_ylabel('sales')
ax.set_title('Total Revenue vs. Revenue from Repeat Customers')

ax.legend(['Total Revenue', 'Repeat Customer Revenue'])

ax.set_ylim([0, max(monthly_revenue_df.values)+100000])

ax2 = ax.twinx()

pd.DataFrame(monthly_rev_perc_repeat_customers_df.values).plot(
    ax=ax2,
    kind='bar',
    color='g',
    alpha=0.2,
)
```

```
ax2.set_ylim([0, max(monthly_rev_perc_repeat_customers_df.values)+30])
ax2.set_ylabel('percentage (%)')
ax2.legend(['Repeat Revenue Percentage'])

ax2.set_xticklabels([
    x.strftime('%m.%Y') for x in monthly_rev_perc_repeat_customers_df.index
])

plt.show()
```

One thing to note in this code is the line, `ax2 = ax.twinx()`. This essentially does the same job as the `secondary_y` flag that we discussed previously. The `twinx` function simply creates a twin y axis that shares the same x axis and has the same effect as the `secondary_y` flag. The resulting graph looks like the following:

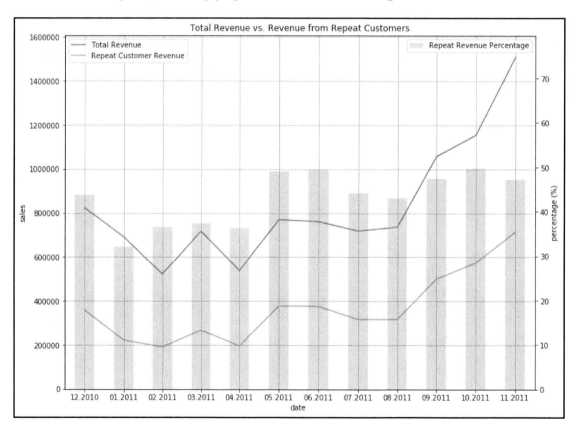

We see a similar pattern as before, where there is a significant increase in the revenue from September 2011. One interesting thing to notice here is the percentage of the monthly revenue from repeat customers. We have seen that roughly 20-30% of the customers who made purchases are repeat customers. However, in this graph, we can see that roughly 40-50% of the **Total Revenue** is from repeat customers. In other words, roughly half of the revenue was driven by the 20-30% of the customer base who are repeat customers. This shows how important it is to retain existing customers.

Trending items over time

So far, we have analyzed the overall time series patterns and how customers engage with the overall business, but not how customers engage with individual products. In this section, we are going to explore and analyze how customers interact with individual products that are sold. More specifically, we will take a look at the trends of the top five best-sellers over time.

For time series trending-item analysis, let's count the number of items sold for each product for each period. Take a look at the following code:

```
date_item_df = df.set_index('InvoiceDate').groupby([
    pd.Grouper(freq='M'), 'StockCode'
])['Quantity'].sum()
```

As you can see from this code snippet, we are grouping the DataFrame, `df`, by month with `StockCode`, which is the unique code for each product, and then summing up the quantities sold for each month and `StockCode`. The first nine records of the result look like the following:

InvoiceDate	StockCode	Quantity
2010-12-31	10002	251
	10120	16
	10125	154
	10133	130
	10135	411
	11001	74
	15034	45
	15036	161
	15039	20

With this data in `data_item_df`, let's see what items were sold the most on November 30, 2011. Take a look at the following code:

```
# Rank items by the last month sales
last_month_sorted_df = date_item_df.loc['2011-11-30'].sort_values(
    by='Quantity', ascending=False
).reset_index()
```

As you can see from this code, we can use the `sort_values` function to sort a `pandas` `DataFrame` by any column we want by providing the column name in the input argument, `by`. Here, we are sorting the data by the column, `Quantity`, in descending order, by setting the `ascending` flag to `False`. The result looks like the following:

	InvoiceDate	StockCode	Quantity
0	2011-11-30	23084	14954
1	2011-11-30	84826	12551
2	2011-11-30	22197	12460
3	2011-11-30	22086	7908
4	2011-11-30	85099B	5909
5	2011-11-30	22578	5366
6	2011-11-30	84879	5254
7	2011-11-30	22577	5003
8	2011-11-30	85123A	4910
9	2011-11-30	84077	4559

As you can see from this result, the products with the codes **23084**, **84826**, **22197**, **22086**, and **85099B** were the top five best-sellers in the month of November 2011.

Now that we know what the top five best-sellers were in November 2011, let's aggregate the monthly sales data for these five products again. Take a look at the following code:

```
date_item_df = df.loc[
    df['StockCode'].isin([23084, 84826, 22197, 22086, '85099B'])
].set_index('InvoiceDate').groupby([
    pd.Grouper(freq='M'), 'StockCode'
])['Quantity'].sum()
```

As you can see from this code, we are still grouping the data by each month and `StockCode`, and summing up the quantities sold. However, one thing to note here is the `isin` operator. The `isin` operator within the `loc` operator checks whether each record matches with one of the elements in the array. In our case, we are checking if the `StockCode` of each record matches with the top five best-sellers' item codes. Using this code, we can aggregate the data by month and product just for the top five best-sellers in November 2011. The first few records of the result look like the following:

InvoiceDate	StockCode	Quantity
2010-12-31	22086	2460
	22197	2738
	84826	366
	85099B	2152
2011-01-31	22086	24
	22197	1824
	84826	480
	85099B	2747
2011-02-28	22086	5
	22197	2666
	84826	66
	85099B	3080

Now that we have this monthly sales data for the top five products, we need to transform this data into a tabular format, where the columns are the individual item codes, the row indexes are the invoice dates, and the values are the number of items sold, so that we can visualize this data as a time series chart. The following code shows you how you can transform this data into a tabular format:

```
trending_itmes_df =
date_item_df.reset_index().pivot('InvoiceDate','StockCode').fillna(0)

trending_itmes_df = trending_itmes_df.reset_index()
trending_itmes_df = trending_itmes_df.set_index('InvoiceDate')
trending_itmes_df.columns = trending_itmes_df.columns.droplevel(0)
```

As you can see in this code, we are using the `pivot` function to `pivot` this `DataFrame`, where the index is the `InvoiceDate` and the columns are individual codes in the `StockCode` column. The result looks like the following:

StockCode	22086	22197	23084	84826	85099B
InvoiceDate					
2010-12-31	2460.0	2738.0	0.0	366.0	2152.0
2011-01-31	24.0	1824.0	0.0	480.0	2747.0
2011-02-28	5.0	2666.0	0.0	66.0	3080.0
2011-03-31	87.0	2803.0	0.0	60.0	5282.0
2011-04-30	13.0	1869.0	0.0	1.0	2456.0
2011-05-31	17.0	6849.0	1131.0	0.0	3621.0
2011-06-30	344.0	2095.0	1713.0	4.0	3682.0
2011-07-31	383.0	1876.0	318.0	2.0	3129.0
2011-08-31	490.0	5421.0	2267.0	72.0	5502.0
2011-09-30	2106.0	4196.0	680.0	0.0	4401.0
2011-10-31	3429.0	5907.0	6348.0	11.0	5412.0
2011-11-30	7908.0	12460.0	14954.0	12551.0	5909.0

With this time series data, we can now visualize the trends over time. You can use the following code to build a time series plot for trending items:

```
ax = pd.DataFrame(trending_itmes_df.values).plot(
    figsize=(10,7),
    grid=True,
)

ax.set_ylabel('number of purchases')
ax.set_xlabel('date')
ax.set_title('Item Trends over Time')

ax.legend(trending_itmes_df.columns, loc='upper left')

plt.xticks(
    range(len(trending_itmes_df.index)),
    [x.strftime('%m.%Y') for x in trending_itmes_df.index],
    rotation=45
)

plt.show()
```

When you run this code, you should see the following chart:

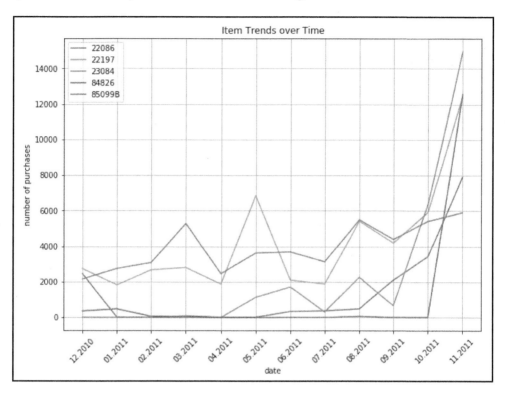

Let's take a closer look at this time series plot. The sales of these five products spiked in November 2011, especially, the sales of the product with the stock code, **85099B**, which were close to **0** from February 2011 to October 2011. Then, it suddenly spiked in November 2011. It might be worth taking a closer look into what might have driven this spike. It could be an item that is highly sensitive to seasonality, such that this item becomes very popular during November, or it could also be due to a genuine change in trends that led this item to become suddenly more popular than before.

The popularity of the rest of the top five products, **22086**, **22197**, **23084**, and **84826**, seem to have built up in the few months prior to November 2011. As a marketer, it would be worthwhile taking a closer look at the potential drivers behind this buildup of rising popularity for these items. You could look at whether these items are typically more popular in colder seasons or whether there is a rising trend for these specific items in the market.

Analyzing the trends and changes in the popularity of products not only helps you understand what your customers like and purchase the most, but also helps you tailor your marketing messages. For example, you can recommend these items with rising popularity in your marketing emails, calls, or advertisements to improve customer engagement. As it has been shown that your customers are more interested and more likely to purchase these items, you might get higher marketing engagement from your customers when you market these items more and you might eventually get higher conversion rates when you target your customers with these trending items. Using these popular and trending items is one way to build a product recommendation engine, which we are going to expand on and experiment with thoroughly in the next chapter.

 The full code for Python exercises in this section can be found at: `https://github.com/yoonhwang/hands-on-data-science-for-marketing/blob/master/ch.5/python/Product%20Analytics.ipynb`.

Product analytics using R

In this section, we are going to discuss how to conduct product analytics using the `dplyr` and `ggplot2` libraries in R. For those readers who would like to use Python, instead of R, you can ignore this section and move to the following section. We will start this section by analyzing the overall time series trends in the revenue, numbers of purchases, and purchasing patterns of repeat purchase customers, and then we will move on to analyzing the trends in products being sold.

For this exercise, we will be using one of the publicly available datasets from the UCI Machine Learning Repository, which can be found at: `http://archive.ics.uci.edu/ml/datasets/online+retail#`. You can follow this link and download the data in Microsoft Excel format, named `Online Retail.xlsx`. Once you have downloaded this data, you can load it by running the following code:

```
# install.packages("readxl")
library(readxl)

#### 1. Load Data ####
df <- read_excel(
  path="~/Documents/research/data-science-marketing/ch.5/data/Online
Retail.xlsx",
  sheet="Online Retail"
)
```

As you may notice from this code, one thing we are doing differently here from previous chapters is using the `readxl` library and the `read_excel` function. Since our data is in Excel format, we cannot use the `read.csv` function that we have been using so far. In order to load a dataset in Excel format, we need to use the `readxl` library that you can install using the `install.packages("readxl")` command in your RStudio. In the `readxl` library, there is a function named `read_excel`, which helps you load an Excel file easily.

Once you have loaded this data into a `DataFrame`, it should look like the following:

	InvoiceNo	StockCode	Description	Quantity	InvoiceDate	UnitPrice	CustomerID	Country	Sales
1	536365	85123A	WHITE HANGING HEART T-LIGHT HOLDER	6	2010-12-01 08:26:00	2.55	17850	United Kingdom	15.30
2	536365	71053	WHITE METAL LANTERN	6	2010-12-01 08:26:00	3.39	17850	United Kingdom	20.34
3	536365	84406B	CREAM CUPID HEARTS COAT HANGER	8	2010-12-01 08:26:00	2.75	17850	United Kingdom	22.00
4	536365	84029G	KNITTED UNION FLAG HOT WATER BOTTLE	6	2010-12-01 08:26:00	3.39	17850	United Kingdom	20.34
5	536365	84029E	RED WOOLLY HOTTIE WHITE HEART.	6	2010-12-01 08:26:00	3.39	17850	United Kingdom	20.34
6	536365	22752	SET 7 BABUSHKA NESTING BOXES	2	2010-12-01 08:26:00	7.65	17850	United Kingdom	15.30
7	536365	21730	GLASS STAR FROSTED T-LIGHT HOLDER	6	2010-12-01 08:26:00	4.25	17850	United Kingdom	25.50
8	536366	22633	HAND WARMER UNION JACK	6	2010-12-01 08:28:00	1.85	17850	United Kingdom	11.10
9	536366	22632	HAND WARMER RED POLKA DOT	6	2010-12-01 08:28:00	1.85	17850	United Kingdom	11.10
10	536367	84879	ASSORTED COLOUR BIRD ORNAMENT	32	2010-12-01 08:34:00	1.69	13047	United Kingdom	54.08

Before we move on to the next step, there is one data-cleaning step we need to take. Let's look quickly at the distribution of the `Quantity` column. We will visualize the distributions of `Quantity` by using the following code:

```
ggplot(df, aes(x="", y=Quantity)) +
  geom_boxplot(outlier.shape = NA) +
  ylim(c(-15, 25))+
  ylab("order quantity") +
  xlab("") +
  ggtitle("Quantity Distribution") +
  theme(plot.title=element_text(hjust=0.5))
```

As you can see from this code, we are visualizing the distribution of the `Quantity` column, in a box plot, using `geom_boxplot`.

The resulting box plot looks like the following screenshot:

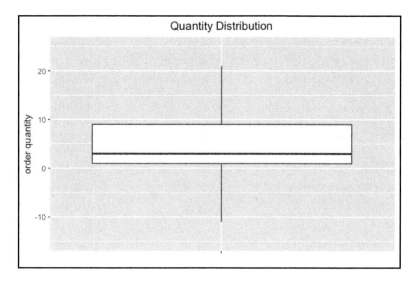

As you can see from this plot, some orders have negative quantities. This is because the cancelled or refunded orders are recorded with negative values in the Quantity column of our dataset. For illustration purposes in this exercise, we are going to disregard the cancelled orders. We can filter out all the cancelled orders in our DataFrame by using the following code:

```
# filter out orders with negative quantity (cancel orders)
df <- df[which(df$Quantity > 0),]
```

Now, we are ready to conduct further analyses and dive into our data.

Time series trends

Before we look at product-level data, as a marketer for an e-commerce business, it will be beneficial to have a better understanding of the overall time series trends in the revenue and the numbers of orders or purchases. This will help us understand whether the business is growing or shrinking in terms of both its overall revenue and the numbers of orders it receives over time.

First, we are going to look into the number of orders over time. Take a look at the following code:

```
# install.packages("lubridate")
library(lubridate)

timeSeriesNumInvoices <- df %>%
    group_by(InvoiceDate=floor_date(InvoiceDate, "month")) %>%
    summarise(NumOrders=n_distinct(InvoiceNo))
```

In this code, we are using the `group_by` function first to group the data by each month. In order to group by each month, we are using the `floor_date` function in the `lubridate` library. If you do not have this library installed already, you can install it using the `install.packages("lubridate")` command. The `floor_date` function simply takes the date and rounds it down by the provided unit. In our case, we are rounding down the `InvoiceDate` column to the first day of the month. Then, for each month, we are counting the number of unique purchase orders by using the `n_distinct` function on the `InvoiceNo` column. The resulting `DataFrame` looks like the following:

	InvoiceDate	NumOrders
1	2010–12–01	1629
2	2011–01–01	1120
3	2011–02–01	1126
4	2011–03–01	1531
5	2011–04–01	1318
6	2011–05–01	1731
7	2011–06–01	1576
8	2011–07–01	1540
9	2011–08–01	1409
10	2011–09–01	1896
11	2011–10–01	2129
12	2011–11–01	2884

Often, time series data is better visualized using line charts. Let's take a look at the following code to see how we can visualize this monthly data as a line chart:

```
ggplot(timeSeriesNumInvoices, aes(x=InvoiceDate, y=NumOrders)) +
  geom_line() +
  ylim(c(0, max(timeSeriesNumInvoices$NumOrders) + 1000)) +
  ylab("number of orders") +
  xlab("date") +
  ggtitle("Number of Orders over Time") +
  theme(plot.title=element_text(hjust=0.5))
```

As you can see from this code, we are using the `ggplot` function in the `ggplot2` library with the `geom_line` function to display the data using a line plot. Let's take a look at the following plot first:

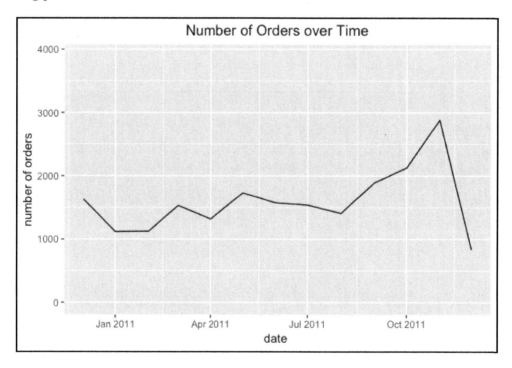

One thing that is noticeable from this chart is that there is a sudden, radical drop in the number of orders in December 2011. If you look closely at the data, this is simply because we do not have the data for the full month of December 2011. We can verify this by using the following code:

```
summary(df[which(df$InvoiceDate >= as.Date("2011-12-01")),"InvoiceDate"])
```

In this code, we get a summary of all invoice dates from December 1, 2011 that looks like the following:

```
> summary(df[which(df$InvoiceDate >= as.Date("2011-12-01")),"InvoiceDate"])
  InvoiceDate
 Min.   :2011-12-01 08:33:00
 1st Qu.:2011-12-04 12:32:00
 Median :2011-12-05 17:28:00
 Mean   :2011-12-05 20:37:49
 3rd Qu.:2011-12-08 09:20:00
 Max.   :2011-12-09 12:50:00
```

As you can see from this output, we only have the data from December 1, to December 9, 2011. It would be a misrepresentation if we used this data for analyzing December sales and revenue, as we cannot get the full picture of this month from the dataset we have. For further analyses, we will disregard any data from December 1, 2011. You can use the following code to remove those data points:

```
df <- df[which(df$InvoiceDate < as.Date("2011-12-01")),]
```

Now that we have filtered out incomplete data for December 2011, we can redraw the line chart using the previous codes. After removing those data points in December 2011, the line chart looks like the following:

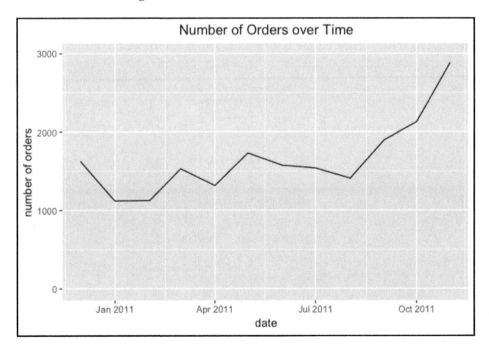

Let's take a closer look at this chart. The monthly number of orders seems to float around 1,500 from December 2010 to August 2011, then increases significantly from September 2011, and almost doubles by November 2011. One explanation for this could be that the business is actually growing significantly from September 2011. Another explanation could be seasonal effects. In e-commerce businesses, it is not rare to see spikes in sales as it approaches the end of the year. Typically, sales rise significantly from October to January for many e-commerce businesses and, without the data from the previous year, it is difficult to conclude whether this spike in sales is due to a growth in business or due to seasonal effects. When you are analyzing your data, we advise you to compare the current year's data against the previous year's data.

Similar to the monthly number of orders, let's take a quick look at the monthly revenue data. Take a look at the following code:

```
df$Sales <- df$Quantity * df$UnitPrice

timeSeriesRevenue <- df %>%
  group_by(InvoiceDate=floor_date(InvoiceDate, "month")) %>%
  summarise(Sales=sum(Sales))
```

As you can see from this code, the first thing we do here is calculate the aggregate sales amount from each order, which is simply the `UnitPrice` multiplied by the `Quantity`. Once we have computed and created this `Sales` column, we can use the `group_by` function with the `floor_date` function to group our data into monthly sales data. Using `sum` as the aggregate function in the `summarise` function, we can get the monthly sales revenue data. The resulting data looks like the following:

	InvoiceDate	Sales
1	2010-12-01	823746.1
2	2011-01-01	691364.6
3	2011-02-01	523631.9
4	2011-03-01	717639.4
5	2011-04-01	537808.6
6	2011-05-01	770536.0
7	2011-06-01	761739.9
8	2011-07-01	719221.2
9	2011-08-01	737014.3
10	2011-09-01	1058590.2
11	2011-10-01	1154979.3
12	2011-11-01	1509496.3

We can visualize this data as a line plot, using the following code:

```
ggplot(timeSeriesRevenue, aes(x=InvoiceDate, y=Sales)) +
  geom_line() +
  ylim(c(0, max(timeSeriesRevenue$Sales) + 10000)) +
  ylab("sales") +
  xlab("date") +
  ggtitle("Revenue over Time") +
  theme(plot.title=element_text(hjust=0.5))
```

As we have seen in previous chapters, we can use the `geom_line` function to build a line chart. The line plot for the monthly revenue data looks like the following:

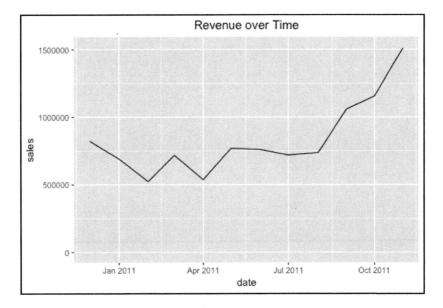

We see a similar pattern to the previous monthly **Number of Orders over Time** chart in this monthly **Revenue over Time** chart. The monthly revenue floats around 700,000 from December 2010 to August 2011 and then it increases significantly from September 2011. As discussed before, to verify whether this significant increase in sales and revenue is due to a growth in business or due to seasonal effects, we need to look further back in the sales history and compare the current year's sales against the previous year's sales.

These types of general and broad time series analyses can help marketers have a better understanding of the overall performance of the business and identify any potential problems that might be occurring within the business. It is generally a good idea to start with broader analyses and then drill down into more granular and specific parts of the business for further product analytics.

Repeat customers

Another important factor of a successful business is how well it is retaining customers and how many repeat purchases and customers it has. In this section, we are going to analyze the number of monthly repeat purchases and how much of the monthly revenue is attributable to these repeat purchases and customers. A typical strong and stable business has a steady stream of sales from existing customers. Let's see how many of the sales are from repeat and existing customers for the online retail business that we are currently analyzing in this chapter.

We are going to look at the number of monthly repeat purchases. This means a customer has placed more than one order within a given month. Let's take a quick look at the data we have:

	InvoiceNo	StockCode	Description	Quantity	InvoiceDate	UnitPrice	CustomerID	Country	Sales
1	536365	85123A	WHITE HANGING HEART T-LIGHT HOLDER	6	2010-12-01 08:26:00	2.55	17850	United Kingdom	15.30
2	536365	71053	WHITE METAL LANTERN	6	2010-12-01 08:26:00	3.39	17850	United Kingdom	20.34
3	536365	84406B	CREAM CUPID HEARTS COAT HANGER	8	2010-12-01 08:26:00	2.75	17850	United Kingdom	22.00
4	536365	84029G	KNITTED UNION FLAG HOT WATER BOTTLE	6	2010-12-01 08:26:00	3.39	17850	United Kingdom	20.34
5	536365	84029E	RED WOOLLY HOTTIE WHITE HEART.	6	2010-12-01 08:26:00	3.39	17850	United Kingdom	20.34
6	536365	22752	SET 7 BABUSHKA NESTING BOXES	2	2010-12-01 08:26:00	7.65	17850	United Kingdom	15.30
7	536365	21730	GLASS STAR FROSTED T-LIGHT HOLDER	6	2010-12-01 08:26:00	4.25	17850	United Kingdom	25.50
8	536366	22633	HAND WARMER UNION JACK	6	2010-12-01 08:28:00	1.85	17850	United Kingdom	11.10
9	536366	22632	HAND WARMER RED POLKA DOT	6	2010-12-01 08:28:00	1.85	17850	United Kingdom	11.10
10	536367	84879	ASSORTED COLOUR BIRD ORNAMENT	32	2010-12-01 08:34:00	1.69	13047	United Kingdom	54.08

As is noticeable from this snapshot of the data, there are multiple records for one purchase order (`InvoiceNo`). However, what we need is the aggregate data for each order, so that one record in the `DataFrame` represents one purchase order. We can aggregate this raw data for each `InvoiceNo` by using the following code:

```
invoiceCustomerDF <- df %>%
  group_by(InvoiceNo, InvoiceDate) %>%
  summarise(CustomerID=max(CustomerID), Sales=sum(Sales))
```

As you can see from this code, we are grouping the `DataFrame`, `df`, by `InvoiceNo` and `InvoiceDate` and summing up all the `Sales`, while taking one value for `CustomerID`. This way, the new `DataFrame`, `invoiceCustomerDf`, has one record for each purchase order. The resulting `DataFrame` looks like the following:

	InvoiceNo	InvoiceDate	CustomerID	Sales
1	536365	2010–12–01 08:26:00	17850	139.12
2	536366	2010–12–01 08:28:00	17850	22.20
3	536367	2010–12–01 08:34:00	13047	278.73
4	536368	2010–12–01 08:34:00	13047	70.05
5	536369	2010–12–01 08:35:00	13047	17.85
6	536370	2010–12–01 08:45:00	12583	855.86
7	536371	2010–12–01 09:00:00	13748	204.00
8	536372	2010–12–01 09:01:00	17850	22.20
9	536373	2010–12–01 09:02:00	17850	259.86
10	536374	2010–12–01 09:09:00	15100	350.40

As you can see here, each record in the `DataFrame` represents all the information we need for each order. Now, we need to aggregate this data for each month and compute the number of customers who made more than one purchase in a given month. Take a look at the following code:

```
timeSeriesCustomerDF <- invoiceCustomerDF %>%
  group_by(InvoiceDate=floor_date(InvoiceDate, "month"), CustomerID) %>%
  summarise(Count=n_distinct(InvoiceNo), Sales=sum(Sales))
```

Similarly to the previous section, we are using the `group_by` and `floor_date` functions to aggregate the data into each month. We are also grouping by `CustomerID`, so that we can count how many orders and how many sales each customer has brought in for each month. This data now looks like the following:

	InvoiceDate	CustomerID	Count	Sales
1	2010–12–01	12347	1	711.79
2	2010–12–01	12348	1	892.80
3	2010–12–01	12370	2	1868.02
4	2010–12–01	12377	1	1001.52
5	2010–12–01	12383	1	600.72
6	2010–12–01	12386	1	258.90
7	2010–12–01	12395	2	679.92
8	2010–12–01	12417	1	291.34
9	2010–12–01	12423	1	237.93
10	2010–12–01	12427	1	303.50

Now, in order to get the number of repeat customers, all we need to do is filter out customers who only have **1** in the **Count** column in this data. The code to perform this operation looks like the following:

```
repeatCustomers <-
na.omit(timeSeriesCustomerDF[which(timeSeriesCustomerDF$Count > 1),])
```

The newly created `DataFrame`, `reapeatCustomers`, now contains all the customers who have made more than one purchase in each month. In order to get the aggregate monthly repeat customer counts, we are going to run the following code:

```
timeSeriesRepeatCustomers <- repeatCustomers %>%
  group_by(InvoiceDate) %>%
  summarise(Count=n_distinct(CustomerID), Sales=sum(Sales))
```

As you can see from this code, we are simply grouping by `InvoiceDate`, which is a date that is rounded down to the first day of each month, and then we are counting the number of unique or distinct customers and summing up the total sales. The result looks like the following:

	InvoiceDate	Count	Sales
1	2010-12-01	263	359170.6
2	2011-01-01	149	219339.8
3	2011-02-01	150	190084.8
4	2011-03-01	201	266773.7
5	2011-04-01	168	194860.1
6	2011-05-01	279	377802.3
7	2011-06-01	219	376084.2
8	2011-07-01	227	317475.0
9	2011-08-01	196	316278.3
10	2011-09-01	271	496818.5
11	2011-10-01	323	573221.8
12	2011-11-01	540	713522.2

Let's now compare these repeat customer numbers against the total number of monthly customers. You can use the following code to compute the total number of monthly customers:

```
# Unique Customers
timeSeriesUniqCustomers <- df %>%
  group_by(InvoiceDate=floor_date(InvoiceDate, "month")) %>%
  summarise(Count=n_distinct(CustomerID))
```

The result looks like the following:

	InvoiceDate	Count
1	2010-12-01	886
2	2011-01-01	742
3	2011-02-01	759
4	2011-03-01	975
5	2011-04-01	857
6	2011-05-01	1057
7	2011-06-01	992
8	2011-07-01	950
9	2011-08-01	936
10	2011-09-01	1267
11	2011-10-01	1365
12	2011-11-01	1666

Lastly, we are going to analyze the percentage of monthly revenue that can be attributed to the repeat customers. Take a look at the following code:

```
timeSeriesRepeatCustomers$Perc <- timeSeriesRepeatCustomers$Sales /
timeSeriesRevenue$Sales*100.0
timeSeriesRepeatCustomers$Total <- timeSeriesUniqCustomers$Count
```

As you can see from this code, we are simply dividing the `Sales` column in the `timeSeriesRepeatCustomers DataFrame` by the `Sales` column in the `timeSeriesRevenue DataFrame` that we created in the previous section. Then, we are appending the number of monthly unique customers to the new column, `Total`, of the `timeSeriesRepeatCustomers DataFrame`.

Let's visualize all of this data in one chart, using the following code:

```
ggplot(timeSeriesRepeatCustomers) +
  geom_line(aes(x=InvoiceDate, y=Total), stat="identity", color="navy") +
  geom_line(aes(x=InvoiceDate, y=Count), stat="identity", color="orange") +
  geom_bar(aes(x=InvoiceDate, y=Perc*20), stat="identity", fill='gray',
alpha=0.5) +
  scale_y_continuous(sec.axis = sec_axis(~./20, name="Percentage (%)")) +
  ggtitle("Number of Unique vs. Repeat & Revenue from Repeat Customers") +
  theme(plot.title=element_text(hjust=0.5))
```

As you can see from this code, we are creating two line plots and one bar plot by using the `geom_line` and `geom_bar` functions in the `ggplot2` library. The first line plot represents the total number of monthly customers, `Total`, and will be drawn with a `navy` color. The second line plot is the number of monthly repeat customers, `Count`, which will be drawn with an `orange` color. Lastly, we are drawing a bar plot with a `gray` color for the percentage of revenue from repeat customers, `Perc`. One thing to note here is the scaling factor, `20`, for the secondary y axis. The `sec_axis` function defines the formula for the scale of the secondary y axis. Here, we are using `~./20`, which means the secondary y axis ranges from 0 to 1/20th of the maximum value of the first axis. Since we are scaling down the secondary y axis by a factor of `20`, we are multiplying this number to `Perc` in the `geom_bar` function to match the scale of our data to the range of the secondary y axis. The result looks like the following:

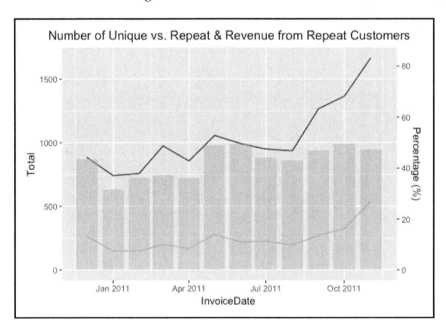

As discussed from the code, we see three plots in this chart: a line of a navy color that represents the total number of monthly customers, a line of an orange color that represents the number of monthly repeat customers, and bars of a gray color that represent the percentage of revenue from the repeat customers. As you can see from this chart, the secondary y axis, labeled as **Percentage (%)**, ranges from **0** to 1/20th of the maximum of the primary y axis, labeled as **Total**, which matches with our scaling factor of `20`.

Let's now take a closer look at the chart. There seems to be an upward trend in both the number of monthly customers and the number of repeat customers from September 2011, and repeat customers are roughly 20-30% of the total monthly customers. However, if you look at the percentage of revenue from these repeat customers, you can see that roughly 40-50% of the total revenue comes from repeat customers. In other words, roughly half of the revenue is driven by the 20-30% of the customer base who are repeat customers. As this online retail business has a large portion of revenue from repeat customers, this business will benefit from this steady stream of revenue from repeat customers. This shows how important it is to retain existing customers. As a marketer, it will be important to keep in mind how to retain existing customers and build up your repeat customer base.

Trending items over time

So far, we have analyzed the overall time series patterns and how customers engage with the overall business, but not how customers engage with individual products. In this section, we are going to explore and analyze how customers interact with individual products that are sold. More specifically, we will take a look at the trends of the top five best-sellers over time.

The first task for analyzing the time series trending items is to count the number of items sold for each product for each period. Take a look at the following code:

```
popularItems <- df %>%
    group_by(InvoiceDate=floor_date(InvoiceDate, "month"), StockCode) %>%
    summarise(Quantity=sum(Quantity))
```

As you can notice from this code, we are grouping the data by the month and the `StockCode`, which is the unique code for each product. Then, we are adding up all the quantities, `Quantity`, sold for the given month and product, by using the `sum` function in the `summarise` function.

Since we are only interested in the top five best-sellers, we will need to subselect those top five products from this `DataFrame`, `popularItems`. Take a look at the following code:

```
top5Items <- popularItems[
    which(popularItems$InvoiceDate == as.Date("2011-11-01")),
    ] %>%
    arrange(desc(Quantity)) %>%
    head(5)

timeSeriesTop5 <- popularItems[
    which(popularItems$StockCode %in% top5Items$StockCode),
    ]
```

Here, we first sort the items in descending order by the number of items sold, `Quantity`, in November 2011. Using the `which` function, we can subselect the data from `popularItems` for November 2011 and then with the `arrange` function, we can sort the data by the column we want, `Quantity`. By having `desc` in the `arrange` function, we can sort the data in descending order. Lastly, we are taking the top five items by using the `head` function. The newly created variable, `top5Items`, now has the top five best-sellers in November 2011. The last thing we need to do is retrieve the time series data for these five items. By using the `which` function and the `%in%` operator, we can subselect the data for those items with `StockCode` in `top5Items`.

To visualize the time series trends of these five products, we can use the following code:

```
ggplot(timeSeriesTop5, aes(x=InvoiceDate, y=Quantity, color=StockCode)) +
  geom_line() +
  ylab("number of purchases") +
  xlab("date") +
  ggtitle("Top 5 Popular Items over Time") +
  theme(plot.title=element_text(hjust=0.5))
```

The chart looks like the following:

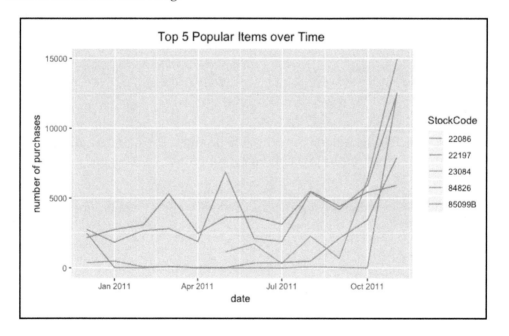

Let's take a closer look at this time series plot. The sales of these five products spiked in November 2011, especially the sales of the product with stock code, **85099B**, which were close to **0** from February 2011 to October 2011. Then, it suddenly spiked in November 2011. It might be worth taking a closer look into what might have driven this spike. It could be an item that is highly sensitive to seasonality, becoming very popular during November, or it could also be that there was a genuine change in trends, which led to this item becoming more popular than before.

The popularity of the other top five products, **22086**, **22197**, **23084**, and **84826**, seems to have built up in the few months prior to November 2011. As a marketer, it would also be worthwhile taking a closer look at the potential drivers behind this buildup and the rising popularity of these items. You could look at whether these items are typically more popular in colder seasons, or whether there is a growing trend for these specific items in the market.

Analyzing the trends and changes in the popularity of products not only helps you understand what your customers like and purchase the most, but it also helps you tailor your marketing messages. For example, you can recommend these items with rising popularity in your marketing emails, calls, or advertisements to improve customer engagement. As your customers are more interested and more likely to purchase these items, you might get higher marketing engagement from your customers when you market these items more, and you might eventually get higher conversion rates when you target your customers with these trending items. Using these popular and trending items is one way to build a product recommendation engine, which we are going to expand on and experiment with thoroughly in the next chapter.

The full code for the R exercise in this section can be found at: `https://github.com/yoonhwang/hands-on-data-science-for-marketing/blob/master/ch.5/R/ProductAnalytics.R`.

Summary

In this chapter, we discussed the concepts and importance of product analytics. We briefly discussed how product analytics starts from tracking events and customer actions, such as website or app visits, page views, and purchases. Then, we discussed some of the common goals of product analytics and how it should be used to generate actionable insights and reports. With these discussions on product analytics, we explored how we can utilize product analytics for customer and product retention in our programming exercises, using e-commerce business data. First, we analyzed the time series trends in the revenue and the numbers of purchase orders. Then, we drilled down to identify the patterns of monthly repeat customers. We have seen from the data that even though monthly repeat customers represent a relatively small portion of the overall customer base, they drive roughly half of the total monthly revenue. This shows the importance of retaining customers and how developing a retention strategy should be taken seriously. Lastly, we discussed how to analyze popular and trending items over time. In this section, we have discussed the potential effects of seasonality and how the analysis of trending items can be used in marketing strategies and in product recommendations.

In the next chapter, we are going to expand and apply our knowledge gained from this chapter to build product recommendation engines. We will learn about the collaborative filtering algorithm and how it can be used for product recommendations.

6
Recommending the Right Products

In this chapter, we are going to dive deeper into building product recommendation systems with which we can target customers better, using product recommendations that are custom-tailored toward individual customers. Studies have shown that personalized product recommendations improve conversion rates and customer retention rates. As we have more data available for utilizing data science and machine learning for target marketing, the importance and effectiveness of customized product recommendations in marketing messages have grown significantly. In this chapter, we are going to discuss the commonly-used machine learning algorithms for developing recommendation systems, collaborative filtering, and the two approaches to implementing collaborative filtering algorithms for product recommendations.

In this chapter, we will cover the following topics:

- Collaborative filtering and product recommendation
- Building a product recommendation algorithm with Python
- Building a product recommendation algorithm with R

Collaborative filtering and product recommendation

According to a study conducted by Salesforce, those customers who are prompted with personalized product recommendations drive 24% of the orders and 26% of the revenue. This signifies how much impact product recommendation has on order volume and the overall sales revenue. In the report that Salesforce published, they have also found that product recommendations lead to repeat visits, purchases with recommendations yield higher average-order value, and customers do buy recommended items. You can view this report at: `https://www.salesforce.com/blog/2017/11/personalized-product-recommendations-drive-just-7-visits-26-revenue`.

Product recommender system

A **product recommender system** is a system with the goal of predicting and compiling a list of items that a customer is likely to purchase. Recommender systems have gained lots of popularity in recent years and have been developed and implemented for various business use cases. For example, the music streaming service, Pandora, utilizes recommender systems for music recommendations for their listeners. The e-commerce company, Amazon, utilizes recommendater systems to predict and show a list of products that a customer is likely to purchase. The media service provider, Netflix, uses recommender systems to recommend movies or TV shows for individual users that they are likely to watch. The usage of a recommender system does not stop here. It can also be used to recommend related articles, news, or books to users. With the potential of being used in a variety of areas, recommender systems play a critical role in many businesses, especially in e-commerce and media businesses, as they directly impact the sales revenue and user engagements.

There are typically two ways to produce a list of recommendations:

- Collaborative filtering
- Content-based filtering

The **collaborative filtering** method is based on previous user behaviors, such as pages that they viewed, products that they purchased, or ratings that they have given to different items. The collaborative filtering approach then uses this data to find similarities between users or items, and recommends the most similar items or contents to the users. The basic assumption behind the collaborative filtering method is that those who have viewed or purchased similar contents or products in the past are likely to view or purchase similar kinds of contents or products in the future. Thus, based on this assumption, if one person purchased items A, B, and C and another person purchased items A, B, and D in the past, then the first person is likely to purchase item D and the other person is likely to purchase the item C, as they share lots of similarities between them.

Content-based filtering, on the other hand, produces a list of recommendations based on the characteristics of an item or a user. It typically looks at the keywords that describe the characteristics of an item. The basic assumption behind the content-based filtering method is that the users are likely to view or purchase items that are similar to those items that they have bought or viewed in the past. For example, if a user has listened to some songs in the past, then the content-based filtering method will recommend similar kinds of songs that share similar characteristics to those songs that the user has already listened to.

In this chapter, we are going to use a collaborative filtering algorithm to build a product recommendation system. Let's take a closer look at how a collaborative filtering algorithm is built in the following section.

Collaborative filtering

As discussed in the previous section, a collaborative filtering algorithm is used to recommend products based on the history of user behaviors and the similarities between users. The first step to implementing a collaborative filtering algorithm for a product recommendation system is building a **user-to-item matrix**. A user-to-item matrix comprises individual users in the rows and individual items in the columns. It will be easier to explain with an example. Take a look at the following matrix:

<table>
<tr><th></th><th></th><th colspan="5">Items</th></tr>
<tr><th></th><th></th><th>A</th><th>B</th><th>C</th><th>D</th><th>E</th></tr>
<tr><th rowspan="5">Users</th><th>1</th><td>0</td><td>1</td><td>0</td><td>1</td><td>0</td></tr>
<tr><th>2</th><td>1</td><td>1</td><td>1</td><td>0</td><td>1</td></tr>
<tr><th>3</th><td>0</td><td>0</td><td>1</td><td>0</td><td>0</td></tr>
<tr><th>4</th><td>1</td><td>0</td><td>1</td><td>0</td><td>1</td></tr>
<tr><th>5</th><td>0</td><td>1</td><td>0</td><td>0</td><td>1</td></tr>
</table>

The rows in this matrix represent each user and the columns represent each item. The values in each cell represent whether the given user bought the given item or not. For example, user **1** has purchased items **B** and **D** and user **2** has purchased items **A, B, C,** and **E**. In order to build a collaborative filtering-based product recommendation system, we need to first build this type of user-to-item matrix. We will discuss how to build such a matrix programmatically in more detail with an example in the programming exercises in the following section.

With this user-to-item matrix, the next step to building a collaborative filtering-based product recommender system is to compute similarities between users. To measure the similarities, **cosine similarity** is frequently used. The equation for computing the cosine similarity between two users looks as follows:

$$\cos(U_1, U_2) = \frac{\sum_{i=1}^{n} P_{1i} P_{2i}}{\sqrt{\sum_{i=1}^{n} P_{1i}^2 \sum_{i=1}^{n} P_{2i}^2}}$$

In this equation, U_1 and U_2 represent user **1** and user **2**. P_{1i} and P_{2i} represent each product, i, that user **1** and user **2** have bought. If you use this equation, you will get 0.353553 as the cosine similarity between users **1** and **2** in the previous example and 0.866025 as the cosine similarity between users **2** and **4**. As you can imagine, the larger the cosine similarity is, the more similar the two users are. So, in our example, users **2** and **4** are more similar to each other than users **1** and **2**. We will discuss how we can compute cosine similarities between users using Python and R in the following programming exercise section.

Lastly, when using a collaborative filtering algorithm for product recommendations, there are two approaches that you can take—a user-based approach and an item-based approach. As the names suggest, the user-based approach to collaborative filtering uses the similarities between users. On the other hand, the item-based approach collaborative filtering uses the similarities between items. This means that when we are calculating similarities between the two users in user-based approach collaborative filtering, we need to build and use a user-to-item matrix, as we have discussed previously. However, for the item-based approach, we need to calculate similarities between the two items, and this means that we need to build and use an item-to-user matrix, which we can get by simply transposing the user-to-item matrix. In the following programming exercise section, we are going to discuss in more detail the differences between these two approaches and how to build recommendation systems based on these two approaches using Python and R.

Building a product recommendation algorithm with Python

In this section, we are going to discuss how to build a product recommendation system using Python. More specifically, we will be learning how to implement a collaborative filtering algorithm in Python using a machine learning library, `scikit-learn`. For those readers who would like to use R instead of Python for this exercise, you can skip to the next section. We will start this section by analyzing some e-commerce business data and then discuss the two approaches to building a product recommendation system with collaborative filtering.

For this exercise, we will be using one of the publicly available datasets from the UCI Machine Learning Repository, which can be found at this link: `http://archive.ics.uci.edu/ml/datasets/online+retail#`. You can follow this link and download the data in Microsoft Excel format, in a file named `Online Retail.xlsx`. Once you have downloaded this data, you can load it into your Jupyter Notebook by running the following command:

```python
import pandas as pd

df = pd.read_excel(io='../data/Online Retail.xlsx', sheet_name='Online
Retail')
```

Similar to `Chapter 5`, *Product Analytics*, we are using the `read_excel` function in the `pandas` package to load the data in Excel format. We provide the path to the data to the argument, `io=`, and the name of the Excel spreadsheet to the argument, `sheet_name`.

Once you have loaded this data into a `pandas` `DataFrame`, it should look as in the following screenshot:

```python
df = pd.read_excel(io='../data/Online Retail.xlsx', sheet_name='Online Retail')
```

```python
df.shape
```

```
(541909, 8)
```

```python
df.head()
```

	InvoiceNo	StockCode	Description	Quantity	InvoiceDate	UnitPrice	CustomerID	Country
0	536365	85123A	WHITE HANGING HEART T-LIGHT HOLDER	6	2010-12-01 08:26:00	2.55	17850.0	United Kingdom
1	536365	71053	WHITE METAL LANTERN	6	2010-12-01 08:26:00	3.39	17850.0	United Kingdom
2	536365	84406B	CREAM CUPID HEARTS COAT HANGER	8	2010-12-01 08:26:00	2.75	17850.0	United Kingdom
3	536365	84029G	KNITTED UNION FLAG HOT WATER BOTTLE	6	2010-12-01 08:26:00	3.39	17850.0	United Kingdom
4	536365	84029E	RED WOOLLY HOTTIE WHITE HEART.	6	2010-12-01 08:26:00	3.39	17850.0	United Kingdom

If you recall from the previous chapter, there are records with negative values in the `Quantity` column, which represent canceled orders. We are going to disregard and remove these records. We can filter out all these records in our `DataFrame` with the following code:

```
df = df.loc[df['Quantity'] > 0]
```

Data preparation

Before we dive into building a product recommender engine using a collaborative filtering algorithm, we need to do the following couple of things:

- Handle `NaN` values in the dataset
- Build a customer-to-item matrix

First, we need to handle `NaN` values in our dataset, especially those `NaNs` in the `CustomerID` field. Without correct values in the `CustomerID` field, we cannot build a proper recommendation system, since the collaborative filtering algorithm depends on the historical item purchase data for individual customers.

Second, we need to build customer-to-item matrix before we move onto implementing the collaborative filtering algorithm for product recommendation. The customer-item matrix is simply tabular data, where each column represents each product or item, each row represents a customer, and the value in each cell represents whether the given customer purchased the given product or not.

Handling NaNs in the CustomerID field

If you look closely at the data, you will notice that there are some records with no `CustomerID`. As we need to build a customer-item matrix where each row is specific to each customer, we cannot include those records with no `CustomerID` in our data. Let's first take a look at how many records do not have `CustomerID`.

Take a look at the following code:

```
df['CustomerID'].isna().sum()
```

The `isna` function that we are using here detects missing values and returns `True` for each missing value. By summing over these values, we can count the number of records with no `CustomerID`. The result looks as follows:

```
df['CustomerID'].isna().sum()
133361
```

As you can see from this output, there are `133,361` records with no `CustomerID`. And some of the data with missing `CustomerID` looks as follows:

```
df.loc[df['CustomerID'].isna()].head()
```

	InvoiceNo	StockCode	Description	Quantity	InvoiceDate	UnitPrice	CustomerID	Country
622	536414	22139	NaN	56	2010-12-01 11:52:00	0.00	NaN	United Kingdom
1443	536544	21773	DECORATIVE ROSE BATHROOM BOTTLE	1	2010-12-01 14:32:00	2.51	NaN	United Kingdom
1444	536544	21774	DECORATIVE CATS BATHROOM BOTTLE	2	2010-12-01 14:32:00	2.51	NaN	United Kingdom
1445	536544	21786	POLKADOT RAIN HAT	4	2010-12-01 14:32:00	0.85	NaN	United Kingdom
1446	536544	21787	RAIN PONCHO RETROSPOT	2	2010-12-01 14:32:00	1.66	NaN	United Kingdom

Now that we know there are records with missing `CustomerID` entries, we need to exclude them from further analysis. One way to drop them from our `DataFrame` is by using the `dropna` function, as in the following:

```
df = df.dropna(subset=['CustomerID'])
```

The `dropna` function in the `pandas` package removes records with missing values from a given DataFrame. As you can see from this code snippet, using the `subset` parameter, we can drop missing values based on specific columns. Here, we are dropping records for those without `CustomerID`. Once you run this code, all the records in the DataFrame, `df`, will now have `CustomerID` values. The dimensions of the DataFrame, `df`, before and after dropping the missing values should look as in the following screenshot:

```
df.shape
(531285, 8)

df = df.dropna(subset=['CustomerID'])

df.shape
(397924, 8)
```

As you can see from this output, the `133,361` records with no `CustomerID` values were dropped from the original `DataFrame`.

Building a customer-item matrix

The data we have now represents individual items purchased by customers. However, in order to build a product recommendation system with a collaborative filtering algorithm, we need to have data where each record contains information on which item each customer has bought. In this section, we are going to transform the data into a customer-item matrix, where each row represents a customer and the columns correspond to different products.

Let's take a look at the following code:

```
customer_item_matrix = df.pivot_table(
    index='CustomerID',
    columns='StockCode',
    values='Quantity',
    aggfunc='sum'
)
```

As you can see from this code snippet, we are using the `pivot_table` function to transform our data into a customer-item matrix. Here, we define the `index` as `CustomerID`, and use `columns` to represent each `StockCode`. By using `sum` as the `aggfunc` and the `Quantity` field for `values`, we can sum all the quantities bought for each item. A snapshot of the resulting `customer_item_matrix` looks as follows:

StockCode	10002	10080	10120	10125	10133	10135	11001	15030	15034	15036
CustomerID										
12481.0	NaN	NaN	NaN	NaN	NaN	NaN	NaN	NaN	NaN	36.0
12483.0	NaN	NaN	NaN	NaN	NaN	NaN	NaN	NaN	NaN	NaN
12484.0	NaN	NaN	NaN	NaN	NaN	NaN	16.0	NaN	NaN	NaN
12488.0	NaN	NaN	NaN	NaN	NaN	10.0	NaN	NaN	NaN	NaN
12489.0	NaN	NaN	NaN	NaN	NaN	NaN	NaN	NaN	NaN	NaN

Let's take a closer look at this data. The customer with `CustomerID 12481` has bought `36` of the item with `StockCode 15036`. Similarly, the customer with `CustomerID 12484` has bought `16` of the item with `StockCode 11001`, and the customer with `CustomerID 12488` has bought `10` of the item with `StockCode 10135`. As you can see from this, we now have a matrix where each row represents the total quantities bought for each product for each customer.

Now, let's `0-1` encode this data, so that the value of `1` means that the given product was purchased by the given customer, and the value of `0` means that the given product was never purchased by the given customer. Take a look at the following code:

```
customer_item_matrix = customer_item_matrix.applymap(lambda x: 1 if x > 0
else 0)
```

As you can see from this code, we are using the `applymap` function, which applies a given function to each element of a DataFrame. The Lambda function that we are using in this code simply encodes all the elements whose values are greater than `0` with `1`, and the rest with `0`. A snapshot of this transformed DataFrame looks as follows:

StockCode	10002	10080	10120	10125	10133	10135	11001	15030	15034	15036
CustomerID										
12481.0	0	0	0	0	0	0	0	0	0	1
12483.0	0	0	0	0	0	0	0	0	0	0
12484.0	0	0	0	0	0	0	1	0	0	0
12488.0	0	0	0	0	0	1	0	0	0	0
12489.0	0	0	0	0	0	0	0	0	0	0

We now have a customer-item matrix that we can use for the collaborative filtering algorithm. Let's now move on to building product recommender engines.

Collaborative filtering

In this section, we are going to explore two approaches to building a product recommender engine—user-based versus item-based. In the user-based approach, we compute similarities between users based on their item purchase history. In the item-based approach, on the other hand, we compute similarities between items based on which items are often bought together with which other items.

To measure the similarity between users or between items, we are going to use the `cosine_similarity` method in the `scikit-learn` package. You can import this function using the following code:

```
from sklearn.metrics.pairwise import cosine_similarity
```

This `cosine_similarity` function in the `sklearn` package computes the pair-wise cosine similarities in the given data. Let's dive in now!

User-based collaborative filtering and recommendations

In order to build a user-based collaborative filtering algorithm, we need to compute cosine similarities between users. Let's take a look at the following code:

```
user_user_sim_matrix = pd.DataFrame(
    cosine_similarity(customer_item_matrix)
)
```

As is noticeable from this code, we are using the `cosine_similarity` function from the `sklearn` package's `metrics.pairwise` module. This function computes pairwise cosine similarities between the samples and outputs the results as an `array` type. Then, we create a `pandas` `DataFrame` with this output array and store it into a variable named `user_user_sim_matrix`, which stands for *user-to-user similarity matrix*. The result looks as follows:

```
user_user_sim_matrix.head()
```

	0	1	2	3	4	5	6	7	8	9	...	4329	4330	4331	4332	4333	4334	4335
0	1.0	0.000000	0.000000	0.000000	0.000000	0.000000	0.0	0.000000	0.000000	0.000000	...	0.0	0.000000	0.000000	0.0	0.000000	0.000000	0.0	0.
1	0.0	1.000000	0.063022	0.046130	0.047795	0.038484	0.0	0.025876	0.136641	0.094742	...	0.0	0.029709	0.052668	0.0	0.032844	0.062318	0.0	0.
2	0.0	0.063022	1.000000	0.024953	0.051709	0.027756	0.0	0.027995	0.118262	0.146427	...	0.0	0.064282	0.113961	0.0	0.000000	0.000000	0.0	0.
3	0.0	0.046130	0.024953	1.000000	0.056773	0.137137	0.0	0.030737	0.032461	0.144692	...	0.0	0.105868	0.000000	0.0	0.039014	0.000000	0.0	0.
4	0.0	0.047795	0.051709	0.056773	1.000000	0.031575	0.0	0.000000	0.000000	0.033315	...	0.0	0.000000	0.000000	0.0	0.000000	0.000000	0.0	0.

5 rows × 4339 columns

As you can see from this snapshot of the user-to-user similarity matrix, the index and column names are not easy to understand. Since each column and each row index stand for individual customers, we are going to rename the index and columns using the following code:

```
user_user_sim_matrix.columns = customer_item_matrix.index

user_user_sim_matrix['CustomerID'] = customer_item_matrix.index
user_user_sim_matrix = user_user_sim_matrix.set_index('CustomerID')
```

Now the result looks as follows:

```
user_user_sim_matrix.head()
```

CustomerID	12346.0	12347.0	12348.0	12349.0	12350.0	12352.0	12353.0	12354.0	12355.0	12356.0	...	18273.0	18274.0	18276.0	18277.0	182
CustomerID																
12346.0	1.0	0.000000	0.000000	0.000000	0.000000	0.000000	0.0	0.000000	0.000000	0.000000	...	0.0	0.000000	0.000000	0.0	0.000
12347.0	0.0	1.000000	0.063022	0.046130	0.047795	0.038484	0.0	0.025876	0.136641	0.094742	...	0.0	0.029709	0.052668	0.0	0.032
12348.0	0.0	0.063022	1.000000	0.024953	0.051709	0.027756	0.0	0.027995	0.118262	0.146427	...	0.0	0.064282	0.113961	0.0	0.000
12349.0	0.0	0.046130	0.024953	1.000000	0.056773	0.137137	0.0	0.030737	0.032461	0.144692	...	0.0	0.105868	0.000000	0.0	0.039
12350.0	0.0	0.047795	0.051709	0.056773	1.000000	0.031575	0.0	0.000000	0.000000	0.033315	...	0.0	0.000000	0.000000	0.0	0.000

5 rows × 4339 columns

Let's take a closer look at this user-to-user similarity matrix. As you can imagine, the cosine similarity between a customer to themselves is 1, and this is what we can observe from this similarity matrix. The diagonal elements in this user-to-user similarity matrix have values of 1. The rest represents the pairwise cosine similarity between two customers. For example, the cosine similarity measure between customers 12347 and 12348 is 0.063022. On the other hand, the cosine similarity between customers 12347 and 12349 is 0.046130. This suggests that customer 12348 is more similar to customer 12347 than customer 12349 is to the customer 12347, based on the products that they purchased. This way, we can easily tell which customers are similar to others, and which customers have bought similar items to others.

These pairwise cosine similarity measures are what we are going to use for product recommendations. Let's work by picking one customer as an example. We will first rank the most similar customers to the customer with ID 12350, using the following code:

```
user_user_sim_matrix.loc[12350.0].sort_values(ascending=False)
```

When you run this code, you will get the following output:

```
user_user_sim_matrix.loc[12350.0].sort_values(ascending=False)

CustomerID
12350.0    1.000000
17935.0    0.183340
12414.0    0.181902
12652.0    0.175035
16692.0    0.171499
16754.0    0.171499
12814.0    0.171499
12791.0    0.171499
16426.0    0.166968
16333.0    0.161690
12475.0    0.161690
```

These are the top 10 customers that are the most similar to customer 12350. Let's pick customer 17935 and discuss how we can recommend products using these results. The strategy is as follows. First, we need to identify the items that the customers 12350 and 17935 have already bought. Then, we are going to find the products that the target customer 17935 has not purchased, but customer 12350 has. Since these two customers have bought similar items in the past, we are going to assume that the target customer 17935 has a high chance of purchasing the items that he or she has not bought, but customer 12350 has bought. Lastly, we are going to use this list of items and recommend them to the target customer 17935.

Let's first take a look at how we can retrieve the items that the customer 12350 has purchased in the past. The code looks as follows:

```
items_bought_by_A = set(customer_item_matrix.loc[12350.0].iloc[
    customer_item_matrix.loc[12350.0].nonzero()
].index)
```

As you can see from this code, we are using the `nonzero` function in the `pandas` package. This function returns the integer indexes of the elements that are non-zero. Using this function on the `customer_item_matrix` for the given customer 12350, we can get the list of items that the customer 12350 has purchased. We can apply the same code for the target customer 17935, as in the following:

```
items_bought_by_B = set(customer_item_matrix.loc[17935.0].iloc[
    customer_item_matrix.loc[17935.0].nonzero()
].index)
```

Now we have two sets of items that customers `12350` and `17935` have purchased. Using a simple set operation, we can find the items that customer `12350` has bought, but customer `17935` has not. The code looks like the following:

```
items_to_recommend_to_B = items_bought_by_A - items_bought_by_B
```

Now the items in the `items_to_recommend_to_B` variable are the items that customer `12350` purchased, but customer `17935` did not purchase (yet). Based on our assumption, these are the items that customer `17935` is likely to purchase. The list of items to recommend to customer `17935` looks like the following:

```
items_to_recommend_to_B

{20615,
 20652,
 21171,
 21832,
 21864,
 21908,
 21915,
 22348,
 22412,
 22620,
 '79066K',
 '79191C',
 '84086C'}
```

In order to get the descriptions of these items, you can use the following code:

```
df.loc[
    df['StockCode'].isin(items_to_recommend_to_B),
    ['StockCode', 'Description']
].drop_duplicates().set_index('StockCode')
```

As you can notice from this code, we are using the `isin` operator to get the records that match with the items in the `items_to_recommend_to_B` variable.

Once you run this code, you will get the following output:

```
df.loc[
    df['StockCode'].isin(items_to_recommend_to_B),
    ['StockCode', 'Description']
].drop_duplicates().set_index('StockCode')
```

StockCode	Description
21832	CHOCOLATE CALCULATOR
21915	RED HARMONICA IN BOX
22620	4 TRADITIONAL SPINNING TOPS
79066K	RETRO MOD TRAY
21864	UNION JACK FLAG PASSPORT COVER
79191C	RETRO PLASTIC ELEPHANT TRAY
21908	CHOCOLATE THIS WAY METAL SIGN
20615	BLUE POLKADOT PASSPORT COVER
20652	BLUE POLKADOT LUGGAGE TAG
22348	TEA BAG PLATE RED RETROSPOT
22412	METAL SIGN NEIGHBOURHOOD WITCH
21171	BATHROOM METAL SIGN
84086C	PINK/PURPLE RETRO RADIO

Using user-based collaborative filtering, we have discussed how we can do targeted product recommendations for individual customers. You can custom-tailor and include these products that each target customer is likely to purchase in your marketing messages, which can potentially drive more conversions from your customers. As discussed so far, using a user-based collaborative filtering algorithm, you can easily do product recommendations for target customers.

However, there is one main disadvantage of using user-based collaborative filtering. As we have seen in this exercise, recommendations are based on the individual customer's purchase history. For new customers, we are not going to have enough data to compare these new customers against the others. In order to handle this problem, we can use item-based collaborative filtering, which we are going to discuss in the following section.

Item-based collaborative filtering and recommendations

Item-based collaborative filtering is similar to the user-based approach, except that it uses the similarity measures between items, instead of between users or customers. We had to compute cosine similarities between users before, but now, we are going to compute cosine similarities between items. Take a look at the following code:

```
item_item_sim_matrix = pd.DataFrame(
    cosine_similarity(customer_item_matrix.T)
)
```

If you compare this code to the previous code, where we computed a user-to-user similarity matrix, the only difference is the fact that we are transposing the `customer_item_matrix` here, so that the row indexes represent individual items and the columns represent the customers. We are still using the `cosine_similarity` function of the `sklearn` package's `metrics.pairwise` module. In order to correctly name the indexes and columns with product codes, you can use the following code:

```
item_item_sim_matrix.columns = customer_item_matrix.T.index

item_item_sim_matrix['StockCode'] = customer_item_matrix.T.index
item_item_sim_matrix = item_item_sim_matrix.set_index('StockCode')
```

Now the result looks as follows:

item_item_sim_matrix														
StockCode	**10002**	**10080**	**10120**	**10125**	**10133**	**10135**	**11001**	**15030**	**15034**	**15036**	**...**	**90214V**	**90214W**	**90214Y**	**90214Z**
StockCode														
10002	1.000000	0.000000	0.094868	0.090351	0.062932	0.098907	0.095346	0.047673	0.075593	0.090815	...	0.000000	0.000000	0.000000	0.000000
10080	0.000000	1.000000	0.000000	0.032774	0.045655	0.047836	0.000000	0.000000	0.082261	0.049413	...	0.000000	0.000000	0.000000	0.000000
10120	0.094868	0.000000	1.000000	0.057143	0.059702	0.041703	0.060302	0.060302	0.095618	0.028718	...	0.000000	0.000000	0.000000	0.000000
10125	0.090351	0.032774	0.057143	1.000000	0.042644	0.044682	0.043073	0.000000	0.051224	0.030770	...	0.000000	0.000000	0.000000	0.000000
10133	0.062932	0.045655	0.059702	0.042644	1.000000	0.280097	0.045002	0.060003	0.071358	0.057152	...	0.000000	0.000000	0.000000	0.000000
10135	0.098907	0.047836	0.041703	0.044682	0.280097	1.000000	0.094304	0.062869	0.074767	0.044911	...	0.073721	0.000000	0.060193	0.000000
11001	0.095346	0.000000	0.060302	0.043073	0.045002	0.094304	1.000000	0.045455	0.072075	0.075765	...	0.000000	0.000000	0.000000	0.000000
15030	0.047673	0.000000	0.060302	0.000000	0.060003	0.062869	0.045455	1.000000	0.108112	0.129884	...	0.000000	0.000000	0.000000	0.000000
15034	0.075593	0.082261	0.095618	0.051224	0.071358	0.074767	0.072075	0.108112	1.000000	0.231694	...	0.000000	0.000000	0.000000	0.000000
15036	0.090815	0.049413	0.028718	0.030770	0.057152	0.044911	0.075765	0.129884	0.231694	1.000000	...	0.000000	0.000000	0.000000	0.000000
15039	0.062284	0.030124	0.026261	0.056274	0.052262	0.054759	0.019795	0.158362	0.235412	0.207400	...	0.000000	0.000000	0.000000	0.000000
16008	0.043033	0.062439	0.027217	0.077762	0.121867	0.014188	0.041030	0.123091	0.081325	0.078161	...	0.000000	0.000000	0.000000	0.000000

As before, the diagonal elements have values of 1. This is because the similarity between an item and itself is 1, meaning the two are identical. The rest of the elements contain the similarity measure values between items based on the cosine similarity calculation. For example, looking at the preceding item-to-item similarity matrix, the cosine similarity between the item with StockCode 10002 and the item with StockCode 10120 is 0.094868. On the other hand, the cosine similarity between the item 10002 and the item 10125 is 0.090351. This suggests that the item with StockCode 10120 is more similar to that with StockCode 10002, than the item with StockCode 10125 is to that with StockCode 10002.

The strategy for doing product recommendation using this item-to-item similarity matrix is similar to what we did using the user-based approach in the previous section. First, for the given product that the target customer bought, we are going to find the most similar items from the item-to-item similarity matrix that we have just built. Then, we are going to recommend these similar items to the customer, since those similar items were bought by other customers who have bought the product that the target customer initially bought. Let's work with an example.

Assume a new customer just bought a product with StockCode 23166, and we want to include some products that this customer is the most likely to purchase in our marketing emails. The first thing we need to do is find the most similar items to the one with StockCode 23166. You can use the following code to get the top 10 most similar items to the item with StockCode 23166:

```
top_10_similar_items = list(
    item_item_sim_matrix\
        .loc[23166]\
        .sort_values(ascending=False)\
        .iloc[:10]\
    .index
)
```

The result looks like the following:

```
top_10_similar_items

[23166, 23165, 23167, 22993, 23307, 22722, 22720, 22666, 23243, 22961]
```

We can get the descriptions of these similar items using the following code:

```
df.loc[
    df['StockCode'].isin(top_10_similar_items),
    ['StockCode', 'Description']
].drop_duplicates().set_index('StockCode').loc[top_10_similar_items]
```

As you can see from this code, we are using the `isin` operator to filter for the items that match the list of similar items in the `top_10_similar_items` variable. Once you run this code, you will see the following output:

StockCode	Description
23166	MEDIUM CERAMIC TOP STORAGE JAR
23165	LARGE CERAMIC TOP STORAGE JAR
23167	SMALL CERAMIC TOP STORAGE JAR
22993	SET OF 4 PANTRY JELLY MOULDS
23307	SET OF 60 PANTRY DESIGN CAKE CASES
22722	SET OF 6 SPICE TINS PANTRY DESIGN
22720	SET OF 3 CAKE TINS PANTRY DESIGN
22666	RECIPE BOX PANTRY YELLOW DESIGN
23243	SET OF TEA COFFEE SUGAR TINS PANTRY
22961	JAM MAKING SET PRINTED

The first item here is the item that the target customer just bought and the other nine items are the items that are frequently bought by others who have bought the first item. As you can see, those who have bought ceramic top storage jars often buy jelly moulds, spice tins, and cake tins. With this data, you can include these items in your marketing messages for this target customer as further product recommendations. Personalizing the marketing messages with targeted product recommendations typically yields higher conversion rates from customers. Using an item-based collaborative filtering algorithm, you can now easily do product recommendations for both new and existing customers.

The full details for this Python exercise can be found at: `https://github.com/yoonhwang/hands-on-data-science-for-marketing/blob/master/ch.6/python/ProductRecommendation.ipynb`

Building a product recommendation algorithm with R

In this section, we are going to discuss how to build a product recommendation system using R. More specifically, we will be learning how to implement a collaborative filtering algorithm in R using the `dplyr`, `reshape2`, and `coop` packages. For those readers who would like to use Python instead of R for this exercise, you can go to the previous section. We will start this section by analyzing some e-commerce business data and then discuss the two approaches to building a product recommendation system with collaborative filtering.

For this exercise, we will be using one of the publicly available datasets from the UCI Machine Learning Repository, which can be found at: `http://archive.ics.uci.edu/ml/datasets/online+retail#`. You can go to this link and download the data, available in Microsoft Excel format, named `Online Retail.xlsx`. Once you have downloaded this data, you can load it into your RStudio by running the following command:

```
library(dplyr)
library(readxl)

df <- read_excel(
  path="~/Documents/research/data-science-marketing/ch.6/data/Online
Retail.xlsx",
  sheet="Online Retail"
)
```

Similar to the previous chapter, we are using the `read_excel` function in the `readxl` package to load the data in Excel format. We provide the path to the data to the argument `path`, and the name of the Excel spreadsheet to the argument `sheet`.

Once you have loaded this data into a `DataFrame`, it should look like the following:

	InvoiceNo	StockCode	Description	Quantity	InvoiceDate	UnitPrice	CustomerID	Country
1	536365	85123A	WHITE HANGING HEART T-LIGHT HOLDER	6	2010-12-01 08:26:00	2.55	17850	United Kingdom
2	536365	71053	WHITE METAL LANTERN	6	2010-12-01 08:26:00	3.39	17850	United Kingdom
3	536365	84406B	CREAM CUPID HEARTS COAT HANGER	8	2010-12-01 08:26:00	2.75	17850	United Kingdom
4	536365	84029G	KNITTED UNION FLAG HOT WATER BOTTLE	6	2010-12-01 08:26:00	3.39	17850	United Kingdom
5	536365	84029E	RED WOOLLY HOTTIE WHITE HEART.	6	2010-12-01 08:26:00	3.39	17850	United Kingdom
6	536365	22752	SET 7 BABUSHKA NESTING BOXES	2	2010-12-01 08:26:00	7.65	17850	United Kingdom
7	536365	21730	GLASS STAR FROSTED T-LIGHT HOLDER	6	2010-12-01 08:26:00	4.25	17850	United Kingdom
8	536366	22633	HAND WARMER UNION JACK	6	2010-12-01 08:28:00	1.85	17850	United Kingdom
9	536366	22632	HAND WARMER RED POLKA DOT	6	2010-12-01 08:28:00	1.85	17850	United Kingdom
10	536367	84879	ASSORTED COLOUR BIRD ORNAMENT	32	2010-12-01 08:34:00	1.69	13047	United Kingdom

If you recall from the previous chapter, there are records with negative values in the `Quantity` column, which represent canceled orders. We are going to disregard and remove those records. We can filter out all these records in our `DataFrame` with the following code:

```
# ignore cancel orders
df <- df[which(df$Quantity > 0),]
```

Data preparation

Before we dive into building a product recommender engine using a collaborative filtering algorithm, there are a couple of things we need to do. First, we need to handle `NaN` values in our dataset, especially those records with `NA` values in the `CustomerID` field. Without correct values in the `CustomerID` field, we cannot build a proper recommendation system, since the collaborative filtering algorithm depends on the historical item purchase data for individual customers. Second, we need to build customer-to-item matrix before we move onto implementing a collaborative filtering algorithm for product recommendation. The customer-item matrix is simply tabular data where each column represents each product or item, each row represents a customer, and the value in each cell represents whether the given customer purchased the given product or not.

Handling NA values in the CustomerID field

If you look closely at the data, you will notice that there are some records with no `CustomerID`. Since we need to build a customer-item matrix, where each row is specific to each customer, we cannot include those records with no `CustomerID` in our data. Let's first take a look at how many records do not have a `CustomerID`.

Take a look at the following code:

```
# there are 133,361 records with no CustomerID
sum(is.na(df$CustomerID))
```

The `is.na` function that we are using here detects missing values and returns `TRUE` for each of the missing values. By summing over these values using the `sum` function, we can count the number of records with no `CustomerID`. The result looks as follows:

```
> sum(is.na(df$CustomerID))
[1] 133361
```

As you can see from this output, there are 133, 361 records with no `CustomerID`. In order to look at those records with no `CustomerID`, you can use the following code:

```
# sneak peek at records with no CustomerID
head(df[which(is.na(df$CustomerID)),])
```

And the output looks like the following code:

```
> head(df[which(is.na(df$CustomerID)),])
# A tibble: 6 x 8
  InvoiceNo StockCode                     Description Quantity         InvoiceDate UnitPrice CustomerID        Country
      <chr>     <chr>                           <chr>    <dbl>              <dttm>     <dbl>      <dbl>          <chr>
1    536414     22139                            <NA>       56 2010-12-01 11:52:00      0.00         NA United Kingdom
2    536544     21773 DECORATIVE ROSE BATHROOM BOTTLE        1 2010-12-01 14:32:00      2.51         NA United Kingdom
3    536544     21774 DECORATIVE CATS BATHROOM BOTTLE        2 2010-12-01 14:32:00      2.51         NA United Kingdom
4    536544     21786               POLKADOT RAIN HAT        4 2010-12-01 14:32:00      0.85         NA United Kingdom
5    536544     21787            RAIN PONCHO RETROSPOT        2 2010-12-01 14:32:00      1.66         NA United Kingdom
6    536544     21790               VINTAGE SNAP CARDS        9 2010-12-01 14:32:00      1.66         NA United Kingdom
```

Now that we know there are records with missing `CustomerID` values, we need to exclude them from further analysis. One way to drop them from our `DataFrame` is by using the `na.omit` function, as in the following:

```
# remove records with NA
df <- na.omit(df)
```

The `na.omit` function in R removes records with missing values (`NA`) from a DataFrame. Once you run this code, all the records in the DataFrame `df` will now have `CustomerID` values. The dimensions of the DataFrame `df` before and after dropping the missing values should look as in the following screenshot:

```
> # current DataFrame shape
> dim(df)
[1] 531285       8
>
> # remove records with NA
> df <- na.omit(df)
> dim(df)
[1] 397924       8
```

As you can see from the outputs of the `dim(df)` commands, the 133, 361 records with no `CustomerID` values were dropped from the original `DataFrame`.

Building a customer-item matrix

The data we have now represents individual items purchased by customers. However, in order to build a product recommendation system with a collaborative filtering algorithm, we need to have data where each record contains information on which item each customer has bought. In this section, we are going to transform the data into a customer-item matrix, where each row represents a customer and the columns correspond to different products.

In order to transform our data into a customer-item matrix, we are going to use the `dcast` function in the `reshape2` package. If you do not already have this package installed in your R environment, you can run the following commands to install and include this package in your R environment:

```
install.packages("reshape2")

library(reshape2)
```

Let's take a look at the following code:

```
customerItemMatrix <- dcast(
    df, CustomerID ~ StockCode, value.var="Quantity"
)
```

The `dcast` function of the `reshape2` package uses a formula to reshape a `DataFrame` into another form of `DataFrame`. In our case, we want our data to be reshaped so that the rows represent individual customers and the columns represent the different products. By defining the formula as `CustomerID ~ StockCode`, the `dcast` function is going to reshape the data, so that the individual codes of the `StockCode` map to columns and each row represents an individual customer. The `value.var` argument defines which value to take. Here, we are telling the `dcast` function to take the values of the `Quantity` field as the values of the elements in the reshaped `DataFrame`. The result looks like the following:

	CustomerID	10002	10080	10120	10123C	10124A	10124G	10125	10133	10135	11001	15030	15034	15036	15039
315	12731	1	0	0	0	0	0	1	0	0	0	0	0	0	0
316	12732	0	0	0	0	0	0	0	0	0	0	0	0	0	0
317	12733	0	0	0	0	0	0	0	0	0	0	0	0	0	0
318	12734	0	0	0	0	0	0	0	0	0	0	0	0	0	0
319	12735	0	0	0	0	0	0	1	0	0	0	0	0	0	0
320	12736	0	0	0	0	0	0	0	0	0	0	0	0	0	0
321	12738	0	0	0	0	0	0	0	0	0	0	0	0	0	0
322	12739	0	0	0	0	0	0	0	0	0	0	0	0	0	0
323	12740	0	0	0	0	0	0	0	0	0	0	0	0	0	0
324	12743	0	0	0	0	0	0	0	0	0	0	0	0	0	0
325	12744	0	0	0	0	0	0	0	0	0	0	0	0	0	0
326	12747	0	0	0	0	0	0	0	0	0	0	0	0	0	0
327	12748	1	0	1	0	0	0	0	1	1	1	1	1	1	1

Let's take a closer look at this data. The customer with `CustomerID 12731` has bought 3 of the item with `StockCode 10002`. Similarly, the customer with `CustomerID 12748` has bought 2 of the item with `StockCode 10080`, and the customer with `CustomerID 12735` has bought 1 of the item with `StockCode 10125`. As you can see from this, we now have a matrix where each row represents the total quantities bought for each product for each customer.

Now, let's 0-1 encode this data, so that the value of 1 means that the given product was purchased by the given customer, and a value of 0 means that the given product was never purchased by the given customer. Take a look at the following code:

```
# 0-1 encode
encode_fn <- function(x) {as.integer(x > 0)}

customerItemMatrix <- customerItemMatrix %>%
  mutate_at(vars(-CustomerID), funs(encode_fn))
```

As you can see from this code, we first define the encoding function, `encode_fn`. This function simply encodes each value as 1 if it is greater than 0, and as 0 if it is not. Then we are using the `muate_at` function of the `dplyr` package, which applies the `encode_fn` encoding function to each element of the matrix, except the `CustomerID` column. The result should look as in the following:

	CustomerID	10002	10080	10120	10123C	10124A	10124G	10125	10133	10135	11001	15030	15034	15036	15039
315	12731	3	0	0	0	0	0	5	0	0	0	0	0	0	0
316	12732	0	0	0	0	0	0	0	0	0	0	0	0	0	0
317	12733	0	0	0	0	0	0	0	0	0	0	0	0	0	0
318	12734	0	0	0	0	0	0	0	0	0	0	0	0	0	0
319	12735	0	0	0	0	0	0	1	0	0	0	0	0	0	0
320	12736	0	0	0	0	0	0	0	0	0	0	0	0	0	0
321	12738	0	0	0	0	0	0	0	0	0	0	0	0	0	0
322	12739	0	0	0	0	0	0	0	0	0	0	0	0	0	0
323	12740	0	0	0	0	0	0	0	0	0	0	0	0	0	0
324	12743	0	0	0	0	0	0	0	0	0	0	0	0	0	0
325	12744	0	0	0	0	0	0	0	0	0	0	0	0	0	0
326	12747	0	0	0	0	0	0	0	0	0	0	0	0	0	0
327	12748	1	0	2	0	0	0	0	5	1	2	1	5	5	2

We now have a customer-item matrix that we can use for a collaborative filtering algorithm. Let's now move on to building product recommender engines.

Collaborative filtering

In this section, we are going to explore two approaches to building a product recommender engine—user-based versus item-based. In the user-based approach, we compute similarities between users based on their item purchase history. In the item-based approach, on the other hand, we compute similarities between items based on which items are often bought together with other items. To measure the similarity between users or between items, we are going to use the `cosine` function in the `coop` library, which is a library for fast implementation of cosine similarity computation in R. You can install and this R library using the following code:

```
install.packages("coop")

library(coop)
```

The `cosine` function in the `coop` library computes the cosine similarity matrix efficiently in R. Let's dive in now!

User-based collaborative filtering and recommendations

In order to build a user-based collaborative filtering algorithm, we need to compute cosine similarities between users. Let's take a look at the following code:

```
# User-to-User Similarity Matrix
userToUserSimMatrix <- cosine(
  as.matrix(
    # excluding CustomerID column
    t(customerItemMatrix[, 2:dim(customerItemMatrix)[2]])
  )
)
colnames(userToUserSimMatrix) <- customerItemMatrix$CustomerID
```

As is noticeable from this code, using the `cosine` function from the `coop` library, you can compute and build a cosine similarity matrix. One thing to note in this code is the fact that we transpose the `customerItemMatrix` before computing cosine similarities. This is to compute user-to-user similarities. Without the transposition, the `cosine` function will be computing item-to-item similarities. Lastly, we are renaming the columns with customer IDs in the last line of this code.

The result looks as follows:

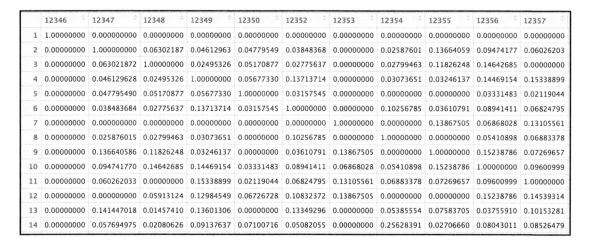

	12346	12347	12348	12349	12350	12352	12353	12354	12355	12356	12357
1	1.00000000	0.000000000	0.00000000	0.00000000	0.00000000	0.00000000	0.00000000	0.00000000	0.00000000	0.00000000	0.00000000
2	0.00000000	1.000000000	0.06302187	0.04612963	0.04779549	0.03848368	0.00000000	0.02587601	0.13664059	0.09474177	0.06026203
3	0.00000000	0.063021872	1.00000000	0.02495326	0.05170877	0.02775637	0.00000000	0.02799463	0.11826248	0.14642685	0.00000000
4	0.00000000	0.046129628	0.02495326	1.00000000	0.05677330	0.13713714	0.00000000	0.03073651	0.03246137	0.14469154	0.15338899
5	0.00000000	0.047795490	0.05170877	0.05677330	1.00000000	0.03157545	0.00000000	0.00000000	0.00000000	0.03331483	0.02119044
6	0.00000000	0.038483684	0.02775637	0.13713714	0.03157545	1.00000000	0.00000000	0.10256785	0.03610791	0.08941411	0.06824795
7	0.00000000	0.000000000	0.00000000	0.00000000	0.00000000	0.00000000	1.00000000	0.00000000	0.13867505	0.06868028	0.13105561
8	0.00000000	0.025876015	0.02799463	0.03073651	0.00000000	0.10256785	0.00000000	1.00000000	0.00000000	0.05410898	0.06883378
9	0.00000000	0.136640586	0.11826248	0.03246137	0.00000000	0.03610791	0.13867505	0.00000000	1.00000000	0.15238786	0.07269657
10	0.00000000	0.094741770	0.14642685	0.14469154	0.03331483	0.08941411	0.06868028	0.05410898	0.15238786	1.00000000	0.09600999
11	0.00000000	0.060262033	0.00000000	0.15338899	0.02119044	0.06824795	0.13105561	0.06883378	0.07269657	0.09600999	1.00000000
12	0.00000000	0.000000000	0.05913124	0.12984549	0.06726728	0.10832372	0.13867505	0.00000000	0.00000000	0.15238786	0.14539314
13	0.00000000	0.141447018	0.01457410	0.13601306	0.00000000	0.13349296	0.00000000	0.05385554	0.07583705	0.03755910	0.10153281
14	0.00000000	0.057694975	0.02080626	0.09137637	0.07100716	0.05082055	0.00000000	0.25628391	0.02706660	0.08043011	0.08526479

Let's take a closer look at this user-to-user similarity matrix. As you can imagine, the cosine similarity between a customer to himself or herself is `1` and this is what we can observe from this similarity matrix. The diagonal elements in this user-to-user similarity matrix have values of `1`. The rest represents the pairwise cosine similarity between two customers. For example, the cosine similarity measure between customers `12347` and `12348` is `0.06302187`. On the other hand, the cosine similarity between customers `12347` and `12349` is `0.04612963`. This suggests that customer `12348` is more similar to customer `12347` than customer `12349` to customer `12347`, based on the products that they purchased previously. This way we can easily tell which customers are similar to which others and which customers have bought similar items to which others.

These pairwise cosine similarity measures are what we are going to use for product recommendations. Let's work by picking one customer as an example. We will first rank the most similar customers to customer with ID 12350 using the following code:

```
top10SimilarCustomersTo12350 <- customerItemMatrix$CustomerID[
  order(userToUserSimMatrix[,"12350"], decreasing = TRUE)[1:11]
]
```

As you can see from this code, we are using the order function to sort the values in the column 12350 of userToUserSimMatrix. With the decreasing = TRUE flag, we can sort the values in descending order.

When you run this code, you will get the following output:

```
> top10SimilarCustomersTo12350
[1] 12350 17935 12414 12652 12791 12814 16692 16754 16426 12475 16333
```

These are the top 10 customers that are the most similar to customer 12350. Let's pick customer 17935 and discuss how we can recommend products using these results. The strategy is as follows. First we need to identify the items that customers 12350 and 17935 have already bought. Then, we are going to find the products that the target customer 17935 has not purchased, but customer 12350 has. Since these two customers have bought similar items in the past, we are going to assume that the target customer 17935 has high chance of purchasing these items that he or she has not bought, but that customer 12350 has bought. Lastly, we are going to use this list of items and recommend them to the target customer 17935.

Let's first take a look at how we can retrieve the items that customer 12350 has purchased in the past. The code looks as follows:

```
itemsBoughtByA <- customerItemMatrix[
  which(customerItemMatrix$CustomerID == "12350"),
]

itemsBoughtByA <- colnames(customerItemMatrix)[which(itemsBoughtByA != 0)]
```

As you can see from this code, we are using the which operator to find the column indexes of the elements that are non-zero. The result of this code looks as follows:

```
> itemsBoughtByA
[1] "CustomerID" "20615"    "20652"    "21171"    "21832"    "21864"    "21866"
[8] "21908"    "21915"    "22348"    "22412"    "22551"    "22557"    "22620"
[15] "79066K"    "79191C"    "84086C"    "POST"
```

Using the following code, we can get the list of items that the customer `17935` has purchased:

```
itemsBoughtByB <- customerItemMatrix[
  which(customerItemMatrix$CustomerID == "17935"),
]

itemsBoughtByB <- colnames(customerItemMatrix)[which(itemsBoughtByB != 0)]
```

The items that customer `17935` has bought are as follows:

```
> itemsBoughtByB
 [1] "CustomerID" "20657"    "20659"    "20828"    "20856"    "21051"    "21866"
 [8] "21867"    "22208"    "22209"    "22210"    "22211"    "22449"    "22450"
[15] "22551"    "22553"    "22557"    "22640"    "22659"    "22749"    "22752"
[22] "22753"    "22754"    "22755"    "23290"    "23292"    "23309"    "85099B"
[29] "POST"
```

Now we have two sets of items that customers `12350` and `17935` have purchased. Using the simple set operation, we can find the items that customer `12350` has bought, but customer `17935` has not. The code looks like the following:

```
itemsToRecommendToB <- setdiff(itemsBoughtByA, itemsBoughtByB)
```

Now the items in the, `itemsToRecommendToB` variable, are the items that customer `12350` purchased, but customer `17935` did not purchase yet. Based on our assumption, these are the items that customer `17935` is likely to purchase. The list of items to recommend to customer `17935` looks as in the following:

```
> itemsToRecommendToB
 [1] "20615"  "20652"  "21171"  "21832"  "21864"  "21908"  "21915"  "22348"  "22412"  "22620"
[11] "79066K" "79191C" "84086C"
```

In order to get the descriptions of these items, you can use the following code:

```
itemsToRecommendToBDescriptions <- unique(
  df[
    which(df$StockCode %in% itemsToRecommendToB),
    c("StockCode", "Description")
    ]
)
itemsToRecommendToBDescriptions <- itemsToRecommendToBDescriptions[
  match(itemsToRecommendToB, itemsToRecommendToBDescriptions$StockCode),
  ]
```

As you can notice from this code, we are using the `%in%` operator to get the records that match with the items in the `itemsToRecommendToB` variable. Once you run this code, you will get the following output that has descriptions of the recommended items:

	StockCode	Description
1	20615	BLUE POLKADOT PASSPORT COVER
2	20652	BLUE POLKADOT LUGGAGE TAG
3	21171	BATHROOM METAL SIGN
4	21832	CHOCOLATE CALCULATOR
5	21864	UNION JACK FLAG PASSPORT COVER
6	21908	CHOCOLATE THIS WAY METAL SIGN
7	21915	RED HARMONICA IN BOX
8	22348	TEA BAG PLATE RED RETROSPOT
9	22412	METAL SIGN NEIGHBOURHOOD WITCH
10	22620	4 TRADITIONAL SPINNING TOPS
11	79066K	RETRO MOD TRAY
12	79191C	RETRO PLASTIC ELEPHANT TRAY
13	84086C	PINK/PURPLE RETRO RADIO

Using user-based collaborative filtering, we have discussed how we can do targeted product recommendations for individual customers. You can custom-tailor and include these products that each target customer is likely to purchase in your marketing messages, which can potentially drive more conversions from your customers. As discussed so far, using a user-based collaborative filtering algorithm, you can easily create product recommendations for target customers.

However, there is one main disadvantage of using user-based collaborative filtering. As we have seen in this exercise, recommendations are based on the individual customer's purchase history. For new customers, we are not going to have enough data to compare them with the others. In order to handle this problem, we can use item-based collaborative filtering that we will be discussing in the following section.

Item-based collaborative filtering and recommendations

Item-based collaborative filtering is similar to the user-based approach, except that it is using the similarity measures between items, instead of between users or customers. We had to compute cosine similarities between users before, but now we are going to compute cosine similarities between items. Take a look at the following code:

```
# Item-to-Item Similarity Matrix
itemToItemSimMatrix <- cosine(
  as.matrix(
    # excluding CustomerID column
    customerItemMatrix[, 2:dim(customerItemMatrix)[2]]
  )
)
```

If you compare this code to the previous code, where we computed user-to-user similarity matrix, the only difference is the fact that we are not transposing the `customerItemMatrix` this time. We are still using the `cosine` function of the `coop` library.

The result looks as follows:

	10002	10080	10120	10123C	10124A	10124G	10125	10133	10135	11001	15030	15034
10002	1.00000000	0.00000000	0.09486833	0.09128709	0.00000000	0.00000000	0.09035079	0.06293168	0.09890707	0.09534626	0.04767313	0.07559289
10080	0.00000000	1.00000000	0.00000000	0.00000000	0.00000000	0.00000000	0.03277368	0.04565544	0.04783649	0.00000000	0.00000000	0.08226127
10120	0.09486833	0.00000000	1.00000000	0.11547005	0.00000000	0.00000000	0.05714286	0.05970223	0.04170288	0.06030227	0.06030227	0.09561829
10123C	0.09128709	0.00000000	0.11547005	1.00000000	0.00000000	0.00000000	0.16495722	0.00000000	0.00000000	0.00000000	0.00000000	0.00000000
10124A	0.00000000	0.00000000	0.00000000	0.00000000	1.00000000	0.44721360	0.06388766	0.04449942	0.00000000	0.00000000	0.00000000	0.00000000
10124G	0.00000000	0.00000000	0.00000000	0.00000000	0.44721360	1.00000000	0.07142857	0.04975186	0.00000000	0.00000000	0.00000000	0.00000000
10125	0.09035079	0.03277368	0.05714286	0.16495722	0.06388766	0.07142857	1.00000000	0.04264445	0.04468166	0.04307305	0.00000000	0.05122408
10133	0.06293168	0.04565544	0.05970223	0.00000000	0.04449942	0.04975186	0.04264445	1.00000000	0.28009746	0.04500225	0.06000300	0.07135782
10135	0.09890707	0.04783649	0.04170288	0.00000000	0.00000000	0.00000000	0.04468166	0.28009746	1.00000000	0.09430419	0.06286946	0.07476672
11001	0.09534626	0.00000000	0.06030227	0.00000000	0.00000000	0.00000000	0.04307305	0.04500225	0.09430419	1.00000000	0.04545455	0.07207500
15030	0.04767313	0.00000000	0.06030227	0.00000000	0.00000000	0.00000000	0.00000000	0.06000300	0.06286946	0.04545455	1.00000000	0.10811250
15034	0.07559289	0.08226127	0.09561829	0.00000000	0.00000000	0.00000000	0.05122408	0.07135782	0.07476672	0.07207500	0.10811250	1.00000000
15036	0.09081532	0.04941327	0.02871833	0.00000000	0.06421613	0.03589791	0.03076964	0.05715161	0.04491139	0.07576539	0.12988352	0.23169352
15039	0.06228411	0.03012376	0.02626129	0.00000000	0.05872202	0.00000000	0.05627419	0.05226191	0.05475857	0.01979519	0.15836152	0.23541181
15044A	0.04343722	0.00000000	0.00000000	0.00000000	0.06142951	0.06868028	0.00000000	0.06833943	0.07160414	0.02070788	0.04141577	0.13134182
15044B	0.07905694	0.00000000	0.00000000	0.00000000	0.00000000	0.00000000	0.00000000	0.03316791	0.03475240	0.02512595	0.05025189	0.11952286
15044C	0.07233642	0.00000000	0.00000000	0.00000000	0.00000000	0.00000000	0.06535653	0.06069670	0.04769723	0.02299002	0.04598005	0.12758946

As before, the diagonal elements have values of 1. This is because the similarity between an item and itself is 1, meaning the two are identical. The other elements contain the similarity measure values between items based on the cosine similarity calculation. For example, looking at the preceding item-to-item similarity matrix, the cosine similarity between the item with StockCode 10002 and the item with StockCode 10120 is 0.09486833. On the other hand, the cosine similarity between item 10002 and item 10125 is 0.09035079. This suggests that the item with StockCode 10120 is more similar to that with StockCode 10002 than the item with StockCode 10125 is to that with StockCode 10002.

The strategy to do product recommendation using this item-to-item similarity matrix is similar to what we did using the user-based approach in the previous section. First, for the given product that the target customer bought, we are going to find the most similar items from the item-to-item similarity matrix that we have just built. Then, we are going to recommend these similar items to the customer, since those similar items were bought by other customers who have bought the product that the target customer initially bought. Let's work with an example.

Assume a new customer just bought a product with StockCode 23166, and we want to include some products that this customer is most likely to purchase in our marketing emails. The first thing we need to do is find the most similar items to the one with StockCode 23166. You can use the following code to get the top 10 most similar items to the item with StockCode 23166:

```
top10SimilarItemsTo23166 <- colnames(itemToItemSimMatrix)[
    order(itemToItemSimMatrix[,"23166"], decreasing = TRUE)[1:11]
]
```

Using the order function with the decreasing = TRUE flag, we can sort the similar items in descending order. Then, with this reverse sorted list of indexes, we can get the top 10 similar items to the item with StockCode 23166.

The result looks as in the following:

```
> top10SimilarItemsTo23166
 [1] "23166" "23165" "23167" "22993" "23307" "22722" "22720" "22666" "23243" "22961"
[11] "23306"
```

We can get the descriptions of these similar items using the following code:

```
top10SimilarItemDescriptions <- unique(
  df[
    which(df$StockCode %in% top10SimilarItemsTo23166),
    c("StockCode", "Description")
  ]
)
top10SimilarItemDescriptions <- top10SimilarItemDescriptions[
  match(top10SimilarItemsTo23166, top10SimilarItemDescriptions$StockCode),
]
```

As you can see from this code, we are using the `%in%` operator to filter for the items that match the list of similar items in the variable `top10SimilarItemsTo23166`. Once you run this code, you will see the following output:

	StockCode	Description
1	23166	MEDIUM CERAMIC TOP STORAGE JAR
2	23165	LARGE CERAMIC TOP STORAGE JAR
3	23167	SMALL CERAMIC TOP STORAGE JAR
4	22993	SET OF 4 PANTRY JELLY MOULDS
5	23307	SET OF 60 PANTRY DESIGN CAKE CASES
6	22722	SET OF 6 SPICE TINS PANTRY DESIGN
7	22720	SET OF 3 CAKE TINS PANTRY DESIGN
8	22666	RECIPE BOX PANTRY YELLOW DESIGN
9	23243	SET OF TEA COFFEE SUGAR TINS PANTRY
10	22961	JAM MAKING SET PRINTED
11	23306	SET OF 36 DOILIES PANTRY DESIGN

The first item here is the item that the target customer just bought, and the remaining 10 items are the items that are frequently bought by others who have bought the first item. As you can see, those who have bought ceramic-top storage jars often buy jelly moulds, spice tins, and cake tins. With this data, you can include these items in your marketing messages for this target customer as further product recommendations. Personalizing the marketing messages with targeted product recommendations typically yields higher conversion rates from customers. Using an item-based collaborative filtering algorithm, you can now easily do product recommendations for both new and existing customers.

The full code for this R exercise can be found in this link: `https://github.com/yoonhwang/hands-on-data-science-for-marketing/blob/master/ch.6/R/ProductRecommendation.R`

Summary

In this chapter, we have discussed product recommender systems. We have learned how personalized product recommendations improve conversion and customer retention rates, according to a study conducted by Salesforce. We have discussed the two approaches, collaborative filtering and content-based filtering, to building product recommendation systems; how they differ from one another; and what their assumptions are. Then, we dove deeper into how we can build collaborative filtering-based recommender systems. As you might recall, the first step to building a collaborative filtering-based recommender system is to build a user-to-item matrix, and then the next step is to use cosine similarity to compute the similarities between the users. We have also discussed the two different approaches to utilizing a collaborative filtering algorithm for product recommendations—a user-based approach and an item-based approach.

From the next chapter, we are going to switch gears and focus on utilizing customer behavior data to our advantage to improve our marketing strategies. In the next chapter, we are going to discuss the benefits and importance of conducting customer analytics.

Section 4: Personalized Marketing

4

In this section, you will learn how to use data to understand customer behavior better, how to use machine learning to predict the likelihood of marketing engagement and the value of individual customers over their lifetime, and how to use data science for better customer retention.

This section consists of the following chapters:

7
Exploratory Analysis for Customer Behavior

In this chapter, as the first step toward future topics in the following chapters, we are going to discuss what customer analytics is, the importance and benefits of analyzing and having a better understanding of the customer base, and the use cases of customer analytics in different aspects of marketing. As we gather and track more data on customers and their behavior regarding individual sales, marketing platforms, and channels, it becomes easier for marketers to analyze and understand how different customers react to different marketing strategies. Customer analytics helps marketers understand their customers better by utilizing this data. Furthermore, it can help marketers to form better marketing strategies that can improve engagement, retention, and conversion rates.

In this chapter, we will cover the following topics:

- Customer analytics: understanding customer behavior
- Conducting customer analytics with Python
- Conducting customer analytics with R

Customer analytics – understanding customer behavior

Customer analytics is a process of understanding and gaining insights into customer behavior through analyzing customer behavior data. It ranges from simple data analysis and visualization to more advanced customer segmentation and predictive analytics. The information and insights gained through customer analytics can then be utilized in forming marketing strategies, optimizing sales channels, and making other key business decisions.

The importance of customer analytics is rising. Because access to customer data became easier for many businesses and also because customers now have easier access to data and information on similar products and contents provided by other competitors, it is critical to many businesses to be able to understand and predict what their customers are likely to purchase or view. The deeper the understanding you have about your customers, the better competitive power you will have against your competitors.

Customer analytics use cases

Customer analytics can be used at any point of the marketing process. It can be used to monitor and track how customers interact with the products or react to different marketing strategies. This typically requires using data analysis and visualization techniques to build reports or dashboards that can easily show **key performance indicators (KPIs)**.

Sales funnel analytics

One of the common use cases of customer analytics is **sales funnel analytics**. By analyzing sales funnel data, we can monitor and track the life cycle of customers, gaining insights such as through which marketing channel they sign up, how often they log into the system, what types of products they browsed and purchased, or how they fall off from each step of the funnel.

Customer segmentation

Customer analytics can also be used to identify different groups of customers based on their behavior. **Customer segmentation** is a good example and outcome of customer analytics. Through identifying subgroups of similar customers, you can better understand the target populations. For example, the marketing strategy for low-engagement customers should be different from the marketing strategy for high-engagement customers. By effectively segmenting the customer base by the level of engagement, you can have a deeper understanding of how different groups of customers behave and react to different marketing strategies. This further helps you better target certain subgroups of customers.

Predictive analytics

Another good use case of customer analytics is using **predictive analytics** on customer data. With customer data, you can have a deeper understanding of what attributes and characteristics of customers are highly correlated with the outcomes of your interest. For example, if you'd like to improve the response and engagement rates, you can analyze the data to identify those characteristics of customers that result in higher responses and engagement rates. Then, you can build predictive models that predict how likely it is that your customers are going to respond to your marketing messages.

Another example of the usage of predictive analytics can be for marketing channel optimization. With the insights gained from customer analytics, you can build predictive models to optimize marketing channels. The customers are going to respond differently to different marketing channels. For instance, younger cohorts, who use smartphones more heavily than the rest of the population, are more likely to respond to marketing via smartphones. On the other hand, more senior cohorts are more likely to respond better to marketing on more traditional media, such as TV or newspaper advertisements. With customer analytics, you can identify correlations between certain attributes of customers and the performances of different marketing channels.

As we have discussed so far, the applications of customer analytics are broad and can be used at any point of the marketing process. In the following programming exercises, we are going to discuss how we can use customer analytics to monitor and track different marketing strategies and see some of the ways to segment and analyze the customer base to gain insights. Then, in the following chapters, we are going to explore other use cases of customer analytics, such as optimizing engagement and retention rates, and customer segmentation.

Conducting customer analytics with Python

In this section, we are going to discuss how to conduct customer analytics using Python. We will be mainly using the `pandas` and `matplotlib` packages to analyze and visualize the customer behavior observed in the dataset. For those readers who would like to use R instead of Python for this exercise, you can skip to the next section. We will start this section by analyzing and understanding the behaviors of engaged customers and then discuss a simple way to segment the customer base by certain criteria.

For this exercise, we will be using one of the publicly available datasets from IBM, which can be found at this link: `https://www.ibm.com/communities/analytics/watson-analytics-blog/marketing-customer-value-analysis/`. You can follow this link and download the data that is available in CSV format, named `WA_Fn UseC_ Marketing Customer Value Analysis.csv`. Once you have downloaded this data, you can load it into your Jupyter Notebook by running the following command:

```
import pandas as pd

df = pd.read_csv('../data/WA_Fn-UseC_-Marketing-Customer-Value-
Analysis.csv')
```

Similar to `Chapter 6`, *Recommending the Right Products*, we are using the `read_csv` function in the `pandas` package to load the data in CSV format. Once you have loaded this data into a `pandas` `DataFrame`, it should look as in the following:

```
df = pd.read_csv('../data/WA_Fn-UseC_-Marketing-Customer-Value-Analysis.csv')
```

```
df.shape
```

```
(9134, 24)
```

```
df.head()
```

	Customer	State	Customer Lifetime Value	Response	Coverage	Education	Effective To Date	EmploymentStatus	Gender	Income	...	Months Since Policy Inception	Number of Open Complaints	Number of Policies
0	BU79786	Washington	2763.519279	No	Basic	Bachelor	2/24/11	Employed	F	56274	...	5	0	1
1	QZ44356	Arizona	6979.535903	No	Extended	Bachelor	1/31/11	Unemployed	F	0	...	42	0	8
2	AI49188	Nevada	12887.431650	No	Premium	Bachelor	2/19/11	Employed	F	48767	...	38	0	2
3	WW63253	California	7645.861827	No	Basic	Bachelor	1/20/11	Unemployed	M	0	...	65	0	7
4	HB64268	Washington	2813.692575	No	Basic	Bachelor	2/3/11	Employed	M	43836	...	44	0	1

5 rows × 24 columns

As you can see from this data, there is a column named `Response`, which contains information about whether a customer responded to the marketing efforts. Also, the `Renew Offer Type` and `Sales Channel` columns represent the type of the renewal offer presented to the customer and which sales channel was used to contact the customer. There are numerous other columns that represent the socio-economic backgrounds of the customers and types of insurance coverage that the customers currently have. We will be utilizing this information to analyze and understand the customer behavior better, especially in regards to their responses and engagement with the marketing and sales efforts.

Analytics on engaged customers

Now that we have loaded the data into our Python environment, we are going to analyze it to understand how different customers behave and react to different marketing strategies. We are going to follow these steps:

1. Overall engagement rate
2. Engagement rates by offer type
3. Engagement rates by offer type and vehicle class
4. Engagement rates by sales channel
5. Engagement rates by sales channel and vehicle size

Overall engagement rate

The first thing we are going to need to understand is the overall marketing response or engagement rate. We can use the following code to get the total number of customers who have responded:

```
df.groupby('Response').count()['Customer']
```

As you have seen from the data, the `Response` column contains information about whether a customer responded to the marketing call or not (`Yes` for those who have responded and `No` for those who have not). We are simply grouping by this column by using the `groupby` function in a `pandas` DataFrame and counting the number of customers in each category with the `count` function in the `pandas` package.

The result looks as in the following:

```
df.groupby('Response').count()['Customer']

Response
No      7826
Yes     1308
Name: Customer, dtype: int64
```

In order to visualize this in a plot, you can use the following code:

```
ax = df.groupby('Response').count()['Customer'].plot(
    kind='bar',
    color='skyblue',
    grid=True,
    figsize=(10, 7),
    title='Marketing Engagment'
)

ax.set_xlabel('Engaged')
ax.set_ylabel('Count')

plt.show()
```

The plot looks as follows:

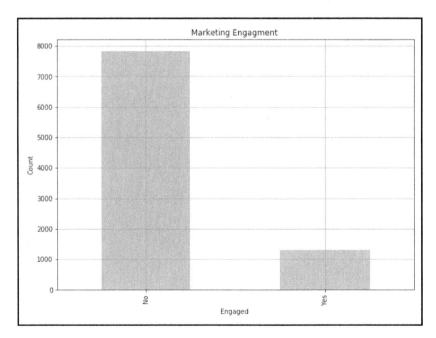

As you can see from these results, the majority of the customers did not respond to the marketing calls. Let's take a look at these numbers in percentages, using the following code:

```
df.groupby('Response').count()['Customer']/df.shape[0]
```

When you run this code, the result looks as follows:

```
df.groupby('Response').count()['Customer']/df.shape[0]

Response
No     0.856799
Yes    0.143201
Name: Customer, dtype: float64
```

From these results, we can see that only about 14% of the customers responded to the marketing calls. Let's dive deeper into the customers who responded and get a better understanding of what worked best for them.

Engagement rates by offer type

Different types of offers will work differently for the customers. In this section, we are going to look into what types of offers worked best for the engaged customers. Take a look at the following code:

```
by_offer_type_df = df.loc[
    df['Response'] == 'Yes'
].groupby([
    'Renew Offer Type'
]).count()['Customer'] / df.groupby('Renew Offer Type').count()['Customer']
```

As you can see from this code, we are grouping by the `Renew Offer Type` column, where we have four different types of offers. We count the number of engaged customers for each type of these renewal offers first by filtering for those with `Yes` values in the `Response` column. Then, we are dividing these numbers by the total number of customers in each renewal offer type to get the engagement rates per renewal offer type. The result looks as follows:

```
by_offer_type_df = df.loc[
    df['Response'] == 'Yes'
].groupby([
    'Renew Offer Type'
]).count()['Customer']/df.groupby('Renew Offer Type').count()['Customer']

by_offer_type_df

Renew Offer Type
Offer1    0.158316
Offer2    0.233766
Offer3    0.020950
Offer4         NaN
Name: Customer, dtype: float64
```

We can visualize these results in a bar plot, using the following code:

```
ax = (by_offer_type_df*100.0).plot(
    kind='bar',
    figsize=(7, 7),
    color='skyblue',
    grid=True
)

ax.set_ylabel('Engagement Rate (%)')

plt.show()
```

The bar plot looks as follows:

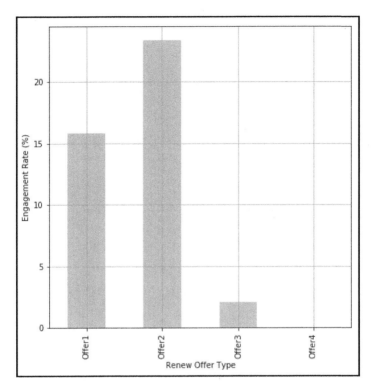

As you can easily notice from this plot, Offer2 had the highest engagement rate among the customers. When conducting customer analytics, as discussed earlier, we often want to know the demographics and attributes of customers for each event, so that we can understand what works best for which type of customers. This can lead to further improvements in the next marketing campaign by better targeting those subgroups of customers. Let's take a step further into this data.

Engagement rates by offer type and vehicle class

In the previous section, we have learned that Renewal Offer Type 2 worked best for the customers. The marketers can benefit from this information itself, as this finding provides a useful insight into which type of offer worked best and had the highest response rate from customers. However, we can gain more insights on how different customers with different backgrounds or characteristics react differently to each offer types. In this section, we will show an example of what you can do as a marketer to understand how customers with different attributes respond differently to different marketing messages.

Let's see whether there is any noticeable difference in the response rates for each offer type for customers with different vehicle classes. We are going to look at the engagement rates by each offer type and `Vehicle Class` using the following code:

```
by_offer_type_df = df.loc[
    df['Response'] == 'Yes'
].groupby([
    'Renew Offer Type', 'Vehicle Class'
]).count()['Customer']/df.groupby('Renew Offer Type').count()['Customer']
```

As you can see from this code, we are grouping the data by two columns, `Renew Offer Type` and `Vehicle Class`, and computing the engagement rates for each group.

The result looks as follows:

```
by_offer_type_df = df.loc[
    df['Response'] == 'Yes'
].groupby([
    'Renew Offer Type', 'Vehicle Class'
]).count()['Customer']/df.groupby('Renew Offer Type').count()['Customer']

by_offer_type_df

Renew Offer Type   Vehicle Class
Offer1             Four-Door Car    0.070362
                   Luxury Car       0.001599
                   Luxury SUV       0.004797
                   SUV              0.044776
                   Sports Car       0.011194
                   Two-Door Car     0.025586
Offer2             Four-Door Car    0.114833
                   Luxury Car       0.002051
                   Luxury SUV       0.004101
                   SUV              0.041012
                   Sports Car       0.016405
                   Two-Door Car     0.055366
Offer3             Four-Door Car    0.016760
                   Two-Door Car     0.004190
Name: Customer, dtype: float64
```

To make this more readable, we can transform this data by using the following code:

```
by_offer_type_df = by_offer_type_df.unstack().fillna(0)
```

As you can see from this code, we are using the unstack function in a pandas DataFrame to pivot the data and extract and transform the inner-level group to columns. It will be easier to look at the result. The result looks as in the following:

```
by_offer_type_df = by_offer_type_df.unstack().fillna(0)
by_offer_type_df
```

Vehicle Class	Four-Door Car	Luxury Car	Luxury SUV	SUV	Sports Car	Two-Door Car
Renew Offer Type						
Offer1	0.070362	0.001599	0.004797	0.044776	0.011194	0.025586
Offer2	0.114833	0.002051	0.004101	0.041012	0.016405	0.055366
Offer3	0.016760	0.000000	0.000000	0.000000	0.000000	0.004190

As you can see here, Vehicle Class now becomes the columns after applying the unstack function. We can visualize this data as a bar plot, using the following code:

```
ax = (by_offer_type_df*100.0).plot(
    kind='bar',
    figsize=(10, 7),
    grid=True
)

ax.set_ylabel('Engagement Rate (%)')

plt.show()
```

The plot looks as follows:

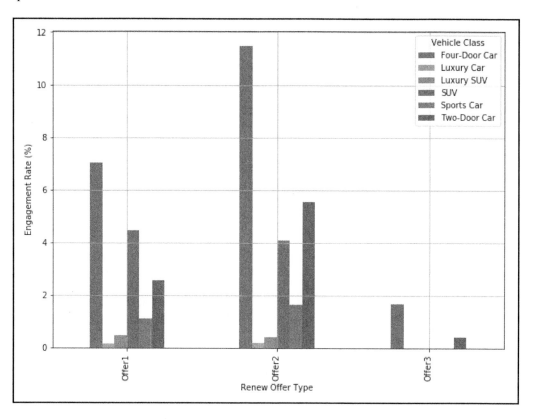

Let's take a closer look at this chart. We have seen that `Offer2` had the highest response rate among the customers in the previous section. Here, we can see how customers with different vehicle classes engage differently with other types of renewal offers. For example, customers with `Four-Door Car` respond the most frequently for all offer types. However, customers with `SUV` respond with a higher chance to `Offer1` than to `Offer2`. As you can see from these results, we can gain more insights by breaking down the customer demographics further. If we see any significant difference in the response rates among different customer segments, we can fine-tune who to target for different sets of offers. In our example, if we believe customers with `SUV` respond to `Offer1` with a significantly higher degree of engagement than to `Offer2`, then we can target `SUV` customers with `Offer1`. On the other hand, if we believe customers with `Two-Door Car` respond to `Offer2` with a significantly higher degree of engagement than to other offer types, then we can target `Two-Door Car` owners with `Offer2`.

Engagement rates by sales channel

Let's take a look at another example. We will analyze how engagement rates differ by different sales channels. Take a look at the following code:

```
by_sales_channel_df = df.loc[
    df['Response'] == 'Yes'
].groupby([
    'Sales Channel'
]).count()['Customer']/df.groupby('Sales Channel').count()['Customer']
```

The result looks as follows:

```
by_sales_channel_df = df.loc[
    df['Response'] == 'Yes'
].groupby([
    'Sales Channel'
]).count()['Customer']/df.groupby('Sales Channel').count()['Customer']

by_sales_channel_df

Sales Channel
Agent          0.191544
Branch         0.114531
Call Center    0.108782
Web            0.117736
Name: Customer, dtype: float64
```

It will be easier to look at this result with a visualization. You can use the following code to visualize this data:

```
ax = (by_sales_channel_df*100.0).plot(
    kind='bar',
    figsize=(7, 7),
    color='skyblue',
    grid=True
)

ax.set_ylabel('Engagement Rate (%)')

plt.show()
```

The plot looks as follows:

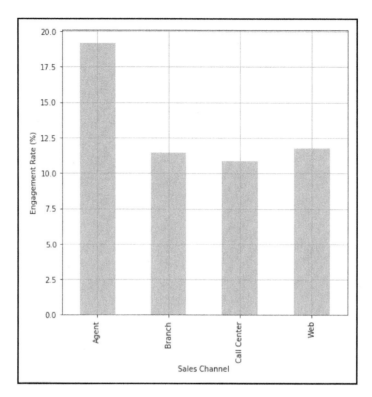

As you can see from this plot, Agent works the best in terms of getting responses from the customers. Then, sales through Web works the second best. As before, let's break down this result deeper and analyze to see whether the behavior change among customers with different characteristics.

Engagement rates by sales channel and vehicle size

In this section, we will take a look at whether customers with various vehicle sizes respond differently to different sales channels. Take a look at the following code to compute the engagement rates per sales channel and vehicle size:

```
by_sales_channel_df = df.loc[
    df['Response'] == 'Yes'
].groupby([
    'Sales Channel', 'Vehicle Size'
]).count()['Customer']/df.groupby('Sales Channel').count()['Customer']
```

The result looks as in the following:

```
by_sales_channel_df = df.loc[
    df['Response'] == 'Yes'
].groupby([
    'Sales Channel', 'Vehicle Size'
]).count()['Customer']/df.groupby('Sales Channel').count()['Customer']

by_sales_channel_df

Sales Channel  Vehicle Size
Agent          Large           0.020708
               Medsize         0.144953
               Small           0.025884
Branch         Large           0.021036
               Medsize         0.074795
               Small           0.018699
Call Center    Large           0.013598
               Medsize         0.067989
               Small           0.027195
Web            Large           0.013585
               Medsize         0.095094
               Small           0.009057
Name: Customer, dtype: float64
```

As before, we can `unstack` this data into a more visible format, using the following code:

```
by_sales_channel_df = by_sales_channel_df.unstack().fillna(0)
```

The result looks as follows:

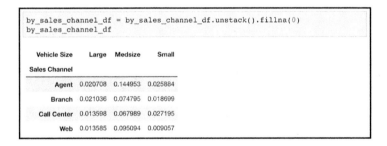

We can visualize these results into a bar chart, using the following code:

```
ax = (by_sales_channel_df*100.0).plot(
    kind='bar',
    figsize=(10, 7),
    grid=True
)

ax.set_ylabel('Engagement Rate (%)')

plt.show()
```

The plot now looks as follows:

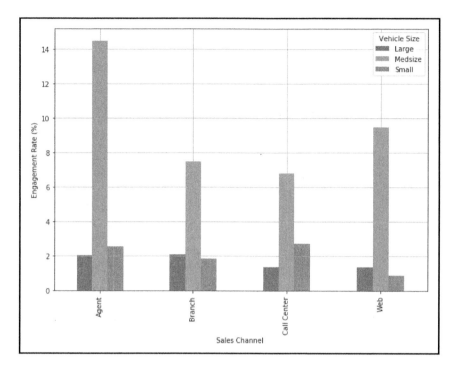

As you can see from this plot, customers with `Medsize` vehicles respond the best to all sales channels. The engagement rates across different sales channels differ slightly between `Large` and `Small` vehicle owners. For example, `Small` vehicle owners respond better through `Agent` and `Call Center` channels, while on the other hand, `Large` vehicle owners respond better through the `Branch` and `Web` channels. As discussed previously, we can utilize this insight in the next marketing efforts. For example, as `Small` car owners respond with a higher chance through `Agent` and `Call Center`, we can utilize those two channels more heavily for `Small` car owners.

Segmenting customer base

We are going to briefly discuss how we can segment the customer base in this section. We are going to expand this concept and discuss further how we can utilize machine learning for customer segmentation in `Chapter 10`, *Data-Driven Customer Segmentation*, but this section will give you some basic idea on what customer segmentation is and what it looks like.

In this section, we will be segmenting our customer base by `Customer Lifetime Value` and `Months Since Policy Inception`. Feel free to try different features for segmenting the customer base. Take a look at the following distribution of the `Customer Lifetime Value` column:

```
df['Customer Lifetime Value'].describe()

count     9134.000000
mean      8004.940475
std       6870.967608
min       1898.007675
25%       3994.251794
50%       5780.182197
75%       8962.167041
max      83325.381190
Name: Customer Lifetime Value, dtype: float64
```

Based on this information, we are going to define those customers with a `Customer Lifetime Value` higher than the median as high-CLV customers and those with a CLV below the median as low-CLV customers. You can use the following code for encoding:

```
df['CLV Segment'] = df['Customer Lifetime Value'].apply(
    lambda x: 'High' if x > df['Customer Lifetime Value'].median() else
'Low'
)
```

We are going to go through the same process for the `Months Since Policy Inception` field. Take a look at the following distribution for `Months Since Policy Inception`:

```
df['Months Since Policy Inception'].describe()

count    9134.000000
mean       48.064594
std        27.905991
min         0.000000
25%        24.000000
50%        48.000000
75%        71.000000
max        99.000000
Name: Months Since Policy Inception, dtype: float64
```

Similarly, we are going to define those customers with `Months Since Policy Inception` higher than the median as high `Policy Age Segment` customers and those below the median as low `Policy Age Segment` customers. You can use the following code for encoding:

```
df['Policy Age Segment'] = df['Months Since Policy Inception'].apply(
    lambda x: 'High' if x > df['Months Since Policy Inception'].median()
else 'Low'
)
```

We can visualize these segments using the following code:

```
ax = df.loc[
    (df['CLV Segment'] == 'High') & (df['Policy Age Segment'] == 'High')
].plot.scatter(
    x='Months Since Policy Inception',
    y='Customer Lifetime Value',
    logy=True,
    color='red'
)

df.loc[
    (df['CLV Segment'] == 'Low') & (df['Policy Age Segment'] == 'High')
].plot.scatter(
    ax=ax,
    x='Months Since Policy Inception',
    y='Customer Lifetime Value',
    logy=True,
    color='blue'
)

df.loc[
    (df['CLV Segment'] == 'High') & (df['Policy Age Segment'] == 'Low')
].plot.scatter(
    ax=ax,
    x='Months Since Policy Inception',
    y='Customer Lifetime Value',
    logy=True,
    color='orange'
)

df.loc[
    (df['CLV Segment'] == 'Low') & (df['Policy Age Segment'] == 'Low')
].plot.scatter(
    ax=ax,
    x='Months Since Policy Inception',
    y='Customer Lifetime Value',
    logy=True,
```

```
        color='green',
        grid=True,
        figsize=(10, 7)
)

ax.set_ylabel('CLV (in log scale)')
ax.set_xlabel('Months Since Policy Inception')

ax.set_title('Segments by CLV and Policy Age')

plt.show()
```

Let's take a closer look at this code. In the first code block, we are creating a scatter plot using the `plot.scatter` function in the `pandas` package for those customers in the `High CLV` and `High Policy Age` segments. By using the `logy=True` flag, we can easily transform the scale to log scale. Log scale is often used for monetary values, as they often have high skewness in their values. We repeat this process four times for the four segments we have created previously.

The resulting scatter plot looks as follows:

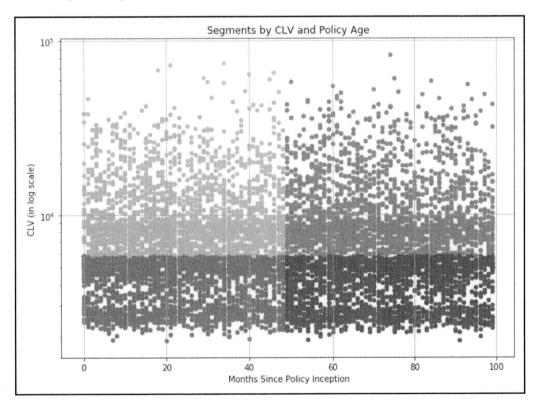

As you can see from this scatter plot, the data points in red represent those customers in the `High CLV` and `High Policy Age` segment. Those in orange represent the `High CLV` and `Low Policy Age` group, those in blue represent the `Low CLV` and `High Policy Age` group, and lastly, those in green represent the `Low CLV` and `Low Policy Age` group.

Now that we have created these four segments, let's see whether there is any noticeable difference in the engagement rates among these four segments. Take a look at the following code:

```
engagment_rates_by_segment_df = df.loc[
    df['Response'] == 'Yes'
].groupby(
    ['CLV Segment', 'Policy Age Segment']
).count()['Customer']/df.groupby(
    ['CLV Segment', 'Policy Age Segment']
).count()['Customer']
```

As you can see from this code, we are grouping by the two newly-created columns, `CLV Segment` and `Policy Age Segment`, and computing the engagement rates for these four segments. The result looks as follows:

```
engagment_rates_by_segment_df = df.loc[
    df['Response'] == 'Yes'
].groupby(
    ['CLV Segment', 'Policy Age Segment']
).count()['Customer']/df.groupby(
    ['CLV Segment', 'Policy Age Segment']
).count()['Customer']

engagment_rates_by_segment_df

CLV Segment    Policy Age Segment
High           High                  0.138728
               Low                   0.132067
Low            High                  0.162450
               Low                   0.139957
Name: Customer, dtype: float64
```

It will be easier to look at the differences in a chart. You can use the following code to create a bar plot for this data:

```
ax = (engagment_rates_by_segment_df.unstack()*100.0).plot(
    kind='bar',
    figsize=(10, 7),
    grid=True
)

ax.set_ylabel('Engagement Rate (%)')
```

```
ax.set_title('Engagement Rates by Customer Segments')

plt.show()
```

Now the plot looks as follows:

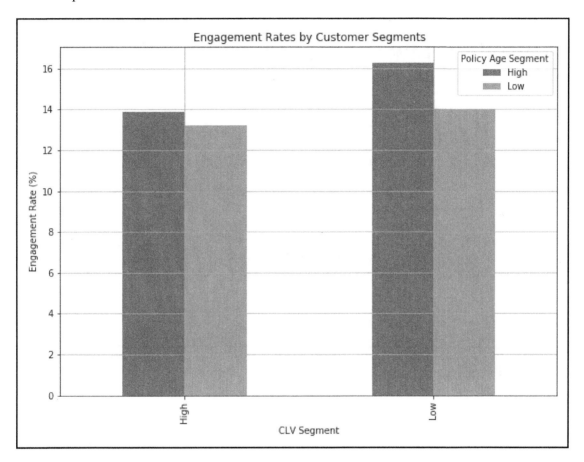

As you can notice from this plot, High Policy Age Segment has higher engagement than the Low Policy Age Segment. This suggests that those customers who have been insured by this company longer respond better. It is also noticeable that the High Policy Age and Low CLV segment has the highest engagement rate among the four segments. By creating different customer segments based on customer attributes, we can better understand how different groups of customers behave differently. We are going to further expand and experiment the concept of customer segmentation in more depth in Chapter 9, *Customer Lifetime Value*.

The full code for this Python exercise can be found in this link: `https://github.com/yoonhwang/hands-on-data-science-for-marketing/blob/master/ch.7/python/CustomerBehaviors.ipynb`

Conducting customer analytics with R

In this section, we are going to discuss how to conduct customer analytics using R. We will be mainly using the `dplyr` and `ggplot2` libraries to analyze and visualize the customer behavior observed in the dataset. For those readers who would like to use Python instead of R for this exercise, you can refer to the previous section. We will start this section by analyzing and understanding the behaviors of engaged customers and then discuss a simple way to segment the customer base by certain criteria.

For this exercise, we will be using one of the publicly available datasets from **IBM**, which can be found at this link: `https://www.ibm.com/communities/analytics/watson-analytics-blog/marketing-customer-value-analysis/`. You can follow this link and download the data that is available in CSV format named `WA_Fn UseC_ Marketing Customer Value Analysis.csv`. Once you have downloaded this data, you can load it into your RStudio by running the following command:

```
library(dplyr)
library(ggplot2)

#### 1. Load Data ####
df <- read.csv(
  file="~/Documents/data-science-for-marketing/ch.7/data/WA_Fn-UseC_-
Marketing-Customer-Value-Analysis.csv",
  header=TRUE
)
```

Similar to the previous chapter, we are using the `read.csv` function in R to load the data in CSV format. Once you have loaded this data into a `DataFrame`, it should look as in the following:

	Customer	State	Customer.Lifetime.Value	Response	Coverage	Education	Effective.To.Date	EmploymentStatus	Gender	Income
1	BU79786	Washington	2763.519	No	Basic	Bachelor	2/24/11	Employed	F	56274
2	QZ44356	Arizona	6979.536	No	Extended	Bachelor	1/31/11	Unemployed	F	0
3	AI49188	Nevada	12887.432	No	Premium	Bachelor	2/19/11	Employed	F	48767
4	WW63253	California	7645.862	No	Basic	Bachelor	1/20/11	Unemployed	M	0
5	HB64268	Washington	2813.693	No	Basic	Bachelor	2/3/11	Employed	M	43836
6	OC83172	Oregon	8256.298	Yes	Basic	Bachelor	1/25/11	Employed	F	62902
7	XZ87318	Oregon	5380.899	Yes	Basic	College	2/24/11	Employed	F	55350
8	CF85061	Arizona	7216.100	No	Premium	Master	1/18/11	Unemployed	M	0
9	DY87989	Oregon	24127.504	Yes	Basic	Bachelor	1/26/11	Medical Leave	M	14072
10	BQ94931	Oregon	7388.178	No	Extended	College	2/17/11	Employed	F	28812
11	SX51350	California	4738.992	No	Basic	College	2/21/11	Unemployed	M	0
12	VQ65197	California	8197.197	No	Basic	College	1/6/11	Unemployed	F	0
13	DP39365	California	8798.797	No	Premium	Master	2/6/11	Employed	M	77026
14	SJ95423	Arizona	8819.019	Yes	Basic	High School or Below	1/10/11	Employed	M	99845
15	IL66569	California	5384.432	No	Basic	College	1/18/11	Employed	M	83689

As you can see from this data, there is a column named `Response`, which contains information about whether a customer responded to the marketing efforts. Also, the `Renew.Offer.Type` and `Sales.Channel` columns represent the type of renewal offer presented to the customer and which sales channel was used to contact the customer. There are numerous other columns that represent the socio-economic backgrounds of the customers and types of insurance coverages that the customers currently have. We will be utilizing this information to analyze and understand the customer behavior better, especially in regards to their responses and engagements with the marketing and sales efforts.

Before we dive into the data, we will encode the `Response` column into numeric values—0 for `No` and 1 for `Yes`. This will make our computations easier for future analyses. You can use the following code for encoding:

```
# Encode engaged customers as 0s and 1s
df$Engaged <- as.integer(df$Response) - 1
```

Analytics on engaged customers

Now that we have loaded the data into our environment, we are going to analyze it to understand how different customers behave and react to different marketing strategies. We are going to follow these steps:

1. Overall engagement rate
2. Engagement rates by offer type
3. Engagement rates by offer type and vehicle class
4. Engagement rates by sales channel
5. Engagement rates by sales channel and vehicle size

Overall engagement rate

The first thing we are going to need to understand is the overall marketing response or engagement rate. We can use the following code to get the total number of customers who have responded:

```
## - Overall Engagement Rates ##
engagementRate <- df %>% group_by(Response) %>%
  summarise(Count=n()) %>%
  mutate(EngagementRate=Count/nrow(df)*100.0)
```

As you have seen from the data, the `Response` column contains information about whether a customer responded to the marketing call or not (`Yes` for those who have responded and `No` for those who have not). We are simply grouping by this column by using the `group_by` function in the `dplyr` library and counting the number of customers in each category with the `n()` function. Then, using the `mutate` function, we compute the engagement rate by dividing `Count` by the total number of records in the `DataFrame`.

The result looks as in the following:

	Response	Count	EngagementRate
1	No	7826	85.67988
2	Yes	1308	14.32012

In order to visualize this in a plot, you can use the following code:

```
ggplot(engagementRate, aes(x=Response, y=EngagementRate)) +
  geom_bar(width=0.5, stat="identity") +
  ggtitle('Engagement Rate') +
```

```
    xlab("Engaged") +
    ylab("Percentage (%)") +
    theme(plot.title = element_text(hjust = 0.5))
```

The plot looks as follows:

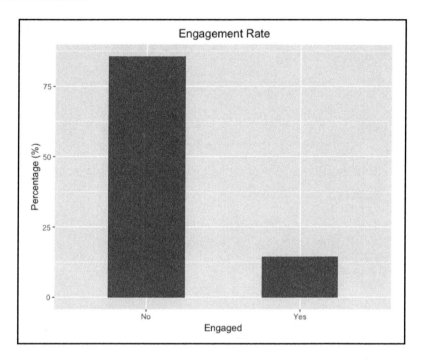

As you can see from these results, the majority of the customers did not respond to the marketing calls. As shown from the data, only about 14% of the customers responded to the marketing calls. We are going to now dive deeper into the customers who responded and get a better understanding of what worked best for them.

Engagement rates by offer type

Different types of offers will work differently for different customers. In this section, we are going to look into what types of offers worked best for the engaged customers. Take a look at the following code:

```
## - Engagement Rates by Offer Type ##
engagementRateByOfferType <- df %>%
  group_by(Renew.Offer.Type) %>%
  summarise(Count=n(), NumEngaged=sum(Engaged)) %>%
  mutate(EngagementRate=NumEngaged/Count*100.0)
```

As you can see from this code, we are grouping by the `Renew.Offer.Type` column, where we have four different types of offers. Then, in the `summarise` function, we count the total number of records using the `n()` function, and we count the number of engaged customers by summing over the encoded column, `Engaged`. Lastly, in the `mutate` function, we compute `EngagementRate` by dividing `NumEngaged` by `Count` and multiplying it by `100.0`.

The result looks as in the following:

	Renew.Offer.Type	Count	NumEngaged	EngagementRate
1	Offer1	3752	594	15.831557
2	Offer2	2926	684	23.376623
3	Offer3	1432	30	2.094972
4	Offer4	1024	0	0.000000

We can visualize these results in a bar plot, using the following code:

```
ggplot(engagementRateByOfferType, aes(x=Renew.Offer.Type,
y=EngagementRate)) +
  geom_bar(width=0.5, stat="identity") +
  ggtitle('Engagement Rates by Offer Type') +
  xlab("Offer Type") +
  ylab("Engagement Rate (%)") +
  theme(plot.title = element_text(hjust = 0.5))
```

The bar plot now looks as follows:

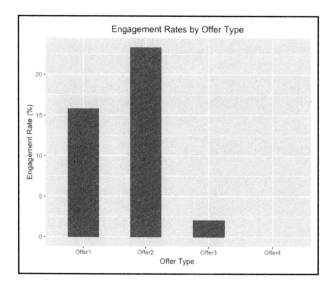

As you can easily notice from this plot, `Offer 2` had the highest engagement rate among the customers. When conducting customer analytics, as discussed earlier, we often want to know the demographics and attributes of customers for each event, so that we can understand what works best for which type of customers. This can lead to further improvements in the next marketing campaign by better targeting those subgroups of customers. Let's take a step further into this data.

Engagement rates by offer type and vehicle class

In the previous section, we have learned that `Renewal Offer Type 2` worked best for the customers. The marketers can benefit from this information itself, as this finding provides a useful insight into which type of offer worked best and had the highest response rate from customers. However, we can gain more insights on how different customers with different backgrounds or characteristics react differently to each offer types. In this section, we will show an example of what you can do as a marketer to understand how customers with different attributes respond differently to different marketing messages.

Let's see whether there is any noticeable difference in the response rates for each offer type for customers with different vehicle classes. We are going to look at the engagement rates by each offer type and vehicle class, using the following code:

```
## - Offer Type & Vehicle Class ##
engagementRateByOfferTypeVehicleClass <- df %>%
  group_by(Renew.Offer.Type, Vehicle.Class) %>%
  summarise(NumEngaged=sum(Engaged)) %>%
  left_join(engagementRateByOfferType[,c("Renew.Offer.Type", "Count")],
by="Renew.Offer.Type") %>%
  mutate(EngagementRate=NumEngaged/Count*100.0)
```

As you can see from this code, we are grouping the data by two columns, `Renew.Offer.Type` and `Vehicle.Class`, and counting the number of engaged customers for each group. Then, we join this data with the `engagementRateByOfferType` variable by the `Renew.Offer.Type` column to get the total number of engaged customers for each offer type. Lastly, we compute the engagement rate in the `mutate` function.

The result looks as follows:

	Renew.Offer.Type	Vehicle.Class	NumEngaged	Count	EngagementRate
1	Offer1	Four–Door Car	264	3752	7.0362473
2	Offer1	Luxury Car	6	3752	0.1599147
3	Offer1	Luxury SUV	18	3752	0.4797441
4	Offer1	Sports Car	42	3752	1.1194030
5	Offer1	SUV	168	3752	4.4776119
6	Offer1	Two–Door Car	96	3752	2.5586354
7	Offer2	Four–Door Car	336	2926	11.4832536
8	Offer2	Luxury Car	6	2926	0.2050581
9	Offer2	Luxury SUV	12	2926	0.4101162
10	Offer2	Sports Car	48	2926	1.6404648
11	Offer2	SUV	120	2926	4.1011620
12	Offer2	Two–Door Car	162	2926	5.5365687
13	Offer3	Four–Door Car	24	1432	1.6759777
14	Offer3	Luxury Car	0	1432	0.0000000
15	Offer3	Luxury SUV	0	1432	0.0000000
16	Offer3	Sports Car	0	1432	0.0000000
17	Offer3	SUV	0	1432	0.0000000
18	Offer3	Two–Door Car	6	1432	0.4189944
19	Offer4	Four–Door Car	0	1024	0.0000000
20	Offer4	Luxury Car	0	1024	0.0000000
21	Offer4	Luxury SUV	0	1024	0.0000000
22	Offer4	Sports Car	0	1024	0.0000000
23	Offer4	SUV	0	1024	0.0000000
24	Offer4	Two–Door Car	0	1024	0.0000000

To make this more readable, we can visualize this data using bar plots. Take a look at the following code:

```
ggplot(engagementRateByOfferTypeVehicleClass, aes(x=Renew.Offer.Type,
y=EngagementRate, fill=Vehicle.Class)) +
  geom_bar(width=0.5, stat="identity", position = "dodge") +
  ggtitle('Engagement Rates by Offer Type & Vehicle Class') +
  xlab("Offer Type") +
  ylab("Engagement Rate (%)") +
  theme(plot.title = element_text(hjust = 0.5))
```

Using this code, we can build a bar plot that looks as follows:

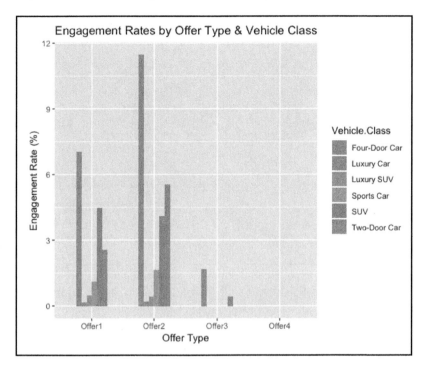

Let's take a closer look at this chart. We have seen that `Offer2` had the highest response rate among the customers in the previous section. Here, we can see how customers with different vehicle classes engage differently with other types of renewal offers. For example, customers with `Four-Door Car` respond the most frequently for all offer types. However, customers with `SUV` respond with a higher chance to `Offer1` than to `Offer2`. As you can see from these results, we can gain more insights by breaking down the customer demographics further. If we see any significant difference in the response rates among different customer segments, we can fine-tune who to target for different sets of offers. In our example, if we believe customers with `SUV` respond to `Offer1` with a significantly higher chance than to `Offer2`, then we can target `SUV` customers with `Offer1`. On the other hand, if we believe customers with `Two-Door Car` respond to `Offer2` with a significantly higher chance than to other offer types, then we can target `Two-Door Car` owners with `Offer2`.

Engagement rates by sales channel

Let's take a look at another example. We will analyze how engagement rates differ by different sales channels. Take a look at the following code:

```
## - Engagement Rates by Sales Channel ##
engagementRateBySalesChannel <- df %>%
  group_by(Sales.Channel) %>%
  summarise(Count=n(), NumEngaged=sum(Engaged)) %>%
  mutate(EngagementRate=NumEngaged/Count*100.0)
```

The result looks as follows:

	Sales.Channel	Count	NumEngaged	EngagementRate
1	Agent	3477	666	19.15444
2	Branch	2567	294	11.45306
3	Call Center	1765	192	10.87819
4	Web	1325	156	11.77358

It will be easier to understand this result with a visualization. You can use the following code to visualize this data:

```
ggplot(engagementRateBySalesChannel, aes(x=Sales.Channel,
y=EngagementRate)) +
  geom_bar(width=0.5, stat="identity") +
  ggtitle('Engagement Rates by Sales Channel') +
  xlab("Sales Channel") +
  ylab("Engagement Rate (%)") +
  theme(plot.title = element_text(hjust = 0.5))
```

The plot looks as follows:

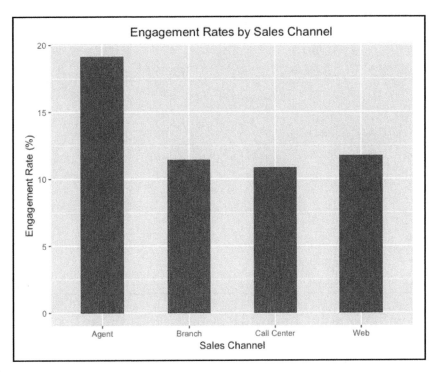

As you can see from this plot, Agent works best in terms of getting responses from the customers. Then, sales through Web works the second best. As before, let's break down this result deeper and analyze it to see whether the behavior changes among customers with different characteristics.

Engagement rates by sales channel and vehicle size

In this section, we will take a look at whether customers with various vehicle sizes respond differently to different sales channels. Take a look at the following code to compute the engagement rates per sales channel and vehicle size:

```
## - Sales Channel & Vehicle Size ##
engagementRateBySalesChannelVehicleSize <- df %>%
  group_by(Sales.Channel, Vehicle.Size) %>%
  summarise(NumEngaged=sum(Engaged)) %>%
  left_join(engagementRateBySalesChannel[,c("Sales.Channel", "Count")],
by="Sales.Channel") %>%
  mutate(EngagementRate=NumEngaged/Count*100.0)
```

The result looks as in the following:

	Sales.Channel	Vehicle.Size	NumEngaged	Count	EngagementRate
1	Agent	Large	72	3477	2.0707506
2	Agent	Medsize	504	3477	14.4952545
3	Agent	Small	90	3477	2.5884383
4	Branch	Large	54	2567	2.1036229
5	Branch	Medsize	192	2567	7.4795481
6	Branch	Small	48	2567	1.8698870
7	Call Center	Large	24	1765	1.3597734
8	Call Center	Medsize	120	1765	6.7988669
9	Call Center	Small	48	1765	2.7195467
10	Web	Large	18	1325	1.3584906
11	Web	Medsize	126	1325	9.5094340
12	Web	Small	12	1325	0.9056604

As before, we can visualize this data in a bar plot to make it easier to read. You can use the following code to visualize this data:

```
ggplot(engagementRateBySalesChannelVehicleSize, aes(x=Sales.Channel,
y=EngagementRate, fill=Vehicle.Size)) +
  geom_bar(width=0.5, stat="identity", position = "dodge") +
  ggtitle('Engagement Rates by Sales Channel & Vehicle Size') +
  xlab("Sales Channel") +
  ylab("Engagement Rate (%)") +
  theme(plot.title = element_text(hjust = 0.5))
```

The plot now looks as follows:

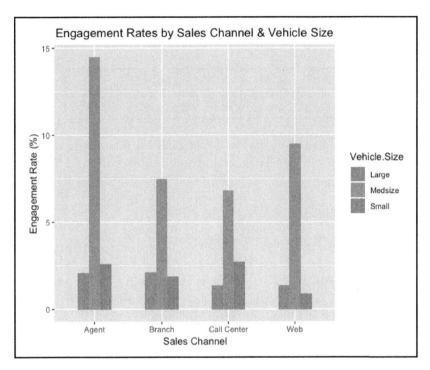

As you can see from this plot, customers with `Medsize` vehicles respond best to all sales channels. The engagement rates across different sales channels differ slightly between `Large` and `Small` vehicle owners. For example, `Small` vehicle owners respond better through `Agent` and `Call Center` channels, while on the other hand, `Large` vehicle owners respond better through the `Branch` and `Web` channels. As discussed previously, we can utilize this insight in the next marketing efforts. For example, as `Small` car owners respond with a higher degree of engagement through `Agent` and `Call Center`, we can utilize those two channels more heavily for `Small` car owners.

Segmenting customer base

We are going to briefly discuss how we can segment the customer base in this section. We are going to expand this concept and discuss further how we can utilize machine learning for customer segmentation in `Chapter 9`, *Customer Lifetime Value*, but this section will give you some basic ideas on what customer segmentation is and what it looks like.

In this section, we will be segmenting our customer base by `Customer.Lifetime.Value` and `Months.Since.Policy.Inception`. Feel free to try different features for segmenting the customer base. Let's first take a look at the following distribution of the `Customer.Lifetime.Value` column:

```
> summary(df$Customer.Lifetime.Value)
  Min. 1st Qu.  Median   Mean 3rd Qu.    Max.
  1898    3994    5780   8005    8962   83325
```

- Based on this information, we are going to define customers with a CLV higher than the median as high-CLV customers and those with a CLV below the median as low-CLV customers. You can use the following code for encoding:

```
clv_encode_fn <- function(x) {if(x > median(df$Customer.Lifetime.Value))
"High" else "Low"}
df$CLV.Segment <- sapply(df$Customer.Lifetime.Value, clv_encode_fn)
```

As you can see from this code, we have defined the `clv_encode_fn` function, which encodes those customers with a CLV higher than the median as `High` and those with a CLV lower than the median as `Low`. Then, using the `sapply` function, we encode the values in the `Customer.Lifetime.Value` column and store those encoded values as a new column named `CLV.Segment`.

We are going to go through the same process for the `Months.Since.Policy.Inception` field. Take a look at the following distribution for `Months.Since.Policy.Inception`:

```
> summary(df$Months.Since.Policy.Inception)
  Min. 1st Qu.  Median   Mean 3rd Qu.    Max.
  0.00   24.00   48.00  48.06   71.00   99.00
```

Similarly, we are going to define those customers with a `Months.Since.Policy.Inception` value higher than the median as high `Policy.Age.Segment` customers and those with a value below the median as low `Policy.Age.Segment` customers. You can use the following code for encoding:

```
policy_age_encode_fn <- function(x) {if(x >
median(df$Months.Since.Policy.Inception)) "High" else "Low"}
df$Policy.Age.Segment <- sapply(df$Months.Since.Policy.Inception,
policy_age_encode_fn)
```

We can visualize these segments, using the following code:

```
ggplot(
    df[which(df$CLV.Segment=="High" & df$Policy.Age.Segment=="High"),],
    aes(x=Months.Since.Policy.Inception, y=log(Customer.Lifetime.Value))
) +
    geom_point(color='red') +
    geom_point(
        data=df[which(df$CLV.Segment=="High" & df$Policy.Age.Segment=="Low"),],
        color='orange'
    ) +
    geom_point(
        data=df[which(df$CLV.Segment=="Low" & df$Policy.Age.Segment=="Low"),],
        color='green'
    ) +
    geom_point(
        data=df[which(df$CLV.Segment=="Low" & df$Policy.Age.Segment=="High"),],
        color='blue'
    ) +
    ggtitle('Segments by CLV and Policy Age') +
    xlab("Months Since Policy Inception") +
    ylab("CLV (in log scale)") +
    theme(plot.title = element_text(hjust = 0.5))
```

Let's take a closer look at this code. We plot the High CLV and High Policy Age segment first in red. Then, we repeat the same process to building scatter plots for the High CLV and Low Policy Age group in orange, the Low CLV and Low Policy Age group in green, and lastly, the Low CLV and High Policy Age group in blue. One thing to note here is how we define the y values in the aes function. As you can see from this code, y=log(Customer.Lifetime.Value), we are transforming the CLV values into log scale. Log scale is often used for monetary values, as they often have high skewness in their values.

The resulting scatter plot looks as follows:

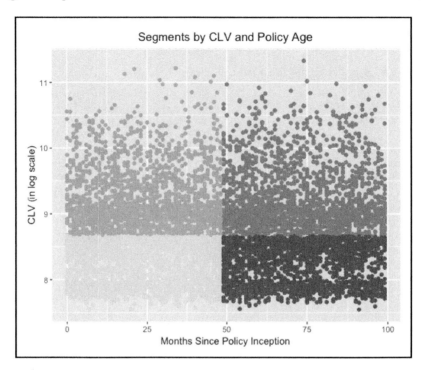

As you can see from this scatter plot, the data points in red represent those customers in the `High CLV` and `High Policy Age` segment. Those in orange represent the `High CLV` and `Low Policy Age` group, those in blue represent the `Low CLV` and `High Policy Age` group, and lastly, those in green represent the `Low CLV` and `Low Policy Age` group.

Now that we have created these four segments, let's see whether there is any noticeable difference in engagement rates among these four segments. Take a look at the following code:

```
engagementRateBySegment <- df %>%
  group_by(CLV.Segment, Policy.Age.Segment) %>%
  summarise(Count=n(), NumEngaged=sum(Engaged)) %>%
  mutate(EngagementRate=NumEngaged/Count*100.0)
```

As you can see from this code, we are grouping by the two newly-created columns, `CLV.Segment` and `Policy.Age.Segment`, and computing the engagement rates for these four segments. The result looks as follows:

	CLV.Segment	Policy.Age.Segment	Count	NumEngaged	EngagementRate
1	High	High	2249	312	13.87283
2	High	Low	2317	306	13.20673
3	Low	High	2253	366	16.24501
4	Low	Low	2315	324	13.99568

It will be easier to understand the differences in a chart. You can use the following code to create a bar plot for this data:

```
ggplot(engagementRateBySegment, aes(x=CLV.Segment, y=EngagementRate,
fill=Policy.Age.Segment)) +
  geom_bar(width=0.5, stat="identity", position = "dodge") +
  ggtitle('Engagement Rates by Customer Segments') +
  ylab("Engagement Rate (%)") +
  theme(plot.title = element_text(hjust = 0.5))
```

Now the plot looks as follows:

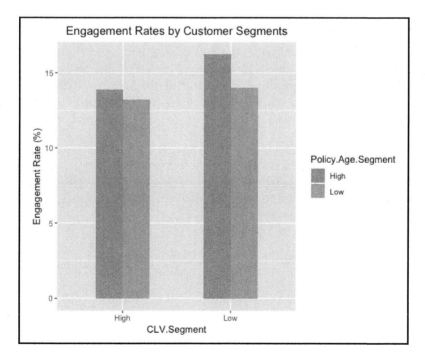

As you can notice from this plot, `High Policy.Age.Segment` has a higher engagement than `Low Policy.Age.Segment`. This suggests that those customers who have been insured by this company longer respond better. It is also noticeable that the `High Policy Age` and `Low CLV` segment has the highest engagement rate among the four segments. By creating different customer segments based on customer attributes, we can better understand how different groups of customers behave differently. We are going to further expand and experiment the concept of customer segmentation in more depth in `Chapter 9`, *Customer Lifetime Value.*

The full code for this R exercise can be found at the following link: `https://github.com/yoonhwang/hands-on-data-science-for-marketing/blob/master/ch.7/R/CustomerBehaviors.R`.

Summary

In this chapter, we have discussed customer analytics. We have learned about what customer analytics is and the importance and benefits of conducting customer analytics, as well as different use cases of customer analytics. We have discussed how the rising accessibility of customer data to businesses and the abundance of data available about customers is resulting in higher competition, and we emphasized the importance of having a good understanding of what customers like. Conducting customer analytics is an important step to gain insights on the behavior of customers, which helps in forming better marketing strategies, optimizing sales channels, and making other key business decisions. Using customer analytics, you can monitor and track KPIs on how customers react to different products and marketing strategies, effectively build segments of similar customers, and build predictive models to improve engagement and retention rates, as well as optimize marketing channels.

In the next chapter, we are going to learn how we can use predictive analytics to forecast the likelihood of marketing engagements. We will discuss some of the machine learning algorithms that are frequently used to build predictive models and experiment with their prediction performances on the dataset.

8
Predicting the Likelihood of Marketing Engagement

In this chapter, we are going to expand the knowledge we gained from the previous chapter and the customer analytics exercise we conducted in Chapter 7, *Exploratory Analysis for Customer Behavior*. For successful and more intelligent marketing strategies, we cannot stop at analyzing customer data. With the advanced technology in data science and machine learning, we can now make intelligent guesses and estimates on customers' future behaviors, such as what types of customers are more likely to engage with marketing efforts, the amount of purchases that customers are likely to make, or which customers are likely to churn. These predictions or intelligent guesses that are built based on historical customer data can help you improve your marketing performance and further tailor your marketing strategies for different target audiences. In this chapter, we are going to learn how we can utilize data science and machine learning to predict future outcomes and how this can help your future marketing efforts.

In this chapter, we will cover the following topics:

- Predictive analytics in marketing
- Evaluating classification models
- Predicting the likelihood of marketing engagement with Python
- Predicting the likelihood of marketing engagement with R

Predictive analytics in marketing

Predictive analytics is a process of analyzing and extracting information from historical data to identify patterns and make predictions about future outcomes. Numerous statistical and machine learning models are typically used to find the relationship between the attributes or features in the dataset and the target variable or behavior that you would like to predict. Predictive analytics can be utilized and applied in many different industries.

For example, it is often used in the financial industry for fraud detection, where machine learning models are trained to detect and prevent potential fraudulent transactions. The healthcare industry can also benefit from predictive analytics to help physicians in their decision-making processes. Furthermore, there are various parts of marketing that can also benefit from predictive analytics, such as customer acquisition, customer retention, and up-selling and cross-selling, to name a few.

In predictive analytics, broadly speaking, there are two types of problems:

- **Classification problems**: A classification problem is where there is a set of categories an observation can belong to. For example, predicting whether a customer is going to open a marketing email or not is a classification problem. There are only two possible outcomes—opening the marketing email or not opening the email.
- **Regression problems**: A regression problem, on the other hand, is where the outcome can take on any range of real numbers. For example, predicting customer lifetime value is a regression problem. One customer can have a lifetime value of $0 and another customer can have a lifetime value of $10,000. This type of problem, where the outcome can take continuous values, is called a regression problem.

In this chapter, we are going to focus on one of the common classification problems in the marketing industry—predicting the likelihood of customer engagement. In the following chapter, Chapter 9, *Customer Lifetime Value*, we are going to tackle one of the frequently appearing regression problems within the marketing industry.

Applications of predictive analytics in marketing

As briefly mentioned previously, there are numerous ways of applying and utilizing predictive analytics in marketing. In this section, we are going to discuss four popular use cases of predictive analytics in marketing:

- **Likelihood of engagement**: Predictive analytics can help marketers forecast the likelihood of customer engagements with their marketing strategies. For example, if your marketing happens a lot in the email space, you can utilize predictive analytics to forecast which customers have a high likelihood of opening your marketing emails and custom-tailor your marketing strategies to those high-likelihood customers to maximize your marketing results. For another example, if you are displaying advertisements on social media, predictive analytics can help you identify certain types of customers that are likely to click on the ads.

- **Customer lifetime value**: Predictive analytics can help you forecast the expected lifetime values of your customers. Using historical transactional data, predictive analytics can help you identify high-value customers within your customer base. With these predictions, you and your firm can focus more on building healthy relationships with those high-value customers. We are going to discuss in more detail how to build predictive models for customer lifetime value forecasts in the following chapter.

- **Recommending the right products and contents**: As we have already discussed in Chapter 6, *Recommending the Right Products*, we can use data science and machine learning to predict which customers are likely to purchase products or view contents. Using these predictions, you can improve customer conversion rates by recommending the right products and contents for individual customers.

- **Customer acquisition and retention**: Predictive analytics has also been heavily used for customer acquisition and retention. Based on the profile data you gathered about your prospects or leads and the historical data of your existing customers, you can apply predictive analytics to identify high-quality leads or rank the leads by their likelihood of being converted into active customers. On the other hand, you can use the customer churn data and the historical data of your existing customers to develop predictive models to forecast which customers are likely to leave or unsubscribe from your products. We are going to discuss in more detail applying predictive analytics for customer retention in Chapter 11, *Retaining Customers*.

On top of these four common use cases of predictive analytics in marketing, there are many other ways you can utilize predictive analytics for your marketing strategies. You should get creative on how and where to use predictive analytics for your future marketing strategies.

Evaluating classification models

When developing predictive models, it is important to know how to evaluate those models. In this section, we are going to discuss five different ways to evaluate the performance of classification models. The first metric that can be used to measure prediction performance is **accuracy**. Accuracy is simply the percentage of correct predictions out of all predictions, as shown in the following formula:

$$Accuracy = \frac{Number\ of\ Correct\ Predictions}{Total\ number\ of\ Records}$$

The second metric that is commonly used for classification problems is **precision**. Precision is defined as the number of true positives divided by the total number of true positives and false positives. True positives are cases where the model correctly predicted as positive, while false positives are cases where the model was predicted as positive, but the true label was negative. The formula looks as follows:

$$Precision = \frac{TP}{TP + FP}$$

Along with precision, **recall** is also commonly used to evaluate the performances of classification models. Recall is defined as the number of true positives divided by the number of true positives plus false negatives. False negatives are cases where the model was predicted as negative, but the true label was positive. Recall can be thought of as a measure of how much of the positive cases are retrieved or found by the model. The formula looks as follows:

$$Recall = \frac{TP}{TP + FN}$$

The final two metrics we are going to discuss are the **receiver operating characteristic (ROC)** curve and the **area under the curve (AUC)**. The ROC curve shows how true positive rates and false positive rates change at different thresholds. The AUC is simply the total area under the ROC curve. The AUC ranges from 0 to 1 and a higher AUC number suggests better model performance. A random classifier has an AUC of 0.5, so any classifier with an AUC higher than 0.5 suggests that the model performs better than random predictions. A typical ROC curve looks as in the following:

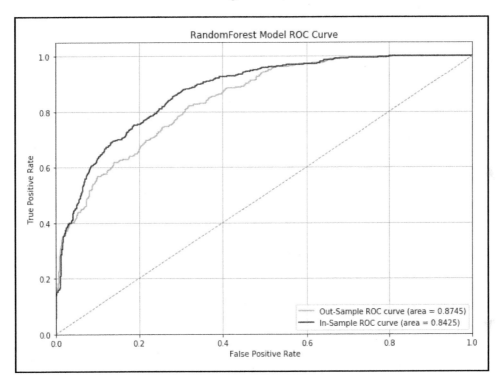

In the following programming exercise, we are going to use these five metrics that we have just discussed to evaluate the performance of the model we build in Python and R. Let's now dive into building machine learning models to predict the likelihood of marketing engagement!

Predicting the likelihood of marketing engagement with Python

In this section, we are going to discuss how to build predictive models using machine learning algorithms in Python. More specifically, we will learn how to build a predictive model using the random forest algorithm, as well as how to tune the random forest model and evaluate the performance of the model. We will be mainly using the `pandas`, `matplotlib`, and `scikit-learn` packages to analyze, visualize, and build machine learning models that predict the likelihood of customer marketing engagement. For those readers who would like to use R instead of Python for this exercise, you can skip to the next section.

For this exercise, we will be using one of the publicly available datasets from IBM, which can be found at this link: `https://www.ibm.com/communities/analytics/watson-analytics-blog/marketing-customer-value-analysis/`. You can follow this link and download the data that is available in CSV format, named `WA_Fn UseC_ Marketing Customer Value Analysis.csv`. Once you have downloaded this data, you can load it into your Jupyter notebook by running the following command:

```
import pandas as pd

df = pd.read_csv('../data/WA_Fn-UseC_-Marketing-Customer-Value-
Analysis.csv')
```

The `df` DataFrame looks as follows:

```
df.head()
```

	Customer	State	Customer Lifetime Value	Response	Coverage	Education	Effective To Date	EmploymentStatus	Gender	Income	...	Months Since Policy Inception	Number of Open Complaints	Number of Policies
0	BU79786	Washington	2763.519279	No	Basic	Bachelor	2/24/11	Employed	F	56274	...	5	0	1
1	QZ44356	Arizona	6979.535903	No	Extended	Bachelor	1/31/11	Unemployed	F	0	...	42	0	8
2	AI49188	Nevada	12887.431650	No	Premium	Bachelor	2/19/11	Employed	F	48767	...	38	0	2
3	WW63253	California	7645.861827	No	Basic	Bachelor	1/20/11	Unemployed	M	0	...	65	0	7
4	HB64268	Washington	2813.692575	No	Basic	Bachelor	2/3/11	Employed	M	43836	...	44	0	1

As you might have noticed, this is the same dataset that we used in the previous chapter, where we conducted customer analytics. With the knowledge we gained about this dataset from the previous chapter, we are going to first prepare our data by encoding the target variable and other categorical variables that we are going to use as features for our machine learning models.

Variable encoding

In order to build machine learning models using the scikit-learn package in Python, all the features in the dataset need to have numerical values. However, in the dataset, we have numerous columns that have non-numerical values. For example, the target variable, Response, which is what we are going to try to predict with machine learning models, is non-numeric. It contains two string values—Yes and No. We will need to encode this Response target variable with numerical values in order to be able to build machine learning models. For another example, the column Gender, which we can use as one of the features for our predictive model, also does not have numerical values. It contains two string values—F for female and M for male. In this section, we are going to discuss how we can encode these non-numeric columns so that we can use them as features for machine learning models.

Response variable encoding

The first thing we are going to do is encode the response variable Response. We are going to encode Yes values with 1s and No values with 0s. Take a look at the following code:

```
df['Engaged'] = df['Response'].apply(lambda x: 1 if x == 'Yes' else 0)
```

As you can see from this code, we are using the apply function of the pandas DataFrame to apply our lambda function on the Response column, so that it encodes Yes values with 1 and No values with 0. We then store these encoded values in a newly-created column, Engaged. In order to get the overall response or engagement rate using this newly-created column, you can use the following code:

```
tdf['Engaged'].mean()
```

The overall engagement rate looks as follows:

```
df['Engaged'].mean()

0.14320122618786948
```

Categorical variable encoding

If you look closely at the data, the following variables are categorical variables:

```
columns_to_encode = [
    'Sales Channel', 'Vehicle Size', 'Vehicle Class', 'Policy', 'Policy
Type',
    'EmploymentStatus', 'Marital Status', 'Education', 'Coverage'
]
```

These variables have a set of different values they can take and those values do not necessarily have orders that differentiate one from another.

If you recall from `Chapter 4`, *From Engagement to Conversion*, there is more than one way to encode categorical variables. In this chapter, the method we are going to use is to create dummy variables for each category of individual categorical variables, using the `get_dummies` function in the `pandas` package. Take a look at the following code:

```
categorical_features = []
for col in columns_to_encode:
    encoded_df = pd.get_dummies(df[col])
    encoded_df.columns = [col.replace(' ', '.') + '.' + x for x in
encoded_df.columns]
    categorical_features += list(encoded_df.columns)
    df = pd.concat([df, encoded_df], axis=1)
```

As you can see from this code snippet, we are iterating through the list of column names of categorical variables, defined in `columns_to_encode`. Then, for each column, we are using the `get_dummies` function in the `pandas` package to build dummy variables. In order to make things clear and cause less confusion, we are renaming the columns of the newly-created and encoded `DataFrame` `encoded_df`, where each column contains information about the original column name and the category it represents. As an example, for the `Sale Channel` column, the newly-created DataFrame `encoded_df` will look as in the following:

	Sales.Channel.Agent	Sales.Channel.Branch	Sales.Channel.Call Center	Sales.Channel.Web
0	1	0	0	0
1	1	0	0	0
2	1	0	0	0
3	0	0	1	0
4	1	0	0	0
5	0	0	0	1
6	1	0	0	0
7	1	0	0	0
8	1	0	0	0
9	0	1	0	0

As you can see from this example, each column of this new `DataFrame` represents each category in the original `Sales Channel` column and the values are one-hot encoded, meaning it assigns a value of 1 if the given record belongs to the given category, and 0 otherwise.

Once we have created dummy variables for the given column, we then store the newly-created columns into a variable named `categorical_features`. Lastly, we concatenate this newly-created `DataFrame` to the original `DataFrame`, by using the `concat` function of the `pandas` package. One of the parameters in the concat function, `axis=1`, tells `pandas` to concatenate the two `DataFrames` by the column.

By now, we have successfully encoded all the categorical variables except `Gender`. Since we do not need to create two dummy variables for the `Gender` column, as there can only be two genders, we are going to create one variable that contains information about the gender of a given record. Take a look at the following code:

```
df['Is.Female'] = df['Gender'].apply(lambda x: 1 if x == 'F' else 0)

categorical_features.append('Is.Female')
```

As you can see from this code, we are creating a new column named `Is.Female`. We are using the apply function of the `pandas DataFrame` and encoding all females with the value of 1 and all males with the value of 0.

Building predictive models

We are almost ready to start building and training machine learning models to predict customer responses or engagements. There are a few things to clean up in our data. Take a look at the following code:

```
all_features = continuous_features + categorical_features
response = 'Engaged'

sample_df = df[all_features + [response]]
sample_df.columns = [x.replace(' ', '.') for x in sample_df.columns]
all_features = [x.replace(' ', '.') for x in all_features]
```

As you can see from this code, we are creating a new `DataFrame` `sample_df`, which contains all the features, `all_features`, and the response variable, `response`. Then, we are cleaning up the column and feature names by replacing all the spaces in the names with dots. After these cleanups, DataFrame `sample_df` now looks as in the following:

```
sample_df.head()
```

	Customer.Lifetime.Value	Income	Monthly.Premium.Auto	Months.Since.Last.Claim	Months.Since.Policy.Inception	Number.of.Open.Complaints	Number.of.Policie
0	2763.519279	56274	69	32	5	0	
1	6979.535903	0	94	13	42	0	
2	12887.431650	48767	108	18	38	0	
3	7645.861827	0	106	18	65	0	
4	2813.692575	43836	73	12	44	0	

5 rows × 51 columns

Now that we have a sample set that we can train and test our machine learning models with, let's split this sample set into two subsets—one for training the models and another for testing and evaluating the trained models. The Python machine learning package, `scikit-learn`, has a function that splits a given sample set into train and test sets. Take a look at the following code:

```
from sklearn.model_selection import train_test_split

x_train, x_test, y_train, y_test =
train_test_split(sample_df[all_features], sample_df[response],
test_size=0.3)
```

In the `model_selection` module of the `scikit-learn` package, there is a function named `train_test_split`. This function takes the sample set and the desired breakdown between train and test set sizes as input parameters and returns train and test sets that are randomly split. As you can see from this code snippet, we are using `70%` of the sample set for training and the remaining `30%` for testing. The following shows the breakdowns of train and test sets from the sample set:

```
sample_df.shape

(9134, 51)

x_train.shape

(6393, 50)

x_test.shape

(2741, 50)
```

As you can see here, there are a total of `9,134` records in `sample_df`, `6,393` records in `x_train`, and `2,741` records in `x_test`, meaning that roughly `70%` of the sample set went into the train set and the remaining `30%` of the sample set went into the test set. We will be using these train and test sets for building and evaluating models in the following sections.

Random forest model

With the data that we have prepared so far, we are going to build a predictive model, using a random forest algorithm, which predicts whether a customer is going to respond or engage with the marketing campaign. In Python's `scikit-learn` package, the random forest algorithm is implemented in the `ensemble` module and you can import the random forest class using the following code:

```
from sklearn.ensemble import RandomForestClassifier
```

You can create a random forest classifier using the following code:

```
rf_model = RandomForestClassifier()
```

However, there are many hyperparameters you can tune for random forest models. Hyperparameters are the parameters you define before you train a machine learning model. For example, in the case of a random forest algorithm, you can define the number of trees you want in your random forest model. As another example, you can define the maximum depth of each tree in the forest, so that you can limit how big each tree in the forest can grow.

There are numerous hyperparameters you can define in `scikit-learn`'s `RandomForestClassifier` class. We will take a look at the following few examples of hyperparameters:

- `n_estimators`: This defines the number of trees you want to build in the forest. Generally speaking, more trees mean better performance results. However, the amount of performance gain for each additional tree decreases as the number of trees in the forest increases. Since having more trees in a forest means higher cost in computations for training additional trees, you should try to find the balance and stop adding trees when the computational cost from training additional trees outweighs the performance gain.

- `max_depth`: This parameter defines the maximum depth of individual trees. The larger the depth is, the more information your tree can capture from the train set, meaning larger trees learn the train set better than smaller trees. However, the larger the tree grows, the more likely it is going to overfit the train set. This means that the trained tree performs and predicts well within the train set, but predicts poorly in the dataset that it has not seen before. In order to avoid overfitting, we would want to limit the depth of the tree to a point where it does not overfit to the train set, but predicts the outcomes well enough.

- `min_samples_split`: This defines the minimum number of data points required to split a node of the tree. For example, if you defined `min_samples_split` to be `50`, but the node only has `40` records, then it will not split the node any further. On the other hand, if the node has more than the predefined minimum number of samples, then it will split the node into child nodes. Similar to the `max_depth` hyperparameter, this helps you manage the amount of overfitting happening in the tree.

- `max_features`: This defines the maximum number of features to be considered for splitting a node. This parameter creates the *randomness* in random forest models. Given the maximum number of features to be considered for a split, the random forest algorithm randomly chooses a subset of the features up to the maximum number and decides how to split a given node of a tree. This helps each tree of a random forest model to learn different information from the train set. When these trees that have learned the train set with slightly different set of features are bagged or ensembled all together, then the resulting forest will become more accurate and robust in its predictions.

For a more detailed description and information on other hyperparameters, you can refer to their official documentation, which can be found at the following link: `https://scikit-learn.org/stable/modules/generated/sklearn.ensemble.RandomForestClassifier.html`.

Training a random forest model

Training a random forest model using `scikit-learn` is simple. Take a look at the following code:

```
rf_model = RandomForestClassifier(
    n_estimators=200,
    max_depth=5
)

rf_model.fit(X=x_train, y=y_train)
```

Using the `RandomforestClasifier` class in the `scikit-learn` package's `ensemble` module, you first need to create a `RandomforestClasifier` object with the hyperparameters. For illustration purposes, we are instructing the model to build 200 trees, where each tree can only grow up to the depth of 5. Then, you can train this model with the `fit` function, which takes two parameters, X and y, where X is for the training samples and y is for the training labels or target values.

When you run this code, you will see an output that looks as follows:

```
from sklearn.ensemble import RandomForestClassifier

rf_model = RandomForestClassifier(
    n_estimators=200,
    max_depth=5
)

rf_model.fit(X=x_train, y=y_train)

RandomForestClassifier(bootstrap=True, class_weight=None, criterion='gini',
            max_depth=5, max_features='auto', max_leaf_nodes=None,
            min_impurity_decrease=0.0, min_impurity_split=None,
            min_samples_leaf=1, min_samples_split=2,
            min_weight_fraction_leaf=0.0, n_estimators=200, n_jobs=1,
            oob_score=False, random_state=None, verbose=0,
            warm_start=False)
```

Once a random forest model is trained or fitted, the model object contains a lot of useful information. One of the useful attributes you can extract from a trained scikit-learn random forest model is the information about individual trees in the forest. Using the estimators_ attribute, you can retrieve the individual trees that are built within the forest. Take a look at the following output:

```
- Individual Trees

rf_model.estimators_

[DecisionTreeClassifier(class_weight=None, criterion='gini', max_depth=5,
            max_features='auto', max_leaf_nodes=None,
            min_impurity_decrease=0.0, min_impurity_split=None,
            min_samples_leaf=1, min_samples_split=2,
            min_weight_fraction_leaf=0.0, presort=False,
            random_state=1182049216, splitter='best'),
 DecisionTreeClassifier(class_weight=None, criterion='gini', max_depth=5,
            max_features='auto', max_leaf_nodes=None,
            min_impurity_decrease=0.0, min_impurity_split=None,
            min_samples_leaf=1, min_samples_split=2,
            min_weight_fraction_leaf=0.0, presort=False,
            random_state=829317093, splitter='best'),
 DecisionTreeClassifier(class_weight=None, criterion='gini', max_depth=5,
            max_features='auto', max_leaf_nodes=None,
            min_impurity_decrease=0.0, min_impurity_split=None,
            min_samples_leaf=1, min_samples_split=2,
            min_weight_fraction_leaf=0.0, presort=False,
            random_state=1398037487, splitter='best'),
 DecisionTreeClassifier(class_weight=None, criterion='gini', max_depth=5,
            max_features='auto', max_leaf_nodes=None,
            min_impurity_decrease=0.0, min_impurity_split=None,
            min_samples_leaf=1, min_samples_split=2,
            min_weight_fraction_leaf=0.0, presort=False,
            random_state=831979291, splitter='best'),
```

As you can see from this output, the `estimators_` attribute returns a list of sub-estimators, which are decision trees. With this information, you can simulate what each of these sub-estimators predicts for each input. For example, the following code shows how you can get the predictions from the first sub-estimator in the forest:

```
rf_model.estimators_[0].predict(x_test)
```

The following output shows some of the predictions from the first five sub-estimators:

```
rf_model.estimators_[0].predict(x_test)[:10]

array([0., 0., 0., 0., 0., 1., 0., 0., 0., 0.])

rf_model.estimators_[1].predict(x_test)[:10]

array([0., 0., 0., 0., 0., 0., 0., 0., 0., 0.])

rf_model.estimators_[2].predict(x_test)[:10]

array([0., 0., 0., 0., 0., 0., 0., 0., 0., 0.])

rf_model.estimators_[3].predict(x_test)[:10]

array([0., 0., 1., 0., 0., 0., 0., 0., 0., 0.])

rf_model.estimators_[4].predict(x_test)[:10]

array([0., 0., 0., 0., 0., 0., 0., 0., 0., 0.])
```

As you can see from this output, different trees predict differently for each record of the test set. This is because each tree is trained with different subsets of features that are randomly selected. Let's take a quick look at the predictions of these individual sub-estimators. The first tree predicts the 6th record in the test set to be a class of 1 and the rest to be a class of 0. On the other hand, the second tree predicts that the first 10 records of the test set to be a class of 0. Using this information, you can see how the final predictions from the random forest model are formed from these individual sub-estimators or trees.

Other useful information that we can gain from the trained RandomForestClassifier object is the feature importances, with which we can understand the importance or the impact of each feature on the final predictions. You can get the feature importances for each feature using the following code:

```
rf_model.feature_importances_
```

The output of this code looks as follows:

```
- Feature Importances

rf_model.feature_importances_

array([0.06054531, 0.09003091, 0.05340668, 0.02954197, 0.05362482,
       0.01076425, 0.02145626, 0.07377831, 0.04641028, 0.00755703,
       0.00755832, 0.00568473, 0.0067975 , 0.01018243, 0.0102477 ,
       0.00495166, 0.00113173, 0.00146122, 0.00683007, 0.00633034,
       0.00360746, 0.00122614, 0.00120962, 0.00099013, 0.00150983,
       0.00156154, 0.00167344, 0.00093062, 0.00100503, 0.00273003,
       0.00141377, 0.00098851, 0.00111641, 0.00475984, 0.03401539,
       0.00604427, 0.29381144, 0.02655533, 0.03369894, 0.01470135,
       0.01590602, 0.00454194, 0.00414489, 0.00268673, 0.0043107 ,
       0.00546048, 0.00556966, 0.00578405, 0.00193898, 0.00781593])
```

In order to associate these feature importances with the corresponding features, you can use the following code:

```
feature_importance_df =
pd.DataFrame(list(zip(rf_model.feature_importances_, all_features)))
feature_importance_df.columns = ['feature.importance', 'feature']
```

The result looks as follows:

```
feature_importance_df = pd.DataFrame(list(zip(rf_model.feature_importances_, all_features)))
feature_importance_df.columns = ['feature.importance', 'feature']

feature_importance_df.sort_values(by='feature.importance', ascending=False)
```

	feature.importance	feature
36	0.293811	EmploymentStatus.Retired
1	0.090031	Income
7	0.073778	Total.Claim.Amount
0	0.060545	Customer.Lifetime.Value
4	0.053625	Months.Since.Policy.Inception
2	0.053407	Monthly.Premium.Auto
8	0.046410	Sales.Channel.Agent
34	0.034015	EmploymentStatus.Employed
38	0.033699	Marital.Status.Divorced
3	0.029542	Months.Since.Last.Claim
37	0.026555	EmploymentStatus.Unemployed
6	0.021456	Number.of.Policies
40	0.015906	Marital.Status.Single
39	0.014701	Marital.Status.Married
5	0.010764	Number.of.Open.Complaints
14	0.010248	Vehicle.Size.Small

As you can see from this output, the `EmploymentStatus.Retired` feature seems to be the most important factor in making the final prediction and the `Income`, `Total.Claim.Amount`, and `Customer.Lifetime.Value` features follow as the second, third, and fourth most important features.

Evaluating a classification model

Earlier in this chapter, we have discussed five different ways to look at the performance of a classification model. In this section, we are going to learn how we can compute and visualize the metrics for evaluating a classification model in Python using the random forest model we have just built.

The first three metrics that we are going to look at are accuracy, precision, and recall. Python's `scikit-learn` package has implemented functions for these three metrics. You can import these functions using the following line of code:

```
from sklearn.metrics import accuracy_score, precision_score, recall_score
```

As you can see from this code snippet, the `metrics` module of the `scikit-learn` package has an `accuracy_score` function for calculating the accuracy of a model, a `precision_score` function for the precision, and a `recall_score` function for the recall.

Before we go ahead and evaluate the model performance, we will need the model prediction results. In order to have the random forest model we have built in the previous section to make predictions on a dataset, we can simply use the `predict` function of the model. Take a look at the following code:

```
in_sample_preds = rf_model.predict(x_train)
out_sample_preds = rf_model.predict(x_test)
```

With these prediction results, we are going to evaluate how well our random forest model performs in the train and test sets. The following code shows how we can use the `accuracy_score`, `precision_score`, and `recall_score` functions in the `scikit-learn` package:

```
# accuracy
accuracy_score(actual, predictions)

# precision
precision_score(actual, predictions)

# recall
recall_score(actual, predictions)
```

As you can see from this code, the `accuracy_score, precision_score,` and `recall_score` functions all take two parameters—truth labels and predicted labels. Take a look at the following output:

```
- Accuracy, Precision, and Recall

from sklearn.metrics import accuracy_score, precision_score, recall_score

in_sample_preds = rf_model.predict(x_train)
out_sample_preds = rf_model.predict(x_test)

print('In-Sample Accuracy: %0.4f' % accuracy_score(y_train, in_sample_preds))
print('Out-of-Sample Accuracy: %0.4f' % accuracy_score(y_test, out_sample_preds))

In-Sample Accuracy: 0.8724
Out-of-Sample Accuracy: 0.8818

print('In-Sample Precision: %0.4f' % precision_score(y_train, in_sample_preds))
print('Out-of-Sample Precision: %0.4f' % precision_score(y_test, out_sample_preds))

In-Sample Precision: 0.9919
Out-of-Sample Precision: 0.9423

print('In-Sample Recall: %0.4f' % recall_score(y_train, in_sample_preds))
print('Out-of-Sample Recall: %0.4f' % recall_score(y_test, out_sample_preds))

In-Sample Recall: 0.1311
Out-of-Sample Recall: 0.1324
```

This output gives us a brief overview of how well our model performs at predicting the responses. For the train set, the accuracy of the overall prediction was 0.8724, meaning the model prediction was correct for about 87% of the time. For the test set, the accuracy of the overall prediction was 0.8818, which is roughly on the same line with the prediction accuracy within the train set. You can also see that the precision for in-sample and out-of-sample predictions were 0.9919 and 0.9423 respectively, and the recalls were 0.1311 and 0.1324. Due to the randomness and the different hyperparameters you might have used, you can get different results.

The next set of metrics we are going to look at are the ROC curve and the AUC. The `metrics` module in the `scikit-learn` package has handy functions for the ROC curve and the AUC. Take a look at the following line of code:

```
from sklearn.metrics import roc_curve, auc
```

The `roc_curve` function in the metrics module of the `scikit-learn` package computes the ROC, and the `auc` function computes the AUC. In order to compute the ROC and AUC using these functions, we need to first get the prediction probabilities from our random forest model. The following code shows how we can get the random forest model's prediction probabilities for both the train and test sets:

```
in_sample_preds = rf_model.predict_proba(x_train)[:,1]
out_sample_preds = rf_model.predict_proba(x_test)[:,1]
```

As you can see from this code, we are using the `predict_proba` function of the random forest model, `rf_model`. This function outputs the predicted probabilities of the given record belonging to each class. Since we only have two possible classes in our case, 0 for no responses and 1 for responses, the output of the `predict_proba` function has two columns, where the first column represents the predicted probability of a negative class, meaning no response for each record, and the second column represents the predicted probability of a positive class, meaning a response for each record. Since we are only interested in the likelihood of responding to the marketing effort, we can take the second column for the predicted probabilities of the positive class.

With these predicted probabilities of the positive class for both the train and test sets, we can now compute the ROC curve and AUC. Let's first take a look at how we can compute the ROC curve using the `roc_curve` function in the following code:

```
in_sample_fpr, in_sample_tpr, in_sample_thresholds = roc_curve(y_train,
in_sample_preds)
out_sample_fpr, out_sample_tpr, out_sample_thresholds = roc_curve(y_test,
out_sample_preds)
```

As you can see from this code snippet, the `roc_curve` function takes two parameters—observed labels and predicted probabilities. This function returns three variables, `fpr`, `tpr`, and `thresholds`. The `fpr` values represent the false positive rates for each given threshold and the `tpr` values represent the true positive rates for each given threshold. The `thresholds` values represent the actual thresholds at which `fpr` and `tpr` are measured.

Next, with these `fpr` and `tpr` values, we can compute the AUC using the following code:

```
in_sample_roc_auc = auc(in_sample_fpr, in_sample_tpr)
out_sample_roc_auc = auc(out_sample_fpr, out_sample_tpr)

print('In-Sample AUC: %0.4f' % in_sample_roc_auc)
print('Out-Sample AUC: %0.4f' % out_sample_roc_auc)
```

As you can see from this code, the `auc` function takes two parameters—`fpr` and `tpr`. Using the previously calculated `fpr` and `tpr` values from the `roc_curve` function, we can easily compute the AUC numbers for both the train and test sets. The output looks as follows:

```
in_sample_roc_auc = auc(in_sample_fpr, in_sample_tpr)
out_sample_roc_auc = auc(out_sample_fpr, out_sample_tpr)

print('In-Sample AUC: %0.4f' % in_sample_roc_auc)
print('Out-Sample AUC: %0.4f' % out_sample_roc_auc)

In-Sample AUC: 0.8745
Out-Sample AUC: 0.8425
```

Depending on the hyperparameters and the randomness within the random forest algorithm, your AUC numbers can look different from these examples. However, in our case, the in-sample train set AUC was `0.8745` and the out-of-sample test set AUC was `0.8425`. If you see a big gap between these two numbers, it is a sign of overfitting and you should try to address it by pruning the trees in the forest by tuning the hyperparameters, such as the maximum depth and minimum number of samples to split.

The last thing we are going to look at for evaluating machine learning models is the actual ROC curve. With the output of the `roc_curve` function, we can plot the actual ROC curves using the `matplotlib` package. Take a look at the following code:

```
plt.figure(figsize=(10,7))

plt.plot(
    out_sample_fpr, out_sample_tpr, color='darkorange', label='Out-Sample
ROC curve (area = %0.4f)' % in_sample_roc_auc
)
plt.plot(
    in_sample_fpr, in_sample_tpr, color='navy', label='In-Sample ROC curve
(area = %0.4f)' % out_sample_roc_auc
)
plt.plot([0, 1], [0, 1], color='gray', lw=1, linestyle='--')
plt.grid()
plt.xlim([0.0, 1.0])
plt.ylim([0.0, 1.05])
plt.xlabel('False Positive Rate')
plt.ylabel('True Positive Rate')
plt.title('RandomForest Model ROC Curve')
plt.legend(loc="lower right")

plt.show()
```

As you can see from this code, we are plotting three line plots—one for the out-of-sample test set ROC curve, another for the in-sample train set ROC curve, and lastly one for a straight line for the benchmark. The result looks as in the following:

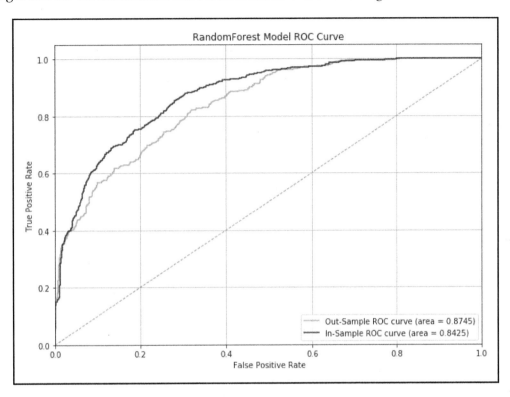

As you can see from this plot, it is easier to see and compare the overall performance of the model between the train and test sets with ROC curves. The larger the gap between the in-sample ROC curve and the out-of-sample ROC curve, the more the model is overfitting to the train set and fails to generalize the findings for unforeseen data.

The full code for this Python exercise can be found at the following link: `https://github.com/yoonhwang/hands-on-data-science-for-marketing/blob/master/ch.8/python/PredictingEngagement.ipynb`

Predicting the likelihood of marketing engagement with R

In this section, we are going to discuss how to build predictive models using machine learning algorithms in R. More specifically, we will learn how to build a predictive model using a random forest algorithm, as well as how to tune the random forest model, and evaluate the performance of the model. We will be mainly using the `caTools`, `ROCR`, and `randomForest` packages to evaluate, visualize, and build machine learning models that predict the likelihood of customer marketing engagement. For those readers who would like to use Python instead of R for this exercise, you can refer to the previous section.

For this exercise, we will be using one of the publicly available datasets from **IBM**, which can be found at this link: `https://www.ibm.com/communities/analytics/watson-analytics-blog/marketing-customer-value-analysis/`. You can follow this link and download the data that is available in CSV format, named `WA_Fn UseC_ Marketing Customer Value Analysis.csv`. Once you have downloaded this data, you can load it into your RStudio by running the following command:

```
#### 1. Load Data ####
df <- read.csv(
    file="~/Documents/data-science-for-marketing/ch.8/data/WA_Fn-UseC_-
Marketing-Customer-Value-Analysis.csv",
    header=TRUE
)
```

`df` looks as follows:

	Customer	State	Customer.Lifetime.Value	Response	Coverage	Education	Effective.To.Date	EmploymentStatus	Gender	Income
1	BU79786	Washington	2763.519	No	Basic	Bachelor	2/24/11	Employed	F	56274
2	QZ44356	Arizona	6979.536	No	Extended	Bachelor	1/31/11	Unemployed	F	0
3	AI49188	Nevada	12887.432	No	Premium	Bachelor	2/19/11	Employed	F	48767
4	WW63253	California	7645.862	No	Basic	Bachelor	1/20/11	Unemployed	M	0
5	HB64268	Washington	2813.693	No	Basic	Bachelor	2/3/11	Employed	M	43836
6	OC83172	Oregon	8256.298	Yes	Basic	Bachelor	1/25/11	Employed	F	62902
7	XZ87318	Oregon	5380.899	Yes	Basic	College	2/24/11	Employed	F	55350
8	CF85061	Arizona	7216.100	No	Premium	Master	1/18/11	Unemployed	M	0
9	DY87989	Oregon	24127.504	Yes	Basic	Bachelor	1/26/11	Medical Leave	M	14072
10	BQ94931	Oregon	7388.178	No	Extended	College	2/17/11	Employed	F	28812
11	SX51350	California	4738.992	No	Basic	College	2/21/11	Unemployed	M	0
12	VQ65197	California	8197.197	No	Basic	College	1/6/11	Unemployed	F	0
13	DP39365	California	8798.797	No	Premium	Master	2/6/11	Employed	M	77026
14	SJ95423	Arizona	8819.019	Yes	Basic	High School or Below	1/10/11	Employed	M	99845
15	IL66569	California	5384.432	No	Basic	College	1/18/11	Employed	M	83689

As you might have noticed, this is the same dataset that we used in the previous chapter, where we conducted customer analytics. With the knowledge we gained about this dataset from the previous chapter, we are going to first prepare our data by encoding the target variable and other categorical variables that we are going to use as features for our machine learning models.

Variable encoding

In order to build machine learning models in R, all the features in the dataset need to have numerical values. However, in the dataset we have numerous columns that have non-numerical values. For example, the target variable, Response, which is what we are going to try to predict with our machine learning models, is non-numeric. It contains two string values—Yes or No. We will need to encode this Response target variable with numerical values in order to be able to build machine learning models. For another example, the Gender column, which we can use as one of the features for our predictive model, also does not have numerical values. It contains two string values—F for female and M for male. In this section, we are going to discuss how we can encode these non-numeric columns, so that we can use them as features in machine learning models.

Response variable encoding

The first thing we are going to do is encode the response variable, Response. We are going to encode Yes values with 1s and No values with 0s. Take a look at the following code:

```
## 2.1. Response Variable: Response
df$Engaged <- as.integer(df$Response) - 1
```

As you can see from this code, we are simply casting the values of the Response column to integer values using the as.integer function. The reason why we are subtracting by 1 is because it encodes values into 1 for No and 2 for Yes, instead of 0 for No and 1 for Yes, as we wanted. We then store these encoded values in a newly-created column, Engaged. In order to get the overall response or engagement rate using this newly-created column, you can use the following code:

```
mean(df$Engaged)
```

The overall engagement rate looks as follows:

```
> mean(df$Engaged)
[1] 0.1432012
```

Categorical variable encoding

If you look closely at the data, the following columns are categorical variables in our dataset:

```
## 2.2. Categorical Features

categoricalVars = c(
  'Sales.Channel', 'Vehicle.Size', 'Vehicle.Class', 'Policy',
'Policy.Type',
  'EmploymentStatus', 'Marital.Status', 'Education', 'Coverage', 'Gender'
)
```

These variables have a set of different values they can take and these values do not necessarily have orders that differentiate one from another.

If you recall from Chapter 4, *From Engagement to Conversion*, we discussed how we can create factor variables for such categorical variables in R. In this chapter, the method we are going to use is to create dummy variables for each category of individual categorical variables, using the model.matrix function in R. Take a look at the following code:

```
encodedDF <- model.matrix(~.-1, df[categoricalVars])
```

As you can see from this code, it is simple to create dummy variables for categorical variables in R. All you need to do is to apply the model.matrix function on the R DataFrame's categorical variable columns. If you look closely at the code, you will notice the ~.-1 formula that we are using here. Without this formula, the model.matrix function will create an unnecessary column named Intercept in the output matrix. In order to avoid having this unnecessary column, we can use the formula in this code example. The first few columns of the newly-created DataFrame encodedDf now look as in the following:

	Sales.ChannelAgent	Sales.ChannelBranch	Sales.ChannelCall Center	Sales.ChannelWeb	Vehicle.SizeMedsize	Vehicle.SizeSmall	Vehicle.ClassLuxury Car
1	1	0	0	0	1	0	0
2	1	0	0	0	1	0	0
3	1	0	0	0	1	0	0
4	0	0	1	0	1	0	0
5	1	0	0	0	1	0	0
6	0	0	0	1	1	0	0
7	1	0	0	0	1	0	0
8	1	0	0	0	1	0	0
9	1	0	0	0	1	0	0
10	0	1	0	0	1	0	0
11	1	0	0	0	0	1	0
12	1	0	0	0	1	0	0
13	1	0	0	0	1	0	0
14	0	1	0	0	1	0	0
15	0	0	1	0	1	0	0

As you can see from this output, each column of this new DataFrame represents each category in the original column. For example, the first column, Sales.ChannelAgent, is encoded with 1 if the given record or customer was reached out by a sales agent and 0 otherwise. For another example, the fifth column, Vehicle.SizeMedsize, is encoded with 1 if the given record or customer has medium-size vehicles and 0 otherwise.

Now that we have successfully encoded all the categorical variables with numerical values, we need to append the continuous variables to this newly-created DataFrame, encodedDF. Take a look at the following code:

```
## 2.3. Continuous Features
continuousFeatures <- c(
  'Customer.Lifetime.Value', 'Income', 'Monthly.Premium.Auto',
  'Months.Since.Last.Claim', 'Months.Since.Policy.Inception',
  'Number.of.Open.Complaints', 'Number.of.Policies', 'Total.Claim.Amount'
)

encodedDF <- cbind(encodedDF, df[continuousFeatures])
```

As you can see from this code, we are using the cbind R function, which combines two DataFrames by columns. We are combining the previously-created DataFrame encodedDF, which contains all the encoded categorical variables with the DataFrame with continuous variables. Then, we are storing this combined DataFrame back to the encodedDF variable.

Building predictive models

We are almost ready to start building and training machine learning models to predict customer responses or engagements. There is one thing we need to do before we start training a random forest model. We need to split the sample set, the `encodedDF` variable, into two subsets—one for training the models and another for testing and evaluating the trained models. The `caTools` R package has a handy function that splits a given sample set into train and test sets. If you do not have this library installed in your R environment, you can install it using the following command:

```
install.packages('caTools')
```

Now, take a look at the following code on how to split the sample set into training and testing:

```
library(caTools)

sample <- sample.split(df$Customer, SplitRatio = .7)

trainX <- as.matrix(subset(encodedDF, sample == TRUE))
trainY <- as.double(as.matrix(subset(df$Engaged, sample == TRUE)))

testX <- as.matrix(subset(encodedDF, sample == FALSE))
testY <- as.double(as.matrix(subset(df$Engaged, sample == FALSE)))
```

Let's take a closer look at this code. The `sample.split` function in the `caTools` package lets us split the dataset into a proportion we would like. As you can see from this code, we defined `SplitRatio` to be `0.7`, which means we are taking 70% of the sample set as a training set and the remaining 30% of the `sample` set as a test set. The resulting variable, sample, now has an array of Boolean values, TRUE or FALSE, where 70% of the arrays are TRUE and the remaining 30% are FALSE.

With this data, we can create train and test sets. As you can see from the code, we are using the `subset` function in R to create train and test sets. First, we take those records that correspond to TRUE values in the `sample` variable as the train set. Then, we take those records whose indexes correspond to FALSE values in the `sample` variable as the test set. The following shows the breakdown of train and test sets from the sample set:

```
> dim(encodedDF)
[1] 9134   42
>
> dim(trainX)
[1] 6393   42
>
> dim(testX)
[1] 2741   42
```

As you can see here, there are a total of 9,134 records in `encodedDF`, 6,393 records in `trainX`, and 2,741 records in `testX`, meaning that roughly 70% of the sample set went into the the train set and the remaining 30% of the sample set went into the test set. We will be using these train and test sets for building and evaluating models in the following sections.

Random forest model

With the data that we have prepared so far, we are going to build a predictive model using a random forest algorithm, which predicts whether a customer is going to respond or engage with the marketing campaign. We are going to use the `randomForest` R library. If you do not have this library installed in your R environment, you can install it using the following command:

```
install.packages('randomForest')
```

Once you have this package installed, you can use the following code to build a random forest model:

```
library(randomForest)

rfModel <- randomForest(x=trainX, y=factor(trainY))
```

However, there are many hyperparameters you can tune for random forest models. Hyperparameters are the parameters you define before you train a machine learning model. For example, in the case of a random forest algorithm, you can define the number of trees you want in your random forest model. As another example, you can define the maximum number of terminal nodes for each tree in the forest, so that you can limit how big each tree in the forest can grow.

There are numerous hyperparameters you can define and fine-tune. We will take a look at a few of these hyperparameters:

- **ntree:** This defines the number of trees you want to build in the forest. Generally speaking, more trees mean better performance results. However, the amount of performance gain for each additional tree decreases as the number of trees in the forest increases. Since having more trees in a forest means higher cost in computations for training additional trees, you should try to find the balance and stop adding trees when the computational cost from training additional trees outweighs the performance gain.

- **sampsize**: This parameter defines the size of the sample to draw for training each tree. This introduces randomness in the forest, while training a random forest model. Having a high sample size results in a less random forest and has a higher chance of overfitting. This means that the trained tree performs and predicts well within the train set, but predicts poorly in the dataset that it has not seen before. Decreasing the sample size can help you avoid overfitting, but the performance of your model usually decreases as you decrease the sample size.
- **nodesize**: This parameter defines the minimum size of the terminal nodes, which means how many samples each terminal node needs to have at the very least. The larger this number is, the smaller the tree can grow. As you increase this number, you can mitigate the overfitting issues, but at the expense of the model performance.
- **maxnodes**: This parameter defines the maximum number of terminal nodes each tree in the forest can have. If you do not set this number, the algorithm is going to grow the tree to the fullest. This can result in overfitting the train set. Reducing the maximum number of terminal nodes can help you overcome overfitting issues.

For a more detailed description and information on other hyperparameters, you can refer to the official documentation that can be found at the following link: `https://www.rdocumentation.org/packages/randomForest/versions/4.6-14/topics/randomForest.`

Training a random forest model

Training a random forest model using the `randomForest` package is simple. Take a look at the following code:

```
rfModel <- randomForest(x=trainX, y=factor(trainY), ntree=200, maxnodes=24)
```

Using the `randomForest` function in the `randomForest` package, you can easily train a random forest model. You just need to supply the train set to the function. For illustration purposes, we are instructing the model to build 200 trees, where each tree can only grow up to 24 terminal nodes.

When you run this code, your model object will look as follows:

Name	Type	Value
⊙ rfModel	list [18] (S3: randomForest)	List of length 18
⊙ call	language	randomForest(x = trainX, y = factor(trainY), ntree = 200, maxnodes = 24)
type	character [1]	'classification'
⊙ predicted	factor	Factor with 6393 levels: "0", "0", "0", "0", "0", "0" , ...
err.rate	double [200 x 3]	0.12019 0.11917 0.12560 0.12535 0.12870 0.12930 0.00884 0.00792 0.00802 0.0...
confusion	double [2 x 3]	5.49e+03 8.06e+02 1.00e+01 8.90e+01 1.82e-03 9.01e-01
votes	double [6393 x 2] (S3: matrix	1.0000 1.0000 1.0000 0.9861 1.0000 1.0000 0.0000 0.0000 0.0000 0.0139 0.0000 ...
oob.times	double [6393]	80 74 75 72 72 68 ...
classes	character [2]	'0' '1'
importance	double [42 x 1]	8.807 1.574 1.074 1.301 0.954 2.164 ...
importanceSD	NULL	Pairlist of length 0
localImportance	NULL	Pairlist of length 0
proximity	NULL	Pairlist of length 0
ntree	double [1]	200
mtry	double [1]	6
⊙ forest	list [14]	List of length 14
y	factor	Factor with 6393 levels: "0", "0", "0", "0", "1", "0" , ...
test	NULL	Pairlist of length 0
inbag	NULL	Pairlist of length 0

Once a random forest model is trained or fitted, the model object contains a lot of useful information. One of the useful attributes you can extract from a trained random forest model is the information about individual trees in the forest. Using the `getTree` function, you can retrieve how the individual trees are built within the forest. Take a look at the following example:

```
> getTree(rfModel, 1)
   left daughter right daughter split var split point status prediction
1             2              3        42   302.37692      1          0
2             4              5         1     0.50000      1          0
3             6              7        35  2017.56718      1          0
4             8              9        39    11.50000      1          0
5            10             11        42    49.16778      1          0
6            12             13        38     9.00000      1          0
7            14             15        39    96.50000      1          0
8            16             17         3     0.50000      1          0
9            18             19        35  3884.07793      1          0
10           20             21        26     0.50000      1          0
11           22             23        24     0.50000      1          0
12            0              0         0     0.00000     -1          1
13           24             25         5     0.50000      1          0
14           26             27        36 10261.50000      1          0
15            0              0         0     0.00000     -1          1
16           28             29         5     0.50000      1          0
17            0              0         0     0.00000     -1          1
18           30             31        36 63155.50000      1          0
19           32             33        22     0.50000      1          0
20           34             35        39    33.50000      1          0
```

Here we are looking at the information about the first tree in the forest. This gives us some information about the structure of the tree. The `left daughter` and `right daughter` columns tell us the location of this node in the given tree. The `status` column tells us whether the node is terminal (-1) or not (1). The `prediction` column tells us the prediction from this node.

Other information we can get from the fitted random forest model is the prediction from each tree in the forest. Take a look at the following code:

```
predict(rfModel, trainX, predict.all=TRUE)
```

By using the `predict.all=TRUE` flag, the `prediction` function returns the predictions from each tree in the forest. Take a look at the following output:

```
> predict(rfModel, trainX, predict.all=TRUE)$individual
  [,1] [,2] [,3] [,4] [,5] [,6] [,7] [,8] [,9] [,10] [,11] [,12] [,13] [,14] [,15] [,16] [,17] [,18] [,19] [,20]
2  "0"  "0"  "0"  "0"  "0"  "0"  "0"  "0"  "0"  "0"   "0"   "0"   "0"   "0"   "0"   "0"   "0"   "0"   "0"   "0"
3  "0"  "0"  "0"  "0"  "0"  "0"  "0"  "0"  "0"  "0"   "0"   "0"   "0"   "0"   "0"   "0"   "0"   "0"   "0"   "0"
4  "0"  "0"  "0"  "0"  "0"  "0"  "0"  "0"  "0"  "0"   "0"   "0"   "0"   "0"   "0"   "0"   "0"   "0"   "0"   "0"
5  "0"  "0"  "0"  "0"  "0"  "0"  "0"  "0"  "0"  "0"   "0"   "0"   "0"   "0"   "0"   "0"   "0"   "0"   "0"   "0"
7  "0"  "0"  "0"  "0"  "0"  "0"  "0"  "0"  "0"  "1"   "0"   "0"   "0"   "0"   "0"   "0"   "0"   "0"   "0"   "0"
```

This output is showing the first 20 trees' predictions for the first five records in the train set. As you can see from this output, the 10th tree in the forest predicted the 5th record in the train set to be a class of 1, but all the other 19 trees predicted the 5th record in the train set to be a class of 0. As you can see from this output, different trees predict differently for each record of the test set. This is because each tree is trained with different subsets of features that are randomly selected. Using this information, you can see how the final predictions from the random forest model are formed from these individual sub-estimators or trees.

Other useful information that we can gain from a trained `randomForest` object is the feature importances, with which we can understand the importance or the impact of each feature on the final predictions. You can get the feature importances for each feature using the following code:

```
# - Feature Importances
importance(rfModel)
```

Part of the output of this code looks as follows:

```
> importance(rfModel)
                                    MeanDecreaseGini
Sales.ChannelAgent                     8.80679847
Sales.ChannelBranch                    1.57399368
Sales.ChannelCall Center               1.07412042
Sales.ChannelWeb                       1.30109148
Vehicle.SizeMedsize                    0.95446772
Vehicle.SizeSmall                      2.16432825
Vehicle.ClassLuxury Car                0.14581500
Vehicle.ClassLuxury SUV                0.09509184
Vehicle.ClassSports Car                0.69120913
Vehicle.ClassSUV                       0.95105991
Vehicle.ClassTwo-Door Car              0.51935534
PolicyCorporate L2                     0.43019126
PolicyCorporate L3                     0.29868539
PolicyPersonal L1                      0.28883213
PolicyPersonal L2                      0.16178421
PolicyPersonal L3                      0.23481424
PolicySpecial L1                       0.36156105
PolicySpecial L2                       0.06004588
PolicySpecial L3                       0.63030395
Policy.TypePersonal Auto               0.16764506
Policy.TypeSpecial Auto                0.36371783
EmploymentStatusEmployed               4.94663314
EmploymentStatusMedical Leave          0.58598988
EmploymentStatusRetired               70.39553508
EmploymentStatusUnemployed             5.81568328
Marital.StatusMarried                  3.86505447
Marital.StatusSingle                   2.64214736
EducationCollege                       1.35925811
EducationDoctor                        0.54873538
EducationHigh School or Below          0.88504666
EducationMaster                        1.09701383
CoverageExtended                       0.89261823
CoveragePremium                        0.57386404
GenderM                                0.87952114
```

As you can see from this output, the `EmploymentStatusRetired` feature seems to be the most important factor in making the final prediction and the `Income`, `Total.Claim.Amount`, and `Customer.Lifetime.Value` features follow as the second, third, and fourth most important features.

Evaluating a classification model

Earlier in this chapter, we discussed five different ways to look at the performance of a classification model. In this section, we are going to learn how we can compute and visualize the metrics for evaluating a classification model in R using the random forest model we have just built.

The first three metrics that we are going to look at are accuracy, precision, and recall. Before we go ahead and evaluate the model performance, we will need the model prediction results. In order to have the random forest model we have built in the previous section make predictions on a dataset, we can simply use the `predict` function. Take a look at the following code:

```
inSamplePreds <- as.double(predict(rfModel, trainX)) - 1
outSamplePreds <- as.double(predict(rfModel, testX)) - 1
```

With these prediction results, we are going to evaluate how well our random forest model performs in the train and test sets. The following code shows how we can compute accuracy, precision, and recall in R:

```
# - Accuracy
accuracy <- mean(testY == outSamplePreds)

# - Precision
precision <- sum(outSamplePreds & testY) / sum(outSamplePreds)

# - Recall
recall <- sum(outSamplePreds & testY) / sum(testY)
```

Using this method, we can compare the in-sample train set `accuracy`, `precision`, and `recall` against the out-of-sample test set's `accuracy`, `precision`, and `recall`. Take a look at the following output:

```
> # - Accuracy, Precision, and Recall
> inSampleAccuracy <- mean(trainY == inSamplePreds)
> outSampleAccuracy <- mean(testY == outSamplePreds)
> print(sprintf('In-Sample Accuracy: %0.4f', inSampleAccuracy))
[1] "In-Sample Accuracy: 0.8756"
> print(sprintf('Out-Sample Accuracy: %0.4f', outSampleAccuracy))
[1] "Out-Sample Accuracy: 0.8636"
>
> inSamplePrecision <- sum(inSamplePreds & trainY) / sum(inSamplePreds)
> outSamplePrecision <- sum(outSamplePreds & testY) / sum(outSamplePreds)
> print(sprintf('In-Sample Precision: %0.4f', inSamplePrecision))
[1] "In-Sample Precision: 0.9717"
> print(sprintf('Out-Sample Precision: %0.4f', outSamplePrecision))
[1] "Out-Sample Precision: 0.8980"
>
> inSampleRecall <- sum(inSamplePreds & trainY) / sum(trainY)
> outSampleRecall <- sum(outSamplePreds & testY) / sum(testY)
> print(sprintf('In-Sample Recall: %0.4f', inSampleRecall))
[1] "In-Sample Recall: 0.1151"
> print(sprintf('Out-Sample Recall: %0.4f', outSampleRecall))
[1] "Out-Sample Recall: 0.1065"
```

This output gives us a brief overview of how well our model performs at predicting the responses. For the train set, the accuracy of the overall prediction was 0.8756, meaning the model prediction was correct for about 88% of the time. For the test set, the accuracy of the overall prediction was 0.8636. You can also find that the precisions for in-sample and out-of-sample predictions were 0.9717 and 0.8980 respectively, and the recalls were 0.1151 and 0.1065. Due to the randomness and the different hyperparameters you might have used, you might get different results.

The next set of metrics we are going to look at are the ROC curve and the AUC. We are going to use the ROCR R package. If you do not have this package installed in your R environment, you can install it using the following command:

```
install.packages('ROCR')
```

Take a look at the following code for the ROC curve and the AUC number first:

```
library(ROCR)

inSamplePredProbs <- as.double(predict(rfModel, trainX, type='prob')[,2])
outSamplePredProbs <- as.double(predict(rfModel, testX, type='prob')[,2])

pred <- prediction(outSamplePredProbs, testY)
perf <- performance(pred, measure = "tpr", x.measure = "fpr")
```

```
auc <- performance(pred, measure='auc')@y.values[[1]]

plot(
  perf,
  main=sprintf('Random Forest Model ROC Curve (AUC: %0.2f)', auc),
  col='darkorange',
  lwd=2
) + grid()
abline(a = 0, b = 1, col='darkgray', lty=3, lwd=2)
```

The first thing we need to do is to get the predicted probabilities from the model we have built. Using the `predict` function and the `type='prob'` flag, we can get the predicted probabilities from the random forest model. Then, we are using the `prediction` function in the ROCR package. This function computes the number of true positives and false positives at different probability cutoffs that we need for the ROC curve. Using the output of the `prediction` function, we can then get the true positive rates and false positive rates at different probability cutoffs with the `performance` function in the ROCR package. Lastly, in order to get the AUC number, we can use the same `performance` function with a different flag, `measure='auc'`.

With this data, we can now plot the ROC curve. Using the `plot` function and the `perf` variable, which is the output of the `performance` function, we can plot the ROC curve. The plot looks as follows:

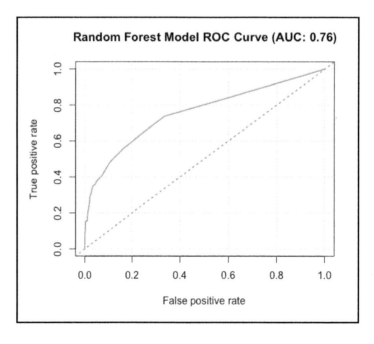

As you can see from this plot, the AUC of our random forest model was `0.76`. Compared to the benchmark straight line, which represents the random line, the model performs much better, and this shows that the model predictions are much better than random predictions.

 The full code for this R exercise can be found at the following link: `https://github.com/yoonhwang/hands-on-data-science-for-marketing/blob/master/ch.8/R/PredictingEngagement.R`.

Summary

In this chapter, we discussed predictive analytics and its applications in marketing. We first discussed what predictive analytics is and how it is used in various other industries, such as in the financial and healthcare industries. Then we discussed four common use cases of predictive analytics in marketing—likelihood of engagement, customer lifetime value, recommending the right products and contents, and customer acquisition and retention. There can be numerous other use cases of predictive analytics in marketing, so we recommend you keep up with the latest news on how predictive analytics can be used in marketing industries. We then discussed five different ways to evaluate the performances of predictive models—accuracy, precision, recall, the ROC curve, and the AUC.

In the following chapter, we are going to expand our knowledge of predictive analytics. We are going to discuss the concept and importance of measuring customer lifetime value, as well as building machine learning models for customer lifetime value predictions.

Customer Lifetime Value

9

In this chapter, we are going to focus on the second use case of predictive analytics in marketing, the customer lifetime value that we discussed in the previous chapter. In marketing, it is always a challenge to budget for marketing campaigns. We do not want to spend too much and result in a negative ROI. However, we also do not want to spend too little and have no visible impact or outcome. When determining the budget for a marketing strategy, it is essential to know what the expected return will be from running a given marketing campaign. Understanding what the **customer lifetime value (CLV)** is for individual customers can help marketers justify their marketing budget, as well as target potential high-value customers. In this chapter, we are going to discuss in more detail the concept and the advantage of calculating the CLV, as well as how to build a predictive machine learning model to predict the expected CLV for individual customers in Python and R.

In this chapter, we will cover the following topics:

- CLV
- Evaluation metrics for regression models
- Predicting the 3 month CLV with Python
- Predicting the 3 month CLV with R

CLV

In marketing, the CLV is one of the key metrics to have and monitor. The CLV measures customers' total worth to the business over the course of their lifetime relationship with the company. This metric is especially important to keep track of for acquiring new customers. It is generally more expensive to acquire new customers than to keep existing customers, so knowing the lifetime value and the costs associated with acquiring new customers is essential in order to build marketing strategies with a positive ROI. For example, if the average CLV of your customer is $100 and it only costs $10 to acquire a new customer, then your business will be generating more revenue as you acquire new customers.

However, if it costs $150 to acquire a new customer and the average CLV of your customer is still $100, then you will be losing money for each acquisition. Simply put, if your marketing spend for new customer acquisition exceeds the CLV, you will be losing money for each acquisition, and it is better to just work with the existing customers.

There are multiple ways to calculate CLV. One way is to find the customer's average purchase amount, purchase frequency, and lifetime span and do a simple calculation to get the CLV. For example, think of a hypothetical case, where a customer's average purchase amount is $100 and he or she makes purchases five times every month on average. Then this customer's average value per month is $500, which is simply multiplying the average purchase amount with the average purchase frequency. Now, we need to know this customer's lifetime span. One way to estimate a customer's lifetime span is to look at the average monthly churn rate, which is the percentage of customers leaving and terminating the relationship with your business. You can estimate a customer's lifetime span by dividing one by the churn rate. Assuming 5% of the churn rate in our hypothetical case, the estimated customer's lifetime span is 20 years. Given the customer's average value per month of $500 and lifetime span of 20 years, the CLV of this customer turns out to be $120,000. This final CLV amount is calculated by multiplying $500, the average value per month, by 12 months and the lifetime span of 20 years.

Because we do not typically know the lifetime span of customers, we often try to estimate CLV over the course of a certain period. It can be done by estimating a customer's 12-month CLV, 24-month CLV, or can also be a 3-month CLV. Aside from the method we discussed through an example, CLV can also be estimated through building predictive models. Using machine learning algorithms and customers' purchase history data, we can build machine learning models that predict customers' CLV over the course of a certain period. In the programming exercises in this chapter, we are going to learn how to build a regression model that predicts customers' 3-month CLV.

Evaluating regression models

We need to use a different set of metrics for evaluating regression models from those for classification model evaluations. This is because the prediction output of a regression model takes continuous values, meaning it can take any value and is not restricted to taking from a predefined set of values. On the other hand, as we have seen in `Chapter 8`, *Predicting the Likelihood of Marketing Engagement*, the prediction output of a classification model can only take a certain number of values. As was the case for the engagement prediction, our classification model from the previous chapter could only take two values—zero for no engagement and one for engagement. Because of this difference, we need to use different metrics to evaluate regression models.

In this section, we are going to discuss four commonly used methodologies to evaluate regression models—**mean squared error (MSE)**, **median absolute error (MAE)**, R^2, and predicted versus actual scatter plot. As the name suggests, MSE measures the average of the squared errors, where the errors are the differences between the predicted and actual values. The equation for *MSE* looks as follows:

$$MSE = \frac{1}{n} \sum_{i=1}^{n} (Y_i - Y_i')^2$$

The Y values in this equation are the actual values and Y' values are the predicted values. Because MSE is an average of squared errors, this measure is sensitive to and highly affected by outliers.

The MAE, on the other hand, is less sensitive to outliers and considered more robust, as the median is affected by the outliers or values at the end tails much less than the average. The equation, borrowed from this `scikit-learn` documentation page, `https://scikit-learn.org/stable/modules/model_evaluation.html#median-absolute-error`, looks as follows:

$$MedAE(y, \hat{y}) = median(|y_1 - \hat{y_1}|, \ldots, |y_n - \hat{y_n}|)$$

The y values in this equation represent the actual values and the $\hat{y}$ values represent the predicted values.

Another frequently used measure for regression models is R^2, also called the coefficient of determination. R^2 measures the goodness of fit. In other words, it measures how well a regression model is fitted to the data. Simply put, R^2 is the percentage of the explained variability of the target variable by the regression model. The equation looks as follows:

$$R^2 = \frac{ExplainedVariation}{TotalVariation}$$

R^2 typically ranges between zero and one. The R^2 value of zero means the model does not explain or capture the target variable variability at all and is not a good fit to the data. On the other hand, the R^2 value of one means that the model captures 100% of the target variable variability and is a perfect fit to the data. The closer to one the R^2 value is, the better the model fit is.

Lastly, a scatter plot of predicted values against actual values is also used to visualize how closely the model fits. An example of this scatter plot looks like the following:

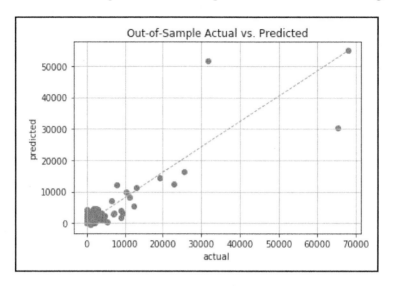

For a good fit, you will see points in this scatter plot that are close to the diagonal line. If the model's R^2 is high, the points will be close to the diagonal line. On the other hand, if the model's R^2 is low, the points will be dispersed away from the diagonal line. In the following programming exercises, we will discuss how to compute and visualize these measures in Python and R, and will use these measures to evaluate our regression model.

Predicting the 3 month CLV with Python

In this section, we are going to discuss how to build and evaluate regression models using machine learning algorithms in Python. By the end of this section, we will have built a predictive model using a linear regression algorithm to predict the CLV, more specifically, the expected 3 month customer value. We will be mainly using the pandas, matplotlib, and scikit-learn packages to analyze, visualize, and build machine learning models that predict the expected 3 month customer value. For those readers who would like to use R instead of Python for this exercise, you can skip to the next section.

For this exercise, we will be using one of the publicly available datasets from the UCI Machine Learning Repository, which can be found at this link: http://archive.ics.uci.edu/ml/datasets/online+retail.

You can follow this link and download the data that is available in XLSX format, named `Online Retail.xlsx`. Once you have downloaded this data, you can load it into your Jupyter Notebook by running the following command:

```
import pandas as pd

df = pd.read_excel('../data/Online Retail.xlsx', sheet_name='Online Retail')
```

The DataFrame, `df`, looks as follows:

```
df = pd.read_excel('../data/Online Retail.xlsx', sheet_name='Online Retail')
```

```
df.shape
```

```
(541909, 8)
```

```
df.head()
```

	InvoiceNo	StockCode	Description	Quantity	InvoiceDate	UnitPrice	CustomerID	Country
0	536365	85123A	WHITE HANGING HEART T-LIGHT HOLDER	6	2010-12-01 08:26:00	2.55	17850.0	United Kingdom
1	536365	71053	WHITE METAL LANTERN	6	2010-12-01 08:26:00	3.39	17850.0	United Kingdom
2	536365	84406B	CREAM CUPID HEARTS COAT HANGER	8	2010-12-01 08:26:00	2.75	17850.0	United Kingdom
3	536365	84029G	KNITTED UNION FLAG HOT WATER BOTTLE	6	2010-12-01 08:26:00	3.39	17850.0	United Kingdom
4	536365	84029E	RED WOOLLY HOTTIE WHITE HEART.	6	2010-12-01 08:26:00	3.39	17850.0	United Kingdom

As you might have noticed, we have used this dataset a few times in the previous chapters. With the knowledge we gained about this dataset from the previous chapters, we are going to first prepare our data by cleaning it up.

Data cleanup

As you might recall, there are a few things we need to clean up in this dataset. The clean-up steps are as follows:

1. **Handling negative quantity**: There are transactions with a negative `Quantity` value, which represent canceled orders. We are going to ignore those canceled orders for this exercise, so we will need to exclude them from our `pandas` DataFrame. The code to exclude these negative values in the `Quantity` column looks as follows:

   ```
   df = df.loc[df['Quantity'] > 0]
   ```

We are simply taking all of those rows with a positive `Quantity` value and storing them back to the `df` variable.

2. **Dropping NaN records**: We need to drop records with no `CustomerID`. Since we are going to build a machine learning model to predict the 3 month customer value, we need to group the data by the `CustomerID` column. Without it, we cannot properly build models for this project. The code to drop records with no `CustomerID` values looks like the following code snippet:

```
df = df[pd.notnull(df['CustomerID'])]
```

As you can see from this code, we are using the `notnull` function in the `pandas` package. This function returns a list of arrays, where `True` values indicate that the value in the given index is not `null` and `False` values indicate that the value in the given index is `null`. We store these records with not null values in the `CustomerID` column back to the `df` variable.

3. **Handling incomplete data**: Another cleanup we need to do is to handle incomplete data. If you recall from previous chapters, the transaction data for the last month is incomplete. Take a look at the following output:

```
print('Date Range: %s - %s' % (df['InvoiceDate'].min(), df['InvoiceDate'].max()))
Date Range: 2010-12-01 08:26:00 ~ 2011-12-09 12:50:00
```

As you can see from this output, the dataset has all of the transactions between December 1, 2010 and December 9, 2011. The data for the last month, December 2011, is not complete. In order to properly build a model for the 3 month customer value predictions, we are going to ignore the transactions in the last month. Take a look at the following code that shows how to drop those records from our DataFrame:

```
df = df.loc[df['InvoiceDate'] < '2011-12-01']
```

We are simply taking all of the transactions that occurred before December 01, 2011 and storing them back to the `df` variable.

4. **Total sales value**: Lastly, we need to create a column for the total sales value for each transaction. Take a look at the following code:

```
df['Sales'] = df['Quantity'] * df['UnitPrice']
```

We are multiplying the `Quantity` column by the `UnitPrice` column to get the total purchase amount for each transaction. Then, we store these values into a column named `Sales`. We have now completed all of the clean-up tasks.

Now we have cleaned up all of the transaction data, let's summarize this data for each order or `InvoiceNo`. Take a look at the following code:

```
orders_df = df.groupby(['CustomerID', 'InvoiceNo']).agg({
    'Sales': sum,
    'InvoiceDate': max
})
```

As you can see from this code, we are grouping the `DataFrame` `df` by two columns, `CustomerID` and `InvoiceNo`. Then, we are summing up all of the `Sales` values for each customer and order, and taking the last transaction time for the given order as `InvoiceDate`. This way we now have a `DataFrame`, `orders_df`, as we need to know about each order that each customer placed. The data looks like the following:

orders_df			
CustomerID	**InvoiceNo**	**Sales**	**InvoiceDate**
12346.0	541431	77183.60	2011-01-18 10:01:00
12347.0	537626	711.79	2010-12-07 14:57:00
	542237	475.39	2011-01-26 14:30:00
	549222	636.25	2011-04-07 10:43:00
	556201	382.52	2011-06-09 13:01:00
	562032	584.91	2011-08-02 08:48:00
	573511	1294.32	2011-10-31 12:25:00
12348.0	539318	892.80	2010-12-16 19:09:00
	541998	227.44	2011-01-25 10:42:00
	548955	367.00	2011-04-05 10:47:00
	568172	310.00	2011-09-25 13:13:00

Before we dive into building models, let's take a closer look at this customer purchase history data.

Data analysis

In order to calculate the CLV, we need to know the frequency, recency, and total amount of purchases by each customer. We are going to compute basic information about each customer's average and lifetime purchase amount, as well as each customer's duration and frequency of purchases. Take a look at the following code:

```
def groupby_mean(x):
    return x.mean()

def groupby_count(x):
    return x.count()

def purchase_duration(x):
    return (x.max() - x.min()).days

def avg_frequency(x):
    return (x.max() - x.min()).days/x.count()

groupby_mean.__name__ = 'avg'
groupby_count.__name__ = 'count'
purchase_duration.__name__ = 'purchase_duration'
avg_frequency.__name__ = 'purchase_frequency'

summary_df = orders_df.reset_index().groupby('CustomerID').agg({
    'Sales': [min, max, sum, groupby_mean, groupby_count],
    'InvoiceDate': [min, max, purchase_duration, avg_frequency]
})
```

We first group by the `CustomerID` column and aggregate the numbers by `Sales` and `InvoiceDate` columns. If you look closely at the aggregation functions, we are using four customer aggregation functions: `groupby_mean`, `groupby_count`, `purchase_duration`, and `avg_frequency`. The first function, `groupby_mean`, simply computes the average for each group and the second function, `groupby_count`, simply counts the number of records in each group. The `purchase_duration` function counts the number of days between the first and last invoice dates in each group and the `avg_frequency` function calculates the average number of days between orders by dividing `purchase_duration` by the number of orders.

The resulting `DataFrame` looks like the following:

```
summary_df
```

| | Sales | | | | | InvoiceDate | | | |
CustomerID	min	max	sum	avg	count	min	max	purchase_duration	purchase_frequency
12346.0	77183.60	77183.60	77183.60	77183.600000	1.0	2011-01-18 10:01:00	2011-01-18 10:01:00	0	0.000000
12347.0	382.52	1294.32	4085.18	680.863333	6.0	2010-12-07 14:57:00	2011-10-31 12:25:00	327	54.500000
12348.0	227.44	892.80	1797.24	449.310000	4.0	2010-12-16 19:09:00	2011-09-25 13:13:00	282	70.500000
12349.0	1757.55	1757.55	1757.55	1757.550000	1.0	2011-11-21 09:51:00	2011-11-21 09:51:00	0	0.000000
12350.0	334.40	334.40	334.40	334.400000	1.0	2011-02-02 16:01:00	2011-02-02 16:01:00	0	0.000000
12352.0	120.33	840.30	2506.04	313.255000	8.0	2011-02-16 12:33:00	2011-11-03 14:37:00	260	32.500000
12353.0	89.00	89.00	89.00	89.000000	1.0	2011-05-19 17:47:00	2011-05-19 17:47:00	0	0.000000
12354.0	1079.40	1079.40	1079.40	1079.400000	1.0	2011-04-21 13:11:00	2011-04-21 13:11:00	0	0.000000
12355.0	459.40	459.40	459.40	459.400000	1.0	2011-05-09 13:49:00	2011-05-09 13:49:00	0	0.000000
12356.0	58.35	2271.62	2811.43	937.143333	3.0	2011-01-18 09:50:00	2011-11-17 08:40:00	302	100.666667

This data gives us an idea of the purchases each customer has made. For example, the customer with ID `12346` only made one purchase on January 18, 2011. However, the customer with ID `12347` has made six purchases that range from December 7, 2010 to October 31, 2011, or over the course of `327` days. The average amount this customer spent on each order is `680` and, on average, this customer made a purchase every `54.5` days.

Let's take a closer look at the distributions of the number of purchases that the repeat customers have made.

Take a look at the following code:

```
summary_df.columns = ['_'.join(col).lower() for col in summary_df.columns]
summary_df = summary_df.loc[summary_df['invoicedate_purchase_duration'] >
0]

ax = summary_df.groupby('sales_count').count()['sales_avg'][:20].plot(
    kind='bar',
    color='skyblue',
    figsize=(12,7),
    grid=True
)

ax.set_ylabel('count')

plt.show()
```

As you can see from this code, we clean up the column names of the DataFrame, `summary_df`, in the first line. Then, we are only taking the customers who have made at least two or more purchases, which represents repeat customers. Lastly, we group by the `sales_count` column and count how many customers belong to each category. The resulting plot looks as follows:

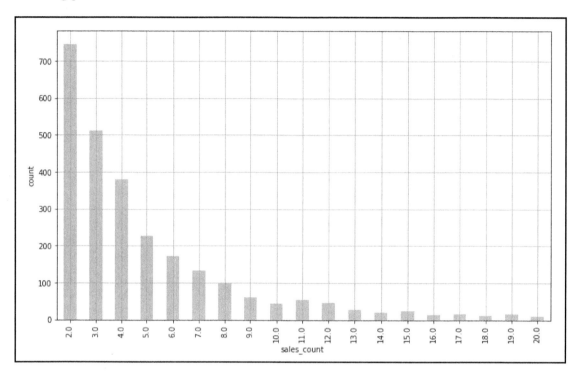

As you can see from this plot, the majority of customers have made 10 or less purchases historically. Let's take a look at the average number of days between purchases for these repeat customers. Take a look at the following code first:

```
ax = summary_df['invoicedate_purchase_frequency'].hist(
    bins=20,
    color='skyblue',
    rwidth=0.7,
    figsize=(12,7)
)

ax.set_xlabel('avg. number of days between purchases')
ax.set_ylabel('count')

plt.show()
```

We are building a histogram with the purchase frequency data using the `hist` function in the `pandas` package. The `bins` parameter defines the number of histogram bins to build. The result looks as follows:

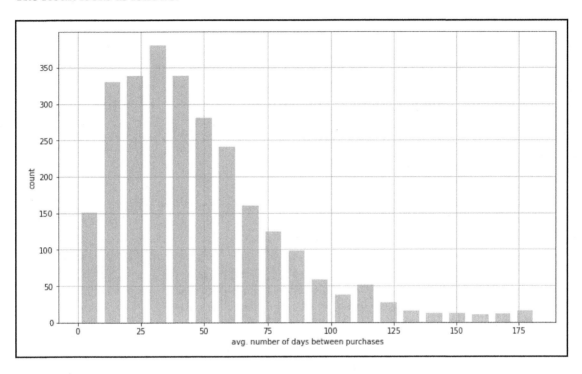

This plot tells us the overall view of how frequently repeat customers made purchases historically. As you can see from this plot, the majority of repeat customers made purchases every 20 to 50 days.

Predicting the 3 month CLV

In this section, we are going to build a model that predicts the 3 month customer value using the `pandas` and `scikit-learn` packages in Python. We are going to first slice the data into chunks of 3 months and take the last 3 months' data as the target for predictions and the rest as the features. We will first prepare our data for model building and then train a linear regression model for the 3 month customer value predictions.

Data preparation

In order to build a predictive model, we need to prepare our data first, so that we can feed the relevant data into the model. Take a look at the following code:

```
clv_freq = '3M'

data_df = orders_df.reset_index().groupby([
    'CustomerID',
    pd.Grouper(key='InvoiceDate', freq=clv_freq)
]).agg({
    'Sales': [sum, groupby_mean, groupby_count],
})

data_df.columns = ['_'.join(col).lower() for col in data_df.columns]
data_df = data_df.reset_index()
```

Since we want to predict the 3 month customer value, we are breaking down the data into chunks of 3 months for each customer. As you can see in the `groupby` function, we group the previously built DataFrame `orders_df` by `CustomerID` and a custom `Grouper`, which groups `InvoiceDate` by every 3 months. Then, for each group of 3 month time windows, we sum up all of the sales to get the total purchase amount, take the average of purchase amount and the total number of purchases for the given period for each customer. This way we have aggregate data that has purchase information for each customer for every 3 months. Lastly, we do some cleanup for the column names. The data in `data_df` now looks like the following:

	CustomerID	InvoiceDate	sales_sum	sales_avg	sales_count
0	12346.0	2011-03-31	77183.60	77183.600	1.0
1	12347.0	2010-12-31	711.79	711.790	1.0
2	12347.0	2011-03-31	475.39	475.390	1.0
3	12347.0	2011-06-30	1018.77	509.385	2.0
4	12347.0	2011-09-30	584.91	584.910	1.0
5	12347.0	2011-12-31	1294.32	1294.320	1.0
6	12348.0	2010-12-31	892.80	892.800	1.0
7	12348.0	2011-03-31	227.44	227.440	1.0
8	12348.0	2011-06-30	367.00	367.000	1.0
9	12348.0	2011-09-30	310.00	310.000	1.0

data_df.head(10)

In order to make things simpler, let's encode the `InvoiceDate` column values so that they are easier to read than the current date format. Take a look at the following code:

```
date_month_map = {
    str(x)[:10]: 'M_%s' % (i+1) for i, x in enumerate(
        sorted(data_df.reset_index()['InvoiceDate'].unique(), reverse=True)
    )
}

data_df['M'] = data_df['InvoiceDate'].apply(lambda x:
date_month_map[str(x)[:10]])
```

As you can see from this code, we are encoding date values into M_1, M_2, M_3, and so forth, where the smaller number represents more recent dates. For example, the date 2011-12-31 is now encoded as M_1 and the date 2011-09-30 is now encoded as M_2. The result looks as follows:

```
data_df.head(10)
```

	CustomerID	InvoiceDate	sales_sum	sales_avg	sales_count	M
0	12346.0	2011-03-31	77183.60	77183.600	1.0	M_4
1	12347.0	2010-12-31	711.79	711.790	1.0	M_5
2	12347.0	2011-03-31	475.39	475.390	1.0	M_4
3	12347.0	2011-06-30	1018.77	509.385	2.0	M_3
4	12347.0	2011-09-30	584.91	584.910	1.0	M_2
5	12347.0	2011-12-31	1294.32	1294.320	1.0	M_1
6	12348.0	2010-12-31	892.80	892.800	1.0	M_5
7	12348.0	2011-03-31	227.44	227.440	1.0	M_4
8	12348.0	2011-06-30	367.00	367.000	1.0	M_3
9	12348.0	2011-09-30	310.00	310.000	1.0	M_2

We are now ready to build a sample set with features and target variables. As briefly mentioned before, we are going to use the last 3 months as the target variable and the rest as the features, meaning we are going to train a machine learning model that predicts the last 3 months' customer value with the rest of the data. In order to train such a model, we need to transform this data into tabular data, where the rows represent the individual customers and the columns represent each feature. Take a look at the following code:

```
features_df = pd.pivot_table(
    data_df.loc[data_df['M'] != 'M_1'],
    values=['sales_sum', 'sales_avg', 'sales_count'],
    columns='M',
```

```
        index='CustomerID'
)

features_df.columns = ['_'.join(col) for col in features_df.columns]
```

As you can see from this code, we use the `pandas` function, `pivot_table`, where the index is going to be `CustomerID` and the columns are going to be `sales_sum`, `sales_avg`, and `sales_count` for each 3 month period. The DataFrame, `features_df`, that we created here looks like the following:

```
features_df.head(10)
```

CustomerID	sales_avg_M_2	sales_avg_M_3	sales_avg_M_4	sales_avg_M_5	sales_count_M_2	sales_count_M_3	sales_count_M_4	sales_count_M_5	sales_sum_M
12346.0	NaN	NaN	77183.600	NaN	NaN	NaN	1.0	NaN	N
12347.0	584.91	509.385	475.390	711.79	1.0	2.0	1.0	1.0	584
12348.0	310.00	367.000	227.440	892.80	1.0	1.0	1.0	1.0	310
12350.0	NaN	NaN	334.400	NaN	NaN	NaN	1.0	NaN	N
12352.0	316.25	NaN	312.362	NaN	2.0	NaN	5.0	NaN	632
12353.0	NaN	89.000	NaN	NaN	NaN	1.0	NaN	NaN	N
12354.0	NaN	1079.400	NaN	NaN	NaN	1.0	NaN	NaN	N
12355.0	NaN	459.400	NaN	NaN	NaN	1.0	NaN	NaN	N
12356.0	NaN	481.460	2271.620	NaN	NaN	1.0	1.0	NaN	N
12358.0	484.86	NaN	NaN	NaN	1.0	NaN	NaN	NaN	484

You might notice that this data has `NaN` values. We can encode these `NaN` values with `0.0` using the following code:

```
features_df = features_df.fillna(0)
```

Now that we have built the features DataFrame, let's build the target variables. Take a look at the following code:

```
response_df = data_df.loc[
    data_df['M'] == 'M_1',
    ['CustomerID', 'sales_sum']
]

response_df.columns = ['CustomerID', 'CLV_'+clv_freq]
```

As you can see from this code, we are taking the last 3 month period, the `M_1` group, as the target variable. The target column will be `sales_sum`, as we want to predict the next 3 month customer value, which is the total purchase amount that a given customer is likely to make in the next 3 months. The target variable looks like the following:

```
response_df.head(10)
```

	CustomerID	CLV_3M
5	12347.0	1294.32
10	12349.0	1757.55
14	12352.0	311.73
20	12356.0	58.35
21	12357.0	6207.67
25	12359.0	2876.85
28	12360.0	1043.78
33	12362.0	2119.85
37	12364.0	299.06
41	12370.0	739.28

There is only one thing left to build, which is a sample set for building machine learning models, combining features and response data together. Take a look at the following code:

```
sample_set_df = features_df.merge(
    response_df,
    left_index=True,
    right_on='CustomerID',
    how='left'
)

sample_set_df = sample_set_df.fillna(0)
```

As you can see here, we are simply joining the two `DataFrames` on `CustomerID`, using the `merge` function. By having the `how='left'` flag, we take all records in the features data, even if there is no corresponding data in the response data. This is a case where the given customer did not make any purchases in the last 3 months, so we encode them as zero. The final sample set now looks as follows:

	CLV_3M	CustomerID	sales_sum_M_5	sales_sum_M_4	sales_sum_M_3	sales_sum_M_2	sales_count_M_5	sales_count_M_4	sales_count_M_3	sales_count
9219	0.00	12346.0	0.00	77183.60	0.00	0.00	0.0	1.0	0.0	
5	1294.32	12347.0	711.79	475.39	1018.77	584.91	1.0	1.0	2.0	
9219	0.00	12348.0	892.80	227.44	367.00	310.00	1.0	1.0	1.0	
9219	0.00	12350.0	0.00	334.40	0.00	0.00	0.0	1.0	0.0	
14	311.73	12352.0	0.00	1561.81	0.00	632.50	0.0	5.0	0.0	
9219	0.00	12353.0	0.00	0.00	89.00	0.00	0.0	0.0	1.0	
9219	0.00	12354.0	0.00	0.00	1079.40	0.00	0.0	0.0	1.0	
9219	0.00	12355.0	0.00	0.00	459.40	0.00	0.0	0.0	1.0	
20	58.35	12356.0	0.00	2271.62	481.46	0.00	0.0	1.0	1.0	
9219	0.00	12358.0	0.00	0.00	0.00	484.86	0.0	0.0	0.0	

With this data, we can now build a model that predicts the next 3 month customer value with historical purchase data.

Linear regression

Similar to the previous chapter, we are going to split the sample set into train and test sets, using the following code:

```
from sklearn.model_selection import train_test_split

target_var = 'CLV_'+clv_freq
all_features = [x for x in sample_set_df.columns if x not in ['CustomerID',
target_var]]

x_train, x_test, y_train, y_test = train_test_split(
    sample_set_df[all_features],
    sample_set_df[target_var],
    test_size=0.3
)
```

As you can see from this code, we are taking 70% of the sample set for training the model and the remaining 30% for testing and evaluating the model performance. In this section, we will be using a linear regression model. However, we recommend experimenting with other machine learning algorithms, such as random forest and **support vector machine (SVM)**.

 More details on how to train these models with the `scikit-learn` package can be found at the following links: `https://scikit-learn.org/stable/modules/generated/sklearn.ensemble.RandomForestRegressor.html` and `https://scikit-learn.org/stable/modules/generated/sklearn.svm.SVR.html`.

In order to train a linear regression model with our dataset, you can use the following code:

```
from sklearn.linear_model import LinearRegression

reg_fit = LinearRegression()
reg_fit.fit(x_train, y_train)
```

This is as simple as it gets. You import the `LinearRegression` class of the `scikit-learn` package and initiate a `LinearRegression` object. Then, you can train a linear regression model using the `fit` function with the `x_train` features and the `y_train` targets.

Once a linear regression model is trained, there is some useful information that you can find in the `LinearRegression` object. First, you can get the intercept of the linear regression equation, using the `intercept_` attribute of the `LinearRegression` object, like the following:

```
reg_fit.intercept_
```

Also, you can find the fitted linear regression model's coefficients, using the `coef_` attribute like the following code:

```
reg_fit.coef_
```

The coefficients of each feature of the fitted regression model look as follows:

```
coef = pd.DataFrame(list(zip(all_features, reg_fit.coef_)))
coef.columns = ['feature', 'coef']

coef
```

	feature	coef
0	sales_avg_M_2	-0.053913
1	sales_avg_M_3	0.162335
2	sales_avg_M_4	0.241964
3	sales_avg_M_5	-0.550508
4	sales_count_M_2	41.247136
5	sales_count_M_3	40.512827
6	sales_count_M_4	62.766692
7	sales_count_M_5	-7.927177
8	sales_sum_M_2	0.533077
9	sales_sum_M_3	0.053559
10	sales_sum_M_4	-0.214531
11	sales_sum_M_5	0.604951

As you can see from this coefficient output, you can easily find which features have negative correlation with the target and which features have positive correlation with the target. For example, the previous 3 month period's average purchase amount, sales_avg_M_2, has negative impacts on the next 3 month customer value. This means that the higher the previous 3 month period's purchase amount is, the lower the next 3 month purchase amount will be. On the other hand, the second and third most recent 3 month period's average purchase amounts, sales_avg_M_3 and sales_avg_M_4, are positively correlated with the next 3 month customer value. In other words, the more a customer made purchases 3 months to 9 months ago, the higher value he or she will bring in the next 3 months. Looking at the coefficients is one way to gain insights on how the expected value will change, given certain features.

Using the 3 month customer value prediction output, you can custom-tailor your marketing strategies in different ways. Since you know the expected revenue or purchase amount from individual customers for the next 3 months, you can set a better informed budget for your marketing campaign. It should be set high enough to reach your target customers, but low enough to be below the expected 3 month customer value, so that you can have a positive ROI marketing campaign. On the other hand, you can also use these 3 month customer value prediction output values to specifically target these high-value customers for the next 3 months. This can help you to create marketing campaigns with a higher ROI, as those high-value customers, predicted by this model, are likely to bring in more revenue than the others.

Evaluating regression model performance

Now that we have a machine learning model that is fitted to predict the 3 month customer value, let's discuss how to evaluate the performance of this model. As discussed previously, we are going to use R^2, MAE, and a scatter plot of predicted versus actual to evaluate our model. We need to get the prediction output from our model first, as shown in the following code:

```
train_preds = reg_fit.predict(x_train)
test_preds = reg_fit.predict(x_test)
```

The `scikit-learn` package has implemented the functions to compute the R^2 and the MAE in their `metrics` module. You can use these functions by importing them into your environment, like the following code:

```
from sklearn.metrics import r2_score, median_absolute_error
```

As the names suggest, the `r2_score` function computes the R^2 and the `median_absolute_error` function computes the MAE. You can compute the R^2 and MAE numbers, using the following code:

```
r2_score(y_true=y_train, y_pred=train_preds)
median_absolute_error(y_true=y_train, y_pred=train_preds)
```

As you can see from here, both functions take two parameters, `y_true` and `y_pred`. The `y_true` parameter is for the actual target values and the `y_pred` parameter is for the predicted target values. Using these codes, the in-sample and out-of-sample values for R^2 and MAE in our case look like the following output:

- R-Squared

```
print('In-Sample R-Squared: %0.4f' % r2_score(y_true=y_train, y_pred=train_preds))
print('Out-of-Sample R-Squared: %0.4f' % r2_score(y_true=y_test, y_pred=test_preds))

In-Sample R-Squared: 0.4445
Out-of-Sample R-Squared: 0.7947
```

- Median Absolute Error

```
print('In-Sample MSE: %0.4f' % median_absolute_error(y_true=y_train, y_pred=train_preds))
print('Out-of-Sample MSE: %0.4f' % median_absolute_error(y_true=y_test, y_pred=test_preds))

In-Sample MSE: 178.2854
Out-of-Sample MSE: 178.7393
```

Due to the randomness in splitting the sample set into train and test sets, your might differ from these results. In our case, the in-sample R^2 was `0.4445` and the out-of-sample R^2 was `0.7947`. On the other hand, the in-sample MAE was `178.2854` and the out-of-sample MAE was `178.7393`. Looking at these numbers, we do not necessarily see a hint of overfitting or a big gap between the in-sample and out-of-sample performances.

Lastly, let's take a look at the scatter plot of predicted versus actual. You can use the following code for this scatter plot:

```
plt.scatter(y_test, test_preds)
plt.plot([0, max(y_test)], [0, max(test_preds)], color='gray', lw=1,
linestyle='--')

plt.xlabel('actual')
plt.ylabel('predicted')
plt.title('Out-of-Sample Actual vs. Predicted')
plt.grid()

plt.show()
```

The resulting plot looks as follows:

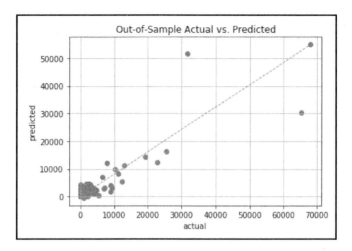

As you can see from this plot, the *x*-values are the actual values and the *y*-values are the predicted values. As discussed earlier, the more the points that are on the straight line, the better the predictions are. This is because points on the straight line suggest that the actual values and the predicted values are close to each other. Looking at this plot, the points seem to be positioned around the straight line, which suggests that the predictions and the actual values are not too far apart from each other.

The full code for this Python exercise can be found at the following repository: `https://github.com/yoonhwang/hands-on-data-science-for-marketing/blob/master/ch.9/python/CustomerLifetimeValue.ipynb`.

Predicting the 3 month CLV with R

In this section, we are going to discuss how to build and evaluate regression models using machine learning algorithms in R. By the end of this section, we will have built a predictive model using a linear regression algorithm to predict the CLV, more specifically, the expected 3 month customer value. We will be using a handful of R packages, such as `dplyr`, `reshape2`, and `caTools`, to analyze, transform, and prepare the data for building machine learning models to predict the expected 3 month customer value. For those readers who would like to use Python instead of R for this exercise, you can refer to the previous section.

For this exercise, we will be using one of the publicly available datasets from the UCI Machine Learning Repository, which can be found at this link: `http://archive.ics.uci.edu/ml/datasets/online+retail`. You can follow this link and download the data that is available in XLSX format, named `Online Retail.xlsx`. Once you have downloaded this data, you can load it into your R environment by running the following command:

```
library(dplyr)
library(readxl)

#### 1. Load Data ####
df <- read_excel(
  path="~/Documents/data-science-for-marketing/ch.9/data/Online
Retail.xlsx",
  sheet="Online Retail"
)
```

The DataFrame, `df`, looks as follows:

	InvoiceNo	StockCode	Description	Quantity	InvoiceDate	UnitPrice	CustomerID	Country
1	536365	85123A	WHITE HANGING HEART T-LIGHT HOLDER	6	2010-12-01 08:26:00	2.55	17850	United Kingdom
2	536365	71053	WHITE METAL LANTERN	6	2010-12-01 08:26:00	3.39	17850	United Kingdom
3	536365	84406B	CREAM CUPID HEARTS COAT HANGER	8	2010-12-01 08:26:00	2.75	17850	United Kingdom
4	536365	84029G	KNITTED UNION FLAG HOT WATER BOTTLE	6	2010-12-01 08:26:00	3.39	17850	United Kingdom
5	536365	84029E	RED WOOLLY HOTTIE WHITE HEART.	6	2010-12-01 08:26:00	3.39	17850	United Kingdom
6	536365	22752	SET 7 BABUSHKA NESTING BOXES	2	2010-12-01 08:26:00	7.65	17850	United Kingdom
7	536365	21730	GLASS STAR FROSTED T-LIGHT HOLDER	6	2010-12-01 08:26:00	4.25	17850	United Kingdom
8	536366	22633	HAND WARMER UNION JACK	6	2010-12-01 08:28:00	1.85	17850	United Kingdom
9	536366	22632	HAND WARMER RED POLKA DOT	6	2010-12-01 08:28:00	1.85	17850	United Kingdom
10	536367	84879	ASSORTED COLOUR BIRD ORNAMENT	32	2010-12-01 08:34:00	1.69	13047	United Kingdom
11	536367	22745	POPPY'S PLAYHOUSE BEDROOM	6	2010-12-01 08:34:00	2.10	13047	United Kingdom
12	536367	22748	POPPY'S PLAYHOUSE KITCHEN	6	2010-12-01 08:34:00	2.10	13047	United Kingdom
13	536367	22749	FELTCRAFT PRINCESS CHARLOTTE DOLL	8	2010-12-01 08:34:00	3.75	13047	United Kingdom
14	536367	22310	IVORY KNITTED MUG COSY	6	2010-12-01 08:34:00	1.65	13047	United Kingdom
15	536367	84969	BOX OF 6 ASSORTED COLOUR TEASPOONS	6	2010-12-01 08:34:00	4.25	13047	United Kingdom

As you might have noticed, we have used this dataset a few times in the previous chapters. With the knowledge we gained about this dataset from the previous chapters, we are going to first prepare our data by cleaning up the data.

Data cleanup

As you might recall, there are a few things we need to clean up in this dataset. The clean-up steps are as follows:

1. **Handling negative quantity**: There are transactions with a negative `Quantity` value, which represent canceled orders. We are going to ignore those canceled orders for this exercise, so we will need to exclude them from our `DataFrame`. The code to exclude these negative values in the `Quantity` column looks as follows:

    ```
    df <- df[which(df$Quantity > 0),]
    ```

    We are simply taking all of those rows with a positive `Quantity` value and storing them back to the variable `df`.

2. **Dropping NA records**: We need to drop records with no value in the `CustomerID` column. Since we are going to build a machine learning model to predict the 3 month customer value, we need to group the data by the `CustomerID` column. Without it, we cannot properly build models for this project. The code to drop records with null values looks like the following code snippet:

    ```
    df <- na.omit(df)
    ```

    As you can see from this code, we are using the `na.omit` function in R. This function returns an object with `null` or `NA` values removed. Then, we store the output back to the original DataFrame, `df` variable.

3. **Handling incomplete data**: If you recall from previous chapters, the transaction data for the last month is incomplete. Take a look at the following output:

    ```
    > sprintf("Date Range: %s ~ %s", min(df$InvoiceDate), max(df$InvoiceDate))
    [1] "Date Range: 2010-12-01 08:26:00 ~ 2011-12-09 12:50:00"
    ```

    As you can see from this output, the dataset has all the transactions between December 1st, 2010 and December 9, 2011. The data for the last month, December of 2011, is not complete. In order to properly build a model for the 3 month customer value predictions, we are going to ignore the transactions in the last month. Take a look at the following code on how to drop those records from our DataFrame:

    ```
    df <- df[which(df$InvoiceDate < '2011-12-01'),]
    ```

We are simply taking all of the transactions that occurred before December 1, 2011 and storing them back to the variable, df.

4. **Total sales value**: Lastly, we need to create a column for the total sales value for each transaction. Take a look at the following code:

```
df$Sales <- df$Quantity * df$UnitPrice
```

We are simply multiplying the Quantity column by the UnitPrice column to get the total purchase amount for each transaction. Then, we store these values into a column named Sales. We have now completed all the cleanup tasks.

Now we have cleaned up all the transaction data, let's summarize this data for each order or InvoiceNo. Take a look at the following code:

```
# per order data
ordersDF <- df %>%
  group_by(CustomerID, InvoiceNo) %>%
  summarize(Sales=sum(Sales), InvoiceDate=max(InvoiceDate))
```

As you can see from this code, we are grouping df by two columns, CustomerID and InvoiceNo. Then, we are summing up all the Sales values for each customer and order, and taking the last transaction time for the given order as the InvoiceDate. This way we now have a DataFrame, ordersDF, that we need to know about each order that each customer placed. The data looks like the following:

	CustomerID	InvoiceNo	Sales	InvoiceDate
1	12346	541431	77183.60	2011-01-18 10:01:00
2	12347	537626	711.79	2010-12-07 14:57:00
3	12347	542237	475.39	2011-01-26 14:30:00
4	12347	549222	636.25	2011-04-07 10:43:00
5	12347	556201	382.52	2011-06-09 13:01:00
6	12347	562032	584.91	2011-08-02 08:48:00
7	12347	573511	1294.32	2011-10-31 12:25:00
8	12348	539318	892.80	2010-12-16 19:09:00
9	12348	541998	227.44	2011-01-25 10:42:00
10	12348	548955	367.00	2011-04-05 10:47:00
11	12348	568172	310.00	2011-09-25 13:13:00
12	12349	577609	1757.55	2011-11-21 09:51:00
13	12350	543037	334.40	2011-02-02 16:01:00
14	12352	544156	296.50	2011-02-16 12:33:00
15	12352	545323	144.35	2011-03-01 14:57:00

Before we dive into building models, let's take a closer look at this customer purchase history data.

Data analysis

In order to calculate the CLV, we need to know the frequency, recency, and total amount of purchases by each customer. We are going to compute basic information about each customer's average and lifetime purchase amount, as well as each customer's duration and frequency of purchases. Take a look at the following code:

```
# order amount & frequency summary
summaryDF <- ordersDF %>%
  group_by(CustomerID) %>%
  summarize(
    SalesMin=min(Sales), SalesMax=max(Sales), SalesSum=sum(Sales),
    SalesAvg=mean(Sales), SalesCount=n(),
    InvoiceDateMin=min(InvoiceDate), InvoiceDateMax=max(InvoiceDate),
    PurchaseDuration=as.double(floor(max(InvoiceDate)-min(InvoiceDate))),
    PurchaseFrequency=as.double(floor(max(InvoiceDate)-
min(InvoiceDate)))/n()
  )
```

We first group by the `CustomerID` column and aggregate the numbers by `Sales` and `InvoiceDate` columns. Using the `min`, `max`, `sum`, `mean`, and n functions in R, we can compute the minimum, maximum, and total purchase amount, as well as the average amount and the number of purchases for each customer. We also use the `min` and `max` functions to get the first and last order dates for each customer. For `PurchaseDuration`, we are taking the number of days between the last and the first order dates. For `PurchaseFrequency`, we are dividing the `PurchaseDuration` number by the number of orders to get the average number of days between purchases.

The resulting DataFrame, `summaryDF`, looks like the following:

	CustomerID	SalesMin	SalesMax	SalesSum	SalesAvg	SalesCount	InvoiceDateMin	InvoiceDateMax	PurchaseDuration	PurchaseFrequency
1	12346	77183.60	77183.60	77183.60	77183.6000	1	2011-01-18 10:01:00	2011-01-18 10:01:00	0	0.000000
2	12347	382.52	1294.32	4085.18	680.8633	6	2010-12-07 14:57:00	2011-10-31 12:25:00	327	54.500000
3	12348	227.44	892.80	1797.24	449.3100	4	2010-12-16 19:09:00	2011-09-25 13:13:00	282	70.500000
4	12349	1757.55	1757.55	1757.55	1757.5500	1	2011-11-21 09:51:00	2011-11-21 09:51:00	0	0.000000
5	12350	334.40	334.40	334.40	334.4000	1	2011-02-02 16:01:00	2011-02-02 16:01:00	0	0.000000
6	12352	120.33	840.30	2506.04	313.2550	8	2011-02-16 12:33:00	2011-11-03 14:37:00	260	32.500000
7	12353	89.00	89.00	89.00	89.0000	1	2011-05-19 17:47:00	2011-05-19 17:47:00	0	0.000000
8	12354	1079.40	1079.40	1079.40	1079.4000	1	2011-04-21 13:11:00	2011-04-21 13:11:00	0	0.000000
9	12355	459.40	459.40	459.40	459.4000	1	2011-05-09 13:49:00	2011-05-09 13:49:00	0	0.000000
10	12356	58.35	2271.62	2811.43	937.1433	3	2011-01-18 09:50:00	2011-11-17 08:40:00	302	100.666667
11	12357	6207.67	6207.67	6207.67	6207.6700	1	2011-11-06 16:07:00	2011-11-06 16:07:00	0	0.000000
12	12358	484.86	484.86	484.86	484.8600	1	2011-07-12 10:04:00	2011-07-12 10:04:00	0	0.000000
13	12359	547.50	2876.85	6372.58	1593.1450	4	2011-01-12 12:43:00	2011-10-13 12:47:00	274	68.500000
14	12360	534.70	1083.58	2662.06	887.3533	3	2011-05-23 09:43:00	2011-10-18 15:22:00	148	49.333333
15	12361	189.90	189.90	189.90	189.9000	1	2011-02-25 13:51:00	2011-02-25 13:51:00	0	0.000000

This data gives us an idea of the purchases each customer has made. For example, the customer with ID `12346` only made one purchase on January 18, 2011. However, the customer with ID `12347` has made six purchases that range from December 7, 2010 to October 31, 2011, or over the course of `327` days. The average amount this customer spent on each order is about `681` and, on average, this customer made a purchase every `54.5` days.

Let's take a closer look at the distributions of the number of purchases that the repeat customers have made. Take a look at the following code:

```
summaryDF <- summaryDF[which(summaryDF$PurchaseDuration > 0),]

salesCount <- summaryDF %>%
  group_by(SalesCount) %>%
  summarize(Count=n())

ggplot(salesCount[1:19,], aes(x=SalesCount, y=Count)) +
  geom_bar(width=0.5, stat="identity") +
  ggtitle('') +
  xlab("Sales Count") +
  ylab("Count") +
  theme(plot.title = element_text(hjust = 0.5))
```

We first exclude customers with only one purchase from our analysis in the first line of code. Then, we count the number of customers for each `SalesCount`. Lastly, we create a bar plot using `ggplot` and `geom_bar` to display this data. The result looks as follows:

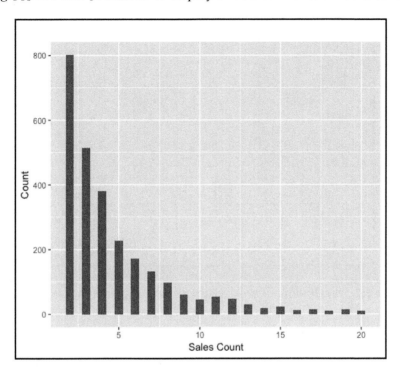

As you can see from this plot, the majority of customers have made 10 or less purchases historically. Let's take a look at the average number of days between purchases for these repeat customers. Take a look at the following code first:

```
hist(
    summaryDF$PurchaseFrequency,
    breaks=20,
    xlab='avg. number of days between purchases',
    ylab='count',
    main=''
)
```

We are building a histogram with the purchase frequency data using the `hist` function in R. The `breaks` parameter defines the number of histogram bins to build. The result looks as follows:

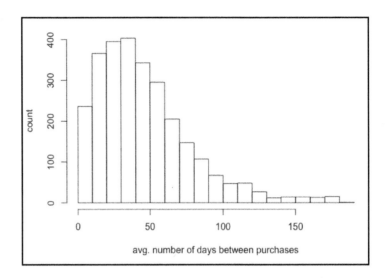

This plot tells us the overall view of how frequently repeat customers made purchases historically. As you can see from this plot, the majority of repeat customers made purchases every 20 to 50 days.

Predicting the 3 month CLV

In this section, we are going to build a model that predicts the 3 month customer value in R. We are going to first slice the data into chunks of 3 months and take the last 3 month data as the target for predictions and the rest as the features. We will first prepare our data for model building and then train a linear regression model for the 3 month customer value predictions.

Data preparation

In order to build a predictive model, we need to prepare our data first, so that we can feed in the relevant data into the model. Take a look at the following code:

```
# group data into every 3 months
library(lubridate)

ordersDF$Quarter = as.character(round_date(ordersDF$InvoiceDate, '3
```

```
months'))

dataDF <- ordersDF %>%
    group_by(CustomerID, Quarter) %>%
    summarize(SalesSum=sum(Sales), SalesAvg=mean(Sales), SalesCount=n())
```

As you can see from this code, we are using the lubridate package that is going to help us to handle data with dates more easily. Using the round_date function in the lubridate package, we first round InvoiceDate to the nearest quarter. Then, we group the data by CustomerID and the newly-created column, Quarter, to get the quarterly sales data for each customer. For each group of 3 month time window, we sum up all of the sales to get the total purchase amount and take the average of purchase amount, and the total number of purchases for the given period for each customer. This way we have aggregate data that has purchase information for each customer for every 3 months. The data in dataDF now looks like the following:

	CustomerID	Quarter	SalesSum	SalesAvg	SalesCount
1	12346	2011-01-01	77183.60	77183.6000	1
2	12347	2011-01-01	1187.18	593.5900	2
3	12347	2011-04-01	636.25	636.2500	1
4	12347	2011-07-01	967.43	483.7150	2
5	12347	2011-10-01	1294.32	1294.3200	1
6	12348	2011-01-01	1120.24	560.1200	2
7	12348	2011-04-01	367.00	367.0000	1
8	12348	2011-10-01	310.00	310.0000	1
9	12349	2012-01-01	1757.55	1757.5500	1
10	12350	2011-01-01	334.40	334.4000	1
11	12352	2011-04-01	1561.81	312.3620	5
12	12352	2011-10-01	944.23	314.7433	3
13	12353	2011-07-01	89.00	89.0000	1
14	12354	2011-04-01	1079.40	1079.4000	1
15	12355	2011-04-01	459.40	459.4000	1

In order to make things simpler, let's encode the Quarter column values to make them easier to read than the current date format. Take a look at the following code:

```
dataDF$Quarter[dataDF$Quarter == "2012-01-01"] <- "Q1"
dataDF$Quarter[dataDF$Quarter == "2011-10-01"] <- "Q2"
dataDF$Quarter[dataDF$Quarter == "2011-07-01"] <- "Q3"
dataDF$Quarter[dataDF$Quarter == "2011-04-01"] <- "Q4"
dataDF$Quarter[dataDF$Quarter == "2011-01-01"] <- "Q5"
```

As you can see from this code, we are encoding the date values into Q1, Q2, Q3, and so forth, where the smaller number represents more recent dates. For example, the date 2012-01-01 is now encoded as Q1 and the date 2011-10-01 is now encoded as Q2. The result looks as follows:

	CustomerID	Quarter	SalesSum	SalesAvg	SalesCount
1	12346	Q5	77183.60	77183.6000	1
2	12347	Q5	1187.18	593.5900	2
3	12347	Q4	636.25	636.2500	1
4	12347	Q3	967.43	483.7150	2
5	12347	Q2	1294.32	1294.3200	1
6	12348	Q5	1120.24	560.1200	2
7	12348	Q4	367.00	367.0000	1
8	12348	Q2	310.00	310.0000	1
9	12349	Q1	1757.55	1757.5500	1
10	12350	Q5	334.40	334.4000	1
11	12352	Q4	1561.81	312.3620	5
12	12352	Q2	944.23	314.7433	3
13	12353	Q3	89.00	89.0000	1
14	12354	Q4	1079.40	1079.4000	1
15	12355	Q4	459.40	459.4000	1

We are now ready to build a sample set with features and target variables. As briefly mentioned before, we are going to use the last 3 months as the target variable and the rest as the features, meaning we are going to train a machine learning model that predicts the last 3 month customer value with the rest of the data. In order to train such a model, we need to transform this data into tabular data, where the rows represent the individual customers and the columns represent each feature. Take a look at the following code:

```
# install.packages('reshape2')
library(reshape2)

salesSumFeaturesDF <- dcast(
    dataDF[which(dataDF$Quarter != "Q1"),],
    CustomerID ~ Quarter,
    value.var="SalesSum"
)
colnames(salesSumFeaturesDF) <- c("CustomerID", "SalesSum.Q2",
"SalesSum.Q3", "SalesSum.Q4", "SalesSum.Q5")

salesAvgFeaturesDF <- dcast(
```

```
      dataDF[which(dataDF$Quarter != "Q1"),],
      CustomerID ~ Quarter,
      value.var="SalesAvg"
   )
   colnames(salesAvgFeaturesDF) <- c("CustomerID", "SalesAvg.Q2",
   "SalesAvg.Q3", "SalesAvg.Q4", "SalesAvg.Q5")

   salesCountFeaturesDF <- dcast(
      dataDF[which(dataDF$Quarter != "Q1"),],
      CustomerID ~ Quarter,
      value.var="SalesCount"
   )
   colnames(salesCountFeaturesDF) <- c("CustomerID", "SalesCount.Q2",
   "SalesCount.Q3", "SalesCount.Q4", "SalesCount.Q5")

   featuresDF <- merge(
      merge(salesSumFeaturesDF, salesAvgFeaturesDF, by="CustomerID"),
      salesCountFeaturesDF, by="CustomerID"
   )
   featuresDF[is.na(featuresDF)] <- 0
```

As you can see from this code, we are using the reshape2 package to pivot the data. For
example, using the dcast function in the reshape2 package, we first transform the
SalesSum data, where the row index represents each customer or CustomerID, the
columns are each quarter, and the values are the total sales or purchase amount for the
given customer and quarter. We repeat this process three times for SalesSum, SalesAvg,
and SalesCount columns and merge the data in the end. Using the merge function, we can
merge these DataFrames by the CustomerID index. Lastly, we encode the null or NA
values with 0, by using the is.na function. The result looks like the following:

	CustomerID	SalesSum.Q2	SalesSum.Q3	SalesSum.Q4	SalesSum.Q5	SalesAvg.Q2	SalesAvg.Q3	SalesAvg.Q4	SalesAvg.Q5	SalesCount.Q2	SalesCount.Q3
1	12346	0.00	0.00	0.00	77183.60	0.0000	0.00000	0.0000	77183.6000	0	0
2	12347	1294.32	967.43	636.25	1187.18	1294.3200	483.71500	636.2500	593.5900	1	2
3	12348	310.00	0.00	367.00	1120.24	310.0000	0.00000	367.0000	560.1200	1	0
4	12350	0.00	0.00	0.00	334.40	0.0000	0.00000	0.0000	334.4000	0	0
5	12352	944.23	0.00	1561.81	0.00	314.7433	0.00000	312.3620	0.0000	3	0
6	12353	0.00	89.00	0.00	0.00	0.0000	89.00000	0.0000	0.0000	0	1
7	12354	0.00	0.00	1079.40	0.00	0.0000	0.00000	1079.4000	0.0000	0	0
8	12355	0.00	0.00	459.40	0.00	0.0000	0.00000	459.4000	0.0000	0	0
9	12356	0.00	0.00	481.46	2271.62	0.0000	0.00000	481.4600	2271.6200	0	0
10	12357	6207.67	0.00	0.00	0.00	6207.6700	0.00000	0.0000	0.0000	1	0
11	12358	0.00	484.86	0.00	0.00	0.0000	484.86000	0.0000	0.0000	0	1
12	12359	2876.85	1109.32	0.00	2386.41	2876.8500	1109.32000	0.0000	1193.2050	1	1
13	12360	1578.48	1083.58	0.00	0.00	789.2400	1083.58000	0.0000	0.0000	2	1
14	12361	0.00	0.00	189.90	0.00	0.0000	0.00000	189.9000	0.0000	0	0
15	12362	2949.84	773.01	974.34	0.00	589.9680	386.50500	487.1700	0.0000	5	2

Now that we have built the features `DataFrame`, let's build the target variables. Take a look at the following code:

```
responseDF <- dataDF[which(dataDF$Quarter == "Q1"),] %>%
    select(CustomerID, SalesSum)

colnames(responseDF) <- c("CustomerID", "CLV_3_Month")
```

As you can see from this code, we are taking the last 3 month period, Q1 group, as the target variable. The target column will be `SalesSum`, as we want to predict the next 3 month customer value, which is the total purchase amount that a given customer is likely to make in the next 3 months. The result looks like the following:

	CustomerID	CLV_3_Month
1	12349	1757.55
2	12356	58.35
3	12375	227.20
4	12380	1040.39
5	12388	286.40
6	12391	460.89
7	12395	265.83
8	12406	1794.05
9	12421	178.48
10	12427	239.72
11	12429	905.52
12	12433	2843.29
13	12437	491.01
14	12438	2016.78
15	12444	936.64

There is only one thing left to build, which is a sample set for building machine learning models, combining features and response data together. Take a look at the following code:

```
sampleDF <- merge(featuresDF, responseDF, by="CustomerID", all.x=TRUE)
sampleDF[is.na(sampleDF)] <- 0
```

As you can see here, we are simply joining the two `DataFrames` on `CustomerID` using the `merge` function. By having the `all.x=TRUE` flag, we take all records in the features data, even if there is no corresponding data in the response data. This is a case where the given customer did not make any purchases in the last 3 months, so we encode them as 0. The final sample set now looks as follows:

SalesSum.Q3	SalesSum.Q4	SalesSum.Q5	SalesAvg.Q2	SalesAvg.Q3	SalesAvg.Q4	SalesAvg.Q5	SalesCount.Q2	SalesCount.Q3	SalesCount.Q4	SalesCount.Q5	CLV_3_Month
0.00	0.00	77183.60	0.0000	0.00000	0.0000	77183.6000	0	0	0	1	0.00
967.43	636.25	1187.18	1294.3200	483.71500	636.2500	593.5900	1	2	1	2	0.00
0.00	367.00	1120.24	310.0000	0.00000	367.0000	560.1200	1	0	1	2	0.00
0.00	0.00	334.40	0.0000	0.00000	0.0000	334.4000	0	0	0	1	0.00
0.00	1561.81	0.00	314.7433	0.00000	312.3620	0.0000	3	0	5	0	0.00
89.00	0.00	0.00	0.0000	89.00000	0.0000	0.0000	0	1	0	0	0.00
0.00	1079.40	0.00	0.0000	0.00000	1079.4000	0.0000	0	0	1	0	0.00
0.00	459.40	0.00	0.0000	0.00000	459.4000	0.0000	0	0	1	0	0.00
0.00	481.46	2271.62	0.0000	0.00000	481.4600	2271.6200	0	0	1	1	58.35
0.00	0.00	0.00	6207.6700	0.00000	0.0000	0.0000	1	0	0	0	0.00
484.86	0.00	0.00	0.0000	484.86000	0.0000	0.0000	0	1	0	0	0.00
1109.32	0.00	2386.41	2876.8500	1109.32000	0.0000	1193.2050	1	1	0	2	0.00
1083.58	0.00	0.00	789.2400	1083.58000	0.0000	0.0000	2	1	0	0	0.00
0.00	189.90	0.00	0.0000	0.00000	189.9000	0.0000	0	0	1	0	0.00
773.01	974.34	0.00	589.9680	386.50500	487.1700	0.0000	5	2	2	0	0.00
0.00	299.10	0.00	252.9000	0.00000	299.1000	0.0000	1	0	1	0	0.00
0.00	0.00	0.00	334.2600	0.00000	0.0000	0.0000	3	0	0	0	0.00
0.00	641.38	0.00	0.0000	0.00000	320.6900	0.0000	0	0	2	0	0.00
0.00	938.39	1868.02	739.2800	0.00000	938.3900	934.0100	1	0	1	2	0.00

With this data, we can now build a model that predicts the next 3 month customer value with historical purchase data.

Linear regression

Similar to the previous chapter, we are going to split the sample set into train and test sets using the following code:

```
# train/test set split
library(caTools)

sample <- sample.split(sampleDF$CustomerID, SplitRatio = .8)

train <- as.data.frame(subset(sampleDF, sample == TRUE))[,-1]
test <- as.data.frame(subset(sampleDF, sample == FALSE))[,-1]
```

As you can see from this code, we are taking 80% of the sample set for training the model and the remaining 20% for testing and evaluating the model performance. In this section, we will be using a linear regression model. However, we recommend experimenting with other machine learning algorithms, such as **random forest** and **support vector machine (SVM)**. You can train a random forest model with the `randomForest` package and an SVM model with the `e1071` package. We highly recommend taking a look at their documentation on the usage.

In order to train a linear regression model with our dataset, you can use the following code:

```
# Linear regression model
regFit <- lm(CLV_3_Month ~ ., data=train)
```

This is as simple as it gets. You simply supply a formula, which is `CLV_3_Month ~ .` in our case, and the data to train with, which is the `train` variable in our case, to the `lm` function. This will instruct your machine to train a linear regression model with the given data.

Once a linear regression model is trained, there is some useful information you can find in the model object. You can use the following command to get detailed information about the model:

```
summary(regFit)
```

The output looks as follows:

```
> summary(regFit)

Call:
lm(formula = CLV_3_Month ~ ., data = train)

Residuals:
    Min      1Q  Median      3Q     Max
-6486.9   -98.5   -17.8    43.8 11969.0

Coefficients:
                Estimate Std. Error t value Pr(>|t|)
(Intercept)   -54.722109  10.987551  -4.980 6.67e-07 ***
SalesSum.Q2     0.120008   0.005131  23.389  < 2e-16 ***
SalesSum.Q3    -0.105788   0.007839 -13.495  < 2e-16 ***
SalesSum.Q4     0.012862   0.012574   1.023 0.306414
SalesSum.Q5    -0.045571   0.015615  -2.918 0.003542 **
SalesAvg.Q2     0.028505   0.022521   1.266 0.205697
SalesAvg.Q3     0.292372   0.026064  11.218  < 2e-16 ***
SalesAvg.Q4    -0.173427   0.031389  -5.525 3.55e-08 ***
SalesAvg.Q5     0.062404   0.016671   3.743 0.000185 ***
SalesCount.Q2  38.608748   6.002764   6.432 1.44e-10 ***
SalesCount.Q3  23.972964   7.543423   3.178 0.001497 **
SalesCount.Q4  21.170655   8.186019   2.586 0.009746 **
SalesCount.Q5  27.466354   7.424798   3.699 0.000220 ***
---
Signif. codes:  0 '***' 0.001 '**' 0.01 '*' 0.05 '.' 0.1 ' ' 1

Residual standard error: 435.8 on 3310 degrees of freedom
Multiple R-squared:  0.4363,    Adjusted R-squared:  0.4342
F-statistic: 213.5 on 12 and 3310 DF,  p-value: < 2.2e-16
```

As you can see from this output, you can easily find the coefficients of each feature and which features have negative or positive correlation with the target. For example, the previous 3 month period's aggregate purchase amount, `SalesSum.Q2`, has positive impacts on the next 3 month customer value. This means that the higher the previous 3 month period's total purchase amount is, the higher the next 3 month purchase amount will be. On the other hand, the second and fourth most recent 3 month period's aggregate purchase amounts, `SalesSum.Q3` and `SalesSum.Q5`, are negatively correlated with the next 3 month customer value. In other words, the more a customer made purchases two quarters or four quarters ago, the lower the value he or she will bring in the next 3 months. Looking at the coefficients is one way to gain insights on how the expected value will change, given certain features.

Using the 3 month customer value prediction output, you can custom-tailor your marketing strategies in different ways. Since you know the expected revenue or purchase amount from individual customers for the next 3 months, you can set a better informed budget for your marketing campaign. It should be set high enough to reach your target customers, but low enough to be below the expected 3 month customer value, so that you can have a positive ROI marketing campaign. On the other hand, you can also use these 3 month customer value prediction outputs to specifically target these high-value customers for the next 3 months. This can help you to create marketing campaigns with a higher ROI, as those high-value customers, predicted by this model, are likely to bring in more revenue than the others.

Evaluating regression model performance

Now that we have a machine learning model that is trained to predict the 3 month customer value, let's discuss how to evaluate the performance of this model. As discussed previously, we are going to use R2, MAE, and a scatter plot of predicted versus actual to evaluate our model. We first need to get the prediction output from our model, like the following code:

```
train_preds <- predict(regFit, train)
test_preds <- predict(regFit, test)
```

We are going to use the `miscTools` package to compute the in-sample and out-of-sample R^2 values. Take a look at the following code:

```
# R-squared
# install.packages('miscTools')
library(miscTools)

inSampleR2 <- rSquared(train$CLV_3_Month, resid=train$CLV_3_Month -
```

```
train_preds)
outOfSampleR2 <- rSquared(test$CLV_3_Month, resid=test$CLV_3_Month -
test_preds)
```

The R^2 values, in our case, look like the following output:

```
> sprintf('In-Sample R-Squared: %0.4f', inSampleR2)
[1] "In-Sample R-Squared: 0.4557"
> sprintf('Out-of-Sample R-Squared: %0.4f', outOfSampleR2)
[1] "Out-of-Sample R-Squared: 0.1235"
```

Due to the randomness in splitting the sample set into train and test sets, your results might differ from these results. In our case, the in-sample R^2 was 0.4557 and the out-of-sample R^2 was 0.1235. The rather big gap between the in-sample and out-of-sample R^2 values suggests that there is some overfitting happening, where the model performs significantly better in the train set and worse in the test set. In case of overfitting, you can try different combinations of features or use more samples for training.

Next, let's take a look at the MAE for in-sample and out-of-sample predictions. Take a look at the following code:

```
# Median Absolute Error
inSampleMAE <- median(abs(train$CLV_3_Month - train_preds))
outOfSampleMAE <- median(abs(test$CLV_3_Month - test_preds))
```

As you can see from this code, we are using the `median` and `abs` functions to get the median of absolute errors in the in-sample and out-of-sample predictions. The result in our case looks like the following:

```
> sprintf('In-Sample MAE: %0.4f', inSampleMAE)
[1] "In-Sample MAE: 69.6753"
> sprintf('Out-of-Sample MAE: %0.4f', outOfSampleMAE)
[1] "Out-of-Sample MAE: 66.9589"
```

Lastly, let's take a look at the scatter plot of predicted versus actual. You can use the following code for this scatter plot:

```
plot(
  test$CLV_3_Month,
  test_preds,
  xlab='actual',
  ylab='predicted',
  main='Out-of-Sample Actual vs. Predicted'
)
abline(a=0, b=1)
```

The resulting plot looks as follows:

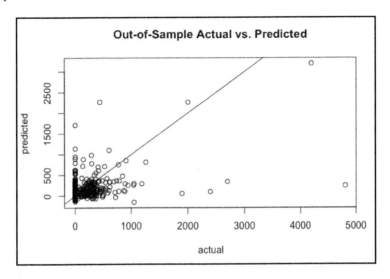

As you can see from this plot, the x-values are the actual values and the y-values are the predicted values. As discussed earlier, the more the points are on the straight line, the better the predictions are. This is because points on the straight line suggest that the actual values and the predicted values are close to each other. Looking at this plot, the points do not seem to be spread around the straight line, which suggest that the predictions are rather poor. This is in line with the low out-of-sample R^2 value that we observed previously. Scatter plot of predicted versus actual values is a good way to visualize the model performance.

The full code for this R exercise can be found at the following repo: https://github.com/yoonhwang/hands-on-data-science-for-marketing/blob/master/ch.9/R/CustomerLifetimeValue.R

Summary

In this chapter, we have learned what CLV is and its importance and usage in marketing. Particularly for justifying the cost of customer acquisition, it is crucial to have a good understanding of how much value each new customer is going to bring to the company. We discussed how CLV calculations can help marketers to develop positive ROI marketing strategies. Then, we went through a hypothetical example to show how we can calculate the CLV, using average purchase amount, purchase frequency, and customer lifetime span. We also mentioned another approach of using machine learning and predictive models to estimate the CLV.

During the programming exercises, we have learned how to build regression models that predict the CLV over the course of a 3 month period. In Python, we used the `scikit-learn` package to build a `LinearRegression` model. In R, we used the built-in `lm` function to train a linear regression model with our data. For regression model evaluations, we have discussed four commonly used measures, MSE, MAE, R^2, and predicted versus actual scatter plot, and what each of these metrics measures and tells us about the performance of regression models. In our programming exercises, we discussed how to compute and visualize MAE, R^2, and predicted versus actual scatter plot in Python and R.

In the following chapter, we are going to cover customer segmentation. We will discuss how segmenting the customer base can help marketers better understand their customers and come up with more efficient marketing strategies.

10
Data-Driven Customer Segmentation

In marketing, we often try to understand the behavior of certain subgroups of the customer base. Especially in targeted marketing, marketers try to segment the customer base in certain ways and focus on each target segment or customer group. This concentration on certain target customer segments results in better performance, as the needs and interests of those customers in the target group align and match better with the business's products, services, or content.

In this chapter, we are going to dive deeper into the concept of customer segmentation. We will discuss what customer segmentation is, the importance and benefits of having a good understanding of different segments of the customer base, and how to utilize customer segment analysis results for different marketing strategies. Aside from a more traditional way of segmenting the customer base, which involves looking at the key statistics of certain attributes of customers and manually cutting the customer base into segments, we can also use machine learning to have machines find the best ways to split the customer base into the desired number of segments. In this chapter, we will learn how we can use the k-means clustering algorithm to build customer segments based on the historical data.

In this chapter, we will cover the following topics:

- Customer segmentation
- Clustering algorithms
- Segmenting customers with Python
- Segmenting customers with R

Customer segmentation

Given today's competition within the market, it is critical to understand the different behaviors, types, and interests of customers. Especially in targeted marketing, understanding and categorizing customers is an essential step in forming effective marketing strategies. By segmenting the customer base, marketers can focus on one segment of customers at a time. It also helps marketers to tailor their marketing messages to one specific audience at a time. Customer segmentation is the backbone of successful targeted marketing, with which you can target specific groups of customers with different pricing options, promotions, and product placements that capture the interests of the target audience in the most cost-effective way.

Any business or industry can benefit from a better understanding of different customer segments. For example, television advertisements that are broadcast across all over the USA for an outerwear brand that sells winter clothes, such as parkas, snow boots, and hats, would not be so cost-effective. People residing in areas that never really get cold, such as Florida, Southern California, or Hawaii, would most likely not be interested in purchasing winter clothes. However, people residing in areas with cold winters, such as Alaska, Minnesota, or North Dakota, would most likely want to buy clothes that will keep them warm. So, for this outerwear brand, instead of sending out marketing mails or emails to all of their customers, it would be better to target those segments of customers, based on their geographic information, that live in places where they would need winter clothes more frequently than other customers.

As another example, if you own a rental building near a college, you might want to target your customers based on their age and education. Marketing to customers between 20 and 30 and who are attending surrounding colleges will have higher return than marketing to others. For hotel businesses, you might want to target those couples who have upcoming anniversaries for romantic package deals. Using social media platforms, such as Facebook or Instagram, you can target this segment of customers.

As we briefly discussed with these three cases, understanding your customers and which segment describes them the best can help you develop effective and efficient marketing strategies. When segmenting the customer base into subgroups, you can use certain characteristics and their statistics, as shown in Chapter 7, *Exploratory Analysis for Customer Behavior*. However, when you are trying to segment your customers with multiple attributes, it becomes exponentially more difficult. In the following sections, we are going to discuss how we can use machine learning for customer segmentation.

Clustering algorithms

Clustering algorithms are frequently used in marketing for customer segmentation. This is a method of unsupervised learning that learns the commonalities between groups from data. Unlike supervised learning, where there is a target and a labeled variable that you would like to predict, unsupervised learning learns from data without any target or labeled variable. Among numerous other clustering algorithms, we are going to explore the usage of the k-means clustering algorithm in this chapter.

The k-means clustering algorithm splits the records in the data into a pre-defined number of clusters, where the data points within each cluster are close to each other. In order to group similar records together, the k-means clustering algorithm tries to find the centroids, which are the centers or means of clusters, to minimize the distances between the data points and the centroids within the clusters. The objective equation (from `https://scikit-learn.org/stable/modules/clustering.html#k-means`) looks like this:

$$\sum_{i=0}^{n} \min_{\mu_j \in C}(||x_i - \mu_j||^2)$$

Here n is the number of records in the dataset, x_i is the ith data point, C is the number of clusters, and μ_j is the jth centroid.

One downside or difficulty of using k-means clustering for customer segmentation is the fact that you need to know the number of clusters beforehand. However, quite often, you do not know what is the optimal number of clusters to create. The silhouette coefficient can be used to evaluate and help you make decisions on what the best number of clusters will be for your segmentation problem. Simply put, the silhouette coefficient measures how close the data points are to their clusters compared to other clusters. The equation is shown here:

$$S = \frac{b - a}{\max(a, b)}$$

Here b is the average of the distance between a point and its closest cluster and a is the average distance among data points within the same cluster. The silhouette coefficient value ranges from -1 to 1, where the closer the values are to 1, the better they are. In the following programming exercises, we will be segmenting the customer base from our dataset, using the k-means clustering algorithm and the silhouette coefficient.

Segmenting customers with Python

In this section, we are going to discuss how to segment the customer base into subgroups using the clustering algorithm in Python. By the end of this section, we will have built a customer segmentation model using the k-means clustering algorithm. We will be mainly using the `pandas`, `matplotlib`, and `scikit-learn` packages to analyze, visualize, and build machine learning models. For those readers, who would like to use R, instead of Python, for this exercise, you can skip to the next section.

For this exercise, we will be using one of the publicly available datasets from the UCI Machine Learning Repository, which can be found at this link: `http://archive.ics.uci.edu/ml/datasets/online+retail`. You can follow this link and download the data, which is available in XLSX format, named `Online Retail.xlsx`. Once you have downloaded this data, you can load it into your Jupyter Notebook by running the following command:

```
import pandas as pd

df = pd.read_excel('../data/Online Retail.xlsx', sheet_name='Online
Retail')
```

The DataFrame, `df`, looks like this:

df.head()								
	InvoiceNo	StockCode	Description	Quantity	InvoiceDate	UnitPrice	CustomerID	Country
0	536365	85123A	WHITE HANGING HEART T-LIGHT HOLDER	6	2010-12-01 08:26:00	2.55	17850.0	United Kingdom
1	536365	71053	WHITE METAL LANTERN	6	2010-12-01 08:26:00	3.39	17850.0	United Kingdom
2	536365	84406B	CREAM CUPID HEARTS COAT HANGER	8	2010-12-01 08:26:00	2.75	17850.0	United Kingdom
3	536365	84029G	KNITTED UNION FLAG HOT WATER BOTTLE	6	2010-12-01 08:26:00	3.39	17850.0	United Kingdom
4	536365	84029E	RED WOOLLY HOTTIE WHITE HEART.	6	2010-12-01 08:26:00	3.39	17850.0	United Kingdom

As you can notice, we have used this dataset a few times in the previous chapters. As you might recall from previous chapters, there are a few things we need to clean up before we proceed.

Data cleanup

Before we can start building clustering models, there are five tasks we need to do to clean up our data and prepare it for modeling. The clean-up steps are as follows:

1. **Dropping canceled orders**: We are going to drop records with negative `Quantity`, using the following code:

   ```
   df = df.loc[df['Quantity'] > 0]
   ```

2. **Dropping records with no** `CustomerID`: There are `133,361` records with no `CustomerID` and we are going to drop those records with the following code:

   ```
   df = df[pd.notnull(df['CustomerID'])]
   ```

3. **Excluding an incomplete month**: As you might recall from previous chapters, the data in the month of December, 2011, is incomplete. You can exclude this data with the following code:

   ```
   df = df.loc[df['InvoiceDate'] < '2011-12-01']
   ```

4. **Computing total sales from the Quantity and UnitPrice columns**: For our analyses, we need the total sales value, so we are going to multiply the two `Quantity` and `UnitPrice` columns, to get the total sales, as shown in the following code:

   ```
   df['Sales'] = df['Quantity'] * df['UnitPrice']
   ```

5. **Per-customer data**: In order to analyze customer segments, we need to transform our data, so that each record represents the purchase history of individual customers. Take a look at the following code:

   ```
   customer_df = df.groupby('CustomerID').agg({
       'Sales': sum,
       'InvoiceNo': lambda x: x.nunique()
   })

   customer_df.columns = ['TotalSales', 'OrderCount']
   customer_df['AvgOrderValue'] =
   customer_df['TotalSales']/customer_df['OrderCount']
   ```

As you can see from this code, we are grouping the `DataFrame`, `df`, by `CustomerID` and computing the total sales and the number of orders for each customer. Then, we also calculate the average per-order value, `AvgOrderValue`, by dividing the `TotalSales` column by the `OrderCount` column. The result is shown in the following screenshot:

CustomerID	TotalSales	OrderCount	AvgOrderValue
12346.0	77183.60	1	77183.600000
12347.0	4085.18	6	680.863333
12348.0	1797.24	4	449.310000
12349.0	1757.55	1	1757.550000
12350.0	334.40	1	334.400000
12352.0	2506.04	8	313.255000
12353.0	89.00	1	89.000000
12354.0	1079.40	1	1079.400000
12355.0	459.40	1	459.400000
12356.0	2811.43	3	937.143333
12357.0	6207.67	1	6207.670000
12358.0	484.86	1	484.860000
12359.0	6372.58	4	1593.145000
12360.0	2662.06	3	887.353333
12361.0	189.90	1	189.900000

Now, as you can see from this data, the three columns, `TotalSales`, `OrderCount`, and `AvgOrderValue`, have different scales. `TotalSales` can take any values from 0 to 26,848, while `OrderCount` takes values between 1 and 201. Clustering algorithms are highly affected by the scales of the data, so we need to normalize this data to be on the same scale. We are going to take two steps to normalize this data. First, we are going to rank the data, so that the values of each column range from 1 to 4298, which is the total number of records. Take a look at the following code:

```
rank_df = customer_df.rank(method='first')
```

The result is shown in the following screenshot:

CustomerID	TotalSales	OrderCount	AvgOrderValue
12346.0	4290.0	1.0	4298.0
12347.0	3958.0	3470.0	3888.0
12348.0	3350.0	2861.0	3303.0
12349.0	3321.0	2.0	4238.0
12350.0	1241.0	3.0	2561.0
12352.0	3630.0	3774.0	2360.0
12353.0	119.0	4.0	201.0
12354.0	2781.0	5.0	4151.0
12355.0	1670.0	6.0	3354.0
12356.0	3724.0	2346.0	4082.0
12357.0	4111.0	7.0	4295.0
12358.0	1738.0	8.0	3447.0
12359.0	4117.0	2862.0	4225.0
12360.0	3680.0	2347.0	4057.0
12361.0	607.0	9.0	1186.0

Next, we are going to normalize this data to center around the mean and have a mean of 0 and a standard deviation of 1. Take a look at the following code:

```
normalized_df = (rank_df - rank_df.mean()) / rank_df.std()
```

The result is shown in the following screenshot:

	TotalSales	OrderCount	AvgOrderValue
CustomerID			
12346.0	1.724999	-1.731446	1.731446
12347.0	1.457445	1.064173	1.401033
12348.0	0.967466	0.573388	0.929590
12349.0	0.944096	-1.730641	1.683093
12350.0	-0.732148	-1.729835	0.331622
12352.0	1.193114	1.309162	0.169639
12353.0	-1.636352	-1.729029	-1.570269
12354.0	0.508917	-1.728223	1.612981
12355.0	-0.386422	-1.727417	0.970690
12356.0	1.268868	0.158357	1.557375
12357.0	1.580746	-1.726611	1.729029
12358.0	-0.331622	-1.725805	1.045637
12359.0	1.585581	0.574194	1.672617
12360.0	1.233409	0.159163	1.537228
12361.0	-1.243079	-1.724999	-0.776471

Take a look at the statistics of each of these columns, shown in the following screenshot:

	TotalSales	OrderCount	AvgOrderValue
count	4.298000e+03	4.298000e+03	4.298000e+03
mean	9.952744e-17	-1.231371e-16	5.719018e-17
std	1.000000e+00	1.000000e+00	1.000000e+00
min	-1.731446e+00	-1.731446e+00	-1.731446e+00
25%	-8.657232e-01	-8.657232e-01	-8.657232e-01
50%	0.000000e+00	0.000000e+00	0.000000e+00
75%	8.657232e-01	8.657232e-01	8.657232e-01
max	1.731446e+00	1.731446e+00	1.731446e+00

You can see that the values are centered around at 0 and have a standard deviation of 1. We are going to use this data for the following clustering analyses.

k-means clustering

The **k-means clustering** algorithm is a frequently used algorithm for drawing insights into the formations and separations within data. In marketing, it is often used to build customer segments and understand the behaviors of these different segments. Let's dive into building clustering models in Python.

In order to use the k-means clustering algorithm in the `scikit-learn` package, we need to import the `kmeans` module, as shown in the following code:

```
from sklearn.cluster import KMeans
```

Then, you can build and fit a k-means clustering model, using the following code:

```
kmeans = KMeans(n_clusters=4).fit(normalized_df[['TotalSales',
'OrderCount', 'AvgOrderValue']])
```

As you can see from this code, we are building a clustering model that splits the data into four segments. You can change the desired number of clusters with the `n_clusters` parameter. Using the `fit` function, you can train a k-means clustering algorithm to learn to split the given data. In this code, we are building four clusters, based on the `TotalSales`, `OrderCount`, and `AvgOrderValue` values. The trained model object, `kmeans`, stores the labels and centers of the clusters in the `labels_` and `cluster_centers_` attributes of the model object. You can retrieve these values as shown in the following code:

```
kmeans.labels_
kmeans.cluster_centers_
```

Now that we have built our first clustering model, let's visualize this data. First, take a look at the following code:

```
four_cluster_df = normalized_df[['TotalSales', 'OrderCount',
'AvgOrderValue']].copy(deep=True)
four_cluster_df['Cluster'] = kmeans.labels_
```

We store the cluster label information for each record into a newly created DataFrame, `four_cluster_df`. With this `DataFrame`, we can visualize the clusters, using the following code:

```
plt.scatter(
    four_cluster_df.loc[four_cluster_df['Cluster'] == 0]['OrderCount'],
```

```
        four_cluster_df.loc[four_cluster_df['Cluster'] == 0]['TotalSales'],
        c='blue'
)

plt.scatter(
        four_cluster_df.loc[four_cluster_df['Cluster'] == 1]['OrderCount'],
        four_cluster_df.loc[four_cluster_df['Cluster'] == 1]['TotalSales'],
        c='red'
)

plt.scatter(
        four_cluster_df.loc[four_cluster_df['Cluster'] == 2]['OrderCount'],
        four_cluster_df.loc[four_cluster_df['Cluster'] == 2]['TotalSales'],
        c='orange'
)

plt.scatter(
        four_cluster_df.loc[four_cluster_df['Cluster'] == 3]['OrderCount'],
        four_cluster_df.loc[four_cluster_df['Cluster'] == 3]['TotalSales'],
        c='green'
)

plt.title('TotalSales vs. OrderCount Clusters')
plt.xlabel('Order Count')
plt.ylabel('Total Sales')

plt.grid()
plt.show()
```

As you can see from this code, we are visualizing the data using scatter plots. The result is shown in the following screenshot:

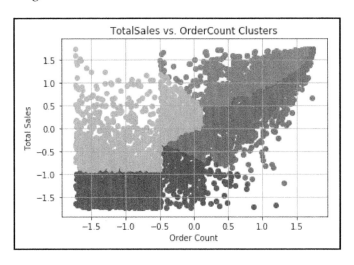

Let's take a closer look at this plot. The cluster in blue is the group of low-value customers, who have not purchased our products so much. On the other hand, the cluster in red is the group of high-value customers, who have purchased the greatest amount and who have purchased products frequently. We can also visualize the clusters with different angles, using the rest of the variables. Take a look at the following plots:

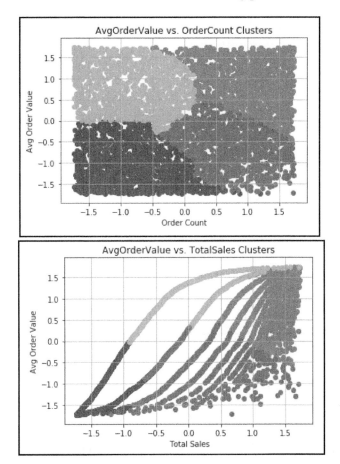

The first plot shows the clusters visualized based on `AvgOrderValue` and `OrderCount`. On the other hand, the second plot shows the clusters visualized based on `AvgOrderValue` and `TotalSales`. As you can see from these plots, the cluster in blue has the lowest average per-order value and the lowest number of orders. However, the cluster in red has the highest average per-order value and the greatest number of orders. Visualizing clusters helps you understand the characteristics of different clusters much more easily and clearly.

Selecting the best number of clusters

Often, we do not know what the best number of clusters to use is when building k-means clustering models. As discussed in an earlier section of this chapter, we can use the silhouette coefficient to determine what the best number of clusters is to split the data. In the `scikit-learn` package, you can use the `silhouette_score` function in the `sklearn.metrics` module to calculate the silhouette score and measure the quality of clusters. Take a look at the following code:

```
from sklearn.metrics import import silhouette_score

for n_cluster in [4,5,6,7,8]:
    kmeans = KMeans(n_clusters=n_cluster).fit(
        normalized_df[['TotalSales', 'OrderCount', 'AvgOrderValue']]
    )
    silhouette_avg = silhouette_score(
        normalized_df[['TotalSales', 'OrderCount', 'AvgOrderValue']],
        kmeans.labels_
    )
    print('Silhouette Score for %i Clusters: %0.4f' % (n_cluster,
silhouette_avg))
```

As you can see from this code, we are experimenting with five different numbers of clusters: 4, 5, 6, 7, and 8. For each amount of clusters, we are going to measure the silhouette score and choose the amount of clusters with the highest score. The output of this code looks like this:

```
Silhouette Score for 4 Clusters: 0.4113
Silhouette Score for 5 Clusters: 0.3771
Silhouette Score for 6 Clusters: 0.3784
Silhouette Score for 7 Clusters: 0.3906
Silhouette Score for 8 Clusters: 0.3810
```

In our case, of the five different numbers of clusters we have experimented with, the best number of clusters with the highest silhouette score was 4. In the following section, we will use 4 as the number of clusters to show how we can interpret the results of the clustering analysis.

Interpreting customer segments

In this section, we are going to discuss different ways to draw insights from the results of the previous clustering analysis. Let's first build a k-means clustering model with four clusters. You can use the following code:

```
kmeans = KMeans(n_clusters=4).fit(
    normalized_df[['TotalSales', 'OrderCount', 'AvgOrderValue']]
)

four_cluster_df = normalized_df[['TotalSales', 'OrderCount',
'AvgOrderValue']].copy(deep=True)
four_cluster_df['Cluster'] = kmeans.labels_
```

As you can see from this code, we are fitting a k-means clustering model with 4 clusters, based on three attributes: `TotalSales`, `OrderCount`, and `AvgOrderValue`. Then, we store the cluster label information into a DataFrame, `four_cluster_df`. This DataFrame is shown in the following screenshot:

CustomerID	TotalSales	OrderCount	AvgOrderValue	Cluster
12346.0	1.724999	-1.731446	1.731446	0
12347.0	1.457445	1.064173	1.401033	2
12348.0	0.967466	0.573388	0.929590	2
12349.0	0.944096	-1.730641	1.683093	0
12350.0	-0.732148	-1.729835	0.331622	0
12352.0	1.193114	1.309162	0.169639	2
12353.0	-1.636352	-1.729029	-1.570269	3
12354.0	0.508917	-1.728223	1.612981	0
12355.0	-0.386422	-1.727417	0.970690	0
12356.0	1.268868	0.158357	1.557375	2
12357.0	1.580746	-1.726611	1.729029	0
12358.0	-0.331622	-1.725805	1.045637	0
12359.0	1.585581	0.574194	1.672617	2
12360.0	1.233409	0.159163	1.537228	2
12361.0	-1.243079	-1.724999	-0.776471	3

The first thing we are going to look at is the centers of each cluster. You can get the cluster centers using the following code:

```
kmeans.cluster_centers_
```

The output of this code is shown in the following screenshot:

```
array([[-0.13330681, -0.84982057,  0.79745159],
       [ 0.21794823,  0.715536  , -0.64337832],
       [ 1.20630621,  1.00552238,  0.86837366],
       [-1.24675221, -0.7971239 , -1.06197333]])
```

Let's take a closer look at this. The fourth cluster has the lowest numbers for all three attributes. This suggests that the fourth cluster contains customers with the smallest amount of sales, smallest number of orders, and lowest average per-order value. This group of customers is one of low-value customers. On the other hand, the third cluster has the highest numbers for all three attributes. The customers in the third cluster have the greatest amount of sales, greatest number of orders, and highest average per-order value. So, these customers in the third cluster purchase expensive items and give the business the highest revenue. You would typically want to focus your marketing efforts on this segment of customers, as it will result in the highest return.

The customers in the second cluster are interesting. They make purchases relatively frequently, as they have a medium-to-high cluster center value for OrderCount, but their average per-order value is low, as the cluster center for AvgOrderValue is low. These are the customers who make frequent purchases of low-value items. So, it would be perfect to market items with low per-item prices to this segment of customers. The customers in the first cluster are also interesting. Their contributions to the revenue and number of orders are medium to low, looking at the centers of this cluster. However, their average per-order value is high. These are the customers who buy expensive items infrequently. Thus, it would be perfect to market expensive items to this segment of customers.

As you can see from this example, looking at the centers of clusters helps us understand different types and segments of customers and how to target them differently. Lastly, we can also find out what the best-selling items are for each customer segment. Take a look at the following code:

```
high_value_cluster = four_cluster_df.loc[four_cluster_df['Cluster'] == 2]

pd.DataFrame(
    df.loc[
        df['CustomerID'].isin(high_value_cluster.index)
    ].groupby('Description').count()[
```

```
            'StockCode'
    ].sort_values(ascending=False).head()
)
```

As we have seen before, the third cluster was the group of high-value customers, and we are going to take a look at the top five best-selling items for this group. The output of this code is as follows:

	StockCode
Description	
JUMBO BAG RED RETROSPOT	1143
REGENCY CAKESTAND 3 TIER	1078
WHITE HANGING HEART T-LIGHT HOLDER	1072
LUNCH BAG RED RETROSPOT	937
PARTY BUNTING	865

For this high-value segment, the best-selling item was JUMBO BAG RED RETROSPOT and the second best-selling item was REGENCY CAKESTAND 3 TIER. You can utilize this information in marketing strategies, when you target this customer segment. In your marketing campaigns, you can recommend items similar to these best-selling items to this segment of customers, as they are the most interested in these types of items.

 You can find the full code for this exercise in the following repository:
https://github.com/yoonhwang/hands-on-data-science-for-marketing/blob/master/ch.10/python/CustomerSegmentation.ipynb.

Segmenting customers with R

In this section, we are going to discuss how to segment the customer base into subgroups using a clustering algorithm in R. By the end of this section, we will have built a customer segmentation model using the k-means clustering algorithm. For those readers who would like to use Python, instead of R, for this exercise, see the previous section.

For this exercise, we will be using one of the publicly available datasets from the UCI Machine Learning Repository, which can be found at this link: `http://archive.ics.uci.edu/ml/datasets/online+retail`. You can follow this link and download the data, which is available in XLSX format, named `Online Retail.xlsx`. Once you have downloaded this data, you can load it into your RStudio by running the following command:

```
library(readxl)

#### 1. Load Data ####
df <- read_excel(
  path="~/Documents/data-science-for-marketing/ch.10/data/Online
Retail.xlsx",
  sheet="Online Retail"
)
```

The DataFrame, `df`, is shown in the following screenshot:

	InvoiceNo	StockCode	Description	Quantity	InvoiceDate	UnitPrice	CustomerID	Country
1	536365	85123A	WHITE HANGING HEART T-LIGHT HOLDER	6	2010-12-01 08:26:00	2.55	17850	United Kingdom
2	536365	71053	WHITE METAL LANTERN	6	2010-12-01 08:26:00	3.39	17850	United Kingdom
3	536365	84406B	CREAM CUPID HEARTS COAT HANGER	8	2010-12-01 08:26:00	2.75	17850	United Kingdom
4	536365	84029G	KNITTED UNION FLAG HOT WATER BOTTLE	6	2010-12-01 08:26:00	3.39	17850	United Kingdom
5	536365	84029E	RED WOOLLY HOTTIE WHITE HEART.	6	2010-12-01 08:26:00	3.39	17850	United Kingdom
6	536365	22752	SET 7 BABUSHKA NESTING BOXES	2	2010-12-01 08:26:00	7.65	17850	United Kingdom
7	536365	21730	GLASS STAR FROSTED T-LIGHT HOLDER	6	2010-12-01 08:26:00	4.25	17850	United Kingdom
8	536366	22633	HAND WARMER UNION JACK	6	2010-12-01 08:28:00	1.85	17850	United Kingdom
9	536366	22632	HAND WARMER RED POLKA DOT	6	2010-12-01 08:28:00	1.85	17850	United Kingdom
10	536367	84879	ASSORTED COLOUR BIRD ORNAMENT	32	2010-12-01 08:34:00	1.69	13047	United Kingdom
11	536367	22745	POPPY'S PLAYHOUSE BEDROOM	6	2010-12-01 08:34:00	2.10	13047	United Kingdom
12	536367	22748	POPPY'S PLAYHOUSE KITCHEN	6	2010-12-01 08:34:00	2.10	13047	United Kingdom
13	536367	22749	FELTCRAFT PRINCESS CHARLOTTE DOLL	8	2010-12-01 08:34:00	3.75	13047	United Kingdom
14	536367	22310	IVORY KNITTED MUG COSY	6	2010-12-01 08:34:00	1.65	13047	United Kingdom
15	536367	84969	BOX OF 6 ASSORTED COLOUR TEASPOONS	6	2010-12-01 08:34:00	4.25	13047	United Kingdom

As you may have noticed, we have used this dataset a few times in the previous chapters. As you might recall from previous chapters, there are a few things we need to clean up before we proceed.

Data cleanup

Before we can start building clustering models, there are five tasks we need to do to clean up our data and prepare it for modeling. The clean-up steps are as follows:

1. **Dropping canceled orders**: We are going to drop records with negative `Quantity`, using the following code:

```
df <- df[which(df$Quantity > 0),]
```

2. **Dropping records with no CustomerID**: There are `133,361` records with no `CustomerID` and we are going to drop those records with the following code:

```
df <- na.omit(df)
```

3. **Excluding an incomplete month**: As you might recall from previous chapters, the data in the month of December, 2011, is incomplete. You can exclude this data with the following code:

```
df <- df[which(df$InvoiceDate < '2011-12-01'),]
```

4. **Computing total sales from the Quantity and UnitPrice columns**: For our analyses, we need the total sales value, so we are going to multiply the `Quantity` and `UnitPrice` columns, to get the total sales, as shown in the following code:

```
df$Sales <- df$Quantity * df$UnitPrice
```

5. **Per-customer data**: In order to analyze customer segments, we need to transform our data, so that each record represents the purchase history of individual customers. Take a look at the following code:

```
# per customer data
customerDF <- df %>%
  group_by(CustomerID) %>%
  summarize(TotalSales=sum(Sales),
OrderCount=length(unique(InvoiceDate))) %>%
  mutate(AvgOrderValue=TotalSales/OrderCount)
```

As you can see from this code, we are grouping the DataFrame, `df`, by `CustomerID` and computing the total sales and the number of orders for each customer. Then, we also calculate the average per-order value, `AvgOrderValue`, by dividing the `TotalSales` column by the `OrderCount` column. The result is shown in the following screenshot:

	CustomerID	TotalSales	OrderCount	AvgOrderValue
1	12346	77183.60	1	77183.6000
2	12347	4085.18	6	680.8633
3	12348	1797.24	4	449.3100
4	12349	1757.55	1	1757.5500
5	12350	334.40	1	334.4000
6	12352	2506.04	8	313.2550
7	12353	89.00	1	89.0000
8	12354	1079.40	1	1079.4000
9	12355	459.40	1	459.4000
10	12356	2811.43	3	937.1433
11	12357	6207.67	1	6207.6700
12	12358	484.86	1	484.8600
13	12359	6372.58	4	1593.1450
14	12360	2662.06	3	887.3533
15	12361	189.90	1	189.9000

Now, as you can see from this data, the `TotalSales`, `OrderCount`, and `AvgOrderValue` columns, have different scales. `TotalSales` can take any values from 0 to 26,848, while `OrderCount` takes values between 1 and 201. Clustering algorithms are highly affected by the scales of the data, so we need to normalize this data to be on the same scale. We are going to take two steps to normalize this data. First, we are going to rank the data, so that the values of each column range from 1 to 4298, which is the total number of records. Take a look at the following code:

```
rankDF <- customerDF %>%
  mutate(TotalSales=rank(TotalSales), OrderCount=rank(OrderCount,
ties.method="first"), AvgOrderValue=rank(AvgOrderValue))
```

The result is shown in the following screenshot:

	CustomerID	TotalSales	OrderCount	AvgOrderValue
1	12346	4290.0	1	4298.0
2	12347	3958.0	3473	3885.0
3	12348	3350.0	2862	3299.0
4	12349	3321.0	2	4237.0
5	12350	1241.0	3	2554.0
6	12352	3630.0	3776	2357.0
7	12353	119.0	4	201.0
8	12354	2781.0	5	4148.0
9	12355	1670.0	6	3347.0
10	12356	3724.0	2346	4079.0
11	12357	4111.0	7	4294.0
12	12358	1738.0	8	3445.0
13	12359	4117.0	2863	4224.0
14	12360	3680.0	2347	4055.0
15	12361	607.0	9	1181.0

Next, we are going to normalize this data to center around the mean, and have a mean of 0 and a standard deviation of 1, using the scale function in R. Take a look at the following code:

```
normalizedDF <- rankDF %>%
  mutate(TotalSales=scale(TotalSales), OrderCount=scale(OrderCount),
AvgOrderValue=scale(AvgOrderValue))
```

The result is shown in the following screenshot:

	CustomerID	TotalSales	OrderCount	AvgOrderValue
1	12346	1.72499932	-1.7314464	1.73144641
2	12347	1.45744512	1.0665903	1.39861543
3	12348	0.96746633	0.5741939	0.92636614
4	12349	0.94409563	-1.7306405	1.68228736
5	12350	-0.73214757	-1.7298346	0.32598095
6	12352	1.19311446	1.3107738	0.16722138
7	12353	-1.63635184	-1.7290287	-1.57026918
8	12354	0.50891711	-1.7282229	1.61056349
9	12355	-0.38642241	-1.7274170	0.96504867
10	12356	1.26886776	0.1583566	1.55495734
11	12357	1.58074570	-1.7266111	1.72822287
12	12358	-0.33162215	-1.7258052	1.04402552
13	12359	1.58558102	0.5749998	1.67181084
14	12360	1.23340877	0.1591625	1.53561607
15	12361	-1.24307940	-1.7249993	-0.78050074

Take a look at the statistics of each of these columns, as shown in the following screenshot:

```
> summary(normalizedDF)
   CustomerID      TotalSales.V1       OrderCount.V1       AvgOrderValue.V1
 Min.   :12346   Min.   :-1.7314464   Min.   :-1.7314464   Min.   :-1.7314464
 1st Qu.:13815   1st Qu.:-0.8660254   1st Qu.:-0.8657232   1st Qu.:-0.8657232
 Median :15300   Median : 0.0000000   Median : 0.0000000   Median : 0.0000000
 Mean   :15302   Mean   : 0.0000000   Mean   : 0.0000000   Mean   : 0.0000000
 3rd Qu.:16781   3rd Qu.: 0.8657232   3rd Qu.: 0.8657232   3rd Qu.: 0.8657232
 Max.   :18287   Max.   : 1.7314464   Max.   : 1.7314464   Max.   : 1.7314464
> sapply(normalizedDF, sd)
   CustomerID    TotalSales   OrderCount AvgOrderValue
     1720.983        1.000        1.000         1.000
```

You can see that the values are centered around at 0 and have a standard deviation of 1. We are going to use this data for the following clustering analyses.

k-means clustering

The **k-means clustering** algorithm is a frequently used algorithm to draw insights on the formations and separations within the data. In marketing, it is often used to build customer segments and understand the behaviors of these different segments. Let's dive into building clustering models in R.

You can build and fit a k-means clustering model using the following code:

```
cluster <- kmeans(normalizedDF[c("TotalSales", "OrderCount",
"AvgOrderValue")], 4)
```

As you can see from this code, we are building a clustering model that splits the data into 4 segments. The first parameter of the `kmeans` function is for the data to be used for k-means clustering and the second parameter is to define the desired number of clusters. In this code, we are building 4 clusters, based on the `TotalSales`, `OrderCount`, and `AvgOrderValue` values. The trained k-means clustering model object, `cluster`, stores the labels and centers of the clusters in the `cluster` and `centers` variables of the model object. You can retrieve these values, as shown in the following code:

```
cluster$cluster
cluster$centers
```

Now that we have built our first clustering model, let's visualize this data. First, we are going to store the cluster labels as a separate column, named `Cluster`, in the `normalizedDF` variable, as shown in the following code:

```
# cluster labels
normalizedDF$Cluster <- cluster$cluster
```

Then, we can visualize the clusters, using the following code:

```
ggplot(normalizedDF, aes(x=AvgOrderValue, y=OrderCount, color=Cluster)) +
  geom_point()
```

As you can see from this code, we are visualizing the data using scatterplots. The result in shown in the following screenshot:

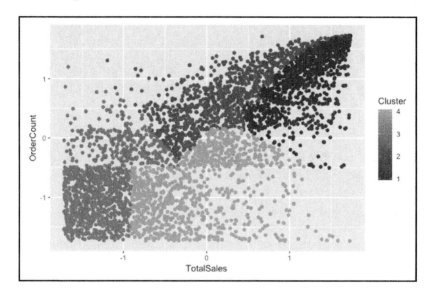

Let's take a closer look at this plot. The cluster in the bottom left is the group of low-value customers, who have not purchased our products so much. On the other hand, the cluster in the top right with the darkest color is the group of high-value customers, who have purchased the greatest amount and who have purchased products frequently. We can also visualize the clusters with different angles, using the rest of the variables. Take a look at the following plots:

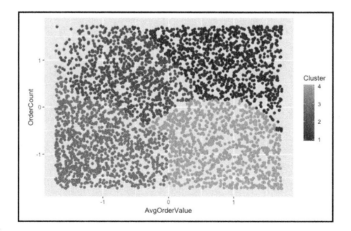

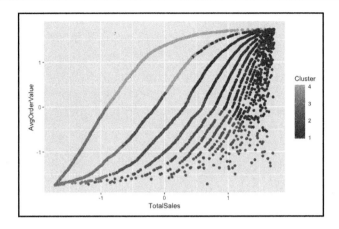

The first plot shows the clusters visualized based on `AvgOrderValue` and `OrderCount`. On the other hand, the second plot the clusters visualized based on `AvgOrderValue` and `TotalSales`. As you can see from these plots, the cluster in the bottom left with the second-lightest color has the lowest average per-order value and the lowest number of orders. However, the cluster in the top right with the darkest color has the highest average per-order value and the greatest number of orders. Visualizing clusters helps you understand the characteristics of different clusters much more easily and clearly.

Selecting the best number of clusters

Quite often, we do not know what the best number of clusters to use is when building k-means clustering models. As discussed in an earlier section of this chapter, we can use the silhouette coefficient to determine what the best number of clusters is to split the data. In R, you can use the `silhouette` function in the `cluster` library to calculate the silhouette score and measure the quality of clusters. Take a look at the following code:

```
# Selecting the best number of cluster
library(cluster)

for(n_cluster in 4:8){
  cluster <- kmeans(normalizedDF[c("TotalSales", "OrderCount",
"AvgOrderValue")], n_cluster)
  silhouetteScore <- mean(
    silhouette(
      cluster$cluster,
      dist(normalizedDF[c("TotalSales", "OrderCount", "AvgOrderValue")],
method = "euclidean")
    )[,3]
  )
```

```
    print(sprintf('Silhouette Score for %i Clusters: %0.4f', n_cluster,
silhouetteScore))
}
```

As you can see from this code, we are experimenting with five different number of clusters: 4, 5, 6, 7, and 8. For each number of clusters, we are going to measure the silhouette score and choose the number of clusters with the highest score. The output of this code is shown in the following screenshot:

```
[1] "Silhouette Score for 4 Clusters: 0.4117"
[1] "Silhouette Score for 5 Clusters: 0.3831"
[1] "Silhouette Score for 6 Clusters: 0.3778"
[1] "Silhouette Score for 7 Clusters: 0.3915"
[1] "Silhouette Score for 8 Clusters: 0.3716"
```

In our case, of the five different numbers of clusters we have experimented with, the best number of clusters with the highest silhouette score was 4. In the following section, we will use 4 for the number of clusters to show how we can interpret the results of clustering analysis.

Interpreting customer segments

In this section, we are going to discuss different ways to draw insights from the results of the previous clustering analysis. Let's first build a k-means clustering model with 4 clusters. You can use the following code:

```
# Interpreting customer segments
cluster <- kmeans(normalizedDF[c("TotalSales", "OrderCount",
"AvgOrderValue")], 4)
normalizedDF$Cluster <- cluster$cluster
```

As you can see from this code, we are fitting a k-means clustering model with 4 clusters, based on the three attributes: TotalSales, OrderCount, and AvgOrderValue. Then, we store the cluster label information into a DataFrame, normalizedDF. This DataFrame is shown in the following screenshot:

	CustomerID	TotalSales	OrderCount	AvgOrderValue	Cluster
1	12346	1.72499932	-1.7314464	1.73144641	4
2	12347	1.45744512	1.0665903	1.39861543	1
3	12348	0.96746633	0.5741939	0.92636614	1
4	12349	0.94409563	-1.7306405	1.68228736	4
5	12350	-0.73214757	-1.7298346	0.32598095	4
6	12352	1.19311446	1.3107738	0.16722138	1
7	12353	-1.63635184	-1.7290287	-1.57026918	3
8	12354	0.50891711	-1.7282229	1.61056349	4
9	12355	-0.38642241	-1.7274170	0.96504867	4
10	12356	1.26886776	0.1583566	1.55495734	1
11	12357	1.58074570	-1.7266111	1.72822287	4
12	12358	-0.33162215	-1.7258052	1.04402552	4
13	12359	1.58558102	0.5749998	1.67181084	1
14	12360	1.23340877	0.1591625	1.53561607	1
15	12361	-1.24307940	-1.7249993	-0.78050074	3

The first thing we are going to look at is the centers of each cluster. You can get the cluster centers using the following code:

```
# cluster centers
cluster$centers
```

The output of this code is shown in the following screenshot:

```
> # cluster centers
> cluster$centers
  TotalSales OrderCount AvgOrderValue
1  0.2132451  0.7112607    -0.6432146
2 -0.1314293 -0.8520880     0.7984693
3 -1.2460079 -0.7960747    -1.0616594
4  1.2059015  1.0076634     0.8661864
```

Let's take a closer look at this. The third cluster has the lowest numbers for all three attributes. This suggests that the third cluster contains customers with the lowest amount of sales, lowest number of orders, and lowest average per-order value. This group of customers is a group of low-value customers. On the other hand, the fourth cluster has the highest numbers for all three attributes. The customers in the fourth cluster have the highest amount of sales, highest number of orders, and highest average per-order value. This suggests that these customers in the fourth cluster purchase expensive items and give the business the highest revenue. You would typically want to focus your marketing efforts on this segment of customers, as it will result in the highest return.

The customers in the first cluster are interesting. They make purchases relatively frequently, as they have a medium to high cluster center value for `OrderCount`, but their average per-order value is low, as the cluster center for `AvgOrderValue` is low. These are the type of customers who make frequent purchases of low-value items. So, it would be perfect to market items with low per-item prices to this segment of customers. The customers in the second cluster are also interesting. Their contributions to the revenue and number of orders are low, looking at the centers of this cluster. However, their average per-order value is high. These are the type of customers who buy expensive items infrequently. Thus, it would be perfect to market expensive items to this segment of customers.

As you can see from this example, looking at the centers of clusters helps us understand different types and segments of customers and how to target them differently. Lastly, we can also find out what the best-selling items are for each customer segment. Take a look at the following code:

```
# High value cluster
highValueCustomers <- unlist(
  customerDF[which(normalizedDF$Cluster == 4),'CustomerID'][,1], use.names
= FALSE
)

df[which(df$CustomerID %in% highValueCustomers),] %>%
  group_by(Description) %>%
  summarise(Count=n()) %>%
  arrange(desc(Count))
```

As we have seen before, the fourth cluster was the group of high-value customers and we are going to take a look at the best-selling items for this group. The output of this code is shown in the following screenshot:

```
> df[which(df$CustomerID %in% highValueCustomers),] %>%
+    group_by(Description) %>%
+    summarise(Count=n()) %>%
+    arrange(desc(Count))
# A tibble: 3,659 x 2
   Description                        Count
   <chr>                              <int>
 1 JUMBO BAG RED RETROSPOT             1147
 2 REGENCY CAKESTAND 3 TIER            1086
 3 WHITE HANGING HEART T-LIGHT HOLDER  1079
 4 LUNCH BAG RED RETROSPOT             938
 5 PARTY BUNTING                       869
 6 ASSORTED COLOUR BIRD ORNAMENT       828
 7 SET OF 3 CAKE TINS PANTRY DESIGN    730
 8 LUNCH BAG  BLACK SKULL.             701
 9 POSTAGE                             696
10 PACK OF 72 RETROSPOT CAKE CASES     690
```

For this high-value segment, the best-selling item was **JUMBO BAG RED RETROSPOT** and the second best-selling item was **REGENCY CAKESTAND 3 TIER**. You can utilize this information in the marketing strategies, when you target this customer segment. In your marketing campaigns, you can recommend items similar to these best-selling items to this segment of customers, as they are the most interested in these types of items.

 You can find the full code for this exercise in the following repository: `https://github.com/yoonhwang/hands-on-data-science-for-marketing/blob/master/ch.10/R/CustomerSegmentation.R`.

Summary

In this chapter, we have learned more about customer segmentation. We worked through three simple scenarios of how customer segmentation could help different businesses to form better and more cost-effective marketing strategies. We have discussed how having a good understanding of different customer segments, how customers in different segments behave, and what they need and are interested in can help you target your audience better. We have also learned about the k-means clustering algorithm, which is one of the most frequently used clustering algorithms for customer segmentation. In order to evaluate the quality of clusters, we have shown how we can use the silhouette coefficient.

During programming exercises, we have experimented with how we can build a k-means clustering model in Python and R. In Python, we could use the KMeans module in the scikit-learn package and in R, we could use the kmeans function to build clustering models. Using the silhouette_score function in Python and the silhouette function in R, we have seen how we could use silhouette coefficients to evaluate the qualities of clusters and have seen how looking at silhouette scores can help us determine the best number of clusters. Lastly, we have discussed how to interpret clustering analysis results, using scatter plots and cluster centroids, and we have seen how to find out the best-selling items for each customer segment.

In the next chapter, we are going to discuss customers at risk of churn and how to retain those customers. We will work together to build neural network models in Python and R, using the keras package, to identify those customers who are likely to churn.

11
Retaining Customers

As customers have more options for similar content to consume or similar products and services to shop for, it has become more difficult for many businesses to retain their customers and not lose them to other competitors. As the cost of acquiring new customers is typically higher than that of retaining and keeping existing customers, customer churn is becoming more and more of a concern than ever before. In order to retain existing customers and not lose them to competitors, businesses should not only try to understand their customers and their customers' needs and interests, but they should also be able to identify which customers are highly likely to churn and how to retain these customers at churn risk.

In this chapter, we are going to dive deeper into customer churn and how it hurts businesses, as well as how to retain existing customers. We will discuss some of the common reasons for customers leaving businesses and look at how data science can help reduce the risk of losing customers. As a way of predicting customer churn, we will learn about what an artificial neural network model is and its applications in different areas, as well as how we can build one using Python and R.

In this chapter, we will cover the following topics:

- Customer churn and retention
- Artificial neural networks
- Predicting customer churn with Python
- Predicting customer churn with R

Customer churn and retention

Customer churn is when a customer decides to stop using services, content, or products from a company. As we have briefly discussed in `Chapter 7`, *Exploratory Analysis for Customer Behavior*, when we discussed customer analytics, it is much less expensive to retain existing customers than to acquire new customers, and the revenue from repeat customers is typically higher than that form new customers. In competitive industries, where a business faces many competitors, the cost of new customer acquisition is even higher, and retaining existing customers becomes more important for such businesses.

There are many reasons behind customers leaving a business. Some of the common reasons why customers churn are poor customer service, not finding enough value in the products or services, lack of communications, and lack of customer loyalty. The first step to retaining these customers is to monitor customer churn rates over time. If the churn rate is generally high or is increasing over time, then it will be a good idea to dedicate some resources to improving customer retention.

In order to improve the customer retention rate, the top priority should be to understand the customer better. You can survey customers who have already churned to understand why they left. You can also survey existing customers to understand what their needs are and what their pain points are. A data science and data analytics approach would be to look into the data. For example, you can look at customers' web activity data and understand where they spend the most time, whether there were errors on the pages that they were looking at, or whether their search results did not return good content. You can also look into the customer service call logs to understand how long their wait time was, what their complaints were, and how their issues were handled. Conducting deep analyses on these data points can reveal the problems that a business is facing in retaining its existing customers.

When analyzing for customer churn, you can also utilize some of the topics we have discussed in this book. You can apply what we have learned from `Chapter 5`, *Product Analytics*, and `Chapter 6`, *Recommending the Right Products*, to understand which products serve the customer needs and interests the best, and recommend the right products so that you can deliver more personalized content. You can also use what we have learned from `Chapter 7`, *Exploratory Analysis for Customer Behavior*, and `Chapter 10`, *Data-Driven Customer Segmentation*, to understand the customer behavior better and the different segments of customers. Another way is to build a machine learning model that can predict which customers are likely to churn and target and retain these specific customers that are at higher risk of churn. In the following sections, we will discuss how to build a neural network model to identify those customers with higher risk of churn for customer retention.

Artificial neural networks

The **artificial neural network (ANN)** model is a machine learning model that is inspired by how a human brain functions. Recent successful applications of ANN models in image recognition, voice recognition, and robotics have proven their predictive power and usefulness in various industries. You might have heard the term **deep learning**. This is a type of ANN model where the number of layers between the input and output layers is large. It is best explained with the following diagram:

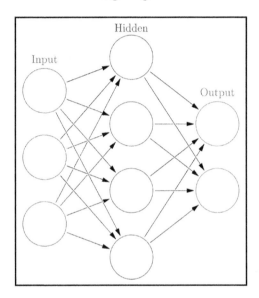

This diagram shows a simple case of an ANN model with one hidden layer. The circles in this diagram represent artificial neurons or nodes, which model those neurons in human brains. The arrows represent how signals are transmitted from one neuron to another. As this diagram suggests, an ANN model learns by finding the patterns or the weights of signals from each input neuron to the neuron in the next layer, which best predicts the output.

The specific type of an ANN model that we will be experimenting with in the following programming exercises is a **multilayer perceptron (MLP)** model. Simply put, an MLP model is a neural network model that has at least one or more hidden layers of nodes. Including one layer for the input and another layer for the output, the MLP model consists of at least three or more layers of nodes. The diagram we just looked at is the simplest case of an MLP model, where there is only one hidden layer.

ANN models can be utilized in many areas of marketing. Using neural network models by BrainMaker, Microsoft increased its direct mail response rate from 4.9% to 8.2%. This helped Microsoft to bring in the same amount of revenue for 35% less cost. Similarly, for the marketing engagement prediction problems we discussed in Chapter 8, *Predicting the Likelihood of Marketing Engagement*, we could have used neural network models, instead of random forest models. We can also use neural network models for the customer segmentation problems that we discussed in Chapter 10, *Data-Driven Customer Segmentation*. In the following programming exercises, we will discuss how we can use ANN models to predict which customers are likely to churn.

Predicting customer churn with Python

In this section, we are going to discuss how to use an ANN model to predict the customers at the risk of leaving, or customers who are highly likely to churn. By the end of this section, we will have built a customer churn prediction model using an ANN model. We will be mainly using the pandas, matplotlib, and keras packages to analyze, visualize, and build machine learning models. For those readers who would like to use R, instead of Python, for this exercise, you can skip to the next section.

For this exercise, we will be using one of the publicly available datasets from the IBM Watson Analytics community, which can be found at this link: https://www.ibm.com/communities/analytics/watson-analytics-blog/predictive-insights-in-the-telco-customer-churn-data-set/. You can follow this link and download the data, which is available in XLSX format, named WA_Fn-UseC_-Telco-Customer-Churn.xlsx. Once you have downloaded this data, you can load it into your Jupyter Notebook by running the following command:

```
import pandas as pd

df = pd.read_excel('../data/WA_Fn-UseC_-Telco-Customer-Churn.xlsx')
```

The DataFrame, `df`, is shown in the following screenshot:

	customerID	gender	SeniorCitizen	Partner	Dependents	tenure	PhoneService	MultipleLines	InternetService	OnlineSecurity	...	DeviceProtection	TechSup
0	7590-VHVEG	Female	0	Yes	No	1	No	No phone service	DSL	No	...	No	
1	5575-GNVDE	Male	0	No	No	34	Yes	No	DSL	Yes	...	Yes	
2	3668-QPYBK	Male	0	No	No	2	Yes	No	DSL	Yes	...	No	
3	7795-CFOCW	Male	0	No	No	45	No	No phone service	DSL	Yes	...	Yes	
4	9237-HQITU	Female	0	No	No	2	Yes	No	Fiber optic	No	...	No	
5	9305-CDSKC	Female	0	No	No	8	Yes	Yes	Fiber optic	No	...	Yes	
6	1452-KIOVK	Male	0	No	Yes	22	Yes	Yes	Fiber optic	No	...	No	
7	6713-OKOMC	Female	0	No	No	10	No	No phone service	DSL	Yes	...	No	
8	7892-POOKP	Female	0	Yes	No	28	Yes	Yes	Fiber optic	No	...	Yes	
9	6388-TABGU	Male	0	No	Yes	62	Yes	No	DSL	Yes	...	No	

There are 21 variables in this dataset, where our goal is to predict the target variable, `Churn`.

Data analysis and preparation

As you may notice by looking at the data, there are a few things we need to do before we can start building machine learning models. In this section, we are going to transform continuous variables that have monetary values and encode the target variable, `Churn`, as well as other categorical variables. To do so, perform the following steps:

1. **Target variable encoding**: As you may have noticed from the data, the target variable, `Churn`, has two values: `Yes` and `No`. We are going to encode these values as `1` for `Yes` and `0` for `No`. The code to encode the target variable looks like the following:

```
df['Churn'] = df['Churn'].apply(lambda x: 1 if x == 'Yes' else 0)
```

To get the overall churn rate, you can simply run the following code:

```
df['Churn'].mean()
```

The output of this code is around 0.27, which suggests that about 27% of customers have churned. A 27% churn rate is not a small number; rather, it is high enough for a business to worry about the overall customer churn and come up with a solution to retain these customers. In the following modeling section, we will discuss how to predict customers who are likely to churn with this data and use these predictions to retain customers.

2. **Handling missing values in the TotalCharges column**: If you looked through the `TotalCharges` column in the dataset, you may have noticed that there are some records with no `TotalCharges` values. Since there are only `11` records with missing `TotalCharges` values, we are going to simply ignore and drop those records with missing values. Take a look at the following code:

```
df['TotalCharges'] = df['TotalCharges'].replace(' ',
                        np.nan).astype(float)

df = df.dropna()
```

As you may notice from this code, we are simply replacing the blank space values with `nan` values. Then, we are dropping all the records with `nan` values by using the `dropna` function.

3. **Transforming continuous variables**: The next step is to scale the continuous variables. Take a look at the following summary statistics for continuous variables:

	tenure	MonthlyCharges	TotalCharges
count	7032.000000	7032.000000	7032.000000
mean	32.421786	64.798208	2283.300441
std	24.545260	30.085974	2266.771362
min	1.000000	18.250000	18.800000
25%	9.000000	35.587500	401.450000
50%	29.000000	70.350000	1397.475000
75%	55.000000	89.862500	3794.737500
max	72.000000	118.750000	8684.800000

You can get these summary statistics using the following code:

```
df[['tenure', 'MonthlyCharges', 'TotalCharges']].describe()
```

As you can see from the summary statistics, the three `tenure`, `MonthlyCharges`, and `TotalCharges` continuous variables all have different scales. The `tenure` variable, ranges from `1` to `72`, while the `TotalCharges` variable, ranges from `18.8` to `8684.8`. ANN models typically perform better with scaled or normalized features. Take a look at the following code for normalizing these three features:

```
df['MonthlyCharges'] = np.log(df['MonthlyCharges'])
df['MonthlyCharges'] = (df['MonthlyCharges'] -
df['MonthlyCharges'].mean())/df['MonthlyCharges'].std()

df['TotalCharges'] = np.log(df['TotalCharges'])
df['TotalCharges'] = (df['TotalCharges'] -
df['TotalCharges'].mean())/df['TotalCharges'].std()

df['tenure'] = (df['tenure'] -
df['tenure'].mean())/df['tenure'].std()
```

As you can see from this code, we apply log-transform first and then normalize the continuous variables by subtracting by the mean and dividing the values by standard deviations. The results look like the following:

```
df[['tenure', 'MonthlyCharges', 'TotalCharges']].describe()
```

	tenure	MonthlyCharges	TotalCharges
count	7.032000e+03	7.032000e+03	7.032000e+03
mean	-1.028756e-16	4.688495e-14	7.150708e-15
std	1.000000e+00	1.000000e+00	1.000000e+00
min	-1.280157e+00	-1.882268e+00	-2.579056e+00
25%	-9.542285e-01	-7.583727e-01	-6.080585e-01
50%	-1.394072e-01	3.885103e-01	1.950521e-01
75%	9.198605e-01	8.004829e-01	8.382338e-01
max	1.612459e+00	1.269576e+00	1.371323e+00

As you see from this output, all the variables now have a mean of `0` and a standard deviation of `1`. We are going to use these normalized variables for future model building.

4. **One-hot encoding categorical variables**: As you can see from the data, there are many categorical variables. Let's first take a look at the number of unique values each column has. Take a look at the following code:

```
for col in list(df.columns):
    print(col, df[col].nunique())
```

You can use the `nunique` function to count the number of unique values in each column. The output of this code looks like the following:

```
customerID 7032
gender 2
SeniorCitizen 2
Partner 2
Dependents 2
tenure 72
PhoneService 2
MultipleLines 3
InternetService 3
OnlineSecurity 3
OnlineBackup 3
DeviceProtection 3
TechSupport 3
StreamingTV 3
StreamingMovies 3
Contract 3
PaperlessBilling 2
PaymentMethod 4
MonthlyCharges 1584
TotalCharges 6530
Churn 2
```

As this output suggests, there are 7032 unique customer IDs, 2 unique genders, 3 unique values for `MultipleLines`, and 6530 unique values for `TotalCharges`. We have handled the `tenure`, `MonthlyCharges`, and `TotalCharges` variables, in the previous step, so we are going to focus on those variables with 2 to 4 unique values.

Let's take a look at the distributions of some of these categorical variables. First, to view the distribution of the data between males and females, you can use the following code for visualization:

```
df.groupby('gender').count()['customerID'].plot(
    kind='bar', color='skyblue', grid=True, figsize=(8,6), title='Gender'
)
plt.show()
```

The plot looks like the following:

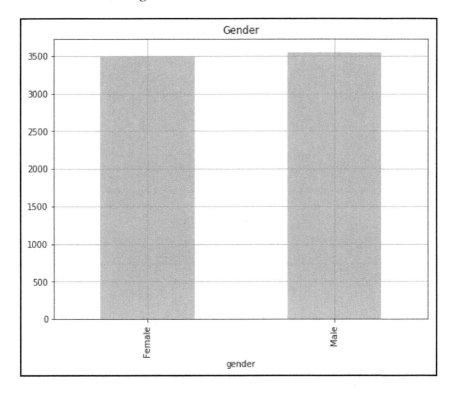

As you can see from this bar plot, the distribution of the data across different genders is roughly equally distributed. You can use the same code to view the distribution of the data across different values of `InternetService` and `PaymentMethod`. Take a look at the following plots:

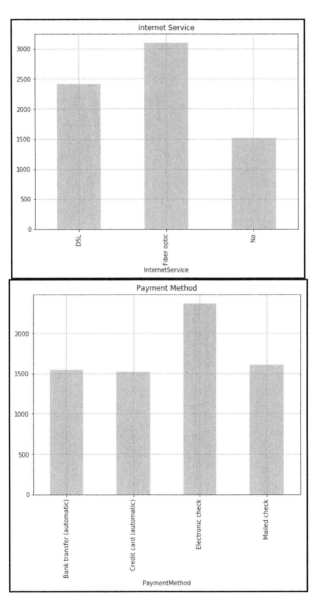

The first plot shows the distribution of the data across three different categories of the `InternetService` variable, and the second plot shows the distribution of the data across four different categories of the `PaymentMethod` variable. As you can see from these plots, we can easily visualize and understand what the distributions of categorical variables look like using bar plots. We recommend that you draw bar plots for other categorical variables to get a better understanding of the data distribution.

Now, we are going to apply one-hot encoding for these categorical variables. Take a look at the following code:

```
dummy_cols = []

sample_set = df[['tenure', 'MonthlyCharges', 'TotalCharges',
'Churn']].copy(deep=True)

for col in list(df.columns):
    if col not in ['tenure', 'MonthlyCharges', 'TotalCharges', 'Churn'] and
df[col].nunique() < 5:
        dummy_vars = pd.get_dummies(df[col])
        dummy_vars.columns = [col+str(x) for x in dummy_vars.columns]
        sample_set = pd.concat([sample_set, dummy_vars], axis=1)
```

As you can see from this code, we are using the `get_dummies` function in the `pandas` package to create dummy variables for each categorical variable. Then, we concatenate these newly created dummy variables back to the `sample_set` variable, which will be used for training models in the following section. The results are shown in the following output:

```
sample_set.head(10)
```

	tenure	MonthlyCharges	TotalCharges	Churn	genderFemale	genderMale	SeniorCitizen0	SeniorCitizen1	PartnerNo	PartnerYes	...	StreamingMoviesYes
0	-1.280157	-1.054244	-2.281382	0	1	0	1	0	0	1	...	0
1	0.064298	0.032896	0.389269	0	0	1	1	0	1	0	...	0
2	-1.239416	-0.061298	-1.452520	1	0	1	1	0	1	0	...	0
3	0.512450	-0.467578	0.372439	0	0	1	1	0	1	0	...	0
4	-1.239416	0.396862	-1.234860	1	1	0	1	0	1	0	...	0
5	-0.994970	0.974468	-0.147808	1	1	0	1	0	1	0	...	1
6	-0.424595	0.786142	0.409363	0	0	1	1	0	1	0	...	0
7	-0.913487	-1.059891	-0.791550	0	1	0	1	0	1	0	...	0
8	-0.180148	1.059269	0.696733	1	1	0	1	0	0	1	...	1
9	1.205048	0.009088	0.783956	0	0	1	1	0	1	0	...	0

Once you have completed these four steps, it is time to start building ANN models for customer churn predictions. Move onto the next section for ANN modeling!

ANN with Keras

For building ANN models in Python, we are going to use `keras` package, which is a high-level neural networks library. For more details, we recommend you visit their official documentation at the following link: `https://keras.io/`. Before we can use this package for building ANN models, we need to install two packages: `tensorflow` and `keras`. The `keras` package uses `tensorflow` as a backend for building neural network models, so we need to install `tensorflow` first. You can install these two packages using the following `pip` commands in your Terminal:

```
pip install tensorflow
pip install keras
```

Once you have installed these two packages, we can finally start building our first neural network models. In this exercise, we are going to build a neural network model with one hidden layer. Take a look at the following code first:

```
from keras.models import Sequential
from keras.layers import Dense

model = Sequential()
model.add(Dense(16, input_dim=len(features), activation='relu'))
model.add(Dense(8, activation='relu'))
model.add(Dense(1, activation='sigmoid'))
```

Let's take a closer look at this code. First, we are using a `Sequential` model here, which is the type of model where the layers are stacked linearly and looks similar to the diagram we saw in the earlier section about the MLP model. The first layer is an input layer, where `input_dim` is simply the number of features or columns in the sample set and the number of output units is `16`. We are using the `relu` activation function for this input layer. Then, in the hidden layer, the number of output units is `8` and the activation function to be used is `relu`. Lastly, the output layer has one output unit, which is the probability of customer churn, and we use the `sigmoid` activation function in this layer. You can experiment with different numbers of output units and activation functions for your exercise.

The final step to build a neural network model with the `keras` package is to compile this model. Take a look at the following code:

```
model.compile(loss='binary_crossentropy', optimizer='adam',
metrics=['accuracy'])
```

Here, we are using the `adam` optimizer, which is one of the most commonly and frequently used optimization algorithms. Since our target variable is binary, we are using `binary_crossentropy` as the loss function. Lastly, this model will use the `accuracy` metric to evaluate model performance during training.

Before we start training this neural network model, we will need to split our sample set into train and test sets. Take a look at the following code:

```
from sklearn.model_selection import train_test_split

target_var = 'Churn'
features = [x for x in list(sample_set.columns) if x != target_var]

X_train, X_test, y_train, y_test = train_test_split(
    sample_set[features],
    sample_set[target_var],
    test_size=0.3
)
```

As you can see from this code, we are using the `train_test_split` function of the `scikit-learn` package. For our exercise, we will use 70% of the sample set for training and 30% for testing. Now we can train our neural network model using the following code:

```
model.fit(X_train, y_train, epochs=50, batch_size=100)
```

Here, we are using `100` samples as `batch_size`, from which the model is going to learn to predict each time, and `50` as the number of `epochs`, which is the number of complete passes through the entire training set. Once you run this code, you will see output that looks like the following:

```
Epoch 1/50
4922/4922 [==============================] - 0s 78us/step - loss: 0.7690 - acc: 0.3779
Epoch 2/50
4922/4922 [==============================] - 0s 14us/step - loss: 0.5783 - acc: 0.7324
Epoch 3/50
4922/4922 [==============================] - 0s 14us/step - loss: 0.4511 - acc: 0.7891
Epoch 4/50
4922/4922 [==============================] - 0s 15us/step - loss: 0.4181 - acc: 0.8046
Epoch 5/50
4922/4922 [==============================] - 0s 15us/step - loss: 0.4093 - acc: 0.8094
Epoch 6/50
4922/4922 [==============================] - 0s 18us/step - loss: 0.4058 - acc: 0.8137
Epoch 7/50
4922/4922 [==============================] - 0s 20us/step - loss: 0.4048 - acc: 0.8070
Epoch 8/50
4922/4922 [==============================] - 0s 16us/step - loss: 0.4027 - acc: 0.8106
Epoch 9/50
4922/4922 [==============================] - 0s 15us/step - loss: 0.4007 - acc: 0.8086
Epoch 10/50
4922/4922 [==============================] - 0s 13us/step - loss: 0.3994 - acc: 0.8094
Epoch 11/50
4922/4922 [==============================] - 0s 13us/step - loss: 0.3984 - acc: 0.8111
Epoch 12/50
4922/4922 [==============================] - 0s 17us/step - loss: 0.3983 - acc: 0.8098
Epoch 13/50
4922/4922 [==============================] - 0s 15us/step - loss: 0.3982 - acc: 0.8133
Epoch 14/50
4922/4922 [==============================] - 0s 13us/step - loss: 0.3972 - acc: 0.8123
Epoch 15/50
4922/4922 [==============================] - 0s 13us/step - loss: 0.3960 - acc: 0.8113
```

As you can see from this output, `loss` typically decreases and the accuracy (`acc`) improves in each epoch. However, the rate of model performance improvement decreases over time. As you can see from this output, there are big improvements in the loss and accuracy measures in the first few epochs and the amount of performance gain decreases over time. You can monitor this process and decide to stop when the amount of performance gain is minimal.

Model evaluations

Now that we have built our first neural network model, let's evaluate its performance. We are going to look at the overall accuracy, precision, and recall, as well as the **receiver operating characteristic (ROC)** curve and area under the curve (AUC). First, take a look at the following code for computing accuracy, precision, and recall:

```
from sklearn.metrics import accuracy_score, precision_score, recall_score

in_sample_preds = [round(x[0]) for x in model.predict(X_train)]
```

```
out_sample_preds = [round(x[0]) for x in model.predict(X_test)]

# Accuracy
print('In-Sample Accuracy: %0.4f' % accuracy_score(y_train,
in_sample_preds))
print('Out-of-Sample Accuracy: %0.4f' % accuracy_score(y_test,
out_sample_preds))

# Precision
print('In-Sample Precision: %0.4f' % precision_score(y_train,
in_sample_preds))
print('Out-of-Sample Precision: %0.4f' % precision_score(y_test,
out_sample_preds))

# Recall
print('In-Sample Recall: %0.4f' % recall_score(y_train, in_sample_preds))
print('Out-of-Sample Recall: %0.4f' % recall_score(y_test,
out_sample_preds))
```

You should be familiar with this code, as we used the same evaluation metrics in `Chapter 8`, *Predicting the Likelihood of Marketing Engagement*. The output of this code in our case looks like the following:

```
In-Sample Accuracy: 0.8151
Out-of-Sample Accuracy: 0.7910

In-Sample Precision: 0.6733
Out-of-Sample Precision: 0.6638

In-Sample Recall: 0.5583
Out-of-Sample Recall: 0.5169
```

Due to some randomness in the model, your results might differ from these numbers. As you can see from this output, the accuracy of predicting whether a customer will churn or not in the test set is about 0.79, suggesting the model is correct roughly about 80% of the time. The out-of-sample precision suggests that the model is correct about 66% of the time that it predicts that the customer is going to churn, and the out-of-sample recall suggests that the model captures roughly 52% of the churn cases.

Next, we can compute the AUC numbers, using the following code:

```
from sklearn.metrics import roc_curve, auc

in_sample_preds = [x[0] for x in model.predict(X_train)]
out_sample_preds = [x[0] for x in model.predict(X_test)]
```

```
in_sample_fpr, in_sample_tpr, in_sample_thresholds = roc_curve(y_train,
in_sample_preds)
out_sample_fpr, out_sample_tpr, out_sample_thresholds = roc_curve(y_test,
out_sample_preds)

in_sample_roc_auc = auc(in_sample_fpr, in_sample_tpr)
out_sample_roc_auc = auc(out_sample_fpr, out_sample_tpr)

print('In-Sample AUC: %0.4f' % in_sample_roc_auc)
print('Out-Sample AUC: %0.4f' % out_sample_roc_auc)
```

The output of this code looks like this:

```
In-Sample AUC: 0.8698
Out-Sample AUC: 0.8352
```

To visualize this data in the ROC curve, you can use the following code:

```
plt.figure(figsize=(10,7))

plt.plot(
    out_sample_fpr, out_sample_tpr, color='darkorange', label='Out-Sample
ROC curve (area = %0.4f)' % in_sample_roc_auc
)
plt.plot(
    in_sample_fpr, in_sample_tpr, color='navy', label='In-Sample ROC curve
(area = %0.4f)' % out_sample_roc_auc
)
plt.plot([0, 1], [0, 1], color='gray', lw=1, linestyle='--')
plt.grid()
plt.xlim([0.0, 1.0])
plt.ylim([0.0, 1.05])
plt.xlabel('False Positive Rate')
plt.ylabel('True Positive Rate')
plt.title('ROC Curve')
plt.legend(loc="lower right")

plt.show()
```

And the output looks like this:

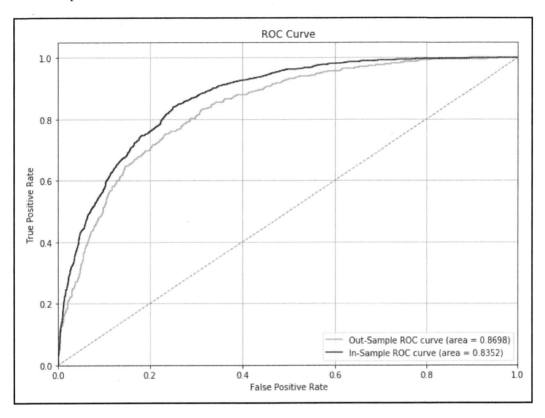

Along with the accuracy, precision, and recall measures that we looked at previously, the AUC and the ROC curve also suggest that the model captures and predicts those customers at churn risk pretty well. As you can see from these evaluation outputs, it is better to use the output of this model for identifying the customers who are likely to churn than simply guessing who they will be. By focusing on those customers with high churn probabilities from this model in your marketing strategies, you can try to retain those customers at churn risks in a more cost-effective way.

The full code for this exercise can be found in this repository: https://github.com/yoonhwang/hands-on-data-science-for-marketing/blob/master/ch.11/python/CustomerRetention.ipynb.

Predicting customer churn with R

In this section, we are going to discuss how to use an ANN model to predict the customers at risk of leaving or customers who are highly likely to churn. By the end of this section, we will have built a customer churn prediction model using the ANN model. We will be mainly using the `dplyr`, `ggplot2`, and `keras` libraries to analyze, visualize, and build machine learning models. For those readers who would like to use Python, instead of R, for this exercise, see the previous section.

For this exercise, we will be using one of the publicly available datasets from the IBM Watson Analytics community, which can be found at this link: `https://www.ibm.com/communities/analytics/watson-analytics-blog/predictive-insights-in-the-telco-customer-churn-data-set/`. You can follow this link and download the data, which is available in XLSX format, named `WA_Fn-UseC_-Telco-Customer-Churn.xlsx`. Once you have downloaded this data, you can load it into your RStudio environment by running the following command:

```
library(readxl)

#### 1. Load Data ####
df <- read_excel(
  path="~/Documents/data-science-for-marketing/ch.11/data/WA_Fn-UseC_-
  Telco-Customer-Churn.xlsx"
)
```

The DataFrame, `df`, should look as in the following screenshot:

	customerID	gender	SeniorCitizen	Partner	Dependents	tenure	PhoneService	MultipleLines	InternetService	OnlineSecurity
1	7590-VHVEG	Female	0	Yes	No	1	No	No phone service	DSL	No
2	5575-GNVDE	Male	0	No	No	34	Yes	No	DSL	Yes
3	3668-QPYBK	Male	0	No	No	2	Yes	No	DSL	Yes
4	7795-CFOCW	Male	0	No	No	45	No	No phone service	DSL	Yes
5	9237-HQITU	Female	0	No	No	2	Yes	No	Fiber optic	No
6	9305-CDSKC	Female	0	No	No	8	Yes	Yes	Fiber optic	No
7	1452-KIOVK	Male	0	No	Yes	22	Yes	Yes	Fiber optic	No
8	6713-OKOMC	Female	0	No	No	10	No	No phone service	DSL	Yes
9	7892-POOKP	Female	0	Yes	No	28	Yes	Yes	Fiber optic	No
10	6388-TABGU	Male	0	No	Yes	62	Yes	No	DSL	Yes
11	9763-GRSKD	Male	0	Yes	Yes	13	Yes	No	DSL	Yes
12	7469-LKBCI	Male	0	No	No	16	Yes	No	No	No internet service
13	8091-TTVAX	Male	0	Yes	No	58	Yes	Yes	Fiber optic	No
14	0280-XJGEX	Male	0	No	No	49	Yes	Yes	Fiber optic	No
15	5129-JLPIS	Male	0	No	No	25	Yes	No	Fiber optic	Yes

There are 21 variables in this dataset, where our goal is to predict the target variable, `Churn`.

Data analysis and preparation

As you may have noticed by looking at the data, there are a few things we need to do before we start building machine learning models. In this section, we are going to transform continuous variables that have monetary values and encode the target variable, `Churn`, as well as other categorical variables. To do so, perform the following steps:

1. **Handling missing values in the data**: If you looked through the `TotalCharges` column in the dataset, you may have noticed that there are some records with no `TotalCharges` values. Since there are only 11 records with missing `TotalCharges` values, we are going to simply ignore and drop those records with missing values. Take a look at the following code:

```
library(tidyr)

df <- df %>% drop_na()
```

As you may notice from this code, we are using the `drop_na` function in the `tidyr` package, which drops all records with `NA` values.

2. **Categorical variables**: As you can see from the data, there are many categorical variables. Let's first take a look at the number of unique values each column has. Take a look at the following code:

```
apply(df, 2, function(x) length(unique(x)))
```

You can use the `unique` function to get the unique values in each column. By applying this function across all the columns in `df`, the output of this code looks like the following:

```
> apply(df, 2, function(x) length(unique(x)))
      customerID          gender    SeniorCitizen         Partner      Dependents
            7032               2                2               2               2
          tenure    PhoneService    MultipleLines  InternetService  OnlineSecurity
              72               2                3               3               3
    OnlineBackup DeviceProtection      TechSupport      StreamingTV StreamingMovies
               3               3                3               3               3
        Contract PaperlessBilling    PaymentMethod   MonthlyCharges    TotalCharges
               3               2                4            1584            6530
           Churn
               2
```

As this output suggests, there are `7032` unique customer IDs, `2` unique genders, `3` unique values for `MultipleLines`, and `6530` unique values for `TotalCharges`. The `tenure`, `MonthlyCharges`, and `TotalCharges` variables, are continuous variables, where each variable can take any value and the rest are the categorical variables.

We are going to take a look at the distributions of some of these categorical variables. First, to view the distribution of the data between male and female, you can use the following code for visualization:

```
ggplot(df %>% group_by(gender) %>% summarise(Count=n()),
  aes(x=gender, y=Count)) +
  geom_bar(width=0.5, stat="identity") +
  ggtitle('') +
  xlab("Gender") +
  ylab("Count") +
  theme(plot.title = element_text(hjust = 0.5))
```

The plot looks like this:

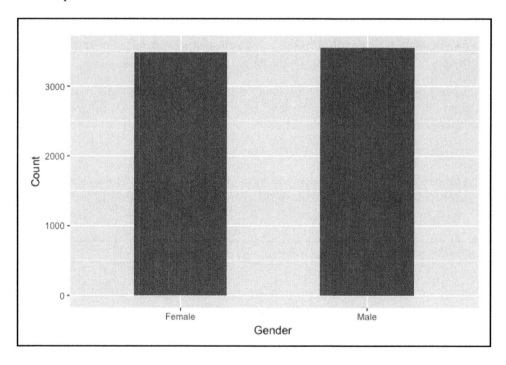

As you can see from this bar plot, the distribution of the data across the two genders is roughly equally distributed. You can use the same code to view the distribution of the data across different values of `InternetService` and `PaymentMethod`. Take a look at the following plots:

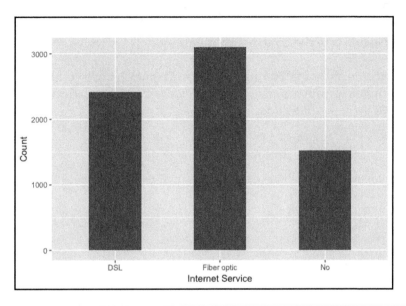

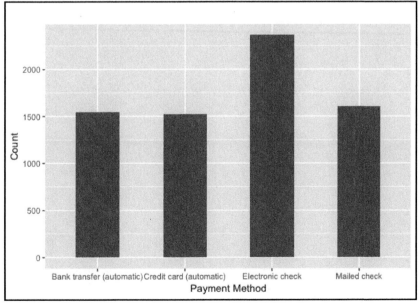

The first plot shows the distribution of the data across three different categories of the `InternetService` variable and the second plot shows the distribution of the data across four different categories of the `PaymentMethod` variable. As you can see from these plots, we can easily visualize and understand what the distributions of categorical variables look like using bar plots. We recommend that you draw bar plots for other categorical variables to get a better understanding of the data distribution.

3. **Transforming and encoding variables**: The next step is to transform the continuous variables and encode the binary-class categorical variables. Take a look at the following code:

```
# Binary & Continuous Vars
sampleDF <- df %>%
 select(tenure, MonthlyCharges, TotalCharges, gender, Partner,
Dependents, PhoneService, PaperlessBilling, Churn) %>%
 mutate(
  # transforming continuous vars
 tenure=(tenure - mean(tenure))/sd(tenure),
  MonthlyCharges=(log(MonthlyCharges) -
mean(log(MonthlyCharges)))/sd(log(MonthlyCharges)),
  TotalCharges=(log(TotalCharges) -
mean(log(TotalCharges)))/sd(log(TotalCharges)),

  # encoding binary categorical vars
 gender=gender %>% as.factor() %>% as.numeric() - 1,
  Partner=Partner %>% as.factor() %>% as.numeric() - 1,
Dependents=Dependents %>% as.factor() %>% as.numeric() - 1,
  PhoneService=PhoneService %>% as.factor() %>% as.numeric() - 1,
  PaperlessBilling=PaperlessBilling %>% as.factor() %>% as.numeric()
- 1,

  Churn=Churn %>% as.factor() %>% as.numeric() - 1
  )
```

As you can see from this code, we are simply encoding those variables with only two categories, `gender`, `Partner`, `Dependents`, `PhoneService`, `PaperlessBilling`, and `Churn`, with 0s and 1s. Then, we apply log transformations to the two continuous variables that have monetary values, `MonthlyCharges` and `TotalCharges`. Also, we standardize all three continuous variables, `tenure`, `MonthlyCharges`, and `TotalCharges`, so that these variables center around 0 and have standard deviations of 1. This is because ANN models typically perform better with scaled or normalized features. After transformations, the distributions of these three continuous variables look as in the following screenshot:

```
> summary(sampleDF[,c("tenure", "MonthlyCharges", "TotalCharges")])
     tenure          MonthlyCharges      TotalCharges
 Min.   :-1.2802   Min.   :-1.8823   Min.   :-2.5791
 1st Qu.:-0.9542   1st Qu.:-0.7584   1st Qu.:-0.6081
 Median :-0.1394   Median : 0.3885   Median : 0.1951
 Mean   : 0.0000   Mean   : 0.0000   Mean   : 0.0000
 3rd Qu.: 0.9199   3rd Qu.: 0.8005   3rd Qu.: 0.8382
 Max.   : 1.6125   Max.   : 1.2696   Max.   : 1.3713
> apply(sampleDF[,c("tenure", "MonthlyCharges", "TotalCharges")], 2, sd)
         tenure MonthlyCharges   TotalCharges
              1              1              1
```

As you can see, the means of these three transformed variables are 0 and the standard deviations are 1. Whereas, before this transformation, the distributions looked like the following:

```
> summary(df[,c("tenure", "MonthlyCharges", "TotalCharges")])
     tenure        MonthlyCharges    TotalCharges
 Min.   : 1.00   Min.   : 18.25   Min.   :  18.8
 1st Qu.: 9.00   1st Qu.: 35.59   1st Qu.: 401.4
 Median :29.00   Median : 70.35   Median :1397.5
 Mean   :32.42   Mean   : 64.80   Mean   :2283.3
 3rd Qu.:55.00   3rd Qu.: 89.86   3rd Qu.:3794.7
 Max.   :72.00   Max.   :118.75   Max.   :8684.8
> apply(df[,c("tenure", "MonthlyCharges", "TotalCharges")], 2, sd)
         tenure MonthlyCharges   TotalCharges
       24.54526       30.08597     2266.77136
```

4. **One-hot encoding categorical variables**: There is one last set of variables we need to transform: multi-class categorical variables that have three or more categories. We are going to apply one-hot encoding and create dummy variables for these variables. Take a look at the following code:

```
# Dummy vars
# install.packages('dummies')
library(dummies)
```

```
         sampleDF <- cbind(sampleDF, dummy(df$MultipleLines, sep="."))
          names(sampleDF) = gsub("sampleDF", "MultipleLines",
names(sampleDF))
```

As you can see from this code, we are using the dummies library to create dummy variables. Using the dummy function of this package, we can apply one-hot encoding and create dummy variables for each multi-class categorical variable. Since the dummy function prepends sampleDF to the names of the newly created dummy variables, we can replace it with corresponding variable name by using the gsub function. We are going to apply the same logic to the rest of the categorical variables, as shown in the following code:

```
         sampleDF <- cbind(sampleDF, dummy(df$InternetService, sep="."))
          names(sampleDF) = gsub("sampleDF", "InternetService",
names(sampleDF))

         sampleDF <- cbind(sampleDF, dummy(df$OnlineSecurity, sep="."))
          names(sampleDF) = gsub("sampleDF", "OnlineSecurity",
names(sampleDF))

         sampleDF <- cbind(sampleDF, dummy(df$OnlineBackup, sep="."))
           names(sampleDF) = gsub("sampleDF", "OnlineBackup",
names(sampleDF))

         sampleDF <- cbind(sampleDF, dummy(df$DeviceProtection, sep="."))
          names(sampleDF) = gsub("sampleDF", "DeviceProtection",
names(sampleDF))

          sampleDF <- cbind(sampleDF, dummy(df$TechSupport, sep="."))
          names(sampleDF) = gsub("sampleDF", "TechSupport", names(sampleDF))

          sampleDF <- cbind(sampleDF, dummy(df$StreamingTV, sep="."))
          names(sampleDF) = gsub("sampleDF", "StreamingTV", names(sampleDF))

          sampleDF <- cbind(sampleDF, dummy(df$StreamingMovies, sep="."))
           names(sampleDF) = gsub("sampleDF", "StreamingMovies",
names(sampleDF))

           sampleDF <- cbind(sampleDF, dummy(df$Contract, sep="."))
           names(sampleDF) = gsub("sampleDF", "Contract", names(sampleDF))

          sampleDF <- cbind(sampleDF, dummy(df$PaymentMethod, sep="."))
          names(sampleDF) = gsub("sampleDF", "PaymentMethod",
names(sampleDF))
```

The results are shown in the following output:

	tenure	MonthlyCharges	TotalCharges	gender	Partner	Dependents	PhoneService	PaperlessBilling	Churn	MultipleLines.No	MultipleLines.No phone service	MultipleLines.Yes	InternetService.DSL
1	-1.28015700	-1.054243906	-2.281382138	0	1	0	0	1	0	0	1	0	1
2	0.06429811	0.032896403	0.389269024	1	0	0	1	0	0	1	0	0	1
3	-1.23941594	-0.061298166	-1.452520489	1	0	0	1	1	1	1	0	0	1
4	0.51244982	-0.467578124	0.372439102	1	0	0	0	0	0	0	1	0	1
5	-1.23941594	0.396862254	-1.234860074	0	0	0	1	1	1	1	0	0	0
6	-0.99496955	0.974467637	-0.147808199	0	0	0	1	1	1	1	0	0	0
7	-0.42459466	0.786142215	0.409363467	1	0	1	1	1	1	0	0	1	0
8	-0.91348743	-1.059891256	-0.791549959	0	0	0	0	0	0	0	1	0	1
9	-0.18014827	1.059268949	0.696733168	0	1	0	1	1	1	0	0	1	0
10	1.20504791	0.009068278	0.783955768	1	0	1	1	1	0	1	0	0	1
11	-0.79126423	-0.187819078	-0.362936119	1	1	1	1	1	1	1	0	0	1
12	-0.66904104	-1.818925526	-0.740522515	1	0	0	0	1	0	1	0	0	0
13	1.04208365	0.986248047	1.098049907	1	1	0	1	0	0	0	0	1	0
14	0.67541407	1.641511473	1.020482172	1	0	0	1	1	1	0	0	1	0
15	-0.30237146	1.070472177	0.615752488	1	0	0	1	1	0	1	0	0	0

Once you have completed these four steps, it is time to start building ANN models for customer churn predictions. Move onto the next section for ANN modeling!

ANN with Keras

For building ANN models in R, we are going to use the keras package, which is a high-level neural networks library. For more details, we recommend you visit their official documentation at the following link: https://keras.io/. Before we can use this package for building ANN models, we need to install two libraries:tensorflow and keras. The keras package uses tensorflow as a backend for building neural network models, so we need to install tensorflow first. You can install these two packages using the following commands in your RStudio:

```
install.packages("devtools")
devtools::install_github("rstudio/tensorflow")
library(tensorflow)
install_tensorflow()

devtools::install_github("rstudio/keras")
library(keras)
install_keras()
```

Once you have installed these two libraries, we can finally start building our first neural network models. In this exercise, we are going to build a neural network model with one hidden layer. Take a look at the following code first:

```
model <- keras_model_sequential()
model %>%
  layer_dense(units = 16, kernel_initializer = "uniform", activation =
'relu', input_shape=ncol(train)-1) %>%
```

```
  layer_dense(units = 8, kernel_initializer = "uniform", activation =
'relu') %>%
  layer_dense(units = 1, kernel_initializer = "uniform", activation =
'sigmoid') %>%
  compile(
    optimizer = 'adam',
    loss = 'binary_crossentropy',
    metrics = c('accuracy')
  )
```

Let's take a closer look at this code. First, we are building a `Sequential` model here, `keras_model_sequential`, which is the type of model where the layers are stacked linearly and looks similar to the diagram we saw in the earlier section about the MLP model. The first layer, `layer_dense`, is an input layer, where `input_shape` is simply the number of features or columns in the sample set and the number of output units is `16`. We are using the `relu` activation function for this input layer. Then, in the hidden layer, the number of output units is `8` and the activation function to be used is `relu`. Lastly, the output layer has one output unit, which is the probability of customer churn, and we use the `sigmoid` activation function in this layer. You can experiment with different numbers of output units and activation functions for your exercise. Lastly, we need to compile this model, using the `compile` function. Here, we are using the `adam` optimizer, which is one of the most frequently used optimization algorithms. Since our target variable is binary, we are using `binary_crossentropy` as the `loss` function. Lastly, this model will use the `accuracy` metric to evaluate model performance during training.

Before we start training this neural network model, we will need to split our sample set into train and test sets. Take a look at the following code:

```
library(caTools)

sample <- sample.split(sampleDF$Churn, SplitRatio = .7)

train <- as.data.frame(subset(sampleDF, sample == TRUE))
test <- as.data.frame(subset(sampleDF, sample == FALSE))

trainX <- as.matrix(train[,names(train) != "Churn"])
trainY <- train$Churn
testX <- as.matrix(test[,names(test) != "Churn"])
testY <- test$Churn
```

As you can see from this code, we are using the `sample.split` function of the `caTools` package. For our exercise, we will use 70% of the sample set for training and 30% for testing. Now we can train our neural network model using the following code:

```
history <- model %>% fit(
  trainX,
  trainY,
  epochs = 50,
  batch_size = 100,
  validation_split = 0.2
)
```

Here, we are using `100` samples as `batch_size`, from which the model is going to learn to predict every time, and `50` as the number of `epochs`, which is the number of complete passes through the entire training set. Once you run this code, you will see the following output:

```
Train on 3937 samples, validate on 985 samples
Epoch 1/50
3937/3937 [==============================] - 1s 202us/step - loss: 0.6851 - acc: 0.7290 - val_loss: 0.6650 - val_acc: 0.7391
Epoch 2/50
3937/3937 [==============================] - 0s 62us/step - loss: 0.6026 - acc: 0.7330 - val_loss: 0.5225 - val_acc: 0.7391
Epoch 3/50
3937/3937 [==============================] - 0s 55us/step - loss: 0.4869 - acc: 0.7330 - val_loss: 0.4533 - val_acc: 0.7391
Epoch 4/50
3937/3937 [==============================] - 0s 52us/step - loss: 0.4520 - acc: 0.7330 - val_loss: 0.4428 - val_acc: 0.7391
Epoch 5/50
3937/3937 [==============================] - 0s 48us/step - loss: 0.4436 - acc: 0.7711 - val_loss: 0.4384 - val_acc: 0.7980
Epoch 6/50
3937/3937 [==============================] - 0s 48us/step - loss: 0.4384 - acc: 0.7917 - val_loss: 0.4359 - val_acc: 0.7929
Epoch 7/50
3937/3937 [==============================] - 0s 49us/step - loss: 0.4350 - acc: 0.7932 - val_loss: 0.4318 - val_acc: 0.7949
Epoch 8/50
3937/3937 [==============================] - 0s 54us/step - loss: 0.4314 - acc: 0.7945 - val_loss: 0.4296 - val_acc: 0.7939
Epoch 9/50
3937/3937 [==============================] - 0s 50us/step - loss: 0.4298 - acc: 0.7971 - val_loss: 0.4272 - val_acc: 0.7919
Epoch 10/50
3937/3937 [==============================] - 0s 46us/step - loss: 0.4278 - acc: 0.7988 - val_loss: 0.4255 - val_acc: 0.7939
```

As you can see from this output, `loss` typically decreases and the accuracy (`acc`) improves in each epoch. However, the rate of model performance improvements decreases over time. As you can see from this output, there are big improvements in the loss and accuracy measures in the first few epochs and the amount of performance gain decreases over time. You can monitor this process and decide to stop when the amount of performance gain is minimal.

Model evaluations

Now that we have built our first neural network model, let's evaluate its performance. We are going to look at the overall accuracy, precision, and recall, as well as the ROC curve and AUC. First, take a look at the following code for computing accuracy, precision, and recall:

```
# Evaluating ANN model
inSamplePreds <- as.double(model %>% predict_classes(trainX))
outSamplePreds <- as.double(model %>% predict_classes(testX))

# - Accuracy, Precision, and Recall
inSampleAccuracy <- mean(trainY == inSamplePreds)
outSampleAccuracy <- mean(testY == outSamplePreds)
print(sprintf('In-Sample Accuracy: %0.4f', inSampleAccuracy))
print(sprintf('Out-Sample Accuracy: %0.4f', outSampleAccuracy))

inSamplePrecision <- sum(inSamplePreds & trainY) / sum(inSamplePreds)
outSamplePrecision <- sum(outSamplePreds & testY) / sum(outSamplePreds)
print(sprintf('In-Sample Precision: %0.4f', inSamplePrecision))
print(sprintf('Out-Sample Precision: %0.4f', outSamplePrecision))

inSampleRecall <- sum(inSamplePreds & trainY) / sum(trainY)
outSampleRecall <- sum(outSamplePreds & testY) / sum(testY)
print(sprintf('In-Sample Recall: %0.4f', inSampleRecall))
print(sprintf('Out-Sample Recall: %0.4f', outSampleRecall))
```

You should be familiar with this code, as we used the same evaluation metrics in `Chapter 8`, *Predicting the Likelihood of Marketing Engagement*. The output of this code in our case looks like the following:

```
> print(sprintf('In-Sample Accuracy: %0.4f', inSampleAccuracy))
[1] "In-Sample Accuracy: 0.8035"
> print(sprintf('Out-Sample Accuracy: %0.4f', outSampleAccuracy))
[1] "Out-Sample Accuracy: 0.8275"
> print(sprintf('In-Sample Precision: %0.4f', inSamplePrecision))
[1] "In-Sample Precision: 0.6638"
> print(sprintf('Out-Sample Precision: %0.4f', outSamplePrecision))
[1] "Out-Sample Precision: 0.7165"
> print(sprintf('In-Sample Recall: %0.4f', inSampleRecall))
[1] "In-Sample Recall: 0.5283"
> print(sprintf('Out-Sample Recall: %0.4f', outSampleRecall))
[1] "Out-Sample Recall: 0.5811"
```

Due to some randomness in the model, your results might differ from these numbers. As you can see from this output, the accuracy of predicting whether a customer will churn or not in the test set is about `0.83`, suggesting the model is correct roughly about 83% of the time. The out-of-sample precision suggests that the model is correct about 72% of the time it predicts that the customer is going to churn, and the out-of-sample recall suggests that the model captures roughly 58% of the churn cases.

Next, we can compute the AUC and plot the ROC curve, using the following code:

```
# - ROC & AUC
library(ROCR)

outSamplePredProbs <- as.double(predict(model, testX))

pred <- prediction(outSamplePredProbs, testY)
perf <- performance(pred, measure = "tpr", x.measure = "fpr")
auc <- performance(pred, measure='auc')@y.values[[1]]

plot(
  perf,
  main=sprintf('Model ROC Curve (AUC: %0.2f)', auc),
  col='darkorange',
  lwd=2
) + grid()
abline(a = 0, b = 1, col='darkgray', lty=3, lwd=2)
```

And the output looks like the following:

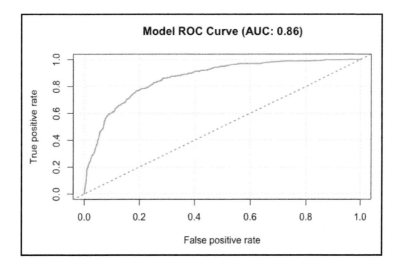

Along with the accuracy, precision, and recall measures that we looked at previously, the AUC and the ROC curve also suggest that the model captures and predicts those customers at churn risk pretty well. As you can see from these evaluation outputs, it is better to use the output of this model for identifying the customers who are likely to churn than simply guessing who they will be. By focusing on those customers with high churn probabilities from this model in your marketing strategies, you can try to retain those customers at churn risk in a more cost-effective way.

The full code for this exercise can be found in this repository: `https://github.com/yoonhwang/hands-on-data-science-for-marketing/blob/master/ch.11/R/CustomerRetention.R`.

Summary

In this chapter, we have learned about customer churn and retention. We have discussed the reasons why customer churn hurts businesses. More specifically, we have learned how retaining existing customers is much less expensive than acquiring new customers. We have shown some of the common reasons why customers leave a company, such as poor customer service, not finding enough value in products or services, lack of communications, and lack of customer loyalty. In order to understand why customers leave, we could conduct surveys or analyze customer data to understand their needs and pain points better. We have also discussed how we can train ANN models to identify those customers who are at risk of churning. Through programming exercises, we have learned how to use the `keras` library to build and train ANN models in Python and R.

In the following chapter, we are going to learn about A/B testing and how it can be used to determine the best marketing strategy among different options. We are going to discuss how to compute statistical significance in Python and R to help marketers decide which marketing strategy to choose among different ideas.

Section 5: Better Decision Making
5

In this section, you will learn a strategy for testing different marketing strategies and choosing the one that works the best.

This section consists of the following chapters:

12
A/B Testing for Better Marketing Strategy

When building different marketing strategies, whether your idea is going to work or not. Typically, there is a lot of guesswork involved when coming up with new marketing ideas, and often there is a lack of tools, resources, or even motivation to test whether any of your marketing ideas will work. However, this way of putting your marketing strategy ideas into work is risky and can be very costly. What if you spent lots of money on your new marketing campaign and it did not help you reach your marketing goal at all? What if you spent hundreds of hours refining your marketing message and it never attracted your prospects to engage with your marketing message?

In this chapter, we are going to discuss a way of testing your marketing ideas before you fully commit to them. More specifically, we are going to learn about what A/B testing is, why running A/B tests is important, and how it can help you reach your marketing goal in a more efficient and less expensive way.

In this chapter, we will cover the following topics:

- A/B testing for marketing
- Statistical hypothesis testing
- Evaluating A/B testing results with Python
- Evaluating A/B testing results with R

A/B testing for marketing

A/B testing plays a critical role in decision-making processes across various industries. A/B testing is essentially a method of comparing and testing the effectiveness and benefits of two different business strategies. It can be considered as an experiment where two or more variants are tested for a set period of time and then the experiment results are evaluated to find the strategy that works best. Running A/B testing before fully committing to a single option helps businesses take the guesswork out of their decision-making processes and saves valuable resources, such as time and capital, that could have been wasted if the chosen strategy did not work.

In a typical A/B testing setting, you would create and test two or more versions of marketing strategies for their effectiveness in achieving your marketing goal. Consider a case where your goal is to improve marketing email open rates. If your hypothesis is that email subject line B will result in higher open rates than email subject line A, then you would run an A/B test with these two subject lines. You will randomly select half of the users and send out marketing emails with subject line A. The other half of randomly selected users will receive emails with subject line B. You will run this test for a predetermined period of time (which could be one week, two weeks, or one month, for instance) or until a predetermined number of users receive the two versions of emails (which is a minimum of 1,000 users to receive each version of the subject line). Once your tests are complete, then you analyze and evaluate the experiment results. When analyzing the results, you will need to check whether there is a statistically significant difference between the results of the two versions. We will cover more about statistical hypothesis testing and statistical significance in the following section. If your experiment results show a clear winner between the two versions of subject line, you can use the winning subject line in your future marketing emails.

Aside from the aforementioned email subject line scenario, A/B testing can be applied in many different areas of marketing. For instance, you can run A/B testing on your advertisements on social media. You can have two or more variants of your ads and run A/B tests to see which variation works better for click-through rates or conversion rates. As another example, you can use A/B testing to test whether product recommendations on your web page result in higher purchase rates. If you have built a different version of your product recommendation algorithm, then you can use and expose the initial version of your product recommendation algorithm to some randomly selected users and the second version to some other randomly selected users. You can gather the A/B test results and evaluate which version of your product recommendation algorithm helps you bring in more revenue.

As you can see from these example use cases, A/B testing plays an important role in decision-making. As you test different scenarios before you fully commit to one, it helps you save your energy, time, and capital that you could have wasted if you had fully committed to it but failed. A/B tests also help you take your guesswork away and quantify the performance gains (or losses) of your future marketing strategy. Whenever you have a new marketing idea that you would like to iterate on, you should consider running A/B tests first.

Statistical hypothesis testing

When you run A/B tests, it is important to test your hypothesis and seek for statistically significant differences among the test groups. Student's t-test, or simply the **t-test**, is frequently used to test whether the difference between two tests is statistically significant. The t-test compares the two averages and examines whether they are significantly different from each other.

There are two important statistics in a t-test—the **t-value** and **p-value**. The t-value measures the degree of difference relative to the variation in the data. The larger the t-value is, the more difference there is between the two groups. On the other hand, the p-value measures the probability that the results would occur by chance. The smaller the p-value is, the more statistically significant difference there will be between the two groups. The equation to compute the t-value is as follows:

$$t = \frac{M_1 - M_2}{\sqrt{\frac{S_1^2}{N_1} + \frac{S_2^2}{N_2}}}$$

In this equation, M_1 and M_2 are the averages of group *1* and *2*. S_1 and S_2 are the standard deviations of group *1* and *2*, and N_1 and N_2 are number of samples in group *1* and *2* respectively.

There is a concept of the null hypothesis and the alternate hypothesis, which you should be familiar with. Generally speaking, the null hypothesis is that the two groups show no statistically significant difference. On the other hand, the alternate hypothesis states that the two groups show a statistically significant difference. When the t-value is larger than a threshold and the p-value is smaller than a threshold, we say that we can reject the null hypothesis and that the two groups show a statistically significant difference. Typically, 0.01 or 0.05 are used as the p-value thresholds for testing statistical significance. If the p-value is less than 0.05, then it suggests that there is less than 5% probability that the difference between the two groups occurs by chance. In other words, the difference is highly unlikely to be by chance.

Evaluating A/B testing results with Python

In this section, we are going to discuss how to evaluate A/B testing results to decide which marketing strategy works the best. By the end of this section, we will have covered how to run statistical hypothesis testing and compute the statistical significance. We will be mainly using the `pandas`, `matplotlib`, and `scipy` packages to analyze and visualize the data, and evaluate the A/B testing results.

For those readers who would like to use R instead of Python for this exercise, you can skip to the next section.

For this exercise, we will be using one of the publicly available datasets from the IBM Watson Analytics community, which can be found at this link: `https://www.ibm.com/communities/analytics/watson-analytics-blog/marketing-campaign-eff-usec_-fastf/`. You can follow this link and download the data, which is available in XLSX format, named `WA_Fn-UseC_-Marketing-Campaign-Eff-UseC_-FastF.xlsx`. Once you have downloaded this data, you can load it into your Jupyter Notebook by running the following command:

```
import pandas as pd

df = pd.read_excel('../data/WA_Fn-UseC_-Marketing-Campaign-Eff-UseC_-
FastF.xlsx')
```

The `df` DataFrame looks as follows:

	MarketID	MarketSize	LocationID	AgeOfStore	Promotion	Week	SalesInThousands
0	1	Medium	1	4	3	1	33.73
1	1	Medium	1	4	3	2	35.67
2	1	Medium	1	4	3	3	29.03
3	1	Medium	1	4	3	4	39.25
4	1	Medium	2	5	2	1	27.81
5	1	Medium	2	5	2	2	34.67
6	1	Medium	2	5	2	3	27.98
7	1	Medium	2	5	2	4	27.72
8	1	Medium	3	12	1	1	44.54
9	1	Medium	3	12	1	2	37.94
10	1	Medium	3	12	1	3	45.49
11	1	Medium	3	12	1	4	34.75
12	1	Medium	4	1	2	1	39.28
13	1	Medium	4	1	2	2	39.80
14	1	Medium	4	1	2	3	24.77

There are a total of seven variables in the dataset. You can find the descriptions of these variables on the IBM Watson Analytics Community page, but we will reiterate in the following:

- `MarketID`: unique identifier for market
- `MarketSize`: size of market area by sales
- `LocationID`: unique identifier for store location
- `AgeOfStore`: age of store in years
- `Promotion`: one of three promotions that was tested
- `week`: one of four weeks when the promotions were run
- `SalesInThousands`: sales amount for specific `LocationID`, `Promotion`, and week

Data analysis

Let's take a deeper look at the data. In this section, we are going to focus on understanding the distributions of sales, market sizes, store locations, and store ages used to test different promotions. The goal of this analysis is to make sure the controls and attributes of each of the promotion groups are symmetrically distributed, so that the promotion performances among different groups are comparable to each other.

The total sales distributions across different promotions can be visualized using the following code:

```
ax = df.groupby(
    'Promotion'
).sum()[
    'SalesInThousands'
].plot.pie(
    figsize=(7, 7),
    autopct='%1.0f%%'
)

ax.set_ylabel('')
ax.set_title('sales distribution across different promotions')

plt.show()
```

As you can see from this code, we are grouping the data by the `Promotion` column and aggregating the total sales amount by summing over the `SalesInThousands` column. Using a pie chart, we can easily visualize how much of the pie each group takes.

The resulting pie chart looks as follows:

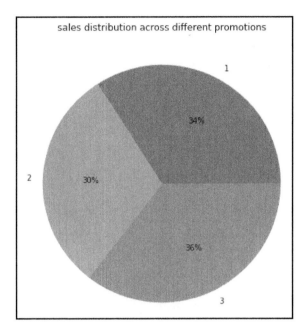

As is easily visible from this pie chart, promotion group **3** has the largest aggregate sales among the three groups. However, each promotion group takes roughly about one third of the total sales during the promotion weeks. Similarly, we can also visualize the compositions of different market sizes in each promotion group. Take a look at the following code:

```
ax = df.groupby([
    'Promotion', 'MarketSize'
]).count()[
    'MarketID'
].unstack(
    'MarketSize'
).plot(
    kind='bar',
    figsize=(12,10),
    grid=True,
)

ax.set_ylabel('count')
ax.set_title('breakdowns of market sizes across different promotions')

plt.show()
```

The bar plot looks as follows:

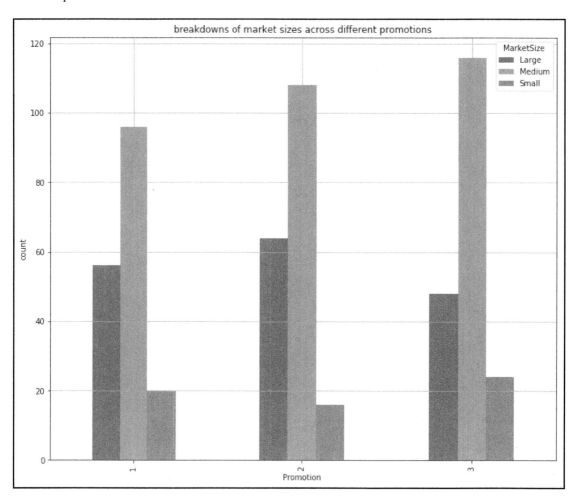

If you think a stacked bar chart will be easier to view, you can use the following code to display this data in a stacked bar plot:

```
ax = df.groupby([
    'Promotion', 'MarketSize'
]).sum()[
    'SalesInThousands'
].unstack(
    'MarketSize'
).plot(
    kind='bar',
    figsize=(12,10),
```

```
        grid=True,
        stacked=True
)

ax.set_ylabel('Sales (in Thousands)')
ax.set_title('breakdowns of market sizes across different promotions')

plt.show()
```

You may notice that the only difference between this code and the previous code is the `stacked=True` flag. The result looks as follows:

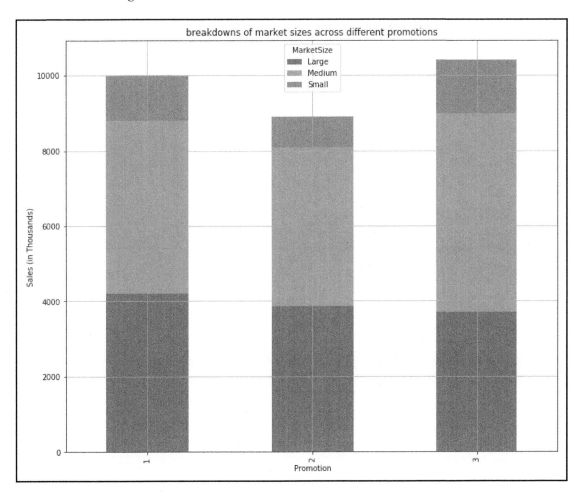

As you can see from this bar chart, the medium market size occupies the most among all three promotion groups, while the small market size occupies the least. We can verify that the compositions of different market sizes are similar among the three promotion groups from this plot.

Another attribute, `AgeOfStore`, and its overall distribution across all different promotions groups, can be visualized by using the following code:

```
ax = df.groupby(
    'AgeOfStore'
).count()[
    'MarketID'
].plot(
    kind='bar',
    color='skyblue',
    figsize=(10,7),
    grid=True
)

ax.set_xlabel('age')
ax.set_ylabel('count')
ax.set_title('overall distributions of age of store')

plt.show()
```

And the result looks as in the following bar plot:

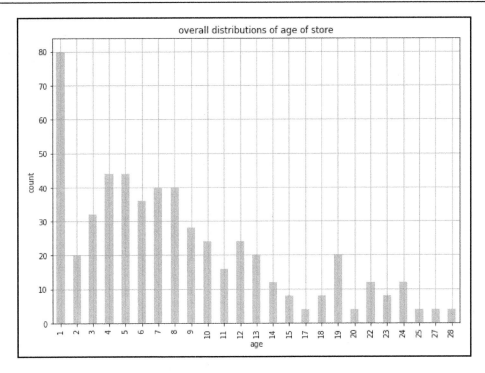

As you can see from this plot, a large number of stores are **1** year old and the majority of stores are **10** years old or less. However, what we are more interested in is whether the stores in the three different promotion groups have similar store age profiles. Take a look at the following code:

```
ax = df.groupby(
    ['AgeOfStore', 'Promotion']
).count()[
    'MarketID'
].unstack(
    'Promotion'
).iloc[::-1].plot(
    kind='barh',
    figsize=(12,15),
    grid=True
)

ax.set_ylabel('age')
ax.set_xlabel('count')
ax.set_title('overall distributions of age of store')

plt.show()
```

Using this code, you will get the following output:

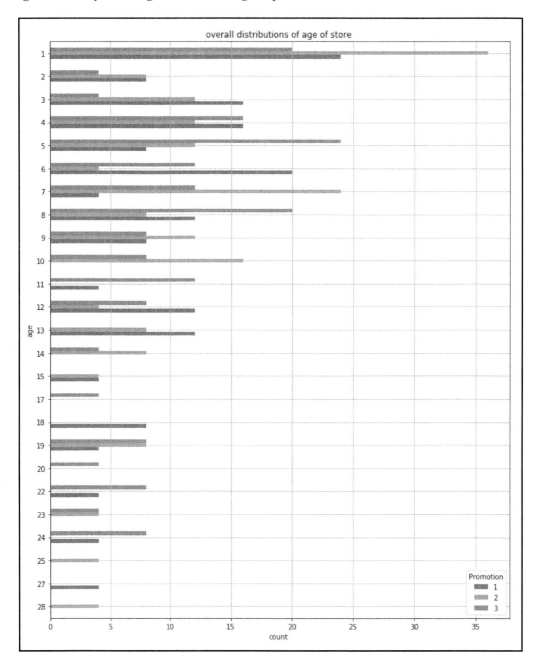

The store age distributions across the three different promotion groups seem to align with each other, but it is quite difficult to digest the information presented from this plot. It will be easier to look at the summary statistics of store ages across the three promotion groups. Take a look at the following code:

```
df.groupby('Promotion').describe()['AgeOfStore']
```

The output of this code looks as follows:

Promotion	count	mean	std	min	25%	50%	75%	max
1	172.0	8.279070	6.636160	1.0	3.0	6.0	12.0	27.0
2	188.0	7.978723	6.597648	1.0	3.0	7.0	10.0	28.0
3	188.0	9.234043	6.651646	1.0	5.0	8.0	12.0	24.0

As you may notice from this output, it is much easier to understand the overall store age distributions from these summary statistics. We can see that all three test groups seem to have similar store age profiles. The average ages of stores for the three groups are 8–9 years old and the majority of the stores are 10–12 years old or younger.

By analyzing how each promotion or test group is comprised, we could verify that the store profiles are similar to each other. This suggests that the sample groups are well controlled and the A/B testing results will be meaningful and trustworthy.

Statistical hypothesis testing

The ultimate goal of A/B testing of different marketing strategies is to find out which strategy is the most efficient and works the best among the others. As briefly discussed in an earlier section, a strategy having a higher response number does not necessarily mean that it outperforms the rest. We will discuss how we can use the t-test to evaluate the relative performances of different marketing strategies and see which strategy wins over the others with significance.

In Python, there are two approaches to computing the t-value and p-value in a t-test. We will demonstrate both approaches in this section, and it is up to you to decide which one works more conveniently for you. The two approaches to compute the t-value and p-value for a t-test are as follows:

- **Computing t-value and p-value from the equations**: The first approach is to manually calculate the t-value using the equation we have learned in the previous section. As you may recall, there are three things we need to compute to get the t-value—the mean, the standard deviation, and the number of samples. Take a look at the following code:

```
means = df.groupby('Promotion').mean()['SalesInThousands']
stds = df.groupby('Promotion').std()['SalesInThousands']
ns = df.groupby('Promotion').count()['SalesInThousands']
```

As you can see from this code, you can easily compute the mean, the standard deviation, and the number of samples in each test group by using the `mean`, `std`, and `count` functions respectively. With these, we can compute the t-value using the previously discussed equation. Take a look at the following code:

```
import numpy as np

t_1_vs_2 = (
    means.iloc[0] - means.iloc[1]
) / np.sqrt(
    (stds.iloc[0]**2/ns.iloc[0]) + (stds.iloc[1]**2/ns.iloc[1])
)
```

Using this code, we can compute the t-value for comparing the performances of promotion 1 and promotion 2. The t-value we get from running the code is `6.4275`. From this t-value, we can get the p-value with the following code:

```
from scipy import stats

df_1_vs_1 = ns.iloc[0] + ns.iloc[1] - 2

p_1_vs_2 = (1 - stats.t.cdf(t_1_vs_2, df=df_1_vs_1))*2
```

As you can see from this code, we first compute the degrees of freedom, which is the sum of the number of samples in both groups minus two. With the t-value calculated previously, we can compute the p-value, using the `t.cdf` function from `scipy` package's `stats` module. The p-value we get from running this code is `4.143e-10`. This is an extremely small number that is close to 0. As discussed earlier, a p-value closer to 0 suggests that there is a strong evidence against the null hypothesis and that the difference between the two test groups is significant.

The average sales (in thousands) for promotion group 1 is about `58.1`, and for promotion group 2 it's about `47.33`. From our t-test, we have shown that the marketing performances for these two groups are significantly different and that promotion group 1 outperforms promotion group 2. However, if we run a t-test between the promotion group 1 and promotion group 3, we see different results.

On the surface, the average sales from promotion group 1 (`58.1`) looks higher than those from promotion group 2 (`55.36`). However, when we run a t-test between these two groups, we get a t-value of `1.556` and a p-value of `0.121`. The computed p-value is much higher than `0.05`, which is a generally accepted cut-off line. This suggests that the marketing performance from promotion group 1 is not statistically different from the marketing performance from promotion group 2. Thus, even though promotion group 1's average sales number is higher than the promotion group 2's from the A/B test, the difference is not statistically significant and we cannot conclude that promotion group 1 performs much better than promotion group 2. From these evaluation results, we can conclude that promotion groups 1 and 3 outperform promotion group 2, but the difference between promotion groups 1 and 3 is not statistically significant.

- **Computing the t-value and p-value using scipy**: Another approach to computing the t-value and p-value is by using the `stats` module from the `scipy` package. Take a look at the following code:

```
t, p = stats.ttest_ind(
    df.loc[df['Promotion'] == 1, 'SalesInThousands'].values,
    df.loc[df['Promotion'] == 2, 'SalesInThousands'].values,
    equal_var=False
)
```

As you can see from this code, the `stats` module from the `scipy` package has a function named `ttest_ind`. This function computes t-value and p-value, given the data. Using this function, we can easily compute t-values and p-values to compare the marketing performances of different promotion or test groups. The results are the same in both approaches. Whether we use the previous approach of manually computing the t-values and p-values from the equation or the approach of using the `ttest_ind` function in the `scipy` package, the t-values we get to compare promotion group 1 against 2 and promotion group 1 against 3 are `6.4275` and `1.556`; whereas, the p-values we get are `4.29e-10` and `0.121` respectively. And, of course, the interpretations of these t-test results are the same as before.

We have shown two approaches to computing t-values and p-values. It may look easier to use the `scipy` package's out-of-the-box solution to compute those values, but it is always helpful to have the equation in the back in your mind.

The full code for this Python exercise can be found at the following link: `https://github.com/yoonhwang/hands-on-data-science-for-marketing/blob/master/ch.12/python/ABTesting.ipynb`.

Evaluating A/B testing results with R

In this section, we are going to discuss how to evaluate A/B testing results to decide which marketing strategy works the best. By the end of this section, we will have covered how to run statistical hypothesis testing and compute the statistical significance. We will be mainly using `dplyr` and `ggplot2` to analyze and visualize the data and evaluate the A/B testing results.

For those readers who would like to use Python instead of R for this exercise, you can refer to the previous section.

For this exercise, we will be using one of the publicly available datasets from the IBM Watson Analytics community, which can be found at this link: `https://www.ibm.com/communities/analytics/watson-analytics-blog/marketing-campaign-eff-usec_-fastf/`. You can follow this link and download the data, which is available in XLSX format, named `WA_Fn-UseC_-Marketing-Campaign-Eff-UseC_-FastF.xlsx`. Once you have downloaded this data, you can load it into your RStudio by running the following command:

```
library(dplyr)
library(readxl)
library(ggplot2)

#### 1. Load Data ####
df <- read_excel(
  path="~/Documents/data-science-for-marketing/ch.12/data/WA_Fn-UseC_-
Marketing-Campaign-Eff-UseC_-FastF.xlsx"
)
```

The `df` DataFrame looks as follows:

	MarketID	MarketSize	LocationID	AgeOfStore	Promotion	Week	SalesInThousands
1	1	Medium	1	4	3	1	33.73
2	1	Medium	1	4	3	2	35.67
3	1	Medium	1	4	3	3	29.03
4	1	Medium	1	4	3	4	39.25
5	1	Medium	2	5	2	1	27.81
6	1	Medium	2	5	2	2	34.67
7	1	Medium	2	5	2	3	27.98
8	1	Medium	2	5	2	4	27.72
9	1	Medium	3	12	1	1	44.54
10	1	Medium	3	12	1	2	37.94
11	1	Medium	3	12	1	3	45.49
12	1	Medium	3	12	1	4	34.75
13	1	Medium	4	1	2	1	39.28
14	1	Medium	4	1	2	2	39.80
15	1	Medium	4	1	2	3	24.77

There are a total of seven variables in the dataset. You can find the descriptions of these variables on the IBM Watson Analytics Community page, but we will reiterate in the following:

- MarketID: unique identifier for market
- MarketSize: size of market area by sales
- LocationID: unique identifier for store location
- AgeOfStore: age of store in years
- Promotion: one of three promotions that was tested
- week: one of four weeks when the promotions were run
- SalesInThousands: sales amount for a specific LocationID, Promotion, and week

Data analysis

Let's take a deeper look at the data. In this section, we are going to focus on understanding the distributions of sales, market sizes, store locations, and store ages used to test different promotions. The goal of this analysis is to make sure that the controls and attributes of each promotion groups are symmetrically distributed, so that the promotion performances among different groups are comparable to each other.

The total sales distributions across different promotions can be visualized using the following code:

```
salesPerPromo <- df %>%
  group_by(Promotion) %>%
  summarise(Sales=sum(SalesInThousands))

ggplot(salesPerPromo, aes(x="", y=Sales, fill=Promotion)) +
  geom_bar(width=1, stat = "identity", position=position_fill()) +
  geom_text(aes(x=1.25, label=Sales), position=position_fill(vjust = 0.5),
color='white') +
  coord_polar("y") +
  ggtitle('sales distribution across different promotions')
```

As you can see from this code, we are grouping the data by the Promotion column and aggregating the total sales amount by summing over the SalesInThousands column. Using a pie chart, we can easily visualize how much of the pie each group takes.

The resulting pie chart looks as follows:

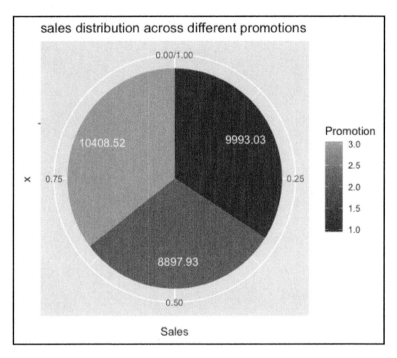

As is easily visible from this pie chart, promotion group **3** has the largest aggregate sales among the three groups. However, each promotion group takes roughly one third of the total sales during the promotion weeks. Similarly, we can also visualize the compositions of different market sizes in each promotion group. Take a look at the following code:

```
marketSizePerPromo <- df %>%
  group_by(Promotion, MarketSize) %>%
  summarise(Count=n())

ggplot(marketSizePerPromo, aes(x=Promotion, y=Count, fill=MarketSize)) +
  geom_bar(width=0.5, stat="identity", position="dodge") +
  ylab("Count") +
  xlab("Promotion") +
  ggtitle("breakdowns of market sizes across different promotions") +
  theme(plot.title=element_text(hjust=0.5))
```

The bar plot looks as follows:

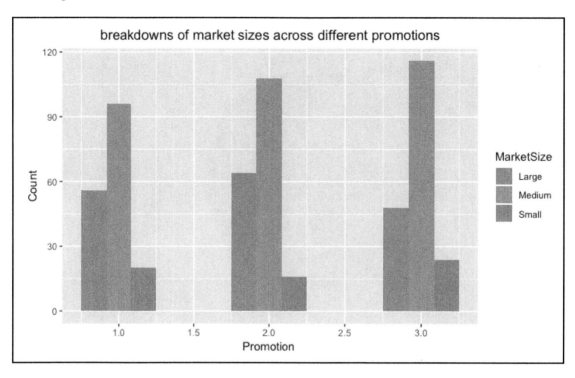

If you think a stacked bar chart will be easier to view, you can use the following code to display this data in a stacked bar plot:

```
ggplot(marketSizePerPromo, aes(x=Promotion, y=Count, fill=MarketSize)) +
    geom_bar(width=0.5, stat="identity", position="stack") +
    ylab("Count") +
    xlab("Promotion") +
    ggtitle("breakdowns of market sizes across different promotions") +
    theme(plot.title=element_text(hjust=0.5))
```

You may notice that the only difference between this code and the previous code is the `position="stack"` flag in the `geom_bar` function. The result looks as follows:

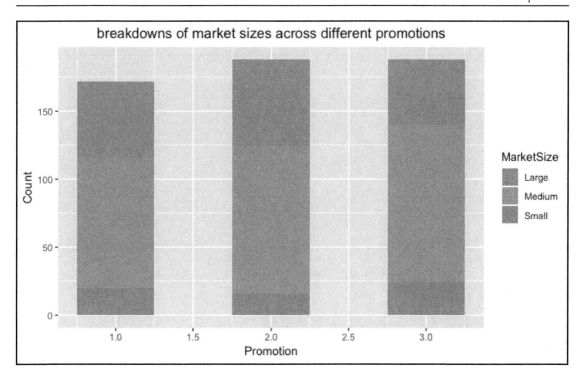

As you can see from this bar chart, the medium market size occupies the most among all three promotion groups, while small market size occupies the least. We can verify that the compositions of different market sizes are similar among the three promotion groups from this plot.

Another attribute, `AgeOfStore`, and its overall distributions across all different promotions groups, can be visualized by using the following code:

```
overallAge <- df %>%
  group_by(AgeOfStore) %>%
  summarise(Count=n())

ggplot(overallAge, aes(x=AgeOfStore, y=Count)) +
  geom_bar(width=0.5, stat="identity") +
  ylab("Count") +
  xlab("Store Age") +
  ggtitle("overall distributions of age of store") +
  theme(plot.title=element_text(hjust=0.5))
```

And the result looks like the following bar plot:

As you can see from this plot, a large number of stores are **1** year old and the majority of stores are **10** years old or less. However, what we are more interested in is whether the stores in the three different promotion groups have similar store age profiles. Take a look at the following code:

```
AgePerPromo <- df %>%
  group_by(Promotion, AgeOfStore) %>%
  summarise(Count=n())

ggplot(AgePerPromo, aes(x=AgeOfStore, y=Count, fill=Promotion)) +
  geom_bar(width=0.5, stat="identity", position="dodge2") +
  ylab("Count") +
  xlab("Store Age") +
  ggtitle("distributions of age of store") +
  theme(plot.title=element_text(hjust=0.5))
```

Using this code, you will get the following output:

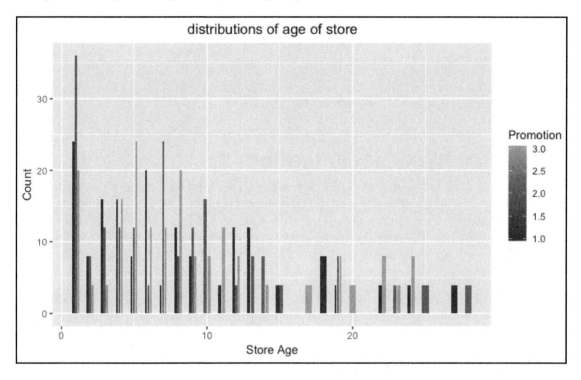

The store age distributions across the three different promotion groups seem to align with each other, but it is quite difficult to digest the information presented from this plot. It will be easier to look at the summary statistics of store ages across the three promotion groups. Take a look at the following code:

```
tapply(df$AgeOfStore, df$Promotion, summary)
```

The output of this code looks as follows:

```
> tapply(df$AgeOfStore, df$Promotion, summary)
$`1`
   Min. 1st Qu.  Median    Mean 3rd Qu.    Max.
  1.000   3.000   6.000   8.279  12.000  27.000

$`2`
   Min. 1st Qu.  Median    Mean 3rd Qu.    Max.
  1.000   3.000   7.000   7.979  10.000  28.000

$`3`
   Min. 1st Qu.  Median    Mean 3rd Qu.    Max.
  1.000   5.000   8.000   9.234  12.000  24.000
```

As you may notice from this output, it is much easier to understand the overall store age distributions from these summary statistics. We can see that all three test groups seem to have similar store age profiles. The average ages of stores for the three groups are 8-9 years old and the majority of the stores are 10-12 years old or younger.

By analyzing how each promotion or test group is comprised, we could verify that the store profiles are similar to each other. This suggests that the sample groups are well controlled and the A/B testing results will be meaningful and trustworthy.

Statistical hypothesis testing

The ultimate goal of A/B testing of different marketing strategies is to find out which strategy is the most efficient and works the best among the others. As briefly discussed in an earlier section, a strategy with a higher response number does not necessarily mean that it outperforms the rest. We will discuss how we can use the t-test to evaluate the relative performances of different marketing strategies and see which strategy wins over the others with significance.

In R, there are two approaches to compute the t-value and p-value for a t-test. We will demonstrate both approaches in this section, and it is up to you to decide which one works more conveniently for you. The two approaches to compute the t-value and p-value for a t-test are as follows:

- **Computing the t-value and p-value from the equations**: The first approach is to manually calculate the t-value using the equation we have learned in the previous section. As you may recall, there are three things we need to compute to get the t-value: the mean, the standard deviation, and the number of samples. Take a look at the following code:

  ```
  promo_1 <- df[which(df$Promotion == 1),]$SalesInThousands
  promo_2 <- df[which(df$Promotion == 2),]$SalesInThousands

  mean_1 <- mean(promo_1)
  mean_2 <- mean(promo_2)
  std_1 <- sd(promo_1)
  std_2 <- sd(promo_2)
  n_1 <- length(promo_1)
  n_2 <- length(promo_2)
  ```

As you can see from this code, you can easily compute the mean, the standard deviation, and the number of samples in each test group by using the mean, sd, and length functions respectively. With these, we can compute the t-value using the previously discussed equation. Take a look at the following code:

```
t_val <- (
  mean_1 - mean_2
) / sqrt(
  (std_1**2/n_1 + std_2**2/n_2)
)
```

Using this code, we can compute the t-value for comparing the performances of promotion 1 and promotion 2. The t-value we get from running the code is 6.4275. From this t-value, we can get the p-value with the following code:

```
df_1_2 <- n_1 + n_2 - 2

p_val <- 2 * pt(t_val, df_1_2, lower=FALSE)
```

As you can see from this code, we first compute the degrees of freedom, which is the sum of the number of samples in both groups minus two. With the t-value calculated previously, we can compute the p-value using the pt function, which returns a probability value from the t-distribution, given the t-value and degree of freedom. The p-value we get from running this code is 4.143e-10. This is an extremely small number that is close to 0. As discussed earlier, a p-value close to 0 suggests that there is strong evidence against the null hypothesis and that the difference between the two test groups is significant.

The average sales (in thousands) for promotion group 1 is about 58.1, and for promotion group 2 it's about 47.33. From our t-test, we have shown that the marketing performances for these two groups are significantly different and that promotion group 1 outperforms promotion group 2. However, if we run a t-test between promotion group 1 and promotion group 3, we see different results.

On the surface, the average sales from promotion group 1 (58.1) looks higher than those from promotion group 2 (55.36). However, when we run a t-test between these two groups, we get a t-value of 1.556 and a p-value of 0.121. The computed p-value is much higher than 0.05, which is a generally accepted cut-off line. This suggests that the marketing performance for promotion group 1 is not statistically different from the marketing performance of promotion group 2. Thus, even though promotion group 1's average sales number is higher than promotion group 2's from the A/B test, the difference is not statistically significant, and we cannot conclude that promotion group 1 performs much better than promotion group 2. From these evaluation results, we can conclude that promotions groups 1 and 3 outperform promotion group 2, but the difference between promotion groups 1 and 3 is not statistically significant.

- **Computing the t-value and p-value using t.test**: Another approach to compute the t-value and p-value is by using the t.test function in R. Take a look at the following code:

```
# using t.test
t.test(
  promo_1,
  promo_2
)
```

As you can see from this code, R has a t.test function, which computes the t-value and p-value, given data. Using this function, we can easily compute t-values and p-values to compare the marketing performances of different promotions or test groups. The results are the same in both approaches. Whether we use the previous approach of manually computing the t-values and p-values from the equation or the approach of using the ttest_ind function in the scipy package, the t-values we get to compare promotion group 1 against promotion group 2 and promotion group 1 against promotion group 3 are 6.4275 and 1.556; whereas, the p-values we get are 4.29e-10 and 0.121 respectively. And, of course, the interpretations of these t-test results are the same as before.

We have shown two approaches to computing t-values and p-values. It may look easier to use the t.test function in R, but it is always helpful to have the equation in the back of your mind.

The full code for this R exercise can be found at the following link: https://github.com/yoonhwang/hands-on-data-science-for-marketing/blob/master/ch.12/R/ABTesting.R.

Summary

In this chapter, we have learned about one of the most frequently used testing methods in marketing for making decisions on future marketing strategies. We have discussed what A/B testing is, why it is important to run A/B tests before you fully commit to one marketing strategy, and how it can help you reach your marketing goal in a more efficient and less expensive way. By working through a sample use case, where your goal was to choose the best email subject line, we learned what a typical process for running A/B tests looks like. A/B testing does not need to happen only once. A/B tests are best used when you consistently test your new ideas against currently running strategies or against other ideas through experiments. Simply put, whenever there is a new idea, it should be A/B tested. Using the t-test and the Python and R tools that we have learned about in this chapter, you should be able to easily evaluate A/B test results and identify which strategy is the winning strategy.

This chapter was the last technical chapter with case studies and programming exercises. In the next chapter, we are going to summarize and review all the topics that we have covered throughout this book. Then, we will discuss some common data science and machine learning applications in marketing and some other Python and R libraries that you can benefit from in your future projects that have not been covered in this book.

13
What's Next?

We have come a long way. We started this book with the basics of data science and its applications in marketing and worked through numerous use cases of data science in marketing. Along the way, we have conducted descriptive analysis, where we used data science techniques to analyze and visualize data to identify patterns. We have also conducted explanatory analysis, where we used machine learning models to draw insights from data, such as finding the drivers behind certain customers' activities and the correlations between customer attributes and their actions. Lastly, we have also looked at predictive analytics, where we trained various machine learning algorithms to make forecasts on certain actions of customers.

The topics we have covered throughout this book are not trivial and were geared toward the practical usage of data science in marketing. Each chapter was meant to showcase how you can use data science and machine learning techniques in actual marketing use cases and guide you through how you might be able to apply the concepts discussed to your specific business cases. As the field of marketing analytics is growing and broadening its reach, we wanted to use this chapter to inform you of some potential challenges you might face and look at some other commonly used technologies, as well as review the topics that we have discussed in this book.

In this chapter, we will cover the following topics:

- Recap of the topics covered in this book
- Real-life data science challenges
- More machine learning models and packages

Recap of the topics covered in this book

We have covered a large amount of material from the beginning of this book, from discussing the trends in marketing and how data science and machine learning have become a crucial part in building marketing strategies, to building various predictive machine learning models for more efficient marketing. It is worth reviewing what we have covered so far and refreshing our memory before we close this book.

Trends in marketing

As you may recall, the first thing we discussed in `Chapter 1`, *Data Science and Marketing*, was the recent trends in marketing. It is important to try to understand and keep up with the trends that are occurring in the industry that you are working and specializing in. Especially in marketing, there is a lot of demand for more data-driven and quantitative marketing, and for the use of the latest and most intelligent technologies for developing more cost-effective marketing strategies.

According to the February, 2018, CMO survey (`https://www.forbes.com/sites/christinemoorman/2018/02/27/marketing-analytics-and-marketing-technology-trends-to-watch/#4ec8a8431b8a`), reliance on marketing analytics has gone up from 30% to 42% in the past 5 years. The three main trends in marketing that can be easily observed are the following:

- **Rising importance of digital marketing**: Lots of marketing activities are now happening more heavily on digital channels, such as search engines, social media, email, and websites, rather than on more traditional mass media, such as TV, radio, and banners at bus stations. As various digital marketing channels are gaining popularity as the choice of marketing channel, it has become more important to have a good understanding of how audience targeting works on social networks, such as Facebook and Instagram, or how to place advertisements on search engines and video streaming services, such as Google and YouTube.

- **Marketing analytics**: Marketing analytics is a way of monitoring and quantifying the results and performances of past marketing efforts. In `Chapter 2`, *Key Performance Indicators and Visualizations*, we learned about various **key performance indicators** (**KPIs**) that we can use to track and quantify the returns from various marketing efforts. Marketing analytics does not just stop at analyzing KPIs. It can also be applied to product and customer analytics, which we discussed in `Chapter 5`, *Product Analytics*, and `Chapter 7`, *Exploratory Analysis for Customer Behavior*.

- **Personalized and target marketing**: As the accessibility of data science and machine learning has become easier, another trend in marketing has arisen: individual-level targeted marketing. Using predictive analytics, we can now predict what types of products that individual customers would like, which we have discussed in Chapter 6, *Recommending the Right Products*. We have also seen how we can target those customers who are likely to churn by building predictive machine learning models in Chapter 11, *Retaining Customers*. As targeted marketing results in higher ROI, there are many **software-as-a-Service (SaaS)** companies, such as Sailthru and Oracle, that provide platforms for personalized and target marketing.

As new strategies and technologies are developed, trends are destined to change. The trends that we have discussed in this book might not be applicable in 20-30 years, time. As a marketing professional, it is critical to follow and understand what others in the same industry do and what other approaches or technologies are being developed and used to achieve higher ROI.

Data science workflow

As a marketing professional or an aspiring data scientist in marketing, it can be challenging to figure out where to start for a data science project. In Chapter 1, *Data Science and Marketing*, we have discussed a typical workflow for a data science project. It is worth reviewing the steps before you embark on your future marketing data science projects. You should be familiar with the following workflow diagram:

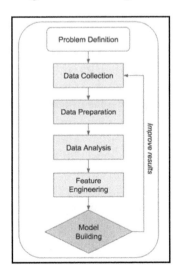

Let's talk a bit more in detail about these six steps:

1. **Problem definition**: Any data science and machine learning project should have a clear problem definition. You will need to have an in-depth understanding of the problem itself, the scope of the project, and approaches to coming up with solutions. This is where you brainstorm what types of analyses and data science techniques to use.

2. **Data collection**: As it is for any data science project, having data is key for success. In this step, you will need to gather all the required data for your data science project. It is common that you will need to implement data collection processes for internal data, purchase third-party data, or scrape data from different websites. Depending on the cases, the data collection step can be trivial or it can also be tedious.

3. **Data preparation**: With the data from the data collection step, the next step is to clean and prepare the data. As we have seen throughout this book, our programming exercises always started with data cleanup and preparation. In the data preparation step, we handled missing values, encoded categorical variables, or transformed other variables, so that this data can be understood by machine learning algorithms.

4. **Data analysis**: As you may recall, we have discovered useful insights from this data analysis step in our programming exercises throughout the book. Through analyzing data, we gain a better understanding of the overall distributions of different variables, and it is often a good idea to visualize data with different plots to identify any noticeable patterns.

5. **Feature engineering**: As we have seen and discussed throughout the book, there are many different ways to approach engineering the features for machine learning models. For monetary values, we have applied log transformations. In some cases, we have normalized the data so that the variables are on the same scale. We have also used one-hot encoding to encode categorical variables. Feature engineering is one of the most important steps in building machine learning models, as the algorithms are going to try to learn from these features to correctly predict the target.

6. **Model building**: The final step in a typical data science workflow is, of course, model building. With the clean data and features that we have built from previous steps, this is where you train your machine learning models. Throughout this book, we have discussed how to evaluate the models. For classification models, we have often used accuracy, precision, recall, the ROC curve, and the AUC. For regression models, we have used MSE, R^2, or a scatterplot of predicted and actual values for model evaluations.

During our programming exercises, our workflow looked almost the same as the workflow that we have just discussed. When unsure about what to do next, we hope this workflow diagram gives you some hints on the next steps.

Machine learning models

As you may recall, we built a number of machine learning models in this book. For example, in Chapter 8, *Predicting the Likelihood of Marketing Engagement*, we trained a random forest model to predict how likely each customer is to engage with marketing calls. In Chapter 11, *Retaining Customers*, we used an **artificial neural network (ANN)** model to identify which customers are likely to churn from the business. In this section, we will review those machine learning models that we have used in this book:

- **Logistic regression**: In Chapter 3, *Drivers behind Marketing Engagement*, we have used a logistic regression model to extract the insights on which factors make customers more likely to engage with marketing campaigns. In Python, we used the statsmodels package to build a logistic regression model, and the code to train a logistic regression model looked like the following:

  ```
  import statsmodels.formula.api as sm

  logit = sm.Logit(
      target_variable,
      features
  )

  logit = logit.fit()
  ```

  From this trained model, we could look at the details and correlations between the features and the target variable by running logit_fit.summary(). On the other hand, in R, we used the following command to train a logistic regression model:

  ```
  logit.fit <- glm(Target ~ ., data = DF, family = binomial)
  ```

  Similar to how we used the summary function in Python, we could run the summary(logit.fit) command to get the details of the logistic regression fit and the correlations between the features and the target variable.

- **Random forest**: As you may recall, we used a random forest algorithm in Chapter 8, *Predicting the Likelihood of Marketing Engagement*, to predict which customers are likely to respond to marketing calls. In Python, we used the `scikit-learn` package to build random forest models. The code to train a random forest model looked like the following:

```
from sklearn.ensemble import RandomForestClassifier

rf_model = RandomForestClassifier()

rf_model.fit(X=x_train, y=y_train)
```

As you may recall, there were numerous hyperparameters you could tune with the random forest algorithm. We have discussed how you can fine-tune the number of estimators in the forest, `n_estimators`, the maximum depth of the tree, `max_depth`, and the minimum of samples needed to be able to split into branches, `min_samples_split`. On the other hand, in R, we used the `randomForest` library to build random forest models. The code for training a random forest model in R looked like the following:

```
library(randomForest)

rfModel <- randomForest(x=trainX, y=factor(trainY))
```

With the `randomForest` package, you could fine-tune the hyperparameters. You could use `ntree` to tune the number of trees in the forest, `sampsize` to tune the size of the sample to draw for training each tree, and `maxnodes` to define the maximum number of terminal nodes in the tree.

- **ANN**: As you may recall, in Chapter 11, *Retaining Customers*, we used an ANN model to predict the customers who are likely to churn from the business. In order to build an ANN model, we used the `keras` package for both Python and R. In Python, training an ANN model looked like the following:

```
from keras.models import Sequential
from keras.layers import Dense

model = Sequential()
model.add(Dense(16, input_dim=
                len(features), activation='relu'))
model.add(Dense(8, activation='relu'))
model.add(Dense(1, activation='sigmoid'))
```

```
model.compile(loss='binary_crossentropy',
              optimizer='adam', metrics=['accuracy'])

model.fit(X_train, y_train, epochs=50, batch_size=100)
```

As you should know already, we first had to add input, hidden, and output layers to the model. Then, we could compile and train an ANN model. In R, the concept is the same, but the syntax looks a bit different. The R code to train an ANN model using the `keras` package looked like the following:

```
library(keras)

model <- keras_model_sequential()
model %>%
  layer_dense(units = 16, kernel_initializer =
  "uniform", activation = 'relu', input_shape=ncol(train)-1) %>%
  layer_dense(units = 8, kernel_initializer =
  "uniform", activation = 'relu') %>%
  layer_dense(units = 1, kernel_initializer =
              "uniform", activation = 'sigmoid') %>%
  compile(optimizer = 'adam',
    loss = 'binary_crossentropy',
    metrics = c('accuracy')
  )

history <- model %>% fit(
  trainX,
  trainY,
  epochs = 50,
  batch_size = 100,
  validation_split = 0.2
)
```

- **k-means clustering**: In Chapter 10, *Data-Driven Customer Segmentation*, we used a k-means clustering algorithm to programmatically build different customer segments. We have seen how analyzing the attributes of these different customer segments can help us understand the different behaviors of the customers and find better ways to target different groups of customers. In Python, we could use the `scikit-learn` package to build a k-means clustering algorithm. The code looked like the following:

```
from sklearn.cluster import KMeans

kmeans = KMeans(n_clusters=4)
kmeans = kmeans.fit(data)
```

As you may recall, you needed to define the number of clusters you would like to build from the data, using the `n_clusters` parameter. In order to get the cluster labels for each record and cluster centroids, we could use `kmeans.labels_` and `kmeans.cluster_centers_`. Similarly, in R, we used the `kmeans` function to build a clustering model, as shown in the following code:

```
cluster <- kmeans(data, 4)
```

In order to get the labels and cluster centroids, we could use `cluster$cluster` and `cluster$centers`.

With these algorithms, we were able to easily build various machine learning models for different use cases in marketing. We hope these brief reviews of the syntax of building these machine learning models helped to refresh your memory.

Real-life data science challenges

Applying data science and machine learning in marketing would be all glamorous and flawless if we were able to just build and use various machine learning models for different marketing use cases. However, that normally is not the case. Quite often, the end-to-end machine learning model building process can be tedious, with lots of barriers and bottlenecks on the way. We are going to discuss some of the most frequently appearing data science challenges in real life, including the following:

- Challenges in data
- Challenges in infrastructure
- Challenges in choosing the right model

Challenges in data

One of the most challenging factors in using data science and machine learning for marketing is getting the right data. As may sound obvious to you, without data, there is no data science or machine learning. Moreover, if the quality of the data is not good, then the quality of your trained machine learning is also going to be bad.

In this section, we are going to discuss some of the common challenges that many data scientists face in getting the right data:

- **Existence of data**: Sometimes you may come up with a great idea of applying data science techniques to solve one of the problems you have in marketing. However, the data you need might not even exist. For example, say your idea was to identify trending web content, such as which web pages are viewed the most and liked the most by your users. However, you might not have the page view data, if the web page tracking functionality was not implemented on your websites. In this case, you will need to implement tracking functionality in your websites to track which users viewed or liked which content. Then, it is only possible to work on your idea after some period of time, when you have gathered enough data for your analysis. This type of case happens relatively frequently, so it is critical to have a good understanding of how well you track user activities and which parts you are missing. If possible, obtaining third-party data is also an option, when the data does not exist internally. There are lots of data vendors who sell data that you might need. If using a third-party data vendor is an option, that can be a good solution when there is no data for your project. Also, there is a lot of publicly available data that you can use freely. It is always worthwhile to see whether the data you need is publicly available or not.

- **Accessibility of data**: Data accessibility can be a barrier for a data science project. Especially in big corporations, access to certain sets of data is strictly restricted to selected subgroups of teams. In this case, even if the required dataset exists, it can be difficult or even impossible for data scientists or marketing professionals to access and use the data. Where the data is being generated from can also cause data accessibility problems. For instance, if the data is streamed into other applications without being stored or archived, then this data can be lost after it has been streamed. The location of the data files can also be a barrier to accessing the data you need. If the data cannot be shared through a network or if you cannot reach the location that the data lives in, then that can also keep you from using this data. This is why the responsibility and importance of data engineering and data engineers is rising. Data engineers work with other data scientists or software developers to specifically work on building data pipelines through which data with accessibility issues can move to other parts of the business. If you are facing issues with data accessibility, it is crucial to first find out what the barrier is and consider working with data engineers to build data pipelines to make the data accessible for your future projects.

- **Messy data**: You can assume the majority of the data you will face in real-life data science projects will be messy. It may be in a format that you cannot easily understand. It may be segmented into smaller parts that cannot easily be joined to each other. Or, there may also be too many missing values or too many duplicate records in the data. The degree of messiness of datasets can significantly increase the amount of time you need to spend on cleaning up the raw data and making it usable. Conducting in-depth data analysis on this messy data is crucial in making the data usable for future steps. Sometimes, it may be worthwhile to work with data engineers to fix the source that causes the messiness in the data and make future data more clean.

Challenges in infrastructure

When working with different datasets for applying data science techniques and using machine learning models for different projects in marketing, you may face some challenges in the system infrastructure that you use for developments. Quite often, datasets are too big to fit into your laptop or computer. As the size of data is grows bigger and bigger everyday, it becomes even more likely that sometime in the future, you will have issues with developing data science models on your laptop, even if you currently do not have this problem.

There are two main things that can slow you down when working on data science projects: shortage of CPU or processing power and shortage of RAM or memory. If you do not have enough processing power, your analysis could take long time. Especially when training machine learning models, it is not uncommon for model training to take days, weeks, or even months. On the other hand, if you do not have enough memory, you might end up getting `Out of Memory` errors while running your analysis. For example, tree-based models, such as decision trees or random forests, can take a large amount of memory, and training such models can fail after hours of training because of shortage of memory.

With the emerging popularity of and developments in cloud computing, there are solutions to these problems. Using one of the cloud computing service providers, such as AWS, Google, or Microsoft Azure, you can, theoretically, get an unlimited amount of computing power and memory. Of course, everything comes with a price. Running large data science jobs on these cloud platforms can cost a fortune, if you do not plan it right. When working with large datasets, it is wise to consider the amount of processing power and memory you would need to successfully run your tasks.

Challenges in choosing the right model

Choosing a machine learning algorithm for a given data science project is more difficult than it sounds. Some algorithms work more like a black box, where you do not know how an algorithm makes predictions or decisions. For example, it is quite difficult to understand how a trained random forest model makes predictions on the output from the input. The decisions are made from hundreds of different decision trees, where each tree works differently with different decision-making criteria, and this makes it difficult for a data scientist to fully understand what happens in between the input and the output.

On the other hand, linear models, such as logistic regression models, tell us exactly how they are making decisions. Once logistic regression models are trained, we know the coefficients given to each feature, and from these coefficients, we can deduce what the predicted output is going to be. Depending on your use cases, you might need to have this kind of explainability, where you need to be able to explain how each feature works and affects the prediction output to your business partners. Quite often, more advanced models work more like a black box, and you will need to make a trade-off between prediction accuracy and explainability.

More machine learning models and packages

In this book, we have mainly used the following five machine learning algorithms that fit into and work the best for our marketing use cases: logistic regression, random forests, ANN, k-means clustering, and collaborative filtering. However, there are many more readily available machine learning algorithms that you may find useful for your future data science and machine learning projects. We will be covering some of the other frequently used machine learning algorithms, what packages to use in Python and R, and where to find more information on these algorithms.

Some of the other machine learning algorithms to consider in your future projects are the following:

- **Nearest neighbors**: This is a machine learning algorithm that finds the pre-defined number of closest samples to a new data point. Even though the concept of this algorithm sounds simple, the nearest neighbors algorithm has been used successfully in various areas, including image recognition. In the `scikit-learn` package of Python, you can use the `KNeighborsClassifier` class in the `neighbors` module to build classification models, or you can use the `KNeighborsRegressor` class to build regression models. For more details on the usage, we recommend you take a look at the following documentation page: `https://scikit-learn.org/stable/modules/neighbors.html`. On the other hand, in R, you can use the `knn` function in the `class` library. For the documentation of this function in R, you can refer to this documentation page: `https://www.rdocumentation.org/packages/class/versions/7.3-15/topics/knn`.

- **Support vector machine (SVM)**: SVM is another machine learning algorithm that you may find useful. The SVM algorithm tries to find a hyperplane that best splits the data into classes or groups. It is especially effective in high-dimensional space. The `scikit-learn` package has the `SVC` and `SVR` classes implemented in Python for classification and regression models. The documentation page can be found at the following link: `https://scikit-learn.org/stable/modules/svm.html`. In R, the `e1071` library has the `svm` function, which you can use to train SVM models. More documentation on its usage can be found here: `https://www.rdocumentation.org/packages/e1071/versions/1.7-0.1/topics/svm`.

- **Gradient-boosted trees (GBT)**: GBT is one of the tree-based machine learning algorithms. Unlike the random forest algorithm, the GBT algorithm learns and trains each tree sequentially, and each tree learns from the mistakes that the previous trees made. It is well known and frequently used for its prediction accuracy and robustness. In Python, you can use the `GradientBoostingClassifier` class in the `scikit-learn` package's `ensemble` module for classification problems and the `GradientBoostingRegressor` class for regression problems. More details about GBT in `scikit-learn` can be found here: `https://scikit-learn.org/stable/modules/ensemble.html#gradient-tree-boosting`. Similarly, in R, the `gbm` package has the GBT algorithm implemented for classification and regression problems. You can use the `gbm` function within the `gbm` package to train a GBT model. More information can be found at the following link: `https://www.rdocumentation.org/packages/gbm/versions/2.1.5/topics/gbm`

Summary

In this chapter, we reviewed the topics that we discussed in this book. We briefly went through the trends that are observable in the marketing industry and how data science and machine learning are becoming more and more important in marketing. Then, we reviewed a typical data science workflow, where you start with problem definition, then move onto data collection, preparation, and analysis, and finally move to feature engineering and model building. While working on future data science projects, it will be worthwhile to keep the workflow diagram we looked at in the back of your head and when stuck with what to do next, refer back to this diagram for ideas. We have also shared some of the challenges you might face when working with real-world datasets. The three main challenges we covered were data issues, infrastructure issues, and choosing the right model. More specifically, we discussed the trade-off between explainability and model accuracy. We have suggested some workarounds and solutions to these challenges, so we hope they help when you face similar challenges. Lastly, we have discussed some other frequently used machine learning models that you may find useful in your future projects. We have briefly showed which Python and R packages to use for each of these models and where you can find more information about the usage of those models.

Throughout the 13 chapters in this book, we have covered the various data science and machine learning techniques you can use in marketing, with a focus on practicality. As you have worked through numerous examples for different use cases in marketing throughout this book, we hope you have gained more confidence in applying data science techniques and building machine learning models for developing more intelligent and efficient marketing strategies. We hope your journey throughout this book was worthwhile and rewarding and that you have gained many new and useful skills.

Other Books You May Enjoy

If you enjoyed this book, you may be interested in these other books by Packt:

Data Science Algorithms in a Week - Second Edition
Dávid Natingga

ISBN: 978-1-78980-607-6

- Understand how to identify a data science problem correctly
- Implement well-known machine learning algorithms efficiently using Python
- Classify your datasets using Naive Bayes, decision trees, and random forest with accuracy
- Devise an appropriate prediction solution using regression
- Work with time series data to identify relevant data events and trends
- Cluster your data using the k-means algorithm

Python Data Science Essentials - Third Edition
Alberto Boschetti, Luca Massaron

ISBN: 978-1-78953-786-4

- Set up your data science toolbox on Windows, Mac, and Linux
- Use the core machine learning methods offered by the scikit-learn library
- Manipulate, fix, and explore data to solve data science problems
- Learn advanced explorative and manipulative techniques to solve data operations
- Optimize your machine learning models for optimized performance
- Explore and cluster graphs, taking advantage of interconnections and links in your data

Leave a review - let other readers know what you think

Please share your thoughts on this book with others by leaving a review on the site that you bought it from. If you purchased the book from Amazon, please leave us an honest review on this book's Amazon page. This is vital so that other potential readers can see and use your unbiased opinion to make purchasing decisions, we can understand what our customers think about our products, and our authors can see your feedback on the title that they have worked with Packt to create. It will only take a few minutes of your time, but is valuable to other potential customers, our authors, and Packt. Thank you!

Index

S

sales channels 79
sales funnel analytics 228
scikit-learn documentation
  reference link 303
simple logistic regression model
  in Python environment 21, 24, 26
  in R environment 31, 34, 36
statistical hypothesis testing 401
support vector machine (SVM)
  about 317, 333
  reference link 438

T

t-test 401
t-value 401
topics

repeating 428
total claim amounts 81, 83

U

UCI Machine Learning Repository
  references 176
UCI's Bank Marketing Data Set 59
user-to-item matrix 195

V

variable encoding, marketing engagement with Python
  categorical variable encoding 272
  response variable encoding 271
variable encoding, marketing engagement with R language
  categorical variable encoding 288
  response variable encoding 287

Printed in Great Britain
by Amazon